A
Political
Education

A Political Education

A Washington Memoir

Harry McPherson

University of Texas Press
Austin

Copyright © 1972, 1988 by Harry McPherson
Copyright © 1995 by the University of Texas Press
All rights reserved
Printed in the United States of America
First University of Texas Press edition, 1995
Requests for permission to reproduce material from this work should be sent to Permissions, University of Texas Press, Box 7819, Austin, TX 78713-7819.

∞ The paper used in this publication meets the minimum requirements of American National Standard for Information Sciences—Permanence of Paper for Printed Library Materials, ANSI Z39.48-1984.

The author wishes to thank Penguin Books for permission to quote from "Elegy of Fortinbras" and "Why the Classics," in *Zbigniew Herbert: Selected Poems,* translated by Czeslaw Milosz and Peter Dale Scott (translation copyright Czeslaw Milosz and Peter Dale Scott, 1968).

Library of Congress Cataloging-in-Publication Data

McPherson, Harry.
   A political education : a Washington memoir / Harry McPherson. — 1st ed.
      p.   cm.
   Includes bibliographical references and index.
   ISBN 978-0-292-75181-1
   1. United States—Politics and government—1963–1969.
2. United States. Congress. Senate. 3. United States—Politics and government—1945–1989. 4. McPherson, Harry.
5. Johnson, Lyndon B. (Lyndon Baines), 1908–1973—Friends and associates. I. Title.
E846.M33   1995
320.973—dc20   94-32805

To My Family

Contents

	Preface, 1995	ix
	Prologue	3
1.	Counsel in Congress	11
2.	Brief Lives	27
3.	Right from Wrong	85
4.	Cold War Democrats	99
5.	Sacred Cows and Racial Justice	121
6.	Johnson for President	156
7.	Racing in Neutral	182
8.	Army and State	205
9.	White House	245
10.	Cities Aflame	334
11.	Democracy Fights a Limited War	384
12.	Dénouement	419
	Epilogue	453
	Postscript, 1988	457
	Index	487

Preface, 1995

MUCH has changed in Washington since the cold winter night of this book's beginning. The capital city is now part of an immense metropolitan region, whose center, the District of Columbia, has actually lost a quarter of its population in the course of becoming architecturally more elaborate, racially more black and Hispanic, culturally more sophisticated, and behaviorally much more violent. What was a Southern city, its pace set by the peaceful tedium of bureaucracy, has become like California: its suburbs wealthy from military spending and real estate development, its core a reef on which the rejected abound, the whole a community only in the geographical sense—far-flung, obsessed with traffic, anonymous.

But as tourists still flock to Hollywood, so do they to Capitol Hill. Both places have been, in their prime, theaters for the projection of the nation's faith in its special relationship with happiness, economic success, and the democratic virtues. On the whole, both had more intriguing performers in the past than they do now, and across the country there are as many complaints about degrading movies as about inadequate politicians. Still people come—among the westward crowds, candidates for the Presidency or for reelection to the Senate, seeking campaign contributions in the Hollywood canyons; and among those on the Hill, the contributors themselves—actors, producers, studio chiefs from Beverly Hills—bearing their generally orthodox liberal opinions to the seat of government.

The Senate that receives them resembles in some respects the place I came to work in thirty-seven years ago. In others it differs markedly.

There is now, as there was then, a majority of lawyers. Since it is a place for attenuated arguments, procedural arcana, narrow ethical distinctions, and ultimately lawmaking, this is unsurprising.

In 1995, as in the late fifties, there is a cadre of temperamentally moderate members who make the place function agreeably, to the degree that it does. Now, as then, there are "characters," some of them charmingly eccentric, others simply petulant and self-absorbed. There are decent Midwestern liberals, as there were three decades ago, though perhaps none today so remarkable for sparkling intellect, sense of purpose, and general irreverence as were Hubert Humphrey, Phil Hart, and Gaylord Nelson. There are richly articulate speech-makers like Dale Bumpers and Fritz Hollings, who at their best remind one of the days when the thundering oratory of Bob Kerr and Joe O'Mahoney filled the chamber. West Virginia once provided the nostalgic rococo of Matthew Neely; it now returns in Robert Byrd, a man of equally florid devotion to the past. At the head of the Foreign Relations Committee is a quaint, kindly, patrician Rhode Islander, Claiborne Pell; exactly the same description fitted Theodore Francis Green in the late fifties. A serious, sometimes austerely conservative Georgian, Richard Russell, then chaired the Armed Services Committee. Another such, Sam Nunn, chairs it now.

There are bêtes noires—Jesse Helms to the liberals, Howard Metzenbaum to the conservatives—as there were decades ago, in the time of Joe McCarthy and Wayne Morse. For scholar-politicians, there is Pat Moynihan, as then there was Paul Douglas—both of them calling up exogenous data in speeches read with admiration outside the chamber and heard with interest or perplexity, depending on the audience, within it. Both found a home on the Finance Committee, though Douglas was forever frustrated there by oil-

PREFACE, 1995 XI

country "whales"* like Johnson, Kerr, and Clinton Anderson, while Moynihan has assumed its chair—which carries with it, even for a scholar, presumptive whaledom.

Similarities and coincidences, as one would expect of a political body with a two-hundred-year history. The differences are more striking. There are six women now, where there was one, or briefly two, in the fifties, and none of today's six is the widow of a senator. Three times as many people work for the Senate now as did when I arrived in 1956. A lot of young lawyers have crossed the Potomac or the Susquehanna, bound for Capitol Hill, since that icy night long ago.

The most significant difference in the makeup of the Senate is not in gender or staff size but in one region's party affiliations. The Confederate South, when I came to Washington, was represented in the Senate by twenty-two Democrats. Many of them held positions of considerable power, since their one-party constituents had returned them often enough to endow them with the essential coin of seniority.

They varied: even among those from the Deep South, there were a few national men, like Lister Hill and John Sparkman of Alabama; on the fringes, where it was possible, a few New Deal–style progressives, such as Albert Gore, Sr. and Estes Kefauver of Tennessee, and Lyndon Johnson of Texas; across the region, the occasional economic populist—Russell Long (Huey's son) and two Carolinians, Kerr Scott of North Carolina and Olin Johnston of South Carolina, who like Hill and Sparkman represented poor hill country people. The rest were pretty thoroughly conservative, whether Burkean intellectuals like Bill Fulbright, crusty legalists like Sam Ervin, John Stennis, John McClellan, and Spessard Holland, or men who would be regarded today as simply and irredeemably racist—Strom Thurmond and Jim Eastland.

They varied, and yet the Deep Southerners among them collected with a single purpose in Dick Russell's office at moments of

---

*See pp. 48–49.

challenge to Southern institutions—when civil rights bills were on the agenda, or when the cloture rule, which protected the filibusters that enabled them to block civil rights bills, was in jeopardy. Then they formed a senatorial British square and prepared to repel attacks. Inevitably the sense of being besieged gave them an even stronger sense of region, and of shared power: ten of those sitting around Russell's table, among the piled books and newspapers of a bachelor's office, were committee chairmen.

If they had become de facto Republicans and determined to block not only civil rights legislation but every other Democratic initiative as well, the result would have been paralysis. It never quite came to that. There was enough Democratic humus in the soil from which they sprang to make a conversion unlikely, and despite President Eisenhower's popularity in the South, his party had not then built a foundation in state and local government sufficient to encourage strong Republican competitors for national office.

So they stayed put. With chairmen like Fulbright, Russell, Hill, Sparkman, Johnston, Byrd and Robertson of Virginia, and Ellender of Louisiana, and with Ike threatening vetoes in the White House, a narrow Democratic majority produced moderate legislation and considerable party unity—purchased, many liberals thought, at the price of obscuring a vigorous national message.

Baker v. *Carr*, the Supreme Court's landmark "one man, one vote" decision of 1963, and the Voting Rights Act of 1965 altered this picture forever. *Baker* made it difficult for Southern legislatures to disenfranchise suburban voters in the paired interests of inner-city and rural organizations. In time congressional districts were reconfigured, and Republican sympathies in the suburbs became more appropriately represented in the House. Inevitably this had an effect on Senate races, as it became plausible to be represented by Republicans there as well. The "solid South" became an agglomeration, its senators divided almost equally between the parties.

The Voting Rights Act also transformed Southern politics. Wherever Democrats survived the growing Republican vote in the suburbs, they needed to be responsive not only to the "good old boys" of the rural areas but also to new black voters throughout the state. When Robert Bork's nomination to the Supreme Court was before the Senate, a Southern Democrat came upon a group of others like himself, in agitated discussion. He asked them what they were arguing about. "What to do about this Bork nomination" was the reply. He laughed. "You're going to do same as I am. You're going to vote the way the people who sent you here want you to." He meant black people, whose leaders strongly opposed the judicial conservative. For the most part, his prediction was correct. On matters in which black Southerners believe their vital interests are at risk, their Democratic representatives, white or black, have no option. That was also true of the fifties, except that Southern Democratic senators then thought they had no option (assuming they might have wished for one) but to sustain the segregated status quo. It would be difficult to find a more complete turnabout.

These days, a politically divided South does not convene in emergency sessions—or in any other. Indeed, there are no regional factions now, at least none that lasts beyond the occasional issue du jour. Nor is there a "liberal" faction that is willing to have its interests negotiated for by a single spokesperson (a role that Hubert Humphrey sometimes played in the fifties and early sixties). The fiercest Senate factions described in this book depended, as many things throughout our history have, on the saliency of race; and racial issues, at least as embodied in the classic dichotomy of human rights/states' rights, do not absorb the Senate as they once did—when they cast many of its members into opposing lines of blue and gray.

A number of behavioral changes have occurred for sheer impact in the working lives of senators—few more significant than the requirement to cast several votes each day. There are four or five times as many roll-call votes each session as there were when I worked in the Senate, making for as many more interruptions in work off the floor. These result, in small part, from a "good government" belief that the public should know where senators stand; in larger part, from the members' wish to demonstrate their own political correctness, and to embarrass their opposition (often on questions of abortion rights and sexual behaviors) in order to raise campaign funds from an aroused constituency. Senator Helms has been particularly aggressive in such efforts, but he now has company on both sides of the ideological aisle.

Filibusters, and the threat of filibusters, have multiplied. Given the cloture rule, the opportunity to disable the Senate until the majority surrenders has always been there; but until very recently it was rarely seized. Why the restraint of the past should have given way to almost weekly obstructions is unclear. The practice is boldly undemocratic, since it requires, on the widest range of issues, a super-majority of sixty to overcome it. This has not embarrassed those who mount filibusters, nor has it generated much public complaint. Maybe the comity that marked the Senate in earlier years has given way, as have manners in general; maybe respect for the mission of the Congress (to pass laws) has succumbed to the quest for partisan, or even personal, advantage. The absence of an urgent agenda, one that millions of Americans believe should be enacted, may have something to do with the public's silence when the desiderata of even the most altruistic interest groups are blocked by filibusters.

Yet the chief cause is probably institutional: Democratic domination of Congress. Republicans have controlled the House for exactly four years in the past sixty-two and the Senate for only eight during the same period. The exasperation of their almost perpetual minority status causes some House Republicans to indulge in puerile procedural tactics, intended more to annoy the majority than to achieve a legislative result. In the Senate, the weapon of choice is the filibuster. A defensive maneuver, once reserved for what was thought to be profound threats to a region's "way of life," has become an almost automatic response to any objectionable legislation.

This expresses, if it does not cause, a quarrelsomeness in the Senate that many of its members complain about. When you join with it the relentless pressure to raise money for reelection campaigning, the inability of the political parties to give them much support, and the often ignorant hostility of the media and the public toward all in public office, you see why "term limits" are not necessary to drive them out. There will always be men—and now women—who wish to remain in the Senate, enjoying the occasional opportunity to make a difference in the lives of their fellow citizens; and they will pay the price to do it. But an increasing number of their colleagues, including some very capable members, sound as if they find the price too high. If there are potential Muskies, Harts, Javitses, and Saltonstalls among them, we shall be the poorer when they retire.

The other part of this book is about life in the Executive Branch, particularly in the White House. Many scholars have published studies of White House organization under the modern Presidents, noting this one's preference for a strong chief-of-staff system, that one's "basketball team" approach in which any senior player could try to score—could inform and try to influence the President directly, without the leave or assistance of a chief of staff. I shall not add to such comparisons, interesting as they are, since I believe the quality of an Administration depends not on its White House organization but on the President: on how the President seizes opportunities, deals with calamity, chooses subordinates, addresses the American people and the Congress, and generally tries to stay on course.

Most of the latter chapters of *A Political Education* are about Lyndon Johnson's stewardship of the office into which he was propelled by the most tragic of circumstances, and which he later won in his own right. As I added a postscript to the book in the summer of 1988, the opinion polls were giving Michael Dukakis an edge over George Bush. As a Democrat, I hoped it was real and would last; but I feared that the "race" question, in all its galling complexity, would continue to bedevil the party in Presidential elections.

The postscript was written before the "Willie Horton" television spot made use of the public's impatience with "soft" liberal responses to the deviant behavior that rots the inner cities. The spot did not cause voters to associate that behavior with black Americans or to identify the Democratic party with both. But it capitalized on impressions that had been building for a quarter-century or more and that once again seemed likely to persuade a majority of white Americans that they were not comfortable with the Democratic nominee.

I did not foresee the nomination, four years later, of a Southerner who would to some degree neutralize those impressions, as Johnson and Jimmy Carter had done in 1964 and 1976. As Carter's evangelical Christianity and naval career made him acceptable to many whites—particularly Southerners—who might otherwise have continued to reject the party's choice, so Bill Clinton declared that he was a "new Democrat," by which he meant to convey that he was not a liberal ideologue on social, particularly race-related, issues. This helped elect him.

Some of his Administration's actions during the early months of 1993 seemed to contradict that message—to imply that race and gender, more than evident merit, were to have priority in appointments. Since it is important that a new Administration, particularly one determined to effect massive social and economic change, show that it is competently managed, it was an error to allow the impression that competence was regarded as secondary, in the selection of senior managers of government, to color and sex. Better to have openly pursued the best, and to have found, *mirabile dictu*, that the best was often black or female. Insisting on changing the military's policy with respect to gay servicemen and servicewomen was not, in itself, an act of "reverse discrimination," but the early focus on it, when more urgent domestic and foreign problems awaited the President's attention, made it seem so. The effect of these misadventures was to distance the President from a constituency (white males) that he had shown promise of winning back to the national Democratic Party.

President Clinton, like millions of other Americans, reveres the memory of President Kennedy—another charming, articulate politician. There are other similarities between them: "Friends of Bill" are almost as numerous as were veterans of PT 109. There are also significant differences. Kennedy's greatest interest and knowledge lay in foreign affairs, Clinton's is in domestic; Kennedy was the scion of a rich family with a long political history on his mother's side, while Clinton is a self-made man; before they reached the White House, Kennedy's arena was the cosmopolitan East and the Congress and Clinton's was the governorship of a poor Southern state. Important differences, and yet emotionally the tie remains strong— perhaps woven of the sentimental wish to recapture days when spirits were high and Vietnam and Watergate still to come, but strong nonetheless.

The President whose name never escapes Clinton's lips is Lyndon Johnson. There are obvious reasons why that should be so. Johnson remains unpopular, dogged with responsibility, in the public's eyes, for America's most lamentable military conflict. Bill Clinton's hatred for that conflict is well known, as is his service, during his Georgetown University years, on the staff of Arkansas Senator Bill Fulbright. The Fulbrights and the Johnsons were among the warmest friends in the Senate during the decade of the fifties and the early sixties. Then came Vietnam and years of reproach, acrimony, and finally bitter mistrust. Small wonder that there is little warmth in Clinton's heart for the memory of Lyndon Johnson, and even less interest in recalling days in which Clinton's military service obligation clashed with his abomination of "Johnson's war."

Yet there are a few reasons why Clinton might consider Johnson, rather than Kennedy, his forerunner. Lyndon Johnson and Bill Clinton rose from the same poor Southwestern soil; they knew the same scrawny little towns, smelled the same sweaty air in the broiling summers, learned history in the same stingily supported public schools, saw the same daily brutalities of racial discrimination make victims out of fellow citizens, and felt the same hot surge of political ambition well up in their chests. They both hungered for high office for its own sake, and they both assumed that once there, they were supposed to use political power to improve living conditions, or at least to improve opportunities, for less-favored Americans. Both cared more about grandma and her grandchildren than about international bureaucracies; both were assumed, with reason, to be indifferent to the daily adjustments in the balance of power that foreign policy specialists told them were critical to world stability. Both did not hesitate to throw themselves into the legislative pit, to fight for their programs. Indeed, they relished the urging and the dealing of it.

Johnson was much coarser, and thus he seemed farther removed from his true self when he put on the Presidential toga. To the young of the late sixties—including Bill Clinton—he was inconceivable as a fraternity brother. If the two of them were serving in today's Senate, Clinton would be the media's favorite, the Sunday talk show regular, the lodestar for young persons of a political bent, and one of several important liberals; Johnson would be the majority leader. Clinton would make fun of him in Georgetown, and seek his help the next morning in passing a bill important to Arkansas, or to some part of the Clintons' wide spectrum of interests. Johnson would give it, after winning Clinton's promise to help him on several matters of importance to the leader, the party, the country, and the free world.

And Johnson could deliver, because he would have firm working relationships with the Republican leaders, and with some of the older, more conservative Democrats who regarded Clinton as prolix and indiscriminately enthusiastic. It would not matter in the slightest to them that Clinton's bill had been written in a Democratic think tank and was supported by a hundred liberal interest groups. What would matter was that a significant player in the game—a reliable trader, who owed many favors and was owed still more—was asking that the bill be passed, for his young friend Bill Clinton.

The importance of such personal networks was one of the lessons in my political education. Clinton surely learned the lesson in Arkansas, dealing with the state legislature. Johnson mastered it in Congress, and made spectacular use of it when he became President. The corollary lesson from those years is that the bolder, more sweeping, more complex the program that a President submits to Congress, the more necessary it is that he and his helpers practice the nonintellectual arts of personal politicking—with men and women of both parties, and of every persuasion save contempt for the President. Grasp of the issues and facility of expression are seldom sufficient. Another former governor, Jimmy Carter, ignored that lesson to his cost.

Clinton can learn much from Johnson's failures and shortcomings; there is a lot that he will not wish to emulate. But I hope he will not altogether reject the notion that one of his direct political forebears is another Southwestern liberal, whose tireless and resourceful hustling helped build the platform on which he stands.

A
Political
Education

Prologue

10 p.m., January 31, 1956

THE long drive from Texas is almost over. It has been raining, and a cold mist still hangs over the highway.

Twenty miles to go. Virginia darkness, hills and white fences, the easy pastoral South.

My back aches. I drive like a robot. The old Buick is full of cigarettes and bags, books and pictures. There is no sound but the roar of its engine and the wet tearing whine of its tires. We have not talked for a long time now, not since the imminence of the frontier filled us with apprehension and thrust us into separate silences.

Then the first bright smears of red and green. Neon throbbing in the mist, an aurora of reflected light in the heavy winter sky, signs and outposts of the Eastern city.

The East! Where it is always cold and wet — where motel rooms are always dim and smoky, and surly night managers wait to intimidate Southerners. I am back in the East again, and tomorrow, after six years' absence, I will confront its quick multitudes once more, its waiters, cab drivers, doormen, business executives, its brilliant hard girls — this competent, cunning, unforgiving East.

Like nomads we swirl down the highway, transients to be used, to be devoured by the omnivorous money-loving Eastern city. I fear our vulnerability, our soft unreadiness, our lack of big-city skills. To be tough, to be wise!

Three miles. Exit for Shirlington, Fairfax Apartments. Images of wealthy Easterners behind picture windows, discussing rich and important affairs, knowing everything about politics, business, tipping, how to get off superhighways at the right exit.

Darkness again. A country club, doubtless much harder to join than the ones at home in Texas.

And then it is there: first the massive unmistakable Pentagon, a few lights burning in its message centers, the middle of an intricate web of secrets that must bind the world submissively to our power. Beyond it, the City.

To the left the Monument; straight ahead, the vast gleaming honeycomb of bureaucracies. To the right, like a fortress on a headland, the Capitol, above its dome a single vivid light. Through the illuminated mist, Washington is a vast stage design — the national dream as seen in a photographic negative.

I slow the car to cross Memorial Bridge. I want to remember this time, this shifting of our lives. We are crossing the wide, black Potomac River, mythic in the January night, leaving the South and its easy permissiveness, its flattering affirmations. We have been young and liberal in Texas, where to be liberal was to be righteously happy under siege. We are entering the North, where one must be astute as well as compassionate.

It is a solemn moment. The smell of power hangs over this city like cordite. Yet for the first time in hours I am more excited than apprehensive.

In the mist beyond the Monument is the White House and General Eisenhower, whom I have mocked for four irreverent liberal years, and hope to help defeat this fall. Tonight, surrounded by this city of power, he seems much more formidable than before, not at all the amiable duck of Herblock's drawings. Eisenhower belongs here. Established residents of this city do his bidding. If there is ultimately a single hand at the lever of power, controlling the warplanes of the Pentagon and the secrets of the State Department, it is his.

I am a devoted reader of the *New Republic,* and so I believe Eisenhower to be the ignorant, if passively benign, figurehead of a conservative party and government. His cabinet, filled with narrow-minded businessmen like George Humphrey, Douglas McKay, and Charlie Wilson, has provided me, and other *New Republic* readers, with almost weekly cause for scorn.

Yet I cannot feel, as we enter the city, the old exuberant confidence in my judgment of these men. It was one thing to sit about the tables of Scholz Garden in Austin, drinking iced Pearl in schooners, and mock their benighted efforts to run the country like a small corporation. It is another to confront this city with its mysteries of authority. Perhaps the presence of power begets ambiguity: in the years ahead I am to see a variety of angry convictions turned to doubt when confronted by power and responsibility.

The most ambiguous figure of all is the man I am to work for — Lyndon Johnson. I have never met him. The one contact I have had with him was by mail: my wife and I had wired him months before from Austin, scolding him for seeming to adopt Senator Knowland's rigid opinions about China. He replied in a long letter that satisfied nothing of our grievance, though the fact that he answered at all — there was his signature — was impressive. It would be several weeks before I understood that such replies were written by his staff, that Senator Johnson had no time to argue China policy with an unknown constituent.

A few months after this exchange-by-proxy, I heard that Johnson had authorized the hiring of a young Texas lawyer for one of his staffs. I was near graduation from law school, and had almost determined to go back home to East Texas and begin practice with a classmate. The chance to go to Washington to deal with great public issues — instead of private injury claims and oil leases — excited me, as it has thousands of others since the 1930's. I applied, was interviewed in the senator's Austin office during the congressional recess, and was hired — all without seeing or speaking to Johnson. There was a curiously detached air to the proceedings; decisions about my salary were relayed as "the Senator says," or "the Senator feels," with the air of having come straight down the mountain from Zeus. It seemed unlikely that I would stay with him very long. As we drove out of Texas that January, I thought of the next two years in Washington as an "experience," to be followed by a return to "real life" in Texas.

Lyndon Johnson. I cannot remember when I first heard his name, though given an early interest in political history and my father's New Deal sympathies, it was probably in 1941, when he lost a Senate race to "Pappy" O'Daniel by a handful of votes. He was young and skinny, and he represented the sainted Roosevelt against a man whom I identified with biscuit dough and country music. He had won his Senate seat in 1948, though with such a narrow margin and after such a struggle in the courts that he scarcely suggested bold and confident leadership. Besides, he had tried to outdo his conservative opponent in opposition to labor; he had embraced, or seemed to embrace, the know-nothing reaction in Texas that was to depress the spirit of a generation of liberals. One heard that he did not really share those right-wing opinions — that he was, in fact, merely trying to gain running room for his progressive instincts. In a way, though one was glad to have even a secret progressive representing Texas in the Senate, his dissembling made it worse. It seemed that he was either turning his back on a decade of commitment to Roosevelt, or trying to placate the new majority of Texans to whom the New Deal and Fair Deal were anathema. Thus Lyndon Johnson was mistrusted by those who, like me, embraced the liberal *Texas Observer* and loathed the *Dallas News*.

Yet he was equally mistrusted by the oilmen and bankers in my hometown. Many of them had found sudden wealth in the oil fields about the time the rest of the country suffered the worst of the Depression. The inability of other Americans to strike it rich was always baffling to them, or attributable solely to malingering; and the idea that the national government should take their tax dollars to help malingerers was outrageous. Anyone who supported Roosevelt must believe in that kind of thievery; Johnson had supported Roosevelt, had been his agent, his defender, his adoring protégé; so Johnson was not to be trusted.

There was another Lyndon Johnson, quite apart from these two polarized, yet similar images in his home state. There was the Johnson of the *Time* cover, already rumored to be the "second most powerful man in America." He had been catapulted into the leadership of Senate Democrats after only four years in the Senate. His legislative skill was already a legend. Most impressive to me, he had secured the unanimous vote of his party in the Senate against Joe McCarthy. Rage against McCarthy had caused me to go to law school. I had thought that sooner or later, McCarthy and his followers would ruin every decent man and institution in the country, unless enough lawyers rallied around to defend them; and so I had set out to acquire the necessary legal weapons to resist him. If I had known more history, and better understood the pendulum of opinion that moves in our democracy, I might not have been so quixotic.

Yet even now, when McCarthy had been subdued, I was grateful to those who had diminished his ugly power. And if Johnson had not cried out against him when McCarthy was in his prime, as had Fulbright and Benton and others, he had done what no other could do: he had caused the Senate to strike him down with an institutional contempt. That wound had been mortal.

There was, of course, more to this Johnson than the victory over McCarthy and primacy among Democrats. He cooperated with Eisenhower, often giving the President stronger support than he received from conservatives in his own party. Yet just as often he carried the banner of progressivism, leading Democrats in attacks on tight money and trickle-down theories of economics. As to race, he was an unknown quantity, at least to me — and my own concerns had not yet shifted from civil liberties to civil rights. He had no reputation as a speaker, but I did not expect to write for him, anyway. I had resigned myself to a vocation and a milieu in which my literary interests would play no part. I would save Yeats and Joyce for the evenings; the days were to be for the United States Code.

Tonight, as we drive down Constitution Avenue toward the Capitol — like pioneers reconnoitering a new campsite at nightfall, trying to remove the threat from an ineffable mystery — it occurs to me that I know very little about the man I am to work for, or about what goes on in the formidable piles that line the street. In that I am probably not much different from most other young men of this time who have emerged from an educational system that fits them equally well for the nineteenth, as for the twentieth century. In my Southern university, the study of literature ended with Hardy. History was British, and its climax was the Reform Bill; in law school, what counted were consideration in a contract and compensation for an injury. I am unschooled in the great issues of modern life, and I know it. I can take positions, strike poses, remember and repeat a number of rhetorical arguments, but I really don't know this world in which interests clash and men struggle to avoid disaster.

Why am I here? Why did I choose this "experience," instead of beginning a law practice and finding a responsible place in a small community? Partly because I want to find out what goes on in the councils of power — very much as a subway straphanger wants to know about scandal among the famous. Partly because I want to "do good," and a decade after Roosevelt it still seems as if Washington is the grand arena for doing good. Partly — perhaps chiefly — because I want to cast a shadow, to feel, however vicariously, that I have affected significant events and therefore exist. Many men find that in small towns, in determining what shall be built and where, in attracting new industry, running a school board, winning an important case, saving a life. But for me, the great game is here, among these men, within these institutions.

The mist has cleared, and it is simply cold and wet. We turn south again, cross the bridge, and find a room for the night.

Two years of casting a shadow, and then home again. I do not feel, as I fall asleep in this exciting, intimidating Eastern city, any premonition of what is to come. I know that my political education is about to begin; how long it is to continue, how diverse and confusing will be its lessons, I cannot imagine.

1

Counsel in Congress

I HAD last seen Washington in August 1950. One suffocating evening in Manhattan, I decided to visit a girl in Georgia, and persuaded a New York Irish couple — Tom Dardis was a fellow graduate student at Columbia, a literary man — to go with me. Next morning we left the train in Washington and decided to hitchhike south. Tom insisted that we visit the Library of Congress first. While he and his wife went inside, I stood on the steps, taking the hot waves of Washington summer, looking across to the Capitol.

Congress was debating the Korean War. The Secretary of State was catching it from the Republicans, allegedly for having left Korea out of his ambit of American concern and thus inviting its invasion. Off-year elections were not far away. The nation was at war, and partisan politics, over there across the park, were intense.

A streetcar banged heavily by. A dozen pigeons slowly avoided a company of tourists. An elderly guard came out for a smoke and asked if it were hot enough for me; he didn't know whether the Democrats were likely to retain control over Congress after November, but he certainly hoped a certain senator made it back, because he was sponsoring a retire-after-thirty-years bill for federal employees. The senator was a profound conservative. That the old library guard, a uniformed member of the proletariat, should be concerned about the return of a conservative Republican senator, was shocking.

I thought that I should have to revise my estimate of political allegiance. I had left out self-interest among blue-collar groups, the kind that I ascribed automatically to banks and the AMA. Apparently not all the working poor read editorials and took up their assigned positions on the barricades.

I was struck, too, by the tranquillity of the scene. The park, with its variety of graceful trees; a few cars, shimmering in the morning sun; beyond, the Capitol. This was the theater, and inside that building was the stage, where the country's passionate preoccupations were acted out: the loss of China, the fight for Korea, the presence or the empty accusation of Communists in government, states' rights, and cruelty to Negroes. Sulphurous issues, the "fury and the mire of human veins."

But if there were conflict and meaning on the stage within, there was, out here, all the complacency of a Southern courthouse square. It was inconceivable that a mob should storm this place. Representative government, I thought, required only that men should sweat and shout and beg and cheat until they were elected to office, whereupon they might quit the small towns, travel to Washington — and enter a mausoleum surrounded by a scene from Fragonard.

The air was colder the next time, and I was something other than an observer from across the park. I had been hired as assistant counsel of the Senate Democratic Policy Committee, and one morning in early February 1956, I made my way among tourists and messengers toward the committee's room on the third floor of the Capitol.

It was crowded. Six or seven people were at desks in a high-ceilinged room whose deeply set windows looked out on the Mall and the Monument, the great mass of official architecture known as the Federal Triangle, and Pennsylvania Avenue down to the Treasury.

It was a breathtaking idea: to work at the very point to which this scene appeared to be tending, and from which it radiated. The view itself was satisfying, in a remote, intellectual way. It was what one expected. One sees Parliament across the Thames, looking just as it does in a thousand drawings and descriptions; the Arc de Triomphe; the Pope's miter. There is nothing human, nothing surprising or moving about such things at first. It takes time before one feels the striving, the inspired foolishness that went into making them. Months later, in a happy, drunken twilight, I looked out and finally felt that scene.

Now to find out what I was hired to do. The counsel of the committee, and my boss, was Gerald W. Siegel, an exceedingly kind and intelligent man who had come to the committee from the staff of the Securities and Exchange Commission. He had worked for Donald Cook, when Cook chaired the SEC by day and briefed Lyndon Johnson in the Senate Preparedness Subcommittee by night. Thereafter Johnson had persuaded Gerry Siegel to become his lawyer.

Gerry had too much on his hands in 1955. Johnson's heart attack had not relieved the pressure on key Senate staff members. If anything, serving Earle Clements, the acting leader, and other members of the Democratic leadership — as well as the convalescent Johnson — had been even more demanding. Gerry asked for help. Johnson agreed, provided he found someone from Texas — I suppose to offset Gerry's Iowa and Yale background, perhaps ultimately to help with Texas problems. So I had been hired.

To do what? To counsel the "Senate Democratic Policy Committee." That had an imposing sound. But what did it mean, why was the committee so rarely in the news?

It had been proposed in 1946, in the LaFollette-Monroney hearings on the reorganization of Congress. It was a political scientists' idea, a structural reform of Congress. Each party was to have a policy committee which would define party doctrine, and take party positions on issues that arose between Presidential elections. It was to be a kind of permanent floating party platform. By this the country would know what Democrats and Republicans thought, who in each party had been faithful to those thoughts, and who had strayed. Clearly the intention was that American politics would more closely approach the ideological mode of Europe. Particularly in mid-term elections, the voters would have a definite choice, not merely between personalities, but between ideas of government.

Those who spoke for this reform in 1946 included not only political scientists, but representatives such as Estes Kefauver and Sherman Adams. Without a word of debate, the Senate adopted it. This was not because it was indisputable, but because senators were more concerned with other matters in the reorganization bill — particularly the size and compensation of Senate staffs. First things first. Few issues command the alert attention of senators as do the salaries and composition of their staffs and of Senate committees.

In the House it was another matter. There was no sign of conflict over the policy committees, but the bill emerged without a mention of them. Pretty clearly the Speaker and Chairman Smith of the Rules Committee had decided that no other entities but themselves should determine policy in the House.

Yet they must have agreed that if senators felt strongly about policy committees, they should have them. Almost at once Congress passed a supplemental appropriations bill in which funds were provided for the staffs of two policy committees. There was no detailed description of their roles. That would be worked out as time went along.

It seemed natural that the Senate Democratic leader would head his policy committee, and so Scott Lucas of Illinois became chairman. Senator Lucas — whom I knew only slightly, long after he had left the Senate — was a kind of Burning Tree Club liberal, generally faithful to President Truman's program, but not inclined to impress his or the President's views on the heterogeneous Democratic membership of the Senate. The original purpose of the policy committees may have been to set policy, to draw lines; but if this was ever possible among Senate Democrats, it was not attempted. Lucas's successor, Ernest McFarland of Arizona, was even less determined to shape a unified party position, and even less capable of it.

The Senate Republicans at that time were far more cohesive in their views. All but a few were generally set against government spending and federal regulation of business. It was therefore relatively easy to establish a Republican position against legislation which would have either effect. The Republican Policy Committee met frequently for lunch and discussion, after which their chairman would emerge to announce Republican opposition to the latest Democratic spending program.

By 1956, the pattern of the Democratic Policy Committee had been fixed. The committee met biweekly, more or less. The counsel explained the bills on the Senate Calendar — the bills that had been reported by the standing committees, and not yet passed. Members of the committee authorized the chairman to call up certain bills for action by the Senate, and asked him to delay others. They debated the merits and politics of each major bill on the Calendar, and of many that were still pending in the standing committees. In effect, they constituted a Senate version of the House Rules Committee. They were a screen of generalists, controlling the flow from the specialist committees.

The thrust of the Reorganization Act had come to this in the Senate Democratic Policy Committee, partly because it was impossible to resolve differences of opinion between men like Hubert Humphrey and Harry Byrd, or Paul Douglas and Richard Russell; partly because Democrats had been in operational control of the Senate during most of the time since the act was passed, and thus it was easy to ignore the ideological problem in favor of the functional job of setting the Senate's program. Republicans, basically more unified in opinion, were also generally in opposition. Having no leadership responsibilities, they had time to be philosophical.

The Republican committee always made news. Opposition to anything in Washington is guaranteed a few lines in the newspaper. Usually all that emerged from the Democratic Policy Committee was a list of bills to be motioned up. Depending on Johnson's mood, that might cover only three or four major bills, or — if the Senate had been accused of dawdling by the press — it might run the gamut from major programs to private immigration bills, their titles read off in the Senate chamber with equal emphasis as if to say, "There, by God, don't say we're not attending to business!"

More than two years passed before I was asked to sit with the committee and brief them on pending legislation. My job at first was to serve as counsel to something called the "Calendar Committee." This was composed of two or three junior senators, who dutifully gathered in the Democratic cloakroom on mornings before the Senate was to have a "Calendar Call."

I often wondered what schoolchildren in the galleries thought of constitutional government when a Calendar Call was in progress. The atmosphere was one of controlled panic, like a tobacco auction. A thin, dark-eyed clerk read off the number and title of every bill — there were sometimes hundreds of them — with a machine-gun rapidity that was interrupted occasionally by a senatorial shout of "Over!" If there was no interruption, the bill passed, by unanimous consent. "Over!" meant that the bill remained on the Calendar.°

In this way the bulk of the Senate's work was done, at least in number of bills passed. Immigration bills, private claim bills, minor statutory amendments, and sometimes even significant legislation which, for one reason or another, senators did not choose

---

° It could, of course, be motioned up later for debate.

to debate, passed the Senate on Calendar Call and made their way to the House or the President.

After a call was announced, usually several days in advance, I read the bills and reports, and prepared myself to brief my small committee. Senators and their staffs phoned to register objections to certain bills — Senator Morse objected to the grant of certain federal land, because the grantee was not required to pay for it; Senator Gore disliked immigration bills for mentally defective girls, mindful, I suppose, of genetics in the Tennessee hills; Senator Magnuson did not object to a lumber marketing bill if the Calendar Committee would offer an amendment to it and secure its adoption. My Calendar was covered with notes as I left, heavy books of bills under both arms, for the cloakroom.

There I would explain the bills and relate the objections I had received. Sometimes an objection raised a problem for the committee members, because they had assured the author of the bill — frequently a powerful congressman — that they would get it through. Then began a great rushing around, seeking out the objector, urging him to withdraw his "hold" on the bill, phoning to warn the congressman, and perhaps writing a last-minute amendment that eased it by.

Ordinarily the members of the Calendar Committee were in agreement on whether or not a bill should pass on the call. Ideological differences did not interfere. One of the best committees was composed of Herman Talmadge and Joseph Clark, whose views of the world could scarcely have been more opposed. In two years of service on the committee, they disagreed no more than twice. Watching them, I learned my first lesson in the nature of the Senate: that the famous "club" atmosphere is based on the members' mutual acceptance of responsibility and concentration on tasks at hand. This governed both a fledgling member of the Establishment, Talmadge, and one who would always be outside it, Joe Clark. For those obsessed with the morality of political opinion, an easy working relationship between a Southern conservative and Northern liberal, even on mundane affairs such as the Calendar Committee, might have suggested a sellout by one or the other. For the men involved, however — though they thrust hard at one another in debate over serious matters — understanding and accommodation in the ordinary course of the Senate day was essential to sanity. Probably the high proportion of lawyers in the Senate, men accustomed to sharing a meal after thrashing one another in court, had something to do with that.

Once on the Senate floor, and the call begun, the tension was terrific. For two or three hours I sat with my committee, reminding them to offer an amendment, whispering information when they were questioned about a bill, all the while praying that I was right. We were onstage, under the professional scrutiny of other senators and staff, with a half-dozen gargoyles of the press leaning over the rail of the gallery directly above us. A less informed but probably perceptive audience sat in the other galleries, waiting, I thought, like the mob in Barrault's *Children of Paradise*, to break into cheers or catcalls at any moment. From time to time I would rush forward to hand the clerk an amendment received from an absent senator, or hoarsely instruct a page to tell another senator in his office that he must come at once if he wanted to be heard on a bill.

At last it would end. Piles of discarded notes and reports lay about us. I would become aware that my shirt was soaking, that I was weary and terribly hungry. But before I went for lunch, I would return to the Policy Committee room and tell the staff, with pride and amazement, that we "passed 175 bills today!" Helping to do that was casting a shadow — very faint, very thin, but a shadow.

I spent a lot of time, in those first two years, walking the halls of the Capitol and of the office buildings, talking with committee professionals and members of the senators' staffs, discussing rules with the parliamentarian. Studying the Senate rules and precedents seemed about as dry as writing a will, but it soon became clear that command of the rules was one of the most powerful weapons in the conservative arsenal. Senator Russell knew them intimately. Senator Lehman did not. And there was nothing to be done with a farsighted liberal amendment, tabled, consigned to committee, ruled not germane, or otherwise held not to be in order, but offer it to the press as something that might have been. Thus I tried to learn the rules.

An ancient, good man tried to teach them to me. Charlie Watkins had been around the Senate for fifty years or more, and his patience was considerable, as it had to be. Often senators who felt themselves abused by a ruling from the chair descended into the well of the Senate — the semicircular depression where I sat, absorbed by the debate or distracted by a pretty girl in the gallery — descended and set upon Charlie with a vehemence that stopped just short of abuse. He listened patiently, and in his old, Pepperidge Farm voice, explained why he had advised the presiding officer to rule as he did. An ultimate respect for Charlie and his knowledge of the rules, and a fervent desire to be on his side next time, sent the senators grumbling back to their seats.

Charlie Watkins and Ed Hickey, the Journal clerk who sat beside him, epitomized the old values of public service by government functionaries. The world needs men of such impartiality and complete dedication to task and institution. It is hell to encounter their opposites — those who must be bought, and if bought, will not stay bought; those so governed by whim or peevishness or simple lust for advancement that they will bend any rule and ignore any precedent in their service. Public life controlled by such men is chaos itself.

Yet as I looked at Ed Hickey, with his lantern jaw and cavernous mouth sprung open with the work of the Journal, on which he scratched like a character in Dickens; or at Charlie himself, crucial as he was; or at the other clerks who maintained the mechanics of the Senate — with little concern for the issues in debate, so often had they heard them, so much bull, so much posturing — I thought that I would avoid such a life at all cost. As Charlie grew very old, it was once suggested that I succeed him. The idea struck me with horror. I thought it was time to be moving on.

We were, nevertheless, a company. There was an esprit de corps among us, something of the irreverence of valets toward great masters, something of their pride in reflected glory. At moments of high drama, late at night, with the galleries packed, the press seats filled, the hour of a historic vote having come, there was no place else to be. Even the pages — droll boys who looked as if they had just sneaked back from a forbidden smoke in the men's room — shared our excitement at such times.

After a while I had two jobs in the Senate, one as a mechanic helping to move legislation through, the other as legislative assistant to the leader. In the latter role I came to know many of the other men, most of them young lawyers, economists, or journalists, who served individual senators as bill-drafters and speechwriters. It was heady work for some. If a senator was an activist, if he served on the right committees or simply had the right interests, his legislative assistant moved in a high-pressure world of cabinet officers, academicians, and Washington lobbyists.

Ben Read, with Senator Clark, became an expert on the issues of nuclear war and peace — an understanding he was to carry into the State Department as its executive secretary. Frank McCulloch and Howard Shuman provided Senator Douglas with limitless information on economic and social matters. When Mike Monroney offered an amendment, Tom Finney sat beside him, feeding him facts and arguments. Ted Sorensen and Mike Feldman with John Kennedy; Oliver Dompierre with Knowland and Dirksen; Steve Horn with Kuchel; John Zentay with Symington; Don McBride with Kerr — such men were indispensable, not only to their senators, but to the entire process of legislating. If their senators were occupied with politics or a thousand constituent chores, the legislative assistants understood and remembered the issues at stake in every vote. We argued for hours over army coffee in the Senate restaurant, challenging each other's judgments, debating — in far simpler terms than those used upstairs on the floor — the merits of pending bills, collecting intelligence on each senator's intentions and motivations. We assumed that the Senate could not do without us. And when an amendment we had prepared or a speech we had written was offered on the floor, we thought we cast an ineluctable shadow.

The committee staffs were a mixed lot. The size and quality of each had much to do with its chairman. Senator Byrd of Virginia, whose ideas of economy reflected those of an eighteenth-century shopkeeper, allowed the Finance Committee a single professional staff member. Senator Russell had not many more on Armed Services, though they were competent and knowledgeable.

Where Southern conservatives predominated — as on the Judiciary Committee — the Southern chairmen were quite permissive about staff. Each of the senior men on Judiciary chaired a subcommittee, where he could entrench a number of faithful retainers. This system had its drawbacks for Chairman Eastland in the case of Senator Kefauver and his Anti-Trust Subcommittee. Conservatives did not want the subcommittee chairmanship, as it was by nature troublesome and aggressive toward business; and yet the demands of committee loyalty required Eastland to defend — halfheartedly, but symbolically — Kefauver's expensive staff requests. It was a dilemma with which Eastland never seemed comfortable.

Committee staff members were inclined to remain in the Senate far longer than were individual assistants to the members. The committees themselves were institutions. Senators came and went, but Appropriations remained. Even men who had migrated to committee staffs because their sponsors had no room on their own, or because of a chairman's solicitude for the staff of a defeated colleague, soon took on the institutional characteristic of their trade: a tired skepticism, often well founded, toward new ideas, whether from the executive branch or from "outside." After a time they embodied a committee's lore, as well as its mannerisms.

They worked in bursts of activity — preparing for hearings, writing reports, negotiating their bills through Senate debates and conferences with the House. These were followed by long, sometimes demoralizing periods of inaction. In such times they assumed the pale uncertain look of men without enough to do, men dependent on the inertia of their relationship to absent lords. Then they might talk of leaving, but most of them were Democrats, and they lacked a viable alternative to Senate work in the Eisenhower government downtown. They were stuck until something better came along.

They were government clerks, and yet they were unlike the civil servants who filled comparable jobs in the departments. A senior civil servant always has a full in-box, a supplicant is always waiting outside his room; there are always committee meetings, from which little may come, but which provide the sense of dealing with important questions. The civil servant's day is full, every day.

But he does not help to write a law. He does not work in an arena where constituent pressures, the threat of election defeat, and the country's needs interact. He rarely encounters the kind of canny, outrageous men whom the voters return to the Senate, men who will not follow an agenda, but proceed by intuition, hearing and believing what they will. The conscientious civil servant moves from written fact to published conclusion. He does not touch or smell. The Senate committee man, working episodically, his livelihood miserably dependent on an eccentric voting public, knows that there is more to government than laws and regulations.

A few years ago, at a country house in England, I took part in an Anglo-American conference on welfare. For two days British and American officials spoke about beneficiaries' needs, the adequacy of remedial assistance, and the merits of a guaranteed income. At last Fred Harris, nurtured in the Oklahoma legislature before coming to the Senate, put it in human terms. "When grandmaw comes in and says she can't get help up at the Oklahoma City office," he began — and in my mind's eye the scene shifted from the small green offices of executive government to the rococo halls of Congress. That was a senator talking, not a bureaucrat. It is the language of the people, and it was spoken and understood by the better committee staffs in Congress.

During that first year in Washington, our friends were mostly Texans like ourselves. Many of them were also émigré liberals, and when we came together we scorned Johnson's compromises and mocked his style. News of my subversion got back to him, and contributed to a long period of coolness on his part. He made no move to fire me, but he was aloof and wary; if I had been more important to him at that time, the consequences would have been more serious.

His staff was competent, but afraid of him. There were few things that Walter Jenkins, his principal assistant, could not do. Apart from managing Johnson's Texas affairs and his senatorial office, Jenkins served as the center-point for a network of influential friends throughout the country. If he was sometimes abused, if his face reddened with the blotches of nervous strain, he was indispensable to Johnson as trustee and friend, and both of them knew it.

George Reedy was the presiding thinker on the staff. Ponderous in speech and movement, he had an uncanny instinct for writing exactly as Johnson wished to speak during his Senate days. His was the doctrine of moderation, of the reasonable center course, repeated and redefined until the listener was ashamed of thinking immoderate thoughts. It was skillful and it worked. George often held forth on the nature of politics in America. I thought him not very exciting then, but I saw many of his analyses proved right — as when he told me, during the civil rights debate of 1957, that it did not necessarily follow that because Wisconsin was a progressive state, its people were without racial prejudice. As a Southern liberal, I thought the South had a patent on bigotry.

There was Pauline Moore, clerk of the Policy Committee, a fragile, tough-minded woman who had descended from Lucas and knew the details of every major bill passed by Congress in her time; Booth Mooney, an urbane countryman, sardonic and matter-of-fact as a city editor; Arthur Perry, who had come to Washington, as I had, to serve a brief tour with a Texas senator, and remained for thirty years to answer a hundred disparate complaints from constituents each day. There was Grace Tully, rich with her experience of the New Deal and FDR, a continuum with the past.

There was Bill Brammer, a small, elfish man with the physique of a diver, answering mail in a corner by day and writing a novel by night. From midnight until dawn — keeping himself alert on a diet of Butterfingers and warm Jell-O and Dr Pepper — he spun a tale of Southwestern politics,* its hero a tall, great-eared, brilliant, and profane politician whose model was never to appreciate the book. At nine each morning, after three hours' sleep, Brammer returned to his typewriter in the Senate Office Building and sympathized with Texans who had been outraged by government.

Finally, there was Bobby Baker. He was a Snopes, a driving, ingenious Southerner who knew the needs and limitations of every member, and who wanted not only wealth and power, but a role in liberal achievement. Officially he was secretary to the majority. Unofficially he was the "97th Senator," when ninety-six

---

* William Brammer, *The Gay Place* (Boston: Houghton Mifflin, 1961).

had been elected. Senators of both parties and of every persuasion were in his debt for favors he had performed over the years — gathering support for their bills, alerting them to pending trouble, offering shrewd advice, finding help for their campaigns. I thought his greatest talent lay in his ability to count. True believers — I was one — were always inclined to attribute more votes to their side than actually existed, simply because they thought people would vote as they "should." Bobby knew better. He would have known, for example, that the liberal, intelligent Frank Church could not support the strict regulation of firearms, even though the facts demanded it, because he came from Idaho. This capacity to resist sentimental analysis is extremely important in the deliberations of political leaders, and Bobby provided it. I envied him his primacy among the Senate staff, but I regretted the turn of fortune that ended his political career. He would have been, I believe, an effective Southern populist senator in the tradition of his original sponsors Burnet Maybank and Olin Johnston.

These were the heart of the sprawling staff that Johnson accrued over time, and he used them according to the bear-pit school of personnel management: most had moments in the sun, each spent time in the shadows, all were exhilarated by contact with him, none was sure for long how well he stood in Johnson's eyes.

After a while, I came to see Washington as something quite different from the forbidding Eastern city I had anticipated on that wintry night of our arrival. In summer, the Capitol was filled with hordes of tourists, ordinary, vulnerable people from the heartland who debarked from cramped buses to march through the Rotunda and Statuary Hall between tours of the FBI and the Lincoln Memorial. The vaulted corridors hummed with their tumult. Everywhere there was an air of permissiveness, of familiarity, real or assumed. Limousines drawing up to the Senate Office

Buildings carried men from New York and Detroit who lost their abrasive sharpness as they entered the Congress's turf — their briefcases filled with prayers to the doyens who might do them well or ill.

Thus on the Hill, at least, and for the people of the Hill, Washington was not intimidating. There was a country zest about the place, a pleasure in personality, a fellow-feeling that came from periodically facing the voters. Downtown in the departments and embassies, and in Georgetown and the suburbs, it might be different. But that did not matter, not yet. I had found a good world on the Hill. I began to relax and enjoy it.

2

Brief Lives

WHAT I have described so far is the environment of the Senate as I found it in 1956. Like the setting of a Renaissance painting — with its courtiers, lords- and ladies-in-waiting, tapestries, columns and forests — the environment was important only as it pointed to a few central figures. In the Senate, those figures were the senators themselves. The staffs, clerks, committees, rules, even the Senate chamber itself, had purpose and meaning only as they served those who had won the right to be called "United States Senator."

What kind of men were they, whom the states had sent as their plenipotentiaries to Washington? Generalizations were easy, and misleading. From time to time I made descriptive notes about them, hoping to build a theory on specific observations. What follows is a distillation of those notes.

THE DEMOCRATS

CLINTON ANDERSON OF NEW MEXICO: tough, tall, shrewd, insurance money. Secretary of Agriculture under Truman. Agreed with Ezra Taft Benson's policy of flexible price supports. Commanded a dozen Democratic votes for that — a few Easterners, like Pastore and Kennedy, and conservatives, like Smathers and Byrd, from states without wheat, corn, and other basic crops. Maverick, though essentially liberal. Horse-and-cattle-trading friend of Kerr, Johnson, and Morse. Near the cloakroom door they sat and complained about the spavined horses and impotent bulls the others had sold them — taking time off from legislation to act out a Faulknerian comedy of abuse and outrage. Urban liberals and Chamber of Commerce conservatives did not share or appreciate their country humor. Anderson fought for a change in Rule 22 at the beginning of each Congress, arguing vehemently for majority cloture. It was one of his few total variances from Establishment views.

ALBEN BARKLEY OF KENTUCKY: once leader of the Senate Democrats and then Vice President, now back as a freshman and by choice seated in the rear. Respected, but not much of a power in Johnson's Senate. A delightful spinner of yarns, he could still turn on the Democratic steam in debate. He died in the midst of a passionate speech at Lexington, Virginia.

ALAN BIBLE OF NEVADA: decent, practical, with something of a GP's bedside manner. A dependable worker, he spoke with mind-stunning deliberation. This was effective in disarming criticism, and enabled him to smother difficult questions. While his opposition seethed, Bible, the soul of accommodation, began: "I feel that a thorough, workmanlike job of studying this proposal has been undertaken by each and every member of the committee . . ." and a warm blanket settled on the fires of controversy.

HARRY BYRD OF VIRGINIA: seemed to be older than he was. Slow, not much drive. His reputation outside the Senate was greater than within, although that public reputation had its impact on other senators. Who would attack Harry Byrd and his Committee on the Reduction of Non-Essential Federal Expenditures? He wore white suits in summer and crepe-soled shoes always. Spoke with a kind of low whistling and sucking sound. A man of great courtesy — deeply reactionary, but so hard to attack personally that when Hubert Humphrey did, shortly after coming to the Senate in 1949, he was temporarily ostracized. Johnson was solicitous of Byrd — respecting his standing in the country, admiring his courtesy, knowing that he would face an uphill battle on every Finance Committee measure without the acquiescence of the chairman. Big bash at his Virginia home every year; all the powers went.

DENNIS CHAVEZ OF NEW MEXICO: fascinating creature — an old Spanish-American pol, whose New Mexico machine was a legend (an AP wire-service reporter in Albuquerque was said to have phoned a county clerk in Chavez territory one election night and asked, "How many votes does Senator Chavez have in your county?" The Spanish-American clerk, believing he was talking to a friend, replied, "How many votes does he nee-eed?"). Chavez chaired the Public Works Committee, fount of all goodness. Nobody wanted to cross old Denny. The bottle was a problem, increasingly as he became ill and was told to lay off. Solid liberal voting record when dry, otherwise unpredictable. Extremely touchy and sentimental. Kerr came to run the committee in time.

JOSEPH CLARK OF PENNSYLVANIA: came to the Senate as a famous reform mayor of Philadelphia. An aristocrat of considerable wealth; small, extremely intense. At first he worked in harness with the Establishment, but through annoyance with its dulling compromises, impatience with Senate procedures, and perhaps thwarted ambition, he became one of its sharpest critics. There was an edge of waspish snobbery to his complaint; it gave sufficient offense to deny him the committees he wanted for almost a decade. His mind was quick, and he cared passionately about arms control and the threat of nuclear war. Together with Douglas and Lehman he was one of the first to describe the plight of the cities and call for federal help.

EARLE CLEMENTS OF KENTUCKY: pol's pol. Back-room man, an embracer, an understander. I'm not sure whether he smoked or not, but I saw him as a George Bellows character in a room full of cigar haze and jousting laughter. He was aggressive and effective as Johnson's whip; not a "modern" politician with an orientation toward issues and PR, but a professional who understood the play of traditional political forces — labor, farmers, and so on.

PRICE DANIEL OF TEXAS: had the demeanor of an established big-city Baptist preacher who had been raised in the country. His reputation as a lawyer was built on his defense of the states' interests in offshore oil and gas against the federal government. Voting record pretty conservative, with practical exceptions for such matters as higher farm supports. Resigned his Senate seat to win the governorship of Texas.

PAUL DOUGLAS OF ILLINOIS: a vivid man, full of apparent contradictions. Intellectual in the extreme, professorial, though carrying an arm half-destroyed in battle as a Marine. Scrupulously honest, a liberal Saint George against the vested-interest dragon. Despite his intellect, fighting spirit, and command of facts, he seldom succeeded on the showdown votes. Like Harry Byrd — whose gentlemanly demeanor he respected as much as he detested his politics — Douglas was a loner, more important in the country than in the councils of the Senate. To many of his colleagues, his committed, serious righteousness was abrasive. In the late afternoons in an empty chamber he stalked the rows, recounting the knavery of the interests and Southern racists, speaking forcefully to an aide and a sleepy press gallery, as if they were a multitude. I remember having a long argument with Ronnie Dugger, editor of the *Texas Observer*, over the respective merits of Douglas and Johnson. Johnson made progress, not issues; Douglas the reverse. Johnson's concern with progress probably helped Democrats win the confidence of the country as a responsible opposition; many of Douglas's issues became the stuff of the Democratic future. The relationship between them was guarded, sometimes openly hostile, but there was always the possibility of rapprochement, and I thought they both desired it. One night in the cloakroom, after Douglas had finished a powerful speech on the evils of the oil depletion allowance, Johnson chided him, "Paul, I just wish you had a few oil wells in Cook County. Then you'd understand." Douglas was courteous to me, though cautious; he thought Baker and I were fundamentally bound to the Establishment that opposed him, and we were. It troubled me that I was not always on the side of one whose views were so close to my own, but I had chosen effectiveness over prophecy, and I was stuck with the consequences. I rationalized that prophecy alone would not help anybody, and I tried to feel contempt for it as a defense against my doubts; but I never could.

JAMES EASTLAND OF MISSISSIPPI: certainly a racist by today's standards; yet it was unlikely that he held the poisonous views of his predecessor Bilbo. He simply had that opinion of Negroes that white Southerners call paternalistic and urban Negroes find infuriating. He could become agitated about the Communist menace, egged on by a mole-like staff man who, like the Romanian heavy in a Grade C thriller, served him up dossiers and intricate organizational charts. Or was Eastland really agitated about that? It was a convenient rationale to explain the new militancy over race, and it put liberals on the defensive. One heard about Byzantine games involving cotton subsidies, judgeships, anticommunism. A thoroughgoing reactionary? What about the afternoon when, in the middle of a speech about cotton prices, he began a long, violent denunciation of the Wall Street bankers who had squeezed the little farmers and businessmen and workers of Mississippi until almost nothing was left, until Franklin

Roosevelt came along and broke their power and saved the people? And there was no one on the floor to defend the Wall Street bankers from that furious tirade but Bill Proxmire, liberal from Wisconsin, who had, it seemed, once worked for J. P. Morgan and Co. and thought they were decent folks.

Interlude and General Observations

Senators were members of the Elks, the Moose, the Eagles, the Lions, Rotary, Kiwanis, the American Legion, VFW, DAV, churches, and bar associations. They were 32nd degree Masons and Knights of Columbus. They had been DA's and county judges and state legislators and attorneys general and congressmen and sometimes governors. They had served in the European theater or as admirals' aides in the Pacific, and they had been awarded the Legion of Merit.

Some had been there so long that whatever they had done before had simply faded as an old letter fades into illegibility; they were just senators now, and the events of their lives were those of classic battles on the Senate floor, in committee, and on the stump winning and defending the right to be there.

The cloakroom at the back of the chamber was a men's club. There were stuffed leather chairs and maybe a dozen phone booths. There was iced mineral water from Maine and West Virginia. Older pages manned the phones, and younger ones hustled in and out with messages summoning the members to the lobby outside, to meet visiting families from home or anxious lawyers and bureaucrats with a cause to press. A few senators read the papers, but mostly the cloakroom was a refuge from great issues and calamitous events. It was a place for a smoke and easy banter. Men driven by causes, such as Douglas and Clark, did not spend much time there; neither did Johnson, who had no time, during the day, for purposeless relaxation. Occasionally, in the late afternoon, a chairman would come back from a conference with the House and tell his colleagues in the cloakroom how tough and mean old Clarence Cannon had been, or how the courtly cunning Albert Thomas had stonewalled the Senate conferees until he got what he wanted. But there was very little debate over the merits of pending legislation.

I spent a lot of time in the cloakroom, listening to stories of bygone campaigns and politicians, and after a time I came to be at ease there. In other places around the building, staff were not wanted: in a baroque room across the way, quiet as a library, where elderly senators napped in the leathery semidarkness; in the secretary of the Senate's office in the late afternoons, when Skeeter Johnston broke out the drinks; and in scattered hideaways throughout the Capitol, the whereabouts of which only a few trusted assistants knew, and where there was as much privacy as a public man is likely to have. The privilege of privacy, to be alone or only with those who shared their status, their responsibilities, their harassments, and their dangers, was guarded like treasure. Senators lived in a world where everyone outside their ranks — staff, constituents, favored interests, the press — wanted something of them, chiefly their attention. They had fought hard to gain admission to that world; its pressures were vital to their self-regard, as it was through them that they were affirmed as consequential. But they also needed to escape, singly or with what the sociologists would call their peer group. Hence those redoubts where no one else was welcome.

ALLEN ELLENDER OF LOUISIANA: made creole gumbo in one of those Capitol hideaways. Small, crotchety man. Was speaker of the Louisiana House under Huey Long and talked to him in that House moments before Huey walked out to be shot in the hall. Once he leaned his head, crinkly-haired, on my shoulder, to hear a suggestion; I thought, my God! Huey Long knew that head, that curly hair, that tough, broad face. Ellender spoke with sharp, chopping motions, as if barely controlling rage. His politics were a mix of Southern conservatism and Louisiana welfarism. Chairman of the Agriculture Committee, he tried to rationalize an instinctive thrift and the depthless needs of farmers and farm-state politicians. He made annual reports to the Senate on his frequent travels abroad; there was blind parochialism in them, but there was also a surprising openness, particularly toward Russia and Eastern Europe. It seemed certain that he would be the first senator to visit Red China. The prospect of that encounter boggled the mind.

SAM ERVIN OF NORTH CAROLINA: a country lawyer and former judge of the North Carolina Supreme Court. At first many people thought he would be Russell's heir as leader of the Southern caucus. But he had little knack for the political business of the Senate, the negotiating; he was an ideologue, with a lawyer's devotion to the "truth" of rigid constitutional formulas. His wit was from the courtroom, and consisted chiefly of stories about old Zeb Vance — not so sharp as Barkley's and more contrived. But withal he had a sharp sense of civil liberties. His scholarly abstractness caused him to bear the burden of many filibusters.

ALLEN FREAR OF DELAWARE: compact little man, from Du Pont country. Wore a jeweled fraternity pin, and shouted "Here!" on quorum calls in a high pitch that made the galleries laugh. Basically conservative, he was nevertheless a sure vote for Johnson and/or Kerr when he was needed.

WILLIAM FULBRIGHT OF ARKANSAS: one of the most perplexing men in the Senate. An eighteenth-century Whig. Bored by the kind of things with which most senators were agreeably concerned. Fulbright was skeptical of man's ability to choose a reasonable course. The space program was absurd and infuriating to him, he said, when compared to more important concerns that went begging. That the country had chosen to go to the moon before properly educating its young made him despair. Did it really? Did he truly care so much? Or had he once cared deeply, and given up? Part senator, part scholar, part Arkansan, and part cosmopolite, he seemed entirely at home nowhere. Like Johnson, Kerr, and Anderson, he had large, rough hands, and I thought he enjoyed ordinary political men more than intellectuals who only wanted to talk. He was always lucid and articulate in debate; his logic was devastating; but he lacked the heat and persistence of a leader. Like Douglas — with whom he regularly contended over social issues — he sometimes seemed to have a stake in losing, in being isolated and right. Johnson had to urge them both to want to win.

WALTER GEORGE OF GEORGIA: old when I arrived, and a Great Figure, he carried, or by encomia was made to seem to carry, the full weight of Bipartisanship, in the tradition of Vandenburg. On the few occasions when he made a set speech, it was something to hear. Powerful tuba-tones, absolutely uninterruptable. The word was that Georgia interests had sacked him for Talmadge, and there was an air of bitterness about his last days in the Senate. Though FDR had once tried to purge him, he was willing to let Johnson use him, on occasion, as the conservative sponsor of liberal causes, as in the Social Security amendment providing disability benefits at fifty. Ike later made him ambassador to NATO.

THEODORE FRANCIS GREEN OF RHODE ISLAND: ancient, tiny, lively, aristocratic man. The fact that he took an active role in the Senate at the age of eighty-five made him a kind of folk hero and extended the range of his effectiveness beyond its natural limits. Loyal Democrat, trustworthy vote. He responded faithfully to Johnson's leadership, on the floor and by proxy in the Foreign Relations Committee he chaired after Walter George retired.

CARL HAYDEN OF ARIZONA: in Congress since 1912. Quiet, manly, very old, did his job and seldom spoke on issues. One of those, like George and Green, whom younger Senate leaders seemed to prop up for their value as monuments. He had done much for Arizona and the West. Once in Skeeter Johnston's office he described his first speech in the House. He had remained silent for many months, perhaps for years, as custom required a new member to do. At last something noncontroversial to the House but vital to Arizona came up, something like money for additional forest rangers. Hayden walked to the well of the House and spoke for a minute — no more. He returned to his seat near a senior member. After a long silence, the senior said scathingly, "Just had to talk, didn't you?" Hayden had been sheriff of Maricopa County, and built his first political machine among other sheriffs in the Arizona Territory with whom he exchanged prisoners. He was a solid vote for unlimited debate, since a filibuster had stopped a bill to bring New Mexico and Arizona into the Union as one state. Born at Hayden's Ferry, Arizona.

THOMAS HENNINGS OF MISSOURI: a walking tragedy, or perhaps high-grade Tennessee Williams. Handsome, black-haired, wearing white suits in summer, once an athlete and an outstanding trial lawyer in St. Louis. He was an alcoholic. Johnson treated him with a surprisingly tender concern, though he was irritated when Hennings failed to show up for important meetings. Liberal, anti-McCarthy, an early and committed friend of civil rights. Booming voice, as if trying to overcome the effects and appearance of his illness.

LISTER HILL OF ALABAMA: courtly, joshing, dedicated to medicine and health care, and a good politician in that field without a taste for wider leadership. Overshadowed by Russell among Southerners. His punctuations came out "Ah-wah." One year he produced his health appropriations bill, swollen as usual far beyond the Administration's request. Styles Bridges, the conservative ranking Republican on Appropriations, asked whether the Senate might hope for an end to such huge overappropriations for health research? "Ah-wah," Hill began, "Mr. President, there is no man in the Senate who has been more dedicated to the health of the American people than the Senator from New Hampshire, ah-wah, and I believe that when we find the answers to heart disease, cancer, stroke, and all these other terrible illnesses that plague our people, ah-wah, that the men and women of America will salute the name of the Senator from New Hampshire, for all the support he has given to research into their causes — Mr. President, I ask for a vote on the bill." Bridges, stopped in his tracks, could only grin and shake his head.

SPESSARD HOLLAND OF FLORIDA: a tough old man, a flyer in World War I. Had an old-fashioned courthouse lawyer–cum–Southern Methodist Board of Stewards style, pedantic and humorless. A conservative, he was surprisingly international-minded in the 1950's; that may have stemmed in part from his admiration of Eisenhower. Like Eisenhower he intruded an "uh" before beginning a sentence. Major figure in agriculture, where generally he followed Benson. His triumph was the passage of the anti–poll tax amendment. All in all, a dependable, responsible man.

HUBERT HUMPHREY OF MINNESOTA: of all senators, the most immediately winning to a young liberal. Warm, open, self-amused, bursting with affirmation of life; sure that men of goodwill, with a little common sense and adventurousness, could solve any problem. A creative legislator, willing to take risks. Spectacular extemporaneous phrasemaker; when genuinely aroused, something to see and hear. Shortcoming an inability to be really cruel. He could be discriminating, but he was unable ruthlessly to carry through with the consequences of his discrimination; he could not make his opponents fear that his anger would have serious long-term costs for them. His stories of Midwestern drugstore life, of his days as a young professor and as mayor of Minneapolis, were funny and moving. He was interested in almost every legislative field, especially agriculture, foreign relations, arms control, and civil rights. After a few years in purgatory, he became the key liberal for negotiations with the Senate Establishment. His farmer-populism attracted Russell, with whom he shared few other opinions. One night, at the end of a week's debate in the course of which the anti-Bensonites had lost vote after vote, Humphrey, tired and angry, rose to make a brief concluding speech. He recited the ills of rural America, and the tiny return small farmers received from days of punishing work. Now the price support levels were to slide down to 60 percent of parity. Russell, who had started out the door, stopped and took a seat in front of Humphrey and told Olin Johnston and John Sparkman to listen. Russell began to beat out a rhythm on Humphrey's desk. He and Johnston and Sparkman said, "That's right" and "Exactly" in the way people say "Amen" at Southern revivals, and when Humphrey ended, saying, "Hubert Humphrey didn't come to the United States Senate to vote for sixty percent of a living wage," they fairly shouted their agreement.

With Lyndon Johnson, Humphrey's relationship was extremely complex. At bottom there was mutual affection and respect. They wanted, or believed they wanted, the same things. To Humphrey, Johnson was the operator who could achieve, sometimes miraculously, what liberals had been seeking in vain for years; he was also the demanding friend who required that Humphrey get his fellow liberals into line for a compromise that represented less than they wished for and more than they could reasonably expect. Humphrey's heart longed for a just and humane society; his mind told him that he must accept something less, some mild improvement, or no change at all in a status quo that offended him deeply. In the pursuit of progress he politicked with his natural enemies. He was tolerant and friendly as he sought to disarm their instinctive mistrust of anyone who cared deeply about remote social ills. He never preached or condemned except in public debate. He was not a "drag" like Douglas, who confronted conservatives on and off the floor in the manner of the WCTU confronting the liquor lobby. He was not so susceptible to liberal opinion and *Times* editorials that he backed away from commitments made in pursuit of a compromised advance; he kept his word. He was often late and disorganized, the result, I thought, of an inordinate desire (which he shared with Johnson) to please his last audience *finally*, end all their doubts, answer all their questions, and convert them totally to himself and the true faith. In 1954 Johnson went out to Minnesota to testify for him in his campaign for reelection. The "speakin'," as Johnson called it, was in a field churned up by a contest of farmer skills. Thousands gathered about a platform where Johnson praised his friend as the "can-do" Hubert Humphrey, the most effective liberal in the Senate. As Humphrey walked to the microphone, storm clouds gathered in the distance. After ten minutes a few big late-summer drops began to fall. Five minutes later the rain was coming strong and the wind was blowing hard, and the crowd began running for cars, and Humphrey, despairing over the weather and this great missed opportunity to convert all of agricultural Minnesota, shouted, "All right, you can go now, but I'll get you later!" And of course he would; he had that indispensable element of a successful politician, tireless energy in pursuit of a political goal.

HENRY JACKSON OF WASHINGTON: serious, steady, ambitious, a hard-liner in military affairs, pretty much a complete liberal on domestic issues. Not a Senate power, as was his colleague Magnuson. "Scoop" Jackson was something of a loner, interested in arcane matters like national security policy machinery. He did not disturb or excite, but he was consistently reasonable; this and his youthful appearance denied him weight in the Senate.

OLIN JOHNSTON OF SOUTH CAROLINA: an extraordinary figure, the apotheosis, in the eyes of *Time*, of all that was wrong about Southern politics. "Flannel-mouthed," "demagogic"—he was that, and more. He was perhaps the most dependable liberal vote among Southerners after Hill and Sparkman, and he spoke for the same Piedmont millworker, sharecropper populism in South Carolina that they did in Alabama. Driven to the right by Strom Thurmond's presence in the Senate, he paid for his liberalism on economic questions by voting consistently against foreign aid and civil rights. Yet his intransigence was skin-deep: once, having dutifully made his contribution to a filibuster against a civil rights bill, he listened for a time to his colleague Thurmond, and then gathered his papers and walked out, winking to me and saying, "Listen to ole Strom. He *believes* that stuff." He seemed a fool out of Molière; when he read a speech his voice dropped at the end of each line of type, as if a sentence had ended. Yet he was shrewd, and understood the price he had to pay to vote as he did. One day in the cloakroom he described an early campaign for governor. At a rally near Spartanburg, his chief local supporter, a county judge, said, "You boys know what to do if the wooly-heads act up. You take you some of those willow branches and you tie you a knot in them and see if you can't beat some sense into those wooly heads. And if somebody comes along and indicts you for criminal assault, you know there ain't a jury in South Carolina that'll convict you. And if there is, there ain't a high court in this state that'll sustain that conviction. And if there is, here's the man who's going to pardon you, the next governor of South Carolina, Olin D. Johnston!" Johnston, his eyes large, said, "You know, I couldn't say no." Once elected, he had done what he could for the poor of South Carolina, black and white, following the policies of "that great man, Franklin D. Roosevelt."

Estes Kefauver of Tennessee: "Estes is the bestes'." Tall, gangling, outgoing in public but fundamentally reserved, he often exasperated those who cared for him: he was usually late, apparently (and sometimes truly) unprepared, asking on arrival to bum a cigarette old buddy, what's going on here, what am I supposed to do. An outsider, he was attractive to others who mistrusted power. This did not derive purely from a shared populism. It demanded a good mind, an impression of lumbering integrity, and an unflagging determination to lay bare the roots of deception. Within the Senate he conveyed a sense of popularity without; that independent, national base made him an object of mistrust among those who lacked it.

John Kennedy of Massachusetts: elegant and casual, he sat in the back row, his knees against his desk, rapping his teeth with a pencil and reading the *Economist* and the *Guardian*. He was treated with affection by most senators, but he was ultimately elusive, finding his way in other worlds outside the chamber. Mythically wealthy, handsome, bright, and well connected, he seemed to regard the Senate grandees as impressive but tedious. In turn, he was regarded by them as something of a playboy, a dilettante. His voting record was moderate and sometimes conservative, especially on trade and agricultural matters. He was not a prime mover in the Senate; only once in early 1960, in handling a labor-management bill, did he seem to emerge as a leader, a *mensch*. Then he stood in the center of the chamber and shouted at his opposition, deriding them, challenging them to match his arguments. I scarcely recognized that cool, glamorous figure. To Johnson, I believe, he was the enviably attractive nephew who sings an Irish ballad for the company, and then winsomely disappears before the table-clearing and dishwashing begin. To Kennedy, Johnson must have seemed a gifted workhorse, an original personality and a conventional politician, incomparably wise about the Senate and luckily uninformed about national politics. They were friends and they respected one another, this ant and grasshopper.

ROBERT KERR OF OKLAHOMA: a combination of swashbuckling Southwestern entrepreneur and populist, with perhaps the most formidable mind in the Senate. He wore dark-colored shirts and in his coat's lapel, a gold "Kerr-McGee" pin, designating his company. Outspoken in defending interests in which both he and Oklahoma had a stake. He seemed to be saying, "If I can be so open in defending those interests, they can't be wrong; and even if they were, none of you has the guts to challenge me." A devout Baptist and a teetotaler. Generally voted with the South, except on economic issues which cut across sectional lines. He was incomparably the Senate's most powerful and effective debater. The fiery Pastore once stood up to him, his eyes on a level with Kerr's third shirt button; Kerr used his great size to back him up the wide shallow steps of the center aisle, like d'Artagnan fencing with a dwarf. He called Homer Capehart a "rancid tub of ignorance" and when Capehart took to the floor next day on a point of personal privilege, complaining that (as he thought) Kerr had called him a "rancid cup of ignorance," Kerr replied that anyone in his right mind would know he never used such an expression; the *Record* would show what anyone who observed Capehart's girth might expect, that he had called him a tub, not a cup. In international affairs he took an isolationist position, voting against American membership in international organizations, foreign aid, and the like. Yet he did a brilliant job of managing the Kennedy trade bill in 1962. At the end of the 1950's it occurred to me that Kerr had become not only chairman of the new Space Committee, but effectively chairman of Public Works — given the age and frequent indisposition of Chavez — and the primary force within the Finance Committee where Harry Byrd presided. I discussed this with Bobby Baker one night on the Senate floor, as the two of us watched Kerr and Johnson stand eye to eye, laughing and trading. I said, "It strikes me that Kerr may really be the most powerful man in the Senate." Bobby looked at me as if I had just discovered the force of gravity. "No kidding," he said.

HERBERT LEHMAN OF NEW YORK: a beloved old liberal. Opinion had it that he had not been much of an administrator as head of UNRRA and governor of New York, and many of his interests in the Senate were quixotic. But his deep compassion for the exploited poor represented Jewish liberalism at its best. Johnson voted against him frequently, and moved to table his amendments swiftly when there was more likely game afoot; to Lehman then he must have appeared the embodiment of heedless power, running roughshod over good. Just as often, however, Johnson was solicitous of him, and he liked to be on Lehman's side when he could; he had long been a friend of the family.

RUSSELL LONG OF LOUISIANA: Huey's son. One night Johnson hung up after a long conversation with Russell Long and said, "I like that boy. I liked his father." Long could be a truly exciting debater. He revealed, or seemed to reveal, the real issues in a Senate debate, as distinct from the legalistic abstractions that were generally disputed. "We all get money from [such and such a source]." "You know the real reason you can't support this bill is because you wouldn't survive the next primary if you did." "The halls outside are full of lobbyists from the insurance companies, and they don't want this amendment because they're afraid somebody will find out what their profits are." He fought continually for higher welfare payments, at least for the old, the lame, and the blind; that was Louisiana policy. It was also Louisiana policy to support the oil and gas industry, and Long was as open as Kerr in acknowledging its beneficience to him. Quick, funny, and smart, he often overreached himself; no one could be quite so brazen as Kerr and get away with it every time.

WARREN MAGNUSON OF WASHINGTON: an archetypal man's man, and a leader in the sense that the Establishment went along with him on matters within his jurisdiction or range of interest. A bachelor in the 1950's, he loved the good life, but he was conscientious in his Senate duties. As Commerce Committee chairman he nurtured the country's ailing and outrageously expensive merchant marine, and handled bills affecting the railroads, the airlines, and the trucking industry. The stakes were high in such matters and "Maggie" knew the game well; usually he managed to produce legislation that satisfied private interests without doing injury to the public conscience. He was a liberal on issues that tapped the main liberal lode, but he voted with the Establishment when Clark, Douglas, or Morse went off on what were considered peripheral crusades. He and Johnson were fast friends. I thought his natural milieu was a convention of transportation interests, where he would give a prepared speech on "The Need to Modernize"; I could imagine him in an elegant hotel lobby, stocky, affable, but not in the least fawning, as he made his way through a hundred handshakes toward the cigar counter. He could be more than this; in the Hell's Canyon fight in 1957 he was a tiger, rough and passionate and driving. That degree of commitment was not required day by day.

MIKE MANSFIELD OF MONTANA: introverted, deeply Catholic. Manly in a Western, Gary Cooper way—taciturn and forthright, a straight shooter. In the sixties, his leader's office was dark and still. On the wall there was a picture of Jacqueline Kennedy, wearing a mantilla of lovely mourning. A gentle old Negro named Morris served coffee from morning until evening. Mansfield's closest assistant, Frank Valeo, was often there to talk about

Asian policy — it was one of Mansfield's passions; he thought the United States was obsessed by a missionary zeal to convert Asia, and that this would be our undoing and Asia's. He was not driven, as Johnson had been, to put his leader's stamp on every major bill that passed. He was not a brilliant debater. Yet he was reasonable, accommodating, and fair, and these qualities, together with the Senate's instinctive practice of following its elected leaders, gave weight to what he said. When he became majority leader, in 1961, he announced that there would be few night or Saturday sessions, very little pressure on the members, and annual summer vacations. The response was what one might expect from boys in a prep school when an old tyrannical headmaster, who believed in the redeeming power of work, was replaced by a permissive young don. No more of Johnson's grinding, inexorable debates leading to a vote at 10 P.M. No more round-the-clock sessions, with their continual taste of ashes, their ache of boredom. It was like a holiday for a time, and it inspired cooperation out of gratitude. Later there was grumbling that his reins were too loose, but there was no move to replace him; he was too much respected, no one else was so broadly accepted, and to discard him would have been a despairing judgment on the Senate itself — for he had permitted it to be what it was, a hundred disparate adults who ought to have been able to deal efficiently and responsibly with public affairs.

JOHN MCCLELLAN OF ARKANSAS: tough as nails and deeply conservative. Virtually every speech he made inscribed a rising curve from the prudent statement of fact to polemical rage, his powerful voice quavering with indignation. He was not so esteemed by the press as was his colleague Fulbright, but he was probably admired by a larger public. McClellan conveyed a prosecutorial vengeance toward wrongdoers. He chaired the Permanent Investigations Subcommittee, where he was at once judge and DA; as he could pick his targets, he chose crooked unions, the Mafia, Negro poverty-program managers who had conned the government — a highly selective and almost indefensible group with few friends in the Southern Establishment. I often wondered what power his investigations gave him among senators. If it gave him any at all, other than self-protection, he did not put it to a programmatic use. McClellan had been hurt beyond any telling by the successive deaths of his sons. Yet this had not made him openly vulnerable; I think he would not have permitted himself that.

PAT MCNAMARA OF MICHIGAN: one could not forget that he had been a plumber and union leader. His voice was gravelly and he smoked continuously. He was old shoe, without *amour propre*. His opinions were deeply and unshakably liberal, and though he was amiable with men of every persuasion, he was deeply offended by the power of Senate conservatism. He lacked brilliance, charisma, and perhaps even interest in the complicated maneuverings that were the substance of the Senate's days. But he embodied the common sense and humanity of the old trade unionists. He was generous and unafraid.

MIKE MONRONEY OF OKLAHOMA: an Oklahoma newspaperman, with the eager, pressing manner of a wire-service reporter. He could feel strongly about issues, and he was a witty and informed debater who conveyed, like Russell Long, a sense of actuality, of the real stakes at issue. Yet he was not a Senate power; one could not imagine Mike Monroney doing anything out of vindictiveness or obsession or self-aggrandizement. Hence it was rarely necessary to defer to him, to cope with him. A liberal, he was constantly tested by the divergence of his views from those of his state's. Oklahoma was becoming increasingly conservative, as Tulsa oil interests replaced those of impoverished farmers. Monroney tried to bridge the gap by attention to civil servants and defense workers, of whom the state had many, but his tenuous hold on the electorate seemed clear to other senators and limited his influence in the chamber. He was a pleasure to know socially, as he was more interested in ideas than position.

WAYNE MORSE OF OREGON: brilliant, tireless, convinced by his own powerful rhetoric. The "Morse hour" was always the last of the day; a few impatient senators and staff waited in the cool, dim chamber as Morse, a former law school dean, lectured on Southern racism, District of Columbia parking fees, South American dictators, and whatever else had recently aroused his displeasure. A gadfly, insensitive to obloquy, he was nevertheless extremely effective when given a leadership role — when managing a labor or education bill he was tolerant and skillful, knowing when to give way and when to resist amendment. He could be easily the most irritating man in the Senate. Yet he was also indispensable: he would fight a bad bill when others wanted to but were afraid, and the threat of his filibusters occasioned many a decent compromise. Morse often voted with Southern conservatives against the passage of progressive bills, because he had earlier lost an issue of principle on amendment. He was Western, a son of the wild jackass.

JAMES MURRAY OF MONTANA: an old liberal, over the hill when I came to the Senate. He had once been considered for majority leader; except for his union connections he would have been manageable, a liberal Ernest McFarland. Dirksen once told of a campaign against Murray in which he had taken part. Flying in a private plane with Murray's opponent, he discovered hundreds of leaflets bound in red and stamped with the hammer and sickle. The message to the voters was that Bolshevism would follow if they elected that copper-union–dominated Jim Murray. "My God," said Dirksen. "This is Montana. You've elected him." As they had.

MATTHEW NEELY OF WEST VIRGINIA: a Bible-quoting, eloquent, old-fashioned Shakespearean, with the smell of the mines and hollows about him. He was old when I came and died not long after.

RICHARD NEUBERGER OF OREGON: an intellectual journalist, whose wife, it was erroneously said, was smarter than he — she was only less willing to compromise. He liked Johnson and ordinarily followed his lead, while continuing to write for the *New Republic*. Neuberger was deeply concerned — in a private, as well as senatorial way — about public issues that affected the quality of life. He was in politics because those issues were most exposed there. His difficulties with Morse increased as the years went by; Morse could not tolerate a junior senator from Oregon who failed to follow his lead. Neuberger was pale and dying for long months in 1959 and 1960.

JOSEPH O'MAHONEY OF WYOMING: a spirit out of the Senate past, of the same mold — if somewhat thinner texture — as Borah, Norris, and Wheeler. A great talker and a constitutionalist; liberal, but as far from urban liberalism as he was from Eastland. Small, with a head that seemed massive and a powerful crowd-challenging voice growing hoarse with age.

Second Interlude and Speculations about Power

One day in early 1963, I sat beside Johnson as he presided over the Senate that he had once led. The Kennedy-Johnson legislative program was ailing, if it had not already expired. Nothing was moving to the satisfaction of the White House, the Administration's supporters in Congress, or the impatient journalists who were beginning to pronounce Kennedy a failure as a political leader. As two young liberal senators rose to praise the President's latest message to Congress, I asked Johnson what was wrong. "We've got all the minnows," he said. "We've got none of the whales."

Who were the whales? Among the senators I have already described, they certainly included Anderson, Kerr, Magnuson, and possibly Hayden and Long; of those to come, Russell and maybe Stennis. Byrd was a fictive whale; Ellender and Eastland could on occasion displace the volume of whales.

Whales were chairmen, but not all chairmen were whales. Whales had the negative power to stop legislation, either because they opposed it or were indifferent to it. A controversial proposal could not pass without their friendly intervention. Not that all of them had to support it; the consent of only one or two was required to give the rest of the Senate confidence that a bill — like a stock issue backed by a respected underwriter — was all right to support.

These are oversimplifications meant to illustrate a point: the interlocking powers of the whales were extremely important in determining the legislative behavior of the minnows (and of other fish in between). Public opinion was also important, and so was the pressure, or lack of it, exerted by the Administration. But the public often had no strong opinion, or was divided and diffused — and the power of the Establishment, of the whales, was constant and palpable. Most senators wanted to be able to see bills bearing their names emerge from committee, and to show people at home that they could get an appropriation for a prized project; for that, good relations with a power were necessary. If a senator had promised to manage an Administration bill, or the bill of some other important group or interest, he would almost certainly have to negotiate with a Senate power. His reputation in the eyes of his clients would be affected by whether he was able to work out a tolerable compromise.

A liberal could answer his angry constituents, when they challenged his position on a recent vote, by writing, "As Sen. Kerr [or Anderson or Russell] said during the debate . . ." Thus the powers offered legitimacy and protective coloration to their colleagues.

Eminence of position was not the only qualification for this kind of power in the Senate. Each of the powers had a special preserve in which his knowledge and experience was unique; but special competence was not enough to confer general authority. Seniority was important, but again, not sufficient in itself.

A power had to be longheaded. He had to be diligent in performing chores for others, and he had to remind them of his diligence often enough to establish a pattern, but not so often as to be oppressive. He had to be secure in his own state. He had to be primarily interested in the legislative process; even if he had national political ambitions, he could not seem to subordinate his senatorial duties to the quest for outside popularity. Some powers had played key roles in the institutional crises of the Senate, as Taft did in the railroad strike legislation of the mid-forties, as Russell did on General MacArthur's return from Korea. Some commanded a fixed block of votes on certain questions, though that was not essential; Russell was the unchallenged leader of the South, but Kerr produced shifting bipartisan majorities on a variety of issues. Hayden's power rested on his chairmanship of Appropriations. That he was fair in performing that role was an additional but not entirely necessary element of his authority. Magnuson had power because he was chairman of the Commerce Committee; still it was necessary that he control, as well as preside over, the resolution of questions affecting the economic lifeblood of every state. Anderson ran the Interior Committee, and therefore was crucial to a substantial minority of the Senate; though America had become predominantly urban, at least thirty Western and Midwestern senators were deeply concerned by whatever increased or decreased the supply of water and arable lands in their states. I have already described the basis of Kerr's power, and of Lyndon Johnson, the preeminent lord of the Senate in the fifties; there will be much more to say.

Beyond these minimum requirements — a chairmanship, longevity in the Senate, devotion to the legislative process, command over the giving or withholding of benefits in which large numbers of senators had an interest — there were other qualities that could not be easily measured. Manliness, perhaps — Big Daddy-ness; the natural assumption of authority; the willingness, in fact the need, to take responsibility; and a tough seriousness about the daily game of making laws. I was often struck by the careful attention that Johnson and Russell and Kerr gave to every bill on the Calendar, when I briefed them in the Policy Committee meetings. It was not for show. They were their only audience. Whether or not a bill fell within the usual scope of their interests, they fastened on it, shook it, questioned it, doubted or approved its wisdom, and rated its chance of passage. They were professional legislators.

Power outside the Senate did not follow from power within, and vice versa. Neither popular favor or significance in the national party flowed from a senator's ability to move a bill. Indeed there were times when they seemed mutually exclusive. The very absorption in legislation, in committee work, and in negotiating, that helped to make a man important within the Senate, made him less sensitive to what was happening in the country. And there was always the potential for a grave political miscalculation: the two senators from Nevada had one vote each, as did the two senators from New York. An active legislator was inclined to weigh them equally on that account. Further, the might of the South in the Senate — nine of the fifteen chairmanships were held by Southerners — made it important to court politicians whose views had little in common with the mass of Democratic voters in the cities. Eastland or Byrd might be won over by a compromise that hurt the compromiser's image in Detroit. What I am describing, of course, is the erroneous basis of Lyndon Johnson's futile campaign for the Presidential nomination in 1960.

To the true Senate man, the successful management of a difficult bill ought to have generated universal praise and a ready-made base of support for national office. It did not; the nation elected General Eisenhower and Senator Kennedy for reasons quite apart from their skill as legislators. What was worse, skill within the Senate implied a knowledge of wheeling and dealing, intricate trade-offs, elaborate posturing — all the black political arts. The nation wanted something different from its Presidents. That a man was unable to negotiate his way in the devious Capitol was not to be held against him. Indeed it was *prima facie* proof of his simple integrity.

At the same time, men such as Kefauver and Kennedy did not capitalize on their national popularity within the Senate. Perhaps they did not really care to. Legislative victories were no match for those won in the polling booths of New Hampshire and Wisconsin.

Of the four announced Democratic candidates for the 1960 nomination — Kennedy, Humphrey, Symington, and Johnson — only the latter was a "Senate man" whose power and reputation were grounded in the body of which all were a part. Kennedy's base was widespread, composed of intellectuals, Catholics, the young, and millions who longed for glamour or the promise of change; Humphrey drew on his years of speaking for Negroes and organized labor, Symington on his career as an effective manager of military and domestic agencies. Only Johnson ran on his record as the man who had made the Senate work. It gained him flattering articles in the magazines, but it did not win him sufficient votes among the parochial, yet — as they were joined in convention — national-minded delegates at Los Angeles. To many sophisticated observers of political men, his effectiveness as the Senate's leader argued for his nomination; in the arena where all four men had worked and sometimes contended, he was clearly the dominant figure — shrewder, tougher, more energetic and imaginative, more assiduous in achieving his purposes. But they — as well as I — were mistaking power in the Senate for power in the country. The cockpit we watched with such fascination was in some respects a paradigm of the country. The issues fought out there were symbolic of those in the street. But it was finally not the street. It was a large room in Washington.

JOHN O. PASTORE OF RHODE ISLAND: an Italian bantamweight with explosives on his tongue. In 1957, walking and gesturing rapidly amid the semicircular rows of Senate desks, he gave the most powerful civil rights speech Congress heard in the decade. Pastore was an astute politician with strong liberal views — not a liberal with political ability. Moustachioed and dapper, he had little independent wealth; yet the Catholic sodalities of Rhode Island called upon him, as they did upon his colleagues Green and, later, Claiborne Pell — both men of great family fortunes — to contribute to their charitable causes, and with sardonic comments about the inequity of it all, he responded. His institutional power lay in his chairmanship of the Communications Subcommittee of Commerce, where he was knowledgeable, if not innovative, in dealing with the networks. Though his small size limited his authority in the men's club of the Senate, his fierceness made him a figure to be conjured with, and he was closer to being a whale than a minnow. He could not be dismissed with patronizing comments about his "scrappiness"; he conveyed gravity and purpose.

WILLIS ROBERTSON OF VIRGINIA: a mix of bluster and manliness, who admired great figures like Churchill and Washington and used their words with a Tory bombast that should have destroyed his opposition in debate, but did not. He was chairman of the Banking Committee, and enjoyed the opportunity it provided him to deal with the great figures of finance. Once in the cloakroom he read aloud, with a kind of amused and astonished rage, a newspaper story of the latest puerile demands by African diplomats in the UN. "McPherson," he said, "these people have dropped out of the trees with umbrellas and attaché cases." I said something about the problems of new nations, their pride and defensiveness; he cleared his throat and went back to reading. Robertson was a great fisherman. He may have been unique among senators for his willingness to confess love for such a frivolous pastime. The Protestant political ethic — selfless devotion to unremitting, frequently unpleasant but always public-spirited work equals goodness, self-justification, and reelection — required most senators to behave as if there were no relief from the grinding demands of their days. Robertson was not a slave to that ethic. Intelligent Virginia squires fish and hunt, and are not afraid to say so. He was conservative, but not so deeply entrenched against modern life as was his senior colleague Byrd — whose primacy in Virginia he deferred to and acknowledged, though with reluctance.

RICHARD RUSSELL OF GEORGIA: in Johnson's office, there was a picture of Russell standing in the doorway of his law office in Georgia, his feet crossed, an arm raised to balance him. He was smiling, intelligent, and easy, at home with the law and the people of Winder, Georgia, to whom he was leader and judge and perhaps a manifestation of God Himself. He had come to the Senate in 1933, young and already a popular governor. In 1952 he made a try for the Presidency, but interest-group politics defeated him before he got off the ground. He returned to the politics of Congress, where he had no peer. Russell was a profoundly attractive man whose Roman bearing, quick mind, and unfeigned courtliness won him the deep respect of people who had little sympathy for his conservative views. He regarded many trends of modern life with truculent disdain; but he had a sophisticated tolerance for those whose constituencies demanded a different response. Institutionally, he was chairman of the Armed Services Committee, the ranking Democrat (behind the venerable Hayden) on Appropriations, and chairman of the Southern caucus. Thus he spoke for the Senate on matters affecting the government's first responsibility, national security; had a great voice in determining where and for what the country should spend one hundred billion dollars; and moved eighteen Southern votes — among whom were nine committee chairmen — as a block, whenever Southern interests were corporately at stake. What sort of a man exercised these powers, out of what inner purpose or conviction, it was difficult to know. He was a bachelor and lived alone in an apartment downtown. I believe he regretted that he had not married. His social life was spare, but not reclusive. He read copiously. Military histories, biographies, and newspapers were scattered about his office, on his desk, on the sofa, and on the large conference table at which Southerners assembled in times of challenge. He read the *Times* and *Post* editorials, and the sports pages as well; he knew batting averages and football scores, and took pleasure in them. He also read county newspapers from Georgia. In fact it was there, in the rural county seats of Georgia, that I thought he discerned the bones of a generous, humane civilization, and like an archaeologist worked them into the present image of a life better than people knew in cities — better than they knew in modern Atlanta, for example. He was the practicing political equivalent of the Fugitive Movement. He was as far from the brutal passions of the Klan as were the fieriest members of the Americans for Democratic Action; yet he treasured a way of life in the course of which whites took responsibility for, and manhood from, millions of blacks. There was rural progressivism in him, a commitment to rural electrification, farmers' loans, and vocational education; but there was no sympathy for the expenditure of billions to remake the steaming cities. In foreign affairs he consistently voted against every statutory involvement of the United States in international organizations, and against the more important treaties. The reason was that treaties and international responsibilities limited America's freedom of action, and hence its autonomy. Like most men, he became more conservative as he grew older. Unlike most men he observed himself doing so — ruefully speculating that it was not the wisdom of age but simply age itself that had driven him inward and rightward. He was a strong speaker, and he knew the Senate, its traditions and rules as none other did. After 1958 his opinions were shared by an ever-smaller fraction of the

Senate, and on some issues he lost the power to affect the outcome by embracing the Republicans. But he remained a great force; nothing could diminish his chairmanships, his cunning, or his integrity. Often I found myself offering counsel to him, seeking to forward his purposes, because his character and professionalism were magnetic to me.

KERR SCOTT OF NORTH CAROLINA: a country gentleman, with a red rose in his lapel. He had been governor of North Carolina, and I thought he embodied the latent progressivism of that state — concerned for the white poor, determined to do right by its blacks, open to new ideas. He might never have grasped the deepest dimensions of what was going on at Chapel Hill, Duke, and Raleigh — an intellectual base was being built where lynchings and red-neck bitterness had held sway for generations — but his heart knew it was right for North Carolina and should be fostered.

JOHN SPARKMAN OF ALABAMA: with Lister Hill, he composed the Senate side of what was — until George Wallace came along and destroyed it — probably the best state delegation in Congress. He was a sharecropper's son. His votes came from the northern Alabama hills where TVA was a holy name, and where it was possible to talk economics instead of race. He was a ranking member of Foreign Relations, but his real concern and authority was in the Banking Committee, where he chaired the Housing Subcommittee. There he proposed and pushed through series of ever more liberal acts to provide housing for the poor and the lower middle class. He napped on the floor during long speeches, but when his time came to speak he was so thorough and reasonable that senators voted for him against the most determined banking interests, certain that he would not lead them astray. He lacked the energy of a whale, but he was an important figure where his interest was strong.

GEORGE SMATHERS OF FLORIDA: Jack Kennedy's best friend in the Senate, a handsome, smooth, elegantly tailored operator who had whipped Claude Pepper in an outrageous campaign (we loved the stories of that campaign, though they were probably apocryphal — Smathers in north Florida town: "Did you know Claude Pepper has committed nepotism with his own wife?" Gasp. "What's more, his daughter is a thespian." More gasps). Smathers was a dependable industry vote on the Finance Committee, but he was also probably as progressive a senator as Florida would tolerate in the fifties and sixties. He moved left when he could, and he brought along several moderate-conservative senators by persuasion and example. He had the glamorous air of a young entrepreneur who casually shoots a round in the high sixties, and later sits about in the club bar with portly millionaires, discounting a feat they consider fantastical.

JOHN STENNIS OF MISSISSIPPI: one day while Stennis was presiding over the Senate, I engaged in a heated conversation with a staff man on the telephone nearby. Bang! went the gavel. Bang! Bang! I hung up. Bang! I sat down. Bang! Bang! Bang! I tried to become invisible. Bang! "Order!" Bang! My face flushed. "Let us have order in the Senate." By this time one could hear nothing but Ed Hickey's pen scratching on the Journal. "Let us have no more of these telephone conversations. The Chair [Chaiah] cannot hear *Senators* because the staff is using the tel-e-phone. Let us have order." Then another Bang! like the coup de grace over my utterly humbled self. Judge Stennis had struck again. He was righteous, he possessed the Judicial Temperament, he was punctilious and straight. Why then was he not resisted as Douglas was? In part because he was Southern, as were most of the powers. In part because he could often be assuaged by courteous conduct and did not demand, as Douglas did, evidence of a repentant change in behavior. Stennis had a trumpet voice and a movie senator's face and carriage. I found it hard to converse with him. He seemed always distracted by larger game — practicing, I thought, his next summation to the jury. Apart from Russell, he was the most impressive Southerner. That they were both identified with the military had something to do with that. Other senators might argue the benefit-cost ratio of public works projects or the level of widows' pensions or the need for urban renewal; Stennis and Russell knew about, and looked after, the country's defense. They did not seem to question the military-industrial complex — indeed, they had seen to it that bases and defense plants were plentifully established in Georgia and Mississippi. They did not publicly challenge the CIA's activities or military assistance programs. They did not try to weigh political estimates of potential wars against the military's requests for arms. But they cared deeply about preparing the country against bluff or attack, and this ultimate gut-concern gave them a standing in the Senate that far transcended that of more fashionable men. Stennis had played, too, a major role in the demise of McCarthy. He was *offended* by McCarthy. If it did not occur to him to protest McCarthy's excesses in hounding former radicals, it infuriated him that senators should be called handmaidens of communism, and it was this sense of outraged decency — aimed and fired by Lyndon Johnson — that inspired in other senators enough courage and self-respect to bring McCarthy down. Stennis represented the white business and professional interests back home in Mississippi. He gave little public evidence of concern for the hundreds of thousands of black Mississippians who were, throughout the fifties and sixties, disenfranchised by new technology and old custom. He was thus a conventional politician of his time and place. He did not offer an ideological defense of the Mississippi way of life; he simply asked others to let his state and people alone. He was truly an ambassador from the cotton kingdom. In the capital to which he had been given credentials, he was also a deeply responsible and important figure.

STUART SYMINGTON OF MISSOURI: an erect, elegant man with an East Coast patrician past; without renouncing it, he related sufficiently to the mountain people of the Ozarks and the blacks and Germans of St. Louis to win their votes, and ultimately to become a Missouri institution. His son Jim — a Yale Whiffenpoof, a delightful, humane spirit with a voice from the Dublin Rising of 1916 — sang mournful country tunes on courthouse steps to draw a crowd for his father at election time. Symington had been Truman's Secretary of the Air Force and administrator of the Reconstruction Finance Corporation. His reputation and demeanor were those of an executive, a manager of larger enterprises; he conveyed a busy impatience in the manner of Forrestal. His interests in the fifties were mainly in the national security field, especially in air power and economic warfare. Like Kennedy, he found his chief constituency outside the Senate. He rarely took part in the bargaining and amending process. One could not easily imagine him holding up someone's bill in order to get his own out of committee. As a consequence, though he had size, he was not a major Senate power. He and Johnson had once been close, but at some point had cooled to one another. Yet his speeches, being free of vagueness or cant, were always thoroughly reported and became realities with which Johnson had to cope. Though his concerns were relatively narrow, compared to those of the powers and of the other candidates in 1960, they were significant, national, perhaps Presidential; I could imagine him in the White House.

STROM THURMOND OF SOUTH CAROLINA: shaped like a medium-range missile, in his sixties but physically a man of thirty-five. He was deeply reactionary. As Olin Johnston said, he believed that stuff. He had tremendous energy and purpose, which made it worse. He reminded me of General Jack D. Ripper in *Dr. Strangelove*, cast as a Carolina pol. His effectiveness in the Senate was that of an intransigent nay-sayer who frustrated unanimous consent agreements and filibustered after other Southerners had determined to compromise. Thus he made them look weak and spineless by comparison; contemptuous and angry, they were nevertheless forced to supplicate him. He had considerable political acumen, courtesy, and no humor. Wound up, he could talk cold war–big bomb–subtle Communist-conspiracy theory for hours, but it was all a canned tape full of mutually reinforcing catchwords; it was without relevance, though it explained everything.

Third Interlude: Questions about Politicians

Mostly extroverted, upwardly mobile personalities. Hungry for acclaim, whether from the newspapers, a football stadium crowd, or a visiting delegation of blue-marcelled DAR's. Maybe the public's expression of approval satisfied a senator's deepest psychological needs; certainly it was evidence that he might survive the next election.

Some senators — I am thinking particularly of Republicans from the Middle West — were so typical of middle-class businessmen or lawyers in their states that there seemed no special reason why they had been chosen to serve in the Senate instead of others. Fate had simply reached down into a bag of identical marbles and selected one at random.

On the other hand, some of the older members — particularly Southerners — were atypical of the ordinary business and professional class to which they belonged, and which they represented. Their style was political-clerical: bar association leaders and Protestant pastors had it, the ones who join Kiwanis. It was a hearty, portentous style, peculiar enough to distinguish a man in a crowd, not so peculiar as to cut him off from the commonality on the Great Issues ("We Americans feel . . .").

Such men were actors, part of a great public show. They could be funny or even ridiculous — Senator Dirksen often walked the edge of the absurd, and he was not only tolerated, but positively welcomed, as a "character." Perhaps the public enjoyed indulging their excesses, enjoyed saying, "You know these politicians," as they might cluck about an eccentric relative in the family.

In the South, especially, there was an old tradition of politics-as-show. Speeches in the town square in late summer — before the Democratic primary that was "tantamount to election" — followed an hour or two of country music by young men whose long sideburns antedated fashion by several decades. When the time came for the candidate to speak, people thought now we'll hear a lot of self-important posturing and belaboring of the obvious; but they expected something thrilling, too, something that organized and gave voice to their discontent. There was an element of priest as well as performer in Southern political men — many of whom adopted red galluses or frock coats or long curling hair, as priests did cassocks and supplices, to set themselves apart from the multitude. (Recognition was vital if they were to be remembered on election day — I don't care what they say about me, so long as they spell my name right.)

But it was dangerous to be set apart too far. After a spectacular performance of jokes, shouts, and tears, a political man had to be ready to salute the accepted verities along with the audience he had just entertained, to lose his voice in their solemn chorus. He had to be Old Bill, familiar, one of us, puts his pants on one leg at a time same as I do. Most of America's millions of veterans were noncoms. They had seen enough of general officers to last them a lifetime. They wanted political representatives who *felt* as they did, though senators might be, and indeed ought to be, more astute about what to do.

How much latitude did a senator have in representing his constituency? How closely did he have to follow the prevailing winds in his state? One of the most common complaints about politicians was that they were obsequious before public opinion. Evasive and insincere, they were forever trimming their words to suit their constituencies. Those who so complained usually believed, or said they believed, in a representative form of government. If they were able to reconcile their complaint with their belief, it was on the ground that politicians should represent *them* — the "good responsible people" — and not the mass. Thus, when they called upon political men to "get out in front" of mass opinion, they generally had in mind getting out just far enough to coincide exactly with their own judgments.

Walter Bagehot expressed it thus, in his essay "The Character of Sir Robert Peel":

> A constitutional statesman is in general a man of common opinions and uncommon abilities. . . . Public opinion, as it is said, rules; and public opinion is the opinion of the average man. Fox used to say of Burke: "Burke is a wise man; but he is wise too soon." The average man will not bear this. . . . Politicians, as has been said, live in the repute of the commonalty. They may appeal to posterity; but of what use is posterity? Years before that tribunal comes into life, your life will be extinct. . . . Those who desire a public career must look to the views of the living public; an immediate exterior influence is essential to the exertion of their faculties. The confidence of others is your *fulcrum*. You cannot, many people wish you could, go into parliament to represent yourself. You must conform to the opinions of others; and they, depend on it, will not be original.
>
> . . . If we wanted to choose an illustration of these remarks out of all the world, it would be Sir Robert Peel. No man has come so near our definition of a constitutional statesman — the powers of a first-rate man and the creed of a second-rate man. From a certain peculiarity of intellect and fortune, he was never in advance of his time. Of almost all the great measures with which his name is associated, he attained great eminence as an opponent before he attained even greater eminence as their advocate. On the corn-laws, on the currency, on the amelioration of the criminal code, on Catholic emancipation, he was not one of the earliest labourers or quickest converts. He did not bear the heat and burden of the day; other men labored, and he entered into their labours. As long as these questions remained the property of first-class intellects, as long as they were confined to philanthropists or speculators, as long as they were only ad-

vocated by austere, intangible Whigs, Sir Robert Peel was against them. So soon as these same measures, by the progress of time, the striving of understanding, the conversion of receptive minds, became the property of second-class intellects, Sir Robert Peel became possessed of them also. He was converted at the conversion of the average man. His creed was, as it had ever been, ordinary; but his extraordinary abilities never showed themselves so much. He forthwith wrote his name on each of these questions, so that it will be remembered as long as they are remembered.

This was, as Bagehot thought, a depressing prospect — if one hoped to be governed by philosopher-kings. But for every Walter Bagehot who longed for brave, creative independence from his elected leaders, there were ten thousand average persons who expected their own views to be reflected in their representative's votes in Congress. The very word "representative" suggested that a senator from Alabama should speak *for* the people of Alabama, should express their convictions and desires. Expressing those of the people of New York was the responsibility of other men.

Many of the struggles I witnessed in the Senate involved this conflict between "statesmanship" and "representation." For many senators there was an almost constant effort to reconcile their own opinions with demands that emerged from the Senate itself — obligations to other senators, due bills for past favors, the need to establish future preference by a present vote — and with the views embodied in letters and phone calls from home. Where public opinion was rigidly fixed and overwhelming, they seldom resisted it. Where it was more evenly balanced, or where it was inchoate and amorphous, their freedom to be independent was correspondingly enhanced.

Perhaps the first question was, as Bagehot suggested, whether a man could be elected whose views were either antithetical to, or advanced beyond, those of his constituency. A Southerner who believed passionately in civil rights, and said so, was almost certain to be defeated — not by an opponent who shared his beliefs, but by one who took advantage of his candor to play on racial fears and animosities among the voters. A Midwesterner who campaigned against the enormous cost of agricultural programs could expect nothing but a trouncing at the hands of farmer-voters. An Easterner who even suggested that the Vikings discovered America could count on prompt retaliation by his Italian constituents.

What a senator had to do, who wanted both to do good and to be elected, was first to bow before the prevailing icons in his state, and having made that obeisance, to turn to more promising endeavors. John Roche has pointed out that the antebellum South was indulgent toward a considerable amount of heterodoxy — a Jew, after all, was secretary of state in the Confederacy — so long as the household god of slavery was accepted. Thus, Lister Hill, John Sparkman, and Olin Johnston could support expensive social programs in the Senate, so long as they took part in filibusters against civil rights. Fulbright could take advanced positions on international questions, so long as he resisted attempts by the federal government to modify racial relations in Arkansas. Proxmire paid his fee of support to the dairy farmers of Wisconsin, Douglas his to the corn growers of Illinois.

Lyndon Johnson faced the same requirement, and he met it in much the same way. He had no special love for the oil and gas industry of Texas; oil men had never been among his most ardent supporters in the days before he became majority leader and acquired such power over their fortunes. Even in his days of supreme authority in the Senate, his efforts in their behalf satisfied only the bare minimum of what was required. His liberal colleague, Ralph Yarborough, was far more outspoken in the industry's defense. Yet Johnson did his part. He helped to lead the fight for state control of the offshore oil lands and against federal regulation of gas prices at the wellhead. He was careful about assignments to the Finance Committee, where the depletion allowance lay like a ruby in a wall safe. Speeches defending the allowance against attacks on the Senate floor were probably unnecessary, so long as there was a heavy majority to protect it.

Having secured the benign indifference — if not the active support — of Texas' most powerful economic interest, Johnson was free to pursue other goals. His refusal in 1956 to sign the Southern Manifesto against the Supreme Court's ruling on school desegregation was possible not only because a substantial minority of Texans were black or brown, but because he was sound on oil and gas. Conservatism on that issue allowed him to work for the Civil Rights Acts of 1957 and 1960, for public housing and urban renewal, and for foreign aid; this at a time when Texas school boards were throwing out textbooks that even discussed the UN, and when the state's most prominent newspaper was espousing views substantially to the right of the *Chicago Tribune*.

In his quest for independence, Johnson had another string to his bow, besides his orthodoxy on oil and gas questions. He was The Leader — a great and famous public figure. Texans were rather proud that one of their own occupied such a position. They allowed him leeway on many issues of less than critical significance to them, and could even tolerate, without accepting, his progressive views on race. He was not a monumental figure, already cast in bronze, as was Russell in Georgia; he was too often *seen* to be operating and maneuvering (as he could not hide his pleasure in those skills). And as I have said, he was mistrusted by many on both sides in the continuous civil war that is Texas politics. But he was national property, and people thought twice about trading him off for an ordinary senator.

There were other senators whose unique political status or personalities gave them a degree of independence and allowed them to vote as they, and not the majority of their constituencies, believed. Arizona was growing steadily more conservative as it became a retirement haven for the wealthy, but Carl Hayden had invented Arizona, and could pretty much vote as he pleased, generally with the liberals. Nothing Dirksen might have done — not all his stunning reversals of position, nor his self-amused, specious justifications for those reversals — could shake his majority in Illinois. Pastore had the same broad and steady base in Rhode Island, and very likely could have espoused free trade in textiles without serious cost in the next election.

Alben Barkley was a permanent part of the Kentucky political scene, and a story about him illustrates a third means of achieving independence while continuing to be elected. It was said that during a campaign in the forties, Barkley was interrupted in the middle of a magnificent town square speech in eastern Kentucky when someone yelled, "How do you stand on FEPC?" Barkley surveyed the crowd. Eastern Kentucky, like eastern Tennessee, had long been divided on the racial issue. There were the grandchildren of Unionists and of Confederates and copperheads in that audience; no one knew how many of each. At last Barkley quietly replied, "I'm all right on FEPC." And went on with his speech.

Put in its worst light, this third road to independence was simply that of the artful dodger — the fancy-footwork, never-laid-a-glove-on-me lightweight, who never answered the question he was asked but always another, who emitted clouds of gas in which he raced about, seeking to placate those whom he had most recently offended. There was something of him in nearly every senator. Unless a man was a living monument, or unless he was at the very end of his career and cared only for his pride or conscience and nothing for his reelection, he did not ignore the political consequences of what he did. He tried not to meet every thrust of public opinion with his chin. Senator Stephen Young made a name for himself by answering foolish or vicious letters with broadsides of contempt; he was widely admired for that, but I thought the public's favorable reaction depended on there being only one of him. A little vagueness on a senator's part seemed necessary for civil discourse with his constituency.

Put more generously, many good men remained in the Senate to perform significant public services because they were able to diffuse or refract the image of their opinions on politically dangerous questions. It would have done the country no ultimate good to know their precise views on birth control, intermarriage, or relations with Eastern Europe, if the consequence of that would have been their defeat and replacement by lesser men. Astute leaders like Johnson often sought to frame issues in ways that did not embarrass their more valuable colleagues; and there were many parliamentary devices — motions to recommit dangerous bills or amendments, points of order, and so on — that could be used to avoid an Armageddon of convictions.

The right timing could give a man independence for a while — so long, to paraphrase Eliot, as the moment lasted. One who had been crying in the wilderness, prophesying economic disaster if present policies were continued, came into his own in a time of recession, and so long as it lasted and the public remembered his position, could do no wrong. A McClellan would have been free to experiment with unusual policies in other fields, because of his identification as a crime-fighter in an age when the fear of criminal violence was widespread.

Independence earned in this way could be short-lived. The issue might pass, or the public grow bored with a senator's reminders that he had foreseen the event. Cassandras were exciting — for a while — but one did not want to live indefinitely in their prophetic presence.

Obeisance to the local household god; a special invulnerability, deriving from personality, historic identification, or position in the Senate; skill in setting the terms of a debate, in avoiding a showdown at sunset; and good timing. These were some of the paths toward independence — perhaps ultimately toward a reputation for statesmanship.

Not every man wanted to be independent of his constituency's views. For many, it was more comfortable to repeat accepted wisdom than to explain variations from it. Nor did every man who achieved independence use it to become a statesman — one to whom the national interest is paramount, and who has the wit and energy to serve it.

In the long history of the Senate, more than a few members had achieved both independence and the stature of statesmen, only to be brought down by the old Adam of politics — the average voter — who simply thought himself no longer well served. The wisest senators I knew did not forget those melancholy examples. Often, when an eager staff man pressed them to cast a particularly difficult but "statesmanlike" vote, acknowledging that it would be hard to explain back home, they calmly voted in a way that required no explaining at all.

Once I urged Johnson to take an unusual position on a pending question, and even suggested how he might rationalize his behavior in the eyes of Texas voters. He showed no interest. I walked over to another senator and made the same argument, this time with success. The senator and I were nodding in enthusiastic agreement when Johnson signaled me back to him. I bowed my head beside him to hear as he whispered something I could not catch at first, until he repeated it with rasping asperity: "You couldn't get elected constable."

Maybe not, but I was learning more and more about those who could.

THE REPUBLICANS

I did not know them as well as I knew the Democrats. The aisle between the two sides was only a few feet wide, but the Republicans had their own Bakers and Siegels and McPhersons, and there were not many occasions when my work required me to cross it.

There was plenty of senatorial traffic across the center aisle, however — mostly Democrats going over to buttonhole Republicans, seeking their support or acquiescence on Democratic bills. Johnson was particularly wide-ranging and seemed to regard the Republican side as quite as much within his domain as the Democratic. A few Republicans did come across from time to time, in search of allies: Knowland, Bridges, or Dirksen to see Russell, Eastland, or Holland; Javits or Keating to see Humphrey, Douglas, Clark, or Morse. But the majority of Republicans seemed content to sit, like melons in a patch, waiting for someone to gather them.

Nevertheless they told much about American politics that could not be learned from the Democrats alone, and for that reason I made notes on some of them.

GEORGE AIKEN OF VERMONT: Robert Frost as a senator; red tie, white hair, blue suit. He would be out early on snowy New England mornings, feeding the animals, stacking wood, checking the maple sap runoff. A man of sturdy independence, with a ready shoulder for a neighbor's bogged-down car. He was Mansfield's great friend (theirs was, I believed, one of the few enduring simple friendships in the Senate). Aiken was a composite of the early American virtues. He could also be intensely partisan — though he often voted with the Democrats, particularly in behalf of rural progressivism and an internationalist foreign policy.

JOHN BRICKER OF OHIO: the Republican as Methodist bishop, smooth skin untouched by turmoil, impregnably respectable, dignified with a few little jokes, his blue polka-dotted tie always cool as the ladies' teas he interrupted with apologies to charm; big law firm, big business conservatism, very sound and attractive in the small Ohio towns as he warned against foreign adventures.

STYLES BRIDGES OF NEW HAMPSHIRE: certainly the most influential Republican among his colleagues. He represented a number of business interests, and professed a hard conservative ideology in the mode of the *Manchester Union-Leader*. Like its publisher, William Loeb, he was intransigent toward the Communist world and those—in his own party and among Democrats—who sought to ease relations with it. Within the Senate he had considerable institutional power—he was the ranking Republican on Appropriations and Armed Services. As a congressional politician, Bridges did not allow reactionary philosophy to prevent his making necessary deals with the Democratic leaders, and in these he kept his word. Many members were in his debt for permitting their legislation to go through without bruising interparty fights. Astute as he was, he was used by equally astute Democrats, who knew him to be as unsympathetic to the "Eisenhower liberals" as they were and just as committed to the Senate's prerogatives. His hostility toward the Administration made the Democrats' role of formal opposition much simpler and more effective. I found him unattractive and suspected his every move, but I knew he was a man with whom my side had to cope.

PRESCOTT BUSH OF CONNECTICUT: a Wall Street banker, a "modern" Republican whom modern Republican journals such as *Time* celebrated because he sensed that the earth was round and that Commodore Vanderbilt was dead. "Pres" Bush was fashionable and decent, a contemporary money aristocrat whom a John Cheever hero would have met at a party, but in whose pool he would not have swum. Johnson in a furious debate once said that he had heard enough from "Bush-league" politicians on a certain issue; Bush was stunned by the roughness of that, but he continued gamely to make his point. He served Eisenhower dutifully.

HOMER CAPEHART OF INDIANA: short, rotund; frustrated, I thought, by the gap between his splenetic emotions and his ability to articulate them. He was typical of many successful businessmen in that his spontaneous views, freely offered on a wide variety of issues, were often simply wrong, misguided, and uninformed; yet when he concentrated on a subject and exposed himself to its history, its perplexities, its ultimate seriousness, he was a valuable and resourceful legislator. This he did in the field of housing, where he was Sparkman's opposite number. He never embraced the need for vast increases in public housing and other direct federal expenditures in urban development, but he knew that more housing had to be built and that new financial devices had to be found to build it. I saw Capehart years later at the Indianapolis 500 race. The rubrous vigor was gone. In defeated retirement, he was quiet, diminished, just another man, wearing a battered broad-brimmed hat and staring with the rest of us as a tower of black smoke grew slowly out of a wreck on the track.

FRANCIS CASE OF SOUTH DAKOTA: somewhere in every public school room in America, there is a little boy who throws and throws his hand up before the teacher, before the child she has called upon has had a chance to think of the answer. He knows the answer at once; his soul cries out for the chance to give it, perhaps because he needs to be praised, or because he must hear the orderly "click" when the right answer fits onto the question. He is oblivious to the scorn of his fellow students; the information is the thing. Francis Case was that little boy grown up, pale, square, and deadly dull. His revelation that a gas lobbyist may have tried to bribe him hit the Senate like a truck loaded with wheat from the hard plains of South Dakota. He could have said "tried to rape me" and been believed; no one would have supposed that Case had the imagination to make it up. When he died, this little man, so tidy and severe, left a monument which archaeologists a millennium from now may find to be proof of our productive genius, or madness, or both — the Interstate Highway System.

EVERETT DIRKSEN OF ILLINOIS: what can be said about him now, that anyone who observed him does not already know or sense? When Dirksen succeeded Knowland as Republican leader, a Democratic power mused, "He will be the ideal Republican in that job. The Republicans are the party of the special interests. Most of them represent one or two. Dirksen represents them all." Through sheer *chutzpah,* he almost made that a virtue: the individual businessman was everywhere oppressed by government, so who was to help him, defend him, seek a fair audience for him, unless it be his elected representative? This struck a sympathetic chord in many members; most of them used the same rationale. It was O.K. so far as it went, but of course it often went too far.

I had a friend who drank a great deal but never suffered a hangover because, he said, hangovers came from moral guilt about drinking, and he had decided that drinking was not bad. Dirksen seemed to feel the same way about his frequent changes of course in matters of public policy — anti–foreign aid, pro–foreign aid, anti–foreign aid, and so on. Change was to be preferred, he said, because "consistency is the hobgoblin of little minds," quoting Emerson. (It was a long time before I realized that Emerson had actually said, *"Foolish* consistency is the hobgoblin of little minds.") Dirksen changed sometimes because his party altered its course behind him, sometimes because he was persuaded to do so by Democratic leaders, and sometimes because Presidents — Eisenhower, Kennedy, and Johnson — made him feel he must, for the country's sake. Moderate Presidents could touch him, though on the Senate floor he might sing the Taft conservative hymn, the I-don't-understand-why-we-should refrain; touch him because he was susceptible to their kindness and appeals to his patriotism. When they said that he alone could sway sufficient votes to redeem the country's honor and insure racial peace, he responded. I admired him for that. Others were less sympathetic. On Dirksen's birthday one year, while the

Senate went through its ritual round of arch or heartfelt congratulations, I asked a Southern power — who had made many arrangements with Dirksen over the years — why he did not join in the celebration. "He is a delightful companion," he said, "but he changes too often for me. I never know where he is." If he was all Politician, as flexible as a reed in the prevailing wind, he was also an individualist who did not yield his personal idiosyncrasies to the common taste, and he was brave in the face of pain.

BARRY GOLDWATER OF ARIZONA: in the Blackstone Hotel coffeeshop in Tyler, Texas, wealthy men with grievances against the government — because it modestly taxed and controlled their extraction of minerals from the earth — sat about on weekday mornings, condemning the tide of socialism that was steadily leveling the giants of the world. Barry Goldwater was such a kaffee-klatsch conservative, though it was hard to be sure what he (or they) cared to conserve. His beliefs, or more precisely his reactions, were wholly negative. There was little he wanted to do, and almost everything he wished to undo. He was manly and attractively casual; a Westerner, he was without personal or class snobbery. As a man he was utterly worldly, and as to the social and economic requirements of modern life, utterly naïve. He was a moralist when it came to the government's relations with individuals or groups (lay off); an amoralist when judging commercial behavior (anything goes). That he was lionized and later nominated for President was not surprising to one who had grown up in Texas. It seemed inevitable that someone would eventually be nominated who represented — again, in the sense of symbolizing — such a large and powerful group of Americans. Orwell said we were anarchists; Goldwater spoke for the respectable anarchists who wrapped the flag about high-speed Cadillacs and called it American individualism. He was not a Senate power, having little interest in legislation that did not involve classic conservative doctrines. He could be stimulated chiefly by labor-management bills. Then he spoke vigorously for businessmen who had endured the hell of labor organization in their plants, and offered a series of amendments as remedies for the many ills inflicted upon them by the NLRB. But he was basically rather lazy in the Senate; not so before the Republican women's groups, who adored him; nor, I am sure, as a military man. If I had served in the CBI theater during the Second World War, as he did, I would have welcomed him as a leader.

WILLIAM KNOWLAND OF CALIFORNIA: the Republican leader in 1956, a strapping man with a great fold of muscle and flesh at the back of his neck. I sometimes feared he would burst out of his skin when the level of contention became high. His mind had a single trajectory — flat — and a point-blank range. His integrity was that of a bull, admirable in its way, but unsuited for political leadership. He was entirely predictable, and permitted more skillful men to tie him (and thus his party) inflexibly in fixed positions. Once, when an issue arose on which his views were in irreconcilable conflict with Eisenhower's, he exchanged his leader's chair for one at the rear of the chamber, and there launched a heated attack on his Administration's policy. It was a respectable and perhaps even logical thing to do, and undoubtedly it served notice on the men in the White House that in Knowland they dealt with an independent spirit. But this they surely knew already, and the effect of his performance was chiefly to demonstrate, through a role-play, the sharp cleavage between traditional and "modern" Republicans. Afterwards I wondered about the best course for a Senate leader when he could not stomach a policy that he might normally be expected to defend. Knowland had chosen a clean break; though he might sleep more easily at night, he had also weakened his party. Mansfield faced the same dilemma in the sixties, over the issue of the Vietnam war. For a long time he simply avoided taking a stand in direct opposition to his Administration. But as his active support was needed, his silence was almost as irritating to the White House as an exposed confrontation; it was not enough for a Democratic leader to look the other way as the line was being drawn in the dirt. In a parliamentary system, a cabinet member caught in such a position would almost certainly resign. Alben Barkley, when leader, once did so, in a conflict with FDR. But that was unusual. In America, the two branches were, after all, separate and coequal. A party leader in the Senate was something more than a spokesman for his Administration. In a showdown even a strong and popular President could not be sure of unseating a man whom senators had chosen as their leader, in favor of one more willing to speak for his policies. The strain of the Senate leader–President relationship — with all its potential for grief, confusion, and mistrust — must have played a considerable role in Johnson's decision to accept the Vice Presidential nomination in 1960. The idea of becoming a powerless shill must have been obnoxious to him, but it promised him freedom from a relationship in which there would have been no peace.

THOMAS KUCHEL OF CALIFORNIA: Earl Warren's man in the Senate. Spokesman for, if not leader of, the Republican liberals. Kuchel (Kee-kul) was iconoclastic and profane about his fellow Republicans, even when talking with the Democratic staff. He was a man in the middle: unwilling to adopt the conventional liberal Democratic dogma, unable to accept the prevailing views of his own party. He sponsored expensive legislation to develop the arid wastelands of California, and voted for civil rights and urban renewal. He was intelligent and articulate, but he was not a Senate power. His was the dilemma of Republican liberals in a period of Democratic control of Congress — without much power to shape the outcome, without will to divert it. I liked him not only for his candor, but because he remained in the ambiguity of his situation and refused to succumb to an ideology that would free him from it.

WILLIAM LANGER OF NORTH DAKOTA: as governor in the thirties, Langer had ordered the borders of the state sealed by force to prevent farmers from selling wheat at depressed prices. He was old, tough, lean, and radical, a Populist who voted isolationist and sometimes left. He chewed on cigars in their wrappers and was almost blind by the time I knew him. Still I felt an unpredictable force in him, even in his age and sickness, that might well have supported a world organization run by farmers and a few of his business friends.

GEORGE MALONE OF NEVADA: often when Johnson was trying to work out a compromise on a bill and needed time before bringing it to a vote, he asked Molly Malone to make a tariff speech. It was basically the same speech, with topical variations. The Reciprocal Trade Agreements Act and the General Agreement on Tariffs and Trade (GATT) were the active agents of evil in the world; they allowed the products of impoverished foreign labor to compete with our own, and so destroyed American jobs. I thought it curious, at first, that a free trader like Johnson should switch on this relic of Smoot-Hawley days. But it was the interlude he wanted, not the message. Years later I learned that Malone, while apparently reactionary, was totally faithful to union labor. At the close of an exhausting week's debate on a labor-management bill, when labor had won most of its battles and was prepared to accept the moderate outcome, I sat in the gallery with a tired and happy union lobbyist, watching the final vote. Everyone — friend and foe — was voting "aye." Suddenly the union man leapt up and said, "My God! I forgot to tell Molly he could vote aye on final passage!" He rushed out of the gallery and down toward the lobby. Too late. "Mr. Malone." "No!" came the reply — the only one.

JOSEPH MCCARTHY OF WISCONSIN: in 1956, soon after I arrived, an elevator operator told me, "Senator McCarthy's one man I like. He doesn't even buzz three times" — the senatorial signal that said come at once. I stared at the young operator in disbelief — didn't he know what this genial, patient senator had done to the country? But he was not alone; many senators regarded McCarthy with something just short of affection. He was, after all, one of the forum, and he affected an aggressive amiability which (since most senators were unwilling to inflict further hurt upon him after the censure) inspired a tolerant condescension in response. He drank a great deal, and his skin normally looked like the pale pulpy underside of a mushroom. He still launched abusive, but-have-you-dropped-your-Communist-party-membership attacks on those who bedeviled him; but these were the roundhouse swings of an old shadow-boxing fighter rocking on his heels, without effect unless one stepped within range. I despised McCarthy and could not imagine why he had been permitted to gain such power in the early fifties. It was disheartening to think it was because he had posed no threat to the solid Rotarians who made up most of the Senate, and who preferred not to engage that part of their constituencies that had been passionately aroused by his talk of Communists in the State Department. The Senate's traditional attitude of laissez-faire was also responsible. So long as McCarthy did not sponsor a bill or an amendment that needed resisting, senators were content to let him go about his malicious games in committee. Besides, those whom he persecuted were often evasive, sometimes intemperate, and almost always unimportant; there was not a straightforward self-made corporate executive among them. One night in 1953, in Wiesbaden, I saw a film about the war in Europe. First came the German attack on France and the Lowlands. The audience was silent. Then June 1941, and the invasion of Russia. A great groan went up from the crowd, and someone nearby said *"Dumm!"* (stupid). So it was with the Senate's reaction to McCarthy: silence when the targets were bureaucrats and insignificant leftists of the past, righteous indignation and reprisal when he became foolish and attacked middle-road respectable members. Perhaps the reason was that McCarthy was merely a crusader-manqué. Sometimes he mocked his own performance when talking to senators, and thus disarmed them; he was, after all, only playing a political game, as they did when they attacked Big Steel or the Agriculture Department. Then there was the environment of his success: the last years of the unpopular Truman, whom few cared to defend, the early years of Ike, whom Democrats enjoyed seeing squirm under Republican attack. There were plenty of reasons, but when I listened to that groaning, cynical voice, pressing for the bruise, the sensitive nerve, the final indecent hold, I thought there was no good reason, and never could be.

JOHN MARSHALL BUTLER OF MARYLAND, WILLIAM JENNER OF INDIANA, and HERMAN WELKER OF IDAHO: with Joe McCarthy, four peas in a bad pod. Butler was a well-dressed lightweight, a "pipsqueak," as Gerald Johnson called him; Jenner was a rough infighter whom Welker, heavy with drinking, followed about the chamber as a malign hound trails a harsh master; McCarthy alone had the energy to convert venom into action. The voters of four states had sent them to the Senate. It was enough to give pause to the most committed believer in the democratic process. One could understand the attractions of conservatism; but why should such small-minded, hostile men, without purpose except to injure, represent the people of those states? There were logical antecedents—their vicious campaigns, and the naïve responses of their opponents; factionalism that destroyed their opposition from within; a national tide of reaction that swept them to shore. But why them? Why not men like Ed Thye, Leverett Saltonstall, or even Martin of Pennsylvania, a captive mouse of industry? If the people of Idaho and Indiana rejected liberal politics and economics, it seemed to me that they might have chosen those of the Union League, instead of an American Falange.

LEVERETT SALTONSTALL OF MASSACHUSETTS: his long, homely face, his simple, self-reliant bearing, and his utter lack of vindictiveness made him the classic exemplar of New England Republicanism. He was as trustworthy and straight as he looked. He was neither brilliant, nor witty, nor inventive; his speeches never excited and seldom surprised. He had no attachment to the rural poor, as did Aiken, and he did not share the urban liberalism of Javits or Kuchel. He was simply true to what men of his heritage believed to be the national interest: a strong defense, an internationalist foreign policy, and a limited government role in the economy. He had no enemies — the result not only of his character, but of his disinclination to enter the trenches where personal feelings were exposed and personal bitterness often resulted. Like Eisenhower, he did not choose to become involved in "personalities." Friction between "personalities" was, of course, fundamental to the Senate. Thus as Saltonstall was spared its unpleasant consequences, he sacrificed the broad effectiveness that might have come from engaging in it. To the Democratic activists he was important, because on a given issue he was a bellwether of the moderate Republican position. The support of Javits, Case of New Jersey, and Kuchel was taken for granted; hence it counted for nothing beyond their individual votes. Saltonstall's support meant something more, both in prestige and in reach — he did not need to vote for progressive measures, as they did because of their liberal constituencies. So his vote was, for moderate conservatives, a sufficient justification for their own apostasy.

ED THYE OF MINNESOTA: a Scandinavian grandfather, warm, benign, a friend of the farmers and in this period a spokesman for their anger against Benson; essentially conservative in other matters. Spoke with a slow, North Country firmness — he was methodical and square, rather like Lawrence Welk. That he and Humphrey represented Minnesota was further proof of a political curiosity: the states often chose utterly different personalities, holding widely varying views, to represent them in the Senate. Hayden and Goldwater from Arizona; Knowland and Kuchel from California; Clark and Martin from Pennsylvania; at almost any moment there were a dozen such anomalies. It was hard to tell whether they stemmed from the voters' instinctive need for balance, or purely from the vicissitudes of timing, compounded by years of seniority in the Senate and familiarity at home.

ALEXANDER WILEY OF WISCONSIN: at some point in the late 1940's Wiley had become "convicted," as the theologians say, of the smallness of the earth. Thereafter he made an almost weekly address on the need for international cooperation. These were platitudinous, but nonetheless welcome because they countered the bellicosity of his colleague Joe McCarthy. In physique and demeanor Wiley reminded me of Victor Moore, standing downstage right and joining as the chorus sang "Wintergreen for President." Still he was a kind man who wished to do well, and by example, as a senior Republican vote for accommodation with other nations, he succeeded.

JOHN WILLIAMS OF DELAWARE: the Republican as C.P.A.—the small businessman (in this case, a successful chicken farmer) outraged by the wastefulness of government and by special-interest chicanery, particularly when performed by Democrats. He could be smug and nit-picking; he could be a valuable public watchdog; he was indiscriminately proud of both roles. His intelligence sources within executive government, particularly in Justice and the Internal Revenue Service, were phenomenal. Like Francis Case, he would object, on a point of narrow principle, to procedures agreed upon by all his colleagues. I remember one such occasion for the light it cast on Lyndon Johnson's character. At the end of a week's desultory argument, Johnson persuaded the Senate to agree on two hours' further debate, followed by a vote. Every base had been touched — all but Williams. The unanimous consent agreement was put to the Senate, and in his high, irritating voice, Williams objected. Johnson sat down with a scowl. Then he rose and, jingling the coins in his pocket in nervous rage, stalked out of the Senate and went to his office. I thought his fury was justified; if I had been he, I would have let the Senate stew in its juice. Five minutes later he came back. He went over to Williams and sat down beside him, staring at the ceiling and talking rapidly, without expression, from the side of his mouth. Then the two rose and went out to the elaborate Johnson office just beyond the chamber. In fifteen minutes they returned. Williams took his seat. Johnson put the same agreement to the Senate — only this time providing for three hours of debate. There was no objection. Williams's principle appeared to have been satisfied; Johnson had his agreement. It was an unforgettable lesson to me — not in the tactics of consent agreements, but in the importance of renouncing the pleasure of righteous indignation when there was practical work to be done.

THE REPUBLICANS AND THE DEMOCRATS

I looked at Republicans through Democratic eyes. I wanted to "win" over them, as years earlier I had wanted the Tyler High School Lions to win over the Longview Lobos. Democrats were my people. I laughed at outrageous Democratic attacks on Republicans, unashamed by a single standard of fairness. I saw nothing wrong in finding Republicans guilty by association with the Liberty Lobby and Dixon-Yates, though I had raged when McCarthy used the same device in tying Democrats to Communists.

In the main, I thought Republicans dull, humorless, complacent, and shortsighted — in league, on the one hand, with exhausted but portentous institutions like the 'church and the Legion; on the other, with selfish business interests. I thought

Democrats by nature festive, original, articulate, and sympathetic to the poor. There were almost as many exceptions to this as there were supporting examples; but that did not prevent me from holding the opinion.

In Southerners I discovered, or devised, a residual populism beneath the racial bigotry. Contrarily, when a Southerner expressed a benighted opinion, I was likely to think it picturesque. When he voted against a needed social reform, I accepted his resistance as natural. Not so with Republicans. What was colorful among Southerners was simply reactionary in those across the aisle.

These were unfair distinctions, and I knew it; but I devised a kind of "literary" basis for them. The South, I believed, was obsessed with character and language; it was violent in thought and action, and yet it was curiously tolerant of extravagant personalities. There was also its ancient — and generally honorable — involvement in international politics, which gave promise that in times of crisis a few Southerners would, through instinct and heritage, serve the country well. Many Southerners in Congress were as plain as a business letter; but the region itself was so vivid that I thought its politics should be judged substantially as art.

There seemed to be no such traditions or obsessions in the Midwest — in the Republican heartland. Respectable as most of them were, Republicans were uninteresting. Hence I judged their views, not in the context of personality or in the realm of art, but purely as ideology — stark and homely as steel-rimmed spectacles, mighty proud to be made in America.

I was easier on Southerners, of course, because I was one. Given the chance, I would have pitched in to fight half of them in their home-state elections. But in Washington, where many Northerners were wet and intolerant toward all things Southern, I found myself defending what I detested back home. Perhaps everyone is inclined to do this, who spent a happy childhood in an identifiable region. The attacks of outsiders, even when intellectually unanswerable, never seem to account for the pleasures of growing up there, and in witnessing to those pleasures one resists hearing what one knows to be true. When the attack is a universal indictment — for example, all Southerners are racial bigots, all Midwesterners are Babbitts — one urges the exceptions, and if the debate goes on long enough, and if there is enough to drink, one romanticizes the exceptions into a universal defense: most Southerners are not racial bigots, most Midwesterners are decent sons of the soil.

For a Southern liberal in Washington, there was another, opposing need, that of being accepted by the political Establishment of the city. Despite Republican control of the White House and Southern control of the Congress, the lively political spirit in Washington was Northern-Democratic; not the Northern democracy of the city bosses, but of those who believed in "taking chances for peace," government intervention in the economy, aid to the distant poor, and civil rights laws. I wanted such people — reporters, columnists, editors, lawyers, and administrators of Roosevelt and Truman days, the staffs of liberal senators — to think me one of them, as in philosophic attitude I was. Often I found myself being introduced at dinner parties in a way that suggested — without, it seemed, intentional condescension — that I was "all right," a Southerner who wanted the right things; and sometimes, to prove my credentials, I responded with sardonic comments about those Southerners with whom I had just been working the Senate chamber. This must have made me uneasy, for I was quick to defend the same men when others joined and intensified the attack.

I envied those who sallied forth with unalloyed spirits, attacking or supporting without hesitation. But I often found my original opinion about a man or an issue to be insufficient, one-sided, or plain wrong, and I became wary about absolute views. And a fascination with personality — with whatever it was that made men strong or weak, driving or passive, hard or vulnerable — made it difficult to concentrate on their philosophies, or even on their actions, as the sole basis for judging them.

In time I found many dull Republicans to be interesting men, worth being "fair" to. And once I started down that road, it became harder to laugh at malicious assaults upon them. Dogma gave way to sympathy; the sharp edge of combat was dulled by fellow feeling. This was perhaps inevitable in any group so tightly circumscribed as was the Senate and its staff, but the threat it posed was ominous: that one would become just another member of the corps of professional political men that invests every capital and city hall, men to whom a slap on the back and a kind exchange are more important than belief. Politics as practiced by such men — the politics of personality without conviction — bears the same relationship to serious governance that a dry grin bears to love. If one abhorred the politics of the doctrinaire, one had also to resist the politics of the club car.

Now, having described some of the Republicans and Democrats in the Senate of 1956, it is time to talk of the work they did there — in what seems today (but did not seem then) a time of innocent tranquillity before the winds of the sixties rose in the land without.

3

Right from Wrong

For Texas liberals in the mid-fifties, political issues were cast in chiaroscuro. On one side were the people, on the other, the reactionaries. In our eyes, the reactionaries were too rich per se, spent lavish sums to elect conservative politicians, and so controlled the state's legislature and regulatory agencies. What was most offensive about this was not that the state as a result spent little on social services — that issue was still to come — but that corruption and favoritism abounded while legislators made wahoo attacks on "un-American" economics and the "intermingling of the races." Wherever liberals looked, they saw hypocrisy — benign or cynical, but everywhere well financed.

An equally bleak view of politics was growing up on the right, determined to resist socialism in all its forms. In the Petroleum Clubs, in the expensive air-conditioned suburbs, the tocsin Joe McCarthy had sounded echoed with a resonance that even he might not have foreseen. A holy war for America began to rage in Dallas and Houston, dividing ordinary citizens into determined crusaders and "innocent dupes." A beloved cousin of mine, a Dallas matron who lived, I believe, at least five miles from the nearest liberal, made thousands of telephone calls in behalf of an archconservative congressman, "maybe the only good one there is," she said. She thought it was he or Khrushchev.

Thus armies of passionate believers were drawn up on opposite sides of the great plain of Texas, as tumultuous with conviction and ardor as were the Christians and Mohammedans of medieval Europe.

The language they used, the issues they pressed (often unjoined by the other side, their salvos of accusations whistling through the air) were primitive indeed, when one considers how complex the world and American society had become. Yet the struggle was not without value for that. Moral certainty is satisfying to the soul. To be able to identify one's enemies is as important to one's political peace of mind as to identify one's friends is to one's social well-being. I knew where I was on the political battlefield of Texas.

In Washington, it was obvious at once that most issues were more complex than those to which I was accustomed. Or perhaps working for someone whose views were not immediately sympathetic to mine forced me to try to understand the other side, and so made the issues "complex." That was unsettling to think about. What if I had faced the necessity of understanding both sides in Texas, instead of responding to the first bugle call of my liberal friends? Would I have found even Texas issues "complex," with something to be said for the "reactionary" view? Maybe so.

In any event, becoming aware of the complexity and ambiguity of great issues did not desiccate them. I still wanted to put down the Republicans; that there was "something to be said for their side" did not render them less odious for saying it.

Why should that have been? Why should an otherwise rational person, who could tolerate opinions different from his own in private matters, become incensed about opposing political views?

It was a long time before I understood that not everyone was so politically excitable. In fact, most people weren't. Even on the Hill, committee clerks and administrative assistants were often oblivious to the great issues which their senators debated with such intensity.

A vivid concern with political questions seemed to require an ability to convert ideas into immediate, visceral significance — in Eliot's terms, to achieve an association of sensibilities. I remember seeing a friend in college weep with anger because Henry VIII had left the Roman Church; had the king remained Catholic, my friend thought, he and his successors might have colonized America with masses of European Catholic labor — thereby obviating the need to import slaves from Africa. That someone could grieve over an ancient might-have-been seemed perfectly natural to me.

Still, an intense concern with politics may have reflected no more than an unwillingness to come to terms with one's personal problems. Political issues were distinct and verbal, if complex; the business of dealing with one's parents, wife, children, boss, colleagues, and friends was far more threatening, as it involved dark tides of emotion into which one might be swept at any moment. One could always "have a view" about a political issue, and even in angry debate there were tacitly accepted ground rules. In an encounter with one's private demons, there was no assurance that one would survive with ego intact.

This analysis seemed to be borne out in the careers of many political men, the failure of whose lives as husbands and fathers matched their success in public affairs. Brilliant in the arena, eager to engage in a contest of ideas and rhetoric, they must have avoided the necessary intimacy by which a family lives — so starved and hostile did their women and children seem.

Whatever the explanation — a special sensitivity to ideas, an unwillingness to confront personal realities, or simply a compelling need to identify with matters of great moment and scope — people with intense political interests were obviously a breed apart.

And generally they were partisan — instinctively supportive of one party or faction, whatever the issue, instinctively antipathetic to the other.

That might derive from history: for a Southerner, old passions surrounded the driest provisions of laws affecting farmers, banks, and tariffs. Memories of the Depression lingered on in the minds of most Democrats, and the mention of FDR's name was enough to arouse the faithful at Democratic dinners. (Indeed, it was sometimes the only thing that did. More than once I heard Johnson, trying to shake a groggy audience out of its torpor, rush to that part of his speech where the names "Franklin D. Roosevelt!" and "Harry S. Truman!" produced a pounding torrent of applause. For Republicans, the magic name was "Bob Taft.")

Partisan emotions might come from personality: that certain leaders were for or against a proposition meant that thousands of people lined up automatically behind them or in opposition to them. If Paul Douglas declared against an economic proposal, most liberals knew they should be against it too (though not so many followed his hard line in foreign affairs). Contrarily, what McCarthy or Knowland were for, liberals were against per se. This hydraulic mechanism served to simplify matters, but it was so powerful that the support of a conservative for a liberal cause made liberals suspect that the cause might not be just after all.

Finally, there was the pressure of professional activists, the party chairmen and staffs who knew that issues had to be produced and the fine edges taken off if the faithful were to be spurred into action. I was often astounded to see a question whose complexities I could barely comprehend converted into the functional equivalent of a picket sign. That was sometimes useful to me, as it reminded me that I was, after all, on one side or the other, and not on both. But it was also enough to make me distrust the work of political promoters as jejune and misleading.

I was a partisan Democrat when I arrived in Washington, and — with many footnotes — I remained one. Yet I never reached the heights of party passion. I was never so sedulous in my devotion as that young man in Austin — call him Smith — who entered the *Daily Texan* office one day to find the staff sitting about in bemused reminiscence of a university guard who had died the night before, after forty years of devoted service. The guard had been a friend to generations of students, and the talk was about his generosity, his wit, his understanding of youthful behavior, and so on. At last Smith asked the vital question: "Was he a Democrat?"

The parties were almost equally divided in the Senate of 1956 — forty-nine Democrats, of whom eighteen were deep Southerners, and forty-seven Republicans, of whom a handful were relatively liberal. Two or three years were to pass by before I understood what those statistics meant, and what they required of the Democratic leader. On the day when Gerry Siegel took me across the floor to meet Lyndon Johnson, I was aware only that my people were on one side of the center aisle, and the Know-Nothings were on the other. I shook hands with Johnson, heard him say, "Do your best," and retreated to the back of the chamber. For the next few hours I listened while my people belabored each other over a proposal about which I knew little, except that I disliked my new employer's position.

The issue was the "gas bill." Its sponsor was Senator Fulbright, and its purpose was to counteract a Supreme Court decision of two years before which had thrust authority upon the Federal Power Commission to regulate natural gas prices at the wellhead. The gas industry had objected violently to this, and its friends in the House had pushed through a bill similar to Fulbright's in the summer of 1955.

By and large, the split in the Senate was geographical, not ideological. Most Northern and Eastern senators of both parties opposed the bill on the ground that unregulated prices at the wellhead would turn up in higher rates for the consumers they represented. Western and Southwestern senators supported it. The Southerners were split, and unusually silent.

For the liberal press, the issue was tailor-made. Oil and gas barons were manipulating the Congress into an unscrupulous attack on helpless home-owners. The *Washington Post,* in an editorial welcoming Johnson back from his convalescence, urged him to let the bill die. Morse and Humphrey disagreed; as parliamentary liberals, they thought every measure, even bad ones such as this, should be fairly debated and decided. How else could they later urge the consideration of civil rights bills and changes in the filibuster rule?

Mike Monroney, speaking for Oklahoma oil and gas, carried the brunt of the case for passage. He knew the industry and all its arguments. FPC regulation would produce a hopeless bureaucratic mess. That would stifle the search for gas. Supplies would be diminished, leading inevitably to higher consumer prices. The real culprits were the distributors — the friendly local gas companies — who bought from the pipelines and methodically overcharged their users. Regulating the producers wouldn't solve that.

Congress, in the Gas Act of 1938, had specifically exempted the production and gathering of natural gas from federal regulation. A divided Supreme Court found that this did not exempt the producers' sale of the gas for resale in interstate commerce. Monroney asked: why else produce it, except to sell it? Justice Douglas, in dissent, had said, "If sales can be regulated, then the Commission could set a rate base (for the producer) which must include all of its producing and gathering properties, and supervision over its production and gathering expenses" (which the Act of 1938 had exempted).

It was amusing to hear conservatives using the arguments of Justice Douglas, in so many other matters their bête noire, as ammunition in the debate. There was a lot of talk about Justices Minton and Black, who had served in the Senate when the Gas Act was debated in the late thirties, and who were therefore thought to possess special wisdom about what Congress had intended to cover. I thought it strange that justices, even former senators, carried such practical information around in their heads, along with the ethereal abstractions with which they dealt in the *Supreme Court Reports.*

The debate, when it was between Monroney, Fulbright, Douglas, and Pastore, was brilliant. There were a hundred exchanges every hour, and each had the best of it on occasion. Following the cut and thrust of their arguments, I changed my mind three or four times daily. Years later I understood that such an intellectual contest was rare in the Senate, that most of what senators said was meant for other audiences — the press, their constituencies, or particular interest groups — and not to provoke debate on the floor.

The gas bill was not a great moral issue, though advocates on both sides tried to make it so. There were captive consumers at one end of the line who had invested in gas-burning furnaces, and there were very rich men at the other end whose intense preoccupation with the bill suggested that they would become richer by its passage. But there remained real doubt about whether imposing utility regulations on the producers made sense. There were no such controls on the production of coal, or of home-heating oil. A key element of utility regulation was the predictable cost of production, and thousands of dry holes in the Southwest testified to the absence of predictability in the search for oil and gas. Gas might look like a utility in Rhode Island; it looked like an uncertain commodity in Texas.

So long as Monroney and Fulbright spoke for the bill, I could appreciate the logic of these arguments, and the tension I had felt on arriving — young Texas liberal joins up with oilman reaction — began to dissipate. I could live with logic, even if its results were obnoxious to liberals.

But I was troubled by tales of heavy pressure from the industry lobby. The campaign for passage took many forms — outwardly and most innocently, in speeches served up for men like Styles Bridges. Representing New Hampshire, a consumer state, he was nevertheless strong for the bill. He made a stunning speech that began with a recitation of "What is America": the Fourth of July, U. S. Grant, Robert E. Lee, John Paul Jones, Hap Arnold, and Carl Spaatz. "All that is America." So was freedom to compete. Our military power was founded on our economic power, which in turn was based on competition and the absence of the kind of regimentation embodied in FPC regulation of natural gas prices at the wellhead. The elisions were breathtaking, as was the summation: "Those who do not care for principle" (that is, the absence of regulation equals boom times for everyone) "but look to their own immediate selfish interest do not appreciate that success in what they seek would mean the slowing down of the flow of natural gas and higher prices for the meager quantities that reach their homes." The combination of Styles Bridges' high principles and the fetid prose of an industry publicist was too much. It corroded Monroney's logic. Speeches such as this — and there were many of them — turned a good debate into a time-killing charade.

But that was only an aesthetic objection. Something more disturbing was going on. A multibillion-dollar industry was conducting a massive political and propaganda campaign with all the finesse of Luis Firpo, and it seemed very likely that it would succeed. Senator Aiken reported, "Never, since I have been in Washington, have I seen such intensive, varied, and ingenious types of lobbying used to promote legislation. I have been badly overlobbied." His letters from Vermont, mostly from oil corporation stockholders and gasoline dealers, were one-sidedly in favor of the bill. He could understand their views and those of oil-state senators: "if I lived in Oklahoma or Kansas, I would probably support it." But the bill seemed bound to increase the price of gas in Vermont. "If it were not intended to raise prices, it would not be here." That seemed logical, too.

At length, all argument spent, the bill headed for an early vote, certain of passage. But then Francis Case rose to tell about the visit of an unnamed lobbyist to his offices, and the lobbyist's subsequent contribution of $2,500 to his campaign. Case had originally favored the bill, but he now felt that if its passage had become "so alluring that dollars are advanced to potential candidates even before the primaries are held, warning signals go up." He would oppose it.

It was a good speech, rather cautious, just one man's experience. I thought he was genuinely disturbed by what I assumed was more or less common practice in Texas. He seemed very square and proud of it. But even if he enjoyed the telling of it, enjoyed the nimbus of righteousness that surrounded each element of the story, it was disturbing. Case had shifted the controversy onto another plane, where substantive arguments about the bill were suddenly irrelevant.

Fulbright was quick to respond. He urged Case to consider that his attitude put the defeat of good legislation into the hands of anyone who might make such an unseemly contribution. It was a good debater's point. But it was insufficient to quiet the storm that Francis Case had broken upon the Senate.

Not that the storm was apparent, for the moment. After a brief colloquy, Douglas began a speech wholly unrelated to Case's disclosure. The Norwegian defense minister was introduced to the applauding members, and Humphrey talked about milk marketing orders. Apparently, the Senate wished to turn its back on this embarrassment, wondering, perhaps, whether it would blow over, never to make the papers, rather to be handled in some quiet way — a mistaken assumption, a perfectly natural error, unauthorized, to be regretted. Even the opponents seemed put off by this tabloid intrusion into an otherwise logical debate.

But the press was galloping after scandal. For the bill's sponsors, hopeful silence would not do. There had to be an answer, something to go out on the wires simultaneously with Case's speech. Fulbright tried again, as did Monroney, complaining that Case's reluctance to name the lobbyist exposed all those who supported the bill to the charge that they had been bought.

Johnson said nothing that day. But when the Senate met again, he was ready with a resolution proposing a committee of investigation. While the committee did its work, the Senate should move ahead to a vote on the bill. It could "ill afford to prostrate itself before phantoms." I was astonished by his audacity. To vote, before the Senate knew exactly what wrong had been done!

I was responding like a journalist, not like a political leader who knew that he had the votes, and that to delay until the scandal could be fully explored would risk those votes in a maelstrom of charge and countercharge — most of it unrelated to the merits of the bill.

In time the Senate approved his resolution. Johnson and Knowland agreed on a four-man committee of such dependability (George, Hayden, Bridges, and Thye) as to quiet the most sensitive nerve in the body of oil and gas. And the Senate moved on toward a vote.

I sat in the Capitol coffee shop one evening, arguing about Case's revelation with other assistants. What effect should it have? Should it defeat the bill? What if educators, or representatives of peace groups, made contributions to senators on the eve of a vote on aid to schools or a treaty with Russia? Many liberal-minded people would find that perfectly acceptable, as a means of "keeping good men in the Senate." How did that differ from the oilman's contribution to Case? If it didn't, if the act itself was neutral, then one's judgment depended on the cause being advanced, and that was a matter of political opinion, not of morality.

A despotic chairman who gaveled "progressive" legislation through his committee was to be admired, while one who did the same for a "reactionary" bill ought to be denounced. A senator who filibustered during a morning committee meeting, until the noon bell rang and further action could be blocked, was to be condemned — unless he were filibustering a bad bill.

Undemocratic procedures, or money given in anticipation of a friendly vote, were therefore only tools to be judged by the uses to which they were put. The logical conclusion was that the successful exercise of power was all that mattered. It was idle to prate about moral standards, hypocritical to impose fixed rules on others when one's own values were wholly relative. If there were such a thing as political integrity, it lay not in clothing desirable results in righteousness, but in acknowledging that ethical judgments simply did not apply to politics.

The "realist" answer had its adherents in the Capitol, in the universities, and in the precincts. It enabled politicians to conduct business without pausing to wrestle with a code of behavior that seemed unnecessarily rigid or irrelevant. A senator might repeat the Ten Commandments and commend the Boy Scout oath with a clear conscience, being himself kind, courteous, and respectful of the property of others; so long as his practical affairs were judged only by success or failure, he could escape the bite of remorse. "Realism" was equally useful to academics, as a means of identifying with the tough world of politics — with things as they are.

Yet if the realists were right, we were all adrift in a sea whose currents no one could predict, much less control. If they were right, there could be no outrage at the arrogant use of money in deciding public questions. The slick distortions of Madison Avenue, the conspiracies of interest groups, the appeals to groundless fear and customary hatreds, the irresponsible grip of a few chairmen on the process of decision — all these were immune from moral criticism, if the realists were right.

This was unnatural to me. I wanted some ground to stand on, some formula by which to judge and be judged. I listened to the prayers of the Senate chaplain, at the beginning of each session

— but I heard nothing but the tumid sanctimonious rhetoric of an aging Methodist, no more related to the moral dilemmas of politics than is the Rotary song to those of business. Columnists and editorial writers were more helpful; they were willing, indeed eager, to pronounce judgment; but often they did it so quickly, with such inherent bias, and on so little evidence (most of it hearsay) that I came to doubt their verdicts instinctively.

There were politicians who professed to experience no problem in distinguishing right from wrong, and thought others devious or obtuse who found it difficult. Some of them were true believers, never troubled by ambiguity; others occupied safe seats, and so escaped the pressures that bear on those who must achieve their majorities from a welter of competing interests. Many of them declined to engage in the dangerous infighting that inevitably took place when the stakes were high. But almost all of them accepted the benefits of that infighting — even when these were produced by autocratic methods or dubious contributions from without.

So did I. I wanted to believe in a consistent moral code, in procedures that would stand examination by any civics class, in judgments made without fear or financial inducement. But when my side prevailed on an issue of great importance to me, I spent little time lamenting the methods by which victory was won. In fact I took pleasure in hearing about them. Ingenious and successful chicanery is almost always attractive, particularly when its result is favorable.

So I often found myself at sea — not because I thought morality was irrelevant to political conduct, but because I knew it was relevant, and still, wishing to win, could not submit entirely to its demands. I sought refuge in the very complexity of issues which, I believed, the moralists could not comprehend; and in thoughts about a "higher morality" which justified any means of arriving at a commonly desirable end. But "higher morality" — besides providing a rationale for every oppressive regime in history — led straight to the swamp of the realists. And though great issues were often too complex for a messianic temperament to understand, that only made more difficult, and did not obviate, the task of moral judgment.

There seemed no way to settle the problem once and for all. Perhaps an intense political commitment and moral sensitivity were irreconcilable.

If they were, then one could choose one or the other, though one led toward a brutal pragmatism, and the other toward ineffectiveness. Unless — one could choose a third way, and remain, as the modern theologians say, "in the ambiguity" — acting forcefully, but conscious always that one's knowledge was insufficient and one's heart slightly corrupt. The best political men I knew seemed to have chosen this way.

Few of them would have expressed it in those terms. Johnson, for one, was put off by a minister's definition of the political life as one lived in ambiguity. His fundamentalist attitude toward "religious" questions did not allow for that, and when he said that a leader's problem was not in doing what was right, but in knowing what was right, he truly believed he had summed up the problem. Yet in dealing with other political men, in finding his way through the labyrinth of their motives — and of his own — in his lust for triumph and in his disabused appreciation of its swift passing, he lived on a far more intricate level. Aggressive, scheming, vehement, his eye fixed on victory and his tremendous energies bent to achieve it, he was also morally aware.

Quite obviously he believed that some ends — particularly the enactment of progressive legislation — required generosity in judging the means that produced them, but he gave no sign that he rejected the legitimacy of judgment. He expected it, and often pronounced it himself. In his own verdicts he was harder on those who condemned the misbehavior of others, without conceding their own vulnerability, than he was on self-admitted scoundrels. But even the former had the power to reach him. He could neither ignore them nor blast them scornfully out of his concern. Ingenious and practical as he was, he was also ethically sentient; he wished to be thought a good man as well as a clever one.

I have gone far afield from the issues before the Senate in 1956. Perhaps it was inevitable, for like most young men who care passionately about politics, I saw political issues in stark moral terms. During the debate over the natural gas bill, a variety of moral questions arose for which I still have no certain answers: the wisdom of the bill itself; loyalty, or opposition, to my employer's policies; the attempted bribe, or whatever it was, and the effect it should have had on the fate of the bill; the relevance of moral standards to political acts. Plato and Machiavelli, Montaigne, Tocqueville, Tolstoy, and Russell all explored the question of right action in public affairs. But I never quite understood its poignancy until I encountered it in the voices of men five or ten feet away, answering "Aye!" or "No!" at the end of a long and troubled debate.

4

Cold War Democrats

EISENHOWER vetoed the natural gas bill, reluctantly. He supported its objectives, but the Case affair and the doubts it raised in the public's mind had tarnished it irreparably. He thought its supporters might try again, this time specifically protecting consumers. . . . It was an empty gesture, and he surely knew it; nobody was ready to try again, this time in a more skeptical Congress.

In a curious way, the matter was resolved to the benefit of everyone, except Johnson and the industry. Eisenhower looked virtuous in an election year; his standing with Eastern consumers was improved. When oilmen called to complain, he could blame the industry for creating its own problems. The bill's supporters in Congress might castigate him for his veto, and its Republican opponents could praise him for it. To the opposition Democrats, the President's action came as a pleasant surprise, especially as it was based on the vulgarity of oil-country wealth.

Johnson was angry, for the veto made him look bad. Confronting the same evidence on which Eisenhower had based his disapproval, he had pushed the bill through to passage. He argued that it was just as meritorious after, as before, Case's disclosure, and of course he was right, as an abstract proposition; but the public is not given to abstract reasoning when scandal is in the air. If he gained anything from the episode, it was a certain freedom from the industry's political requirements. He had taken risks in its behalf, and suffered a degree of political discredit because of its clumsiness. For the time being, nothing more could fairly be asked of him. He had also gained the right to suggest to Texans that Republicans were untrustworthy friends — not that this was to count for much in the fall election.

I was glad to see the issue behind us. After listening to Monroney's arguments, I had vigorously defended the bill, and accused liberal friends of conducting an emotional crusade in defiance of the facts. With the bill's Southwestern supporters I opposed it with equal heat. Like the town crank, I was dissatisfied with both positions; my opinion, like his, was without consequence to the outcome; and I rather enjoyed the ironies and on-the-other-hands.

But I wanted to participate in "larger" issues, about which I thought positions would be much clearer and more satisfying: foreign and economic policy, civil liberties, defense. In these, at least, the good guys would not break ranks. Whatever the merits of "living in ambiguity," I looked forward to the pleasures of righteous solidarity.

Not many senators were interested in foreign countries as such. Other histories and cultures, like the arts and sciences of our own, were remote from their daily concerns. A deep preoccupation with intellectual matters would probably have struck their voters as evidence of impracticality.

Nevertheless most of them were interested in foreign policy. They were absorbed, as were millions of private citizens, with what people in other countries thought about us. (Tocqueville described the same consuming interest in the Americans of his day. Other peoples were considered friendly to the extent they envied America's freedom and prosperity.)

Senators, like ordinary citizens, expected gratitude from others as a result of our participation in the century's European and Asian wars and our subsequent aid to impoverished countries.

Like ordinary citizens they became indignant when it was not forthcoming. The notion that such assistance was in our national interest, whether or not it inspired gratitude, was not widely embraced.

With few exceptions, senators accepted two broad principles as governing our relations with the Soviet Union. First, that Russia's military power and its acquisitive ideology posed a constant threat to American interests. Second, that this threat could not be removed by an attack upon Russia without intolerable risk to civilization itself. By the mid-fifties, few public men were bold enough to talk about a preemptive strike on Moscow.

It was also generally agreed that America required a massive airborne nuclear deterrent, and that alliances with non-Communist states on the periphery of Russia gave us our best chance of containing Soviet expansion on the ground. The importance of NATO was an article of faith; so was that of SEATO, which was aimed at both the Chinese and the Russians.

Beyond these principles, there was disagreement — in tone and degree, if not in essence. The Presbyterian rage of Secretary Dulles toward "neutrals" in the struggle between darkness and the light inspired mockery among many liberals. Some senators believed in foreign economic assistance as the key to a safer world; others put their faith in the Strategic Air Command. Some thought the results of the Second War might be undone, and Eastern Europe liberated from Communist rule, by threat — of what, it was never made specific; others looked to diplomatic agreements, and the softening of Russian attitudes after Stalin, for an acceptable détente.

Because senators made so many speeches about foreign policy, I assumed — before coming to Washington — that they had considerable power over the direction of that policy. In time I saw that there were simply not enough levers for the Senate to manipulate if it was to be a consistent force in making foreign policy. Presidents, State Department officials, and editorial writers often complained about the Congress's interference in foreign affairs, and there was occasional justification for that. But there was a great difference between making a speech on the Senate floor, and sending a cable that gave critical guidance to an ambassador. In the daily business of policy-making, Congress might urge or complain; it could not instruct.

Yet there were two levers of consequence by which weight could be given to congressional views. One was the annual protracted decision on the level of foreign aid, with subsidiary instructions as to who should (or who should not) receive it. The other was the resolution of support for, or opposition to, Presidential initiatives. The authority of the first lay in the traditional power of Congress over the purse — its final and greatest power, and the basis for its claim to equality among the branches. The second, the "sense of Congress resolution" was important for what it told the President about public opinion.

The foreign aid debates — there were two of them each year, one over the authorization of funds, the other over their appropriation — held an attraction for all manner of senatorial opinion. In the cloakroom, I heard it said that "getting involved in foreign aid debates never helped anybody politically"; there was no way to satisfy both the League of Women Voters lady and the small home-owner who resented having his tax dollars spent on ungrateful foreigners. But something about foreign aid — its combination of philanthropy and self-interest, colossal need and shameful waste, evangelism and realpolitik, perhaps above all its susceptibility to congressional control—made the debates and votes irresistible.

Everyone knew that the squabble each year would end with foreign aid being continued. The question was, at what level, and with what restrictions. Because economic aid had the characteristics of a community chest drive — the need was undeniable, whatever the inefficiencies of the program that responded to it — the sharpest controversy centered around the military aid which we provided nations in Asia, the Middle East, and Latin America. Typically the committees involved supported a figure close to what the Administration requested. When their recommendation reached the floor, there began a salami-slicing in which an increasing number of senators joined: a cut of $500 million in military aid received twenty votes; a cut of $300 million, thirty votes; and so on until a majority favored reducing by $100 million the value of the tanks, planes, mortars, and rifles which we shipped about the world. Statesmanship required that the deepest cuts be resisted. Practical politics required that a man should show his constituents at least one prudent vote on foreign aid.

In the late fifties, the coalition for military assistance included the Administration's Republicans and Douglas, Fulbright, Hayden, Johnson, Kennedy, Lehman, Neuberger, Pastore, and Sparkman. Southern Democrats generally voted to reduce military assistance on grounds of economy, and a few Western and border-state men — Mansfield, Gore, Morse, O'Mahoney — joined them for ideological reasons. They opposed the arming of military regimes to whom the threat of Communist aggression was remote, and who wanted arms principally to put down domestic insurgencies.

Liberals instinctively disliked military regimes unless they set about vast programs of social reform and ran over landowners in the process. The image of jack-booted generals locking up leftist politicians, closing universities, seizing the press, and reviewing American tanks on parade was deeply offensive. But when the same generals pointed to their peasant origins, expropriated the holdings of American corporations, and announced programs of land distribution, the picture changed. Liberals began to ask whether parliamentary democracy was appropriate to all societies. If the same generals then declared their immutable opposition to international communism, a coalition of approval formed in the Pentagon, the State Department, and on Capitol Hill. The generals become, in the language of the trade, our sons-of-bitches, deserving our support. They were entitled to military aid.

In the late fifties, the rationale for military aid was based on the containment theory, and on the practical argument that it was better to arm friendly states for self-defense than to endanger American lives, and drain America's wealth, in distant conflicts. A few voices warned that this kind of surrogate commitment would lead inevitably to direct American involvement if the client governments proved unable to defend themselves. The answer of Secretary Dulles, having the unpopular Korean example in mind, was that Communist aggression anywhere might provoke our "massive retaliation." For the Secretary, as for the liberals, the commonly accepted threat was of a land invasion across free world borders — the Red Army moving over the north German plain, the Chinese pouring into South Asia. That the trouble might come in a different form, in a mixture of indigenous rebellion and outside support, and that it might not prove amenable to either massive retaliation or American-equipped local forces, was doubtless considered by planners on the Joint Staff; but it did not affect the conventional view of America's responsibilities. The impotence of our power was a nightmare, and practical men do not deal in nightmares.

So military aid continued. Liberals remained uneasy about it, and introduced into the *Congressional Record* articles that exposed its misuse by various tyrants, the danger of providing one non-Communist state with the arms to attack another, the general failure of its recipients to meet social needs, and so on. But they were not prepared to say that some of the world's territory, and the fate of some of its people, were of no consequence to America. That would have contradicted humane philosophy, and in any case would have been terrible politics — in the rhetoric of the day, we could not yield one foot of freedom. Therefore, like it or not, the liberals voted for military aid. They had no alternative to offer. Neither did I.

I followed a restless course in this, as in other matters. I derided prevailing policy; made fun of Eisenhower, Dulles, and conservative Republican senators; traded horror stories about the repressive regimes we armed and endorsed; believed that the "real" problems abroad were economic and social; doubted whether the Communists really intended to launch a new war, and thought that diplomacy would reduce the threat more effectively than military confrontation; and then faced the tough imperatives of a worldwide political and military struggle — in the light of which my objections seemed aesthetic, if not irrelevant. Unless one was prepared to risk the extension of Communist power into nations that did not choose to be controlled by it, one had to support the giving of arms to those nations, and hope that reform would come after. The contrary argument — that by supplying reactionary governments, we sacrificed the friendship of democrats who might, in time, replace them — was persuasive; and yet the votes came, and the admonitions that without arms for self-defense, weak nations, however governed, might fall under totalitarian Communist rule. In which event the issue of reform would become academic.

I thought of my father, saying, you must earn a living; and of my answer, that I wanted to do good; and again, you must earn a living . . . over and over, like a dull theme in the music of Mahler that drowns a promising obbligato. It was the same in politics: liberal speculations, followed by conservative compromise; the luxury of talking about what ought to be, the necessity of doing what apparently had to be done. To yield to that necessity was to act responsibly.

In the late fifties, all the potential Democratic candidates for the Presidency — Kennedy, Johnson, Humphrey, and Symington — thought it responsible to support military aid. Even when Proxmire moved to cut off aid to the Dominican Republic because of the escapades of Trujillo's son, they stood fast. If they were uncomfortable in that position, they could rationalize it as being faithful to Truman's policies. In any event, they thought prudence required them to provide a more popular President with what he said he required for peace-keeping.

A more subtle, and at this time a more difficult issue, concerned the giving of aid to Poland and Yugoslavia. The accepted device for providing such aid was to deny it, unless the President found that the recipient nation was not participating in "any policy or program for the Communist conquest of the world." In the light of Tito's efforts to plot an independent course, the language was an embarrassing relic of the past. But it worked. It took Congress off the hook, and gave the Administration the flexibility it needed to improve our relations with Eastern Europe.

One morning in 1959 I sat in the Republican cloakroom with Hickenlooper, Curtis, and other conservative senators, trying to find a magic phrase that would permit them to support their President without doing violence to their anticommunism. Dirksen had invited me in to "search for a little compromise language." He was eager for a solution, but he rejected each of my suggestions as too permissive — not for him, but for his right wing. I sensed that his colleagues were uncomfortable about my taking part in their family debate, and I thought them intransigent and shortsighted; but I would not have missed the chance to see that the Republican leader had the same political problems in his cloakroom as Johnson did across the way.

There were many justifications for foreign aid, and Johnson used them all at one time or another, depending on his audience. He had a favorite story about an unemployed schoolteacher who applied for a job in the Texas hill country during the Depression. The school board was composed of ranchers and farmers — red-faced men with upper foreheads as white as Herefords'. Their notions of right learning were extremely simple. After the teacher described his training, experience, and need for the job, one of the ranchers asked him: "How do you teach, is the world round or flat?" The teacher looked at each man in turn, seeking some sign, some indication of what was desired. There was none — nothing but the hard agate stare of eyes that had looked on more cows and goats than books. It was a desperate moment. The teacher's mouth was dry as the chalky dust on the road outside. At last he replied, in a low, steady voice, "I can teach it either way."

Johnson might warn a Chamber of Commerce audience that since communism preyed on ignorance, a massive educational program abroad was our first line of defense. The entire third world was trembling on the brink. Who could say how long it would remain there, before toppling into Communist arms? Foreign needs (he might say to REA district managers) were colossal and urgent; and these should be met (as the bankers before him would know) by loans, not by grants, which denied self-respect. But foreign aid was ultimately justified (as he would tell a sympathetic crowd of journalists) not because it fended off communism, but because it was right. America was rich and skilled, and as a matter of morality ought to share its technology and wealth with poor nations.

He could teach it round or flat, but the important thing was, he taught it.

Two principles of foreign policy guided most Democrats during the Eisenhower years. First, that communism should be regarded as detestable and dangerous; second, that the President should be given the power and the flexibility to resist it.

For Lyndon Johnson, these principles were not the fruit of abstract speculation, but of personal experience. As a young congressman he had witnessed the country's failure to prepare for World War II, a failure caused in part by isolationist members of Congress. As a freshman senator he had observed the savage punishment of President Truman when officials sympathetic to communism were discovered in his Administration. The first experience made him a fervent believer in a strong defense establishment and broad Presidential discretion, in order that the President might respond effectively to the threat of aggression. The second convinced him that progressive Democrats could not endure association with the far left. I experienced the full force of that conviction in 1958.

In that year, shocked by the Russian Sputnik, Congress rushed to provide the country with an adequate supply of scientists and mathematicians. A National Defense Education Act — so called in order to clothe a controversial subject with the mantle of national security — was passed, making thousands of fellowships available in selected fields. The American Legion patriots, led by Senator Mundt, succeeded in attaching a loyalty oath requirement to the bill. Within a year several universities announced that they would not accept funds under the act because the oath transgressed upon freedom of thought. John Kennedy, spurred by Mark de Wolfe Howe of Harvard, introduced a bill to repeal the oath. The Senate Labor Committee reported it to the Senate Calendar. There it sat, week after week.

As the Calendar's list of bills grew thin, I began to include the oath repeal in my daily memoranda to Johnson, as a proper subject for action. He ignored it, choosing instead a bill to provide emergency feed-cake relief for drought-stricken cattle, an amendment to the District of Columbia code, and the like. After a while there was nothing more to be motioned up except Kennedy's bill. One day at noon, as I walked with Johnson toward the Senate floor, he asked me for a program of bills, and I said, "There's nothing but the loyalty oath repeal. And we really ought to pass it. It's a damned McCarthyite oath and the universities are up in arms . . ." He wheeled on me, and leaning over until we were nose to nose, said, "No, sir. I'm not going to do it. You liberals want me to get the Democratic party into a national debate: 'Resolved: That the Communist party is good for the United States,' with the Democrats taking the affirmative. I'm not going to do it."

In time he did motion up the bill, but voted with the majority to send it back to committee. (Years later he told a group one evening, pointing to me, "When I voted to recommit that bill, Harry turned white as a sheet"; which was probably true, though I thought I had concealed the awful sickness I felt in my stomach as Johnson voted.)

I could not understand his antipathy to the bill. He was not a professional anti-Communist; indeed I had heard him laugh about the "bomb-throwers" he used to run around with back in the thirties, "some of them," he said, "about halfway to Moscow." His civil liberties voting record was good, and so far as I knew, he had no special reason to side with the Mundts against the Kennedys. It was possible that he simply wanted to defeat his rival on a matter with which Kennedy was closely identified, as a means of showing that in a crunch, Johnson, and not Kennedy, controlled the Senate. But he joined with Kennedy and cleared his path during debates on labor bills, so pure obstructionism seemed an insufficient explanation. He may have wanted to consolidate his position with the conservatives, and with those moderates who looked to Johnson before voting; that would leave Kennedy with the committed liberals, the university deans, and the *New York Times*. But it was not long before Johnson himself would reach for liberal support at the Democratic convention, where Karl Mundt had no delegates.

I came to believe that his reply in the corridor expressed his true position. President Truman's domestic program, and his ability to lead the country, had suffered grievously because of Alger Hiss, Harry Dexter White, and other sensational cases in the late forties. The presence of Communist sympathizers in a Democratic Administration had clouded all that it sought to achieve at home. Social reform came to be identified with socialism. The AMA's phrase for the proposed national health program, "socialized medicine," sounded credible to voters worried about leftist influence in the government.

Thus for Johnson the rule was that if Democrats wanted social progress, they should be seen to abhor communism. They should not indulge in national debates in which their position could be made to appear "soft" on Communists. They could safely resist egregious laws that impinged upon civil liberties, but if such a law passed — as the price for securing a larger goal, like the National Defense Education Act — then it was best to leave it alone for a while, at least until the country quit worrying about Communists in government.

Johnson also believed that President Eisenhower should be given the means and the compass to prosecute American interests abroad. He should have enough military equipment to disperse, and enough foreign aid to dispense, to meet demands as they arose; and he should not be made to wear a congressional halter. He should not go abroad to conferences confined to a narrow agenda by sense-of-Congress resolutions.

In part, Johnson's solicitude for the President was careful politics. Eisenhower's popularity was still very great in the mid-fifties. If he were afflicted by partisan attacks — a smiling, earnest general hamstrung by cunning politicians — there could be no doubt about the public's sympathies. Thus Johnson dramatized his support for the President, and compared it with the sedulous resistance of Bridges, McCarthy, Jenner, and others of the President's own party.

But there were other reasons for backing the President. He was, after all, trying to reduce the danger of Armageddon. He was speaking more in terms of conciliation than of holy war. Having no need to prove his patriotism, he was teaching America to muddle through a period of global tension, to seek points of accommodation with a hostile superpower. While bombast continued on his right, the distinguished soldier in the White House spoke, in his casual syntax, of his hopes for peace. When he left for Geneva to meet with Khrushchev, he carried with him not only the Democrats' discreet support, but their belief in his purposes. They may have thought him something less than a brilliant negotiator (there were already those in Johnson's camp who marveled at the thought of the wily Texan succeeding Eisenhower and bargaining the Russians out of their hostility and aggressiveness, and perhaps out of Eastern Europe as well). But of his good intentions and international reputation they had no doubt.

From time to time, the rhetoric of the Cold War surfaced in Congress and was not to be put down. A "Captive Nations" resolution passed the Senate each year, full of resounding talk about liberating oppressed peoples; but few Americans, even among the consanguinary ethnics, wanted to risk a nuclear exchange to achieve that. Republicans and a few Southerners joined to deny funds to the International Labor Organization if it permitted a Communist representative to vote. Senator Russell discerned a threat to the Republic in a reported RAND study of "when and how the U.S. should surrender to a foreign power," and the Senate solemnly voted to halt such a study in its tracks.

These were nit-picks, and only emphasized the inability and unwillingness of the Senate majority to reverse the prevailing flow of foreign policy. With a popular President who spoke of nuclear war as unthinkable and of coexistence as necessary, the Democrats were not inclined to play dog-in-the-manger. And Lyndon Johnson, for his part, was not interested in becoming the Henry Cabot Lodge, Sr., of his day.

As a result, in matters that involved American relations with the Soviet Union, the Senate gave Eisenhower the widest possible discretion. Senators complained, warned, and praised as they saw fit, but the majority did not try to assume his responsibilities as executor of foreign policy. I saw them sigh and shrug their shoulders, as private citizens did, when the great game of international chicken produced a crisis. On such occasions I thought they were glad to grant the President the possibility of glory, along with the certainty of anxiety.

But there were other crises, not involving a direct confrontation with the Red Army, in which the Senate's views were both pertinent and important.

The typical situation arose from a sudden tumult — a coup d'etat, or a marshaling of forces by one small country on the border of another — which produced an apparent threat to American interests. Either a friendly state had its back to the wall, or the Soviets were offered an opportunity for mischief. Within hours our ambassadors in the region sent alarming cables to the State Department; the British began to speak, in their practiced way, of the need for common action; ministers to Washington from the affected countries passed into a frenzy of supplication; and senior officials from State and the Pentagon began to haunt the White House.

After a time, Johnson, Rayburn, and a few other ranking members were invited to meet with the President and the Secretary of State in the Cabinet Room. I never heard Johnson speak of these meetings on his return to the Hill. No doubt he considered what he heard there too important to be broadcast on the circuits of staff gossip. But from what followed during the next few days — and from personal experience years later — I thought I could reconstruct the scene in the Cabinet Room.

The Executive presented the facts — cables, foreign government reactions, friendly and enemy orders of battle. Experts from the bureaucracy put the facts into perspective. The recent history of American involvement in the area was described in such a way as to demonstrate that nothing had been done to provoke the crisis, and nothing left undone which might have prevented it.

The Executive's tone was urgent. It had the constitutional responsibility to deal with such incidents, and it was ready. Long-developed contingency plans were waiting to be effectuated.

The Executive also had superior access to the press. In background briefings it could reveal the gravity of the crisis, and make any procrastination by Congress appear dangerous to the national interest.

But though it had the facts, the responsibility, the power, and the ability to take its case to the people, the Executive wanted something more. It wanted the active consent of the Congress, preferably embodied in a resolution that endorsed whatever future action the Executive might take to deal with the situation. It wanted an expression of political unity at the outset, so that it would not have to fear political harassment if the going became tough.

The congressional leaders who came down to the Cabinet Room brought no facts about the crisis with them. They had no ambassadors abroad, no communications systems, no array of experts to match those of the State and Defense Departments.

Very likely the Congress had spent the day debating price support levels for farm commodities, or interest rates for low-cost housing. On such matters the facts were easily obtainable. Communications with farmers, builders, and housing authorities were good. In a discussion with the President and the Secretary of Agriculture or the budget director, the congressional leaders would have been prepared. Armed with figures about farm prices and housing starts, they might have taken the offensive. They might have forced the Executive to compromise; yielding on one issue, they might have exacted concessions on others.

But in a foreign crisis they were at a hopeless disadvantage. The difference between the parochial, "political" issues which they had debated during the day on the Hill and the cosmic events that were laid before them in the Cabinet Room was intimidating. When they emerged to meet the press, they knew that they must not carp or scold. They sacrificed the skepticism and humor with which they responded to other confrontations with the Executive. In a time of international crisis, the country wanted its leaders to speak with an appropriate solemnity. It wanted a uniform tone. The Executive set the tone, and the Congress adopted it. This was "bipartisanship."

The accepted rationale for it was that the country should speak with one voice abroad. The truth was that in an emergency, Congress had little choice. Its role, so its leaders believed, was to free the President to play America's hand as he saw fit. By performing that role, Congress relinquished the right effectively to criticize the President's initial assessment of the crisis, his judgment that vital American interests were truly involved, and his deployment of our forces.

Later, senators could make historical reevaluations of these matters and find that the President had erred. Second thoughts were of interest to those who hoped that "next time" Congress might withhold its approval until it had thoroughly examined the premises on which the President proposed to act — in other words, to those who had not weighed the relative strengths of the two branches in a time of sudden turbulence abroad.

The one thing Congress had to give, except best wishes, was the one thing the President wanted: the resolution of endorsement. Why this was of such importance, when apparently there was no alternative, made a nice question. I supposed it was useful in convincing the Russians that they could not expect the Congress to undermine the President; though given the members' anticommunism, it was unlikely that Moscow had ever relied on that. The resolution did suggest national unity, which was reassuring to the worried man in the White House. And there was even something in it for Congress. It represented action, response — without ultimate responsibility.

The Middle East crisis of 1957–1958 produced a classic resolution of support. No one was quite sure what was happening in the area, but the Suez debacle, the absence of British or French power, and the fury of Arab nationalism were all unsettling. It was feared that Communists would move into the "vacuum" — a term frequently and often erroneously used when Western colonial authority departed an area; that they would exploit Arab grievances and make the region inhospitable to Western interests. Egypt, Syria, Lebanon, Iraq, and Jordan all seemed ripe for seizure by a pan-Arabist movement dominated by radical, later Communist, elements. The anti-Zionism of the Arab world had made enemies of many American Democrats. Its anticapitalism (for which read anti-oil) had stirred resentment among Republicans. The British and French were profoundly concerned, for economic and political reasons, but they could do little about it. If anyone could, it was the Americans.

Possibly there were those in Congress who believed that the Arabs were passing through an unavoidable period of tumult, in the aftermath of a long colonial era. That they were hostile not only to Western imperialism, but to that of the Communists. That they were disorganized and faction-ridden, and unlikely to establish a single monolithic state. That the wisest course for America was one of restraint and patience.

But the agreed wisdom of the day required a different response. "Munich" was the controlling experience of Western statesmen, conjuring images of disaster after appeasement and delay. The Arabs spoke with Hitlerian violence against the Israelis; threatened the West's supply of oil; had power to sever Western commerce at the canal; and in the case of Egypt had accepted massive Communist aid. America should be prepared to act, in the event the situation grew worse.

The Middle East resolution endorsed action in the broadest terms. The United States, when the President determined it to be necessary, was prepared to use its military forces, consistent with its treaty obligations and the Constitution, to assist any nation in the Middle East requesting such assistance, against armed aggression from any country controlled by international communism. The resolution was to be effective until the President determined that the authority granted was no longer necessary, or until it was terminated by another resolution of Congress.

Debate on the resolution focused almost exclusively upon the proper roles of Congress and the President. Senator Morse proposed that the President give notice to Congress prior to the employment of American armed forces. If he were unable to do so because of an emergency, he should subsequently submit the reasons for his action to Congress for its approval or disapproval. Those who supported Morse — among them Byrd, Ellender, Russell, Douglas, Kefauver, Symington, and Jenner — did so for widely disparate reasons: jealousy of congressional authority, disapproval of Dulles's policy toward Israel, opposition to the President. They lost to a coalition that included Johnson, Kennedy, Mansfield, Gore, Clark — together with Thurmond, Eastland, Robertson, and most Republicans. The majority was regarded as "internationalist," because it did not circumscribe the President's authority to intervene in a foreign conflict. Remembering Wilson and the League, FDR and Lend-Lease, I thought it a great victory.

The following year, after force was used in the Middle East — the Marines had gone ashore at Beirut to stabilize Lebanon and give pause to the war-dancing Iraqi — an item on the news ticker outside the chamber caught my eye. It suggested that the President needed something more than a free rein from Congress if he were to take effective action in a foreign crisis. Several days after the guns were quiet in Lebanon, American tanks intended to support the operation were still rolling down the Apennines from their base in Germany. With all its vaunted power, our military Establishment lacked the mobility to match our political commitments.

And mobility was not the only problem. As far as most Democrats at the time were concerned, the Administration was perilously slow to strengthen our military forces across the board, particularly to develop new weapons. The attitude of Defense Secretary Wilson toward basic research seemed unimaginative, shortsighted, and therefore typically Republican. "If they want to go ahead and have pure research," he said, "let somebody else subsidize it. Let us not put the burden on the Defense Department. I am not very interested, as a military project, in why potatoes turn brown when they are fried." His words had the ring of willful ignorance, and they were thrown back at the Administration many times after the Russian successes in space. (The liberal complaint, that Defense dominated scientific research to the detriment of other, independent inquiries, was still to come.)

The defense appropriations bill ordinarily took about a day to pass. It was so vast, so complex, and it was managed by one of such esteem — Senator Russell — that few tried to halt its momentum, take it apart, and weigh its priorities. On occasion there was a move to reduce it on grounds of economy. In 1957, those who voted to cut military appropriations were the traditional economizers of the Senate, the conservatives: Ellender, Lausche, Robertson, Smathers, Thurmond (Thurmond?), Bricker, Curtis, and Goldwater. Douglas, who every year made a special plea for a larger Marine Corps, nevertheless voted for an across-the-board reduction in the bill. But most of the liberals stood by Russell's figure — unless, as happened in 1959, they moved to increase it. In that year Symington tried to add $230 million for army modernization — for exactly the kind of equipment needed to fight brushfire wars. He failed, though he was ardently supported by an army of liberal senators. Church, Clark, Fulbright, Hart, Kennedy, Mansfield, Gene McCarthy, Morse, Muskie, Young of Ohio, all thought the army needed better equipment if it was to fight effectively in the Lebanons of tomorrow. The economizers — among them Byrd and Eastland, Lausche and Stennis and Russell — remained unconvinced, and prevailed.

Liberal Democrats were also concerned about what came to be known as the "missile gap" between the United States and the Soviet Union. Our lack of readiness was a good stick for belaboring Republicans; it was a useful way to show the voters that liberals were tough; and it was also believed. In 1960 Senator Clark complained that the Administration's manned bomber program had been reduced, "imperiling our deterrent power during the years when the missile gap will continue to favor the Soviet Union." The Administration could not be left to its own devices. It needed prodding if we were to close the gap. Scoop Jackson made a long speech about our shortcomings in long-range missiles, and John Kennedy praised him, saying, "It is not desirable to leave the development of these important matters completely in the hands of the Executive . . . if there had not been action by Congress [by Jackson and Brien McMahon, impelled by Edward Teller] the United States would have been behind the Soviet Union in the development of the bomb." Of course much depended on who was President.

Johnson played a great role in making the Democrats the party of defense preparedness. He had few close friends in the Pentagon, and little respect for many generals and admirals; but he had always worked closely with leaders of the Armed Services committees — Carl Vinson in the House, Russell and Stennis in the Senate. He attacked wasteful spending by the military with a vengeance, but he was often in the vanguard of the fight for larger appropriations. Urging more for defense was bulletproof for a Texan. Like support for the oil depletion allowance, it made up for a great many questionable votes on housing, welfare, foreign aid, and education bills. It was tough, anti-Communist, it was even productive for the state's economy; besides, Johnson's experience in the thirties had told him that America should be preeminently strong. There was no such thing as too much defense.

By 1960, the congressional Democrats had written an extensive record in national security affairs.

- They had supported a popular Republican President, often against the congressional leaders of his own party, as he tried to reduce the threat of general war.
- They had insisted on greater spending for defense, in order to match the Soviet effort, and to enable the United States to respond swiftly in limited conflicts.
- They had given the President wide latitude in using American forces abroad.
- They had erased any legitimate concern that their party was infiltrated by Communist sympathizers.
- They had continued the foreign aid program, and resisted attempts to limit its use on ideological grounds.
- A few of them — Hubert Humphrey, in particular — had begun to explore the elements of a workable disarmament agreement with the Soviet Union. The militant advocates of a stronger defense, Johnson, Kennedy, Symington, and Clark, did not try to dissuade him; they saw no inconsistency between their efforts and his.

All in all, it was a highly responsible record. And it was politically attractive. In the campaign of 1960, there was nothing in it for which Kennedy needed to apologize, and there was much to be proud of.

Many of the assumptions on which it was based were shaken in the 1960's. Optimism faded about foreign aid. Alliances with other states became burdens, instead of rallying points. Democratic Presidents increased our military power, but found it ineffectual in resolving small wars. The public no longer feared Communists in government. It worried about liberal sympathies for violent radicals. Congress became hesitant about endorsing Presidential actions abroad, past or future.

By 1970, the Democratic national security policy of the fifties was regarded (by many Democrats) as just as benighted as that of Foster Dulles and Charles Wilson. If only Democrats had risen above the Cold War, ignored Southeast Asia, spent for the cities instead of for armaments —

But that was not just hindsight. It was reading the experience of the sixties into the choices of the fifties. The Cliveden set was not proved right before the war, because the West Germans afterwards produced a democracy. Neither did Vietnam discredit the Democrats' genuine concerns, and excellent politics, in Eisenhower's second term.

5

Sacred Cows and Racial Justice

A FIERCE clatter filled the room. Fifty robo-type machines — three to an operator — emitted personal congratulatory letters from Senator Lyndon B. Johnson to the graduating seniors of every Texas high school and college class of 1957. Tens upon tens of thousands of seniors.

Senator Joe Bailey had sent such a letter to his young constituent Johnson nearly thirty years before. The effect was inspirational and lasting. Now — in my second year on the Johnson staff — I sat in the blinding glare of the robo room, typing Bobby Lee Floyd, Route 2, Stamford, Texas, then pressing a key and letting the robo-typewriter do the rest. On to the next machine; the trick, for a clumsy typist, was to finish the address on the third machine by the time the first rapped out the signature line.

Ten o'clock. Empty Coke bottles, piles of mistyped pages, ashes and pallor. Bill Brammer's eyes, as he waited for a machine to finish so that he might begin the cycle once more, were large and red. "Do you love it, Brammer?" I shouted. "I love it, I love it!" he replied. After a while we switched off the current and went out for a beer.

We speculated on this unusual turn in our careers. Brammer the editor, the high diver, the budding novelist, the staff assistant; McPherson the lawyer, the almost-poet, the sometimes theologian–tennis player–raconteur; suddenly Brammer and McPherson the night-shift robo-typists. It was hard to tell what this implied for our futures.

What it implied about Johnson was somewhat clearer. One conclusion was that he was callous toward his staff, and used it wastefully; we drew that conclusion. But there was more to it. When Johnson came to Washington in the early thirties, he drove an elevator on Capitol Hill. So to ask his professional staff to robo-type letters of congratulation to the class of 1957 would not strike him as unusual. Perhaps it was vengeance, but who could say?

Certainly it was consistent with his attitude toward the people of the Hill: an indefatigable worker himself, he saw his staff, and senators themselves, as fungible parts of an army whose purpose was to serve, equip, and sustain its general in his infinite tasks.

Earlier that year I had prepared a long list of questions for a hearing with Secretary Dulles. I was proud of them, and waited anxiously through long hours of testimony for Johnson's turn to come. I saw him thumb through my memorandum and make a few comments in the margin. He looked up; I caught his eye; he motioned me up to the dais with him. Excited, I rushed around behind senators and staff and bent to hear him whisper: "Go up to my office and get me a few of those orange sourballs." I was furious but I did what he said, bringing them back sealed in an immense manila envelope which, I hoped, he would have trouble opening discreetly.

His interchangeable assignments were legendary. A speech handed to his chauffeur, Norman Holmes, for comment; senior assistants asked to perform menial jobs of repair or delivery; a young secretary instructed to tell a cabinet member that he was a damned fool. Apparently he regarded his staff as an indistinguishable rabble of talents.

This spared him many of the mechanical and psychological problems of managing an office. But it was also confusing, and painful to the egos of those who worked there. Speaker Rayburn, it was said, had upbraided him about his treatment of his staff. Johnson had responded with a hurt surprise that was probably genuine. He had paid the extensive medical bills of this man, and traveled far to see that man's new baby. All true, and unusual, as I was to learn, among political men; but Rayburn was talking about something else.

Every leader bent on great enterprises consumes his staff as fuel. There is reciprocal benefit in this, since the staff enjoys the prestige of contributing to events beyond its inherent reach.

Yet wise leaders regard their staffs as something more than a mass; more, even, than as individual objects of their care and concern. They individualize, not only in bestowing favor, but in receiving it. They recognize the special talents and interests of those who serve them, and they understand that it is more important to a man to be asked for what he has particularly to give, than to be singled out for generosity. Perhaps the Speaker was aiming at Johnson's celebrated rages, his denunciations, sometimes before others, of staff incompetence or delay. These were hard to take; but I thought it worse when, with asperity or benevolence, he appeared to regard us as an aggregate entity called "the staff."

The graduation-letter project was never repeated. But nothing — not his rise to great congressional power, nor his candidacy for President — diminished Johnson's concern for keeping in touch with Texas.

Minutes after a bill passed that affected the state or any of its citizens, word was telephoned to someone down there, with instructions to pass it on. It was implicit by the very speed of our report that Johnson had played a role in passing the bill. The Pentagon told us of procurement contracts to Texas firms in advance of its public announcements, giving us time to spread the good news; again, this suggested that Johnson had been an effective advocate for Texas interests. Letters bearing complicated entreaties were acknowledged at once, though the case might drag on for months or years.

These were all gimmicks, all public relations devices; yet they conveyed an essential truth — that Johnson was not only the Senate's leader, a national Democrat, and an ambitious politician, but a tireless worker for his state.

Few senators lasted long who did not convey the same message to their own people. Extended careers in Congress were built on more than momentous debates and right answers to critical questions. They rested, as well, upon files of social security cases, immigrant appeals, draft and military discharge problems, applications for small business loans and drought relief, appointments made with bureaucrats, and the frequent publication of local views in the *Congressional Record*. Trivia — except to those who were immediately concerned with such things, and to their relatives, friends, employers, and fellow workers.

So Arthur Perry sat folded in his chair, his white head bent low to a stenograph mike, beginning one hundred times a day, "Senator Johnson has asked me to respond to your letter . . ." I did my share of casework and answering letters from Texas, and thought it repetitious and boring. Yet it could also be rewarding. When I succeeded in breaking the paper-jam on a desk downtown, and actually helped someone get his overdue check, his undesirable discharge changed to general, his loan approved, I knew I had achieved something undisputable. The results of writing a memorandum or a speech were usually not so clear. For the citizen who was helped, there was no comparison. To him, "responsive government" wrote him at once that his letter had been received, and that calls on his behalf had been made. Even if he was ultimately unsuccessful, he was far happier to connect with his politician-ombudsman, than to receive a brisk form letter stamped at the bottom by an agency figure of speech.

For a Southwestern senator, there was another lifeline to the folks at home, one that required constant attention. Pork-barrel appropriations bills brought scores of Stetson-wearing, string-tied old boys to Washington each year, in delegations that urged the building of dams, levees, irrigation ditches, the dredging and widening of waterways, and all the other monuments to progress which local interests and the Corps of Engineers could devise. For the visitors it was a time of festivity downtown in the evening, and of red-eyed humility in the committee room next morning. The staff had much to do, making sure the delegation saw the senator, helping with hotel accommodations, relaying messages from home, preparing earnest statements for submission to the committee — this dam might save a hundred lives in a dozen years, or the other way around, this reservoir will enable us to add another ten thousand bales of cotton to the national surplus.

As I became an Easterner I grew critical of vast expenditures for concrete in remote rural areas. But in the late fifties, I was strongly for them, and worked hard to help secure more than a fair share for Texas. We needed water for the long droughts, and protection against floods when the wild rains swept the gullies. Besides, it was a good political issue. In the agricultural counties, there was no limit to the public's support of water and power projects; when the conservative city papers complained of too much spending for "pork," we replied that Texas received a larger proportionate share of the pie than it paid in federal taxes. As a friend said, we "country-slicked" the Easterners when it came to federal spending, and that always helped back home.

Paul Douglas and John Kennedy often voted to reduce the pork bill, and Senator Proxmire once conducted a day-long filibuster against a Kansas project with a particularly suspicious "benefit-cost" ratio. That was a mystical number that supposedly defined with precision how valuable a project would be, compared to what it would cost. A large number of projects barely made the grade, that is, they had a benefit-cost ratio of about 1.1 to 1, which suggested creativity on the Corps' part and drew fire from those who thought the dollars could better be spent elsewhere.

It was foolish to be mathematically "right" in matters of public works spending. Proxmire, after his conversion to thrift, once tried to eliminate an appropriation for new post offices in Tupelo, Mississippi; Dyersburg, Tennessee; Montpelier, Vermont; and Pittsburgh. The Administration had not recommended the appropriation, which had been added in committee. By moving to cut it, Proxmire strengthened himself with Wisconsin taxpayers. But he annoyed the majority of senators by forcing them to support an obvious piece of pork. He won seventeen votes to his side on that question, and alienated eight men — representing the affected states — for the indefinite future.

With Kerr and Johnson behind it — Kerr had already begun to think about making the Arkansas River navigable clear across Oklahoma; Johnson had attached a Southwestern River Basin Study to a minor bill, following an example of Russell's in the Southeast (with the impatience of a man determined to own the second Cadillac in town) — with support from the powers and a broad constituency in the states, pork — or as Senator Morse called it, Congress's investment in the future — prevailed. In 1959 an Eisenhower veto of a pork-barrel bill was overridden. The President made a good argument that it was wasteful, but its proponents answered that the country could use the construction jobs in a lingering recession. One could always count on the Corps having a full shelf of meritorious projects. When spending was needed, the plans, the builders, and the delegations were ready. So was the Congress.

Some sacred cows were regional, like dams and oil to Texas, aircraft to the Pacific coast, cotton to the South. I was shocked when Kennedy and Pastore opposed a bill levying fines for the misbranding of textiles, until I realized that sacred cows grazed in New England as elsewhere.

Others were national: pay increases for federal workers, for one. And these had to be uniform. The salaries of civil servants could not be raised unless those of postal workers were raised simultaneously. Separate treatment was once tried; when a remedial amendment was offered on the floor, the gallery was packed with postmen in shirt-sleeved blue, their weight upon the men below as palpable as a late-returning precinct. I half expected someone to speak out against this menacing pressure, so foreign to the measured deliberations of the Senate. No one did, and the amendment was overwhelmingly adopted.

Road building was a sacred cow; so was the idea that America must maintain a merchant marine at whatever expense, and the costly yards in which to build it. Indeed, the very act of building often conveyed a certain cachet to a proposition. Whatever aroused the interest of the general contractors, the trade unions, the steel and cement makers, et al., had a fighting chance of passage. My colleague Jim Wilson — a Texas lawyer with a fecund, irreverent mind — thought aid to education would have passed long since if it had been cast purely in terms of school-building and with none of that nonsense about improving the curriculum or attracting good teachers. We tried without success to conceive a similar approach for civil rights.

There were some limitations on the Senate's eagerness to build. Adding a second office building, and a grand new subway to the Capitol, aroused opposition in the newspapers and apprehension among the members, most of whom welcomed the improvements once they were accomplished. I was skeptical of these constructions at first, and talked about Versailles. But I admired Johnson and Stennis and Bridges as they argued for them. Big daddies, they were convinced that their institution required better facilities, and they pushed the necessary appropriations through in a storm of derision and complaint. Stennis was convincing when he said, "I think it is time to stand up and tell the American people that these improvements are not for our convenience and comfort. Personally, I never would use the tunnel, unless it were raining, if I had the time to walk back and forth . . . this has to do with senatorial work, not play." His defense of good working conditions for senators earned him credit in other battles. Two lessons were to be learned from this: political men did not live only on issues, or even on public favor; most of them were also concerned about their physical well-being and were grateful to those who provided it. And arguments over the building of new structures, even over architectural abominations, did not last. People used them, and after a time few could remember the controversy that surrounded their beginnings.

For some members, the purpose of serving in the Senate was to remain there. Keeping in touch with home, taking care of constituents, and tending sacred cows was a full-time occupation. They performed these tasks so that they might be retained to perform them again.

But for most senators, these were only requirements, not purposes. For them, a senator's purpose was to legislate on matters of concern to the country.

How a particular issue came to command the Senate's attention and absorb its energies was a question of great intricacy — though at the time it seemed simple and even inevitable. Why other issues were avoided was equally complex. A decade later, it appeared that the chief event of the 1950's had been the epic migration of Negroes from the rural South to the cities, bringing with them the accumulated hopes, needs, and debilities of ten generations in subservience. The cities were as unprepared for this tide of humanity as were the Negroes for urban life. Senators knew that the movement was taking place, but few grasped its consequences. They saw it through the screen of their preconceptions: Northern liberals as proof that the Southern "system" was intolerable, Southern conservatives as the first step in "educating" the North to the realities of race. Thus the event was viewed rhetorically, and without prescience. And as it occurred in stages, as the result of hundreds of thousands of private decisions, it did not impress itself suddenly and concretely upon the public mind as a crisis from which misery and stress, as well as opportunity, would come.

Therefore little or nothing was done to assure that there would be job training programs in every major city. That there would be compensatory schooling, including adult literacy classes; adequate medical care, particularly for mothers and children; a public and private commitment of jobs for men able to work, and a living income for others. That the cities would not be impoverished trying to provide enough welfare and public services to meet demands they had not consciously invited and could not avoid.

There was, to be sure, a classic debate over civil rights in 1957. Perhaps it persuaded many Southern Negroes that at last the Congress intended to do them justice, and that they might confidently await it in the region of their birth. But the great migration was already past. Assuring the right to vote was important morally, and gave promise that one day black political power would change the South; but it would not train, employ, house, teach, and feed the population already resettled in the cities.

Congress did not meet those needs in the 1950's — in part because the plight of the cities had not yet crystallized into specific issues of policy. The domestic issues which did preoccupy senators during most of those years — agriculture, labor, the structure of the economy — had been debated and legislated for at least three decades. By the time men arrived in Congress, they had fixed ideas, or at least fixed tendencies, with regard to them. The issues were cast in terms of price supports, union power, taxation, and interest rates — known and measurable quanta, whose results were fairly predictable. It was possible to act on these questions without a Royal Commission inquiry into first principles; without a debate over social conscience and the Puritan work ethic; and with some assurance of party cohesion.

The latter was particularly important to the Democratic leader. With the Senate evenly divided, and with eighteen

Southerners on his side of the aisle, Johnson needed to stress those issues which united his party. Once I heard him define his chief concern as "keeping Dick Russell from walking across the aisle and embracing Everett Dirksen." A Senate whose Democratic committee chairmen were totally allied to conservative Republicans, and totally opposed to the national party's program, would have been impossible to lead with credit to the party and to himself.

The Southerners, like other Democrats, supported TVA, most of the big farm subsidy programs, heavy spending for health research, and the Rural Electrification Administration. Johnson capitalized on these shared views when the opportunity arose. One of the few Eisenhower vetoes to be overridden concerned a bill giving the REA administrator independence of the Secretary of Agriculture in making loans to cooperatives. It was not a profound issue, but it enabled the Democrats to act as a unified party. Blasting Ezra Taft Benson was righteous sport for all of them — and it could set a precedent for more important questions.

In the annual debates over farmer subsidies, Humphrey and Ellender were often allied for higher supports, and the big-city Democrats were content to go along for the sake of political unity. The number of farmers was declining, but the farm issue remained. Johnson once growled to me, "In thirty years, I've never heard of a farmer who didn't complain," but he took to television after Eisenhower vetoed a 90 percent price support bill. Ten years later, that would have been inconceivable for a congressional leader, but in 1959 it made sense. "Solving" the farm problem was a common cause for older Southerners like Russell and Johnston, who remembered the Depression, and for Midwesterners like Humphrey and Proxmire, to whom it was a political necessity.

So the Democratic leader concentrated on issues which held the maximum number of Democrats together. He (and they) were for quick spending when the economy needed priming. He (and they) were parsimonious and cut deeply into the Administration's budget requests, after Eisenhower attacked Democrats as "reckless spenders."

I thought civil liberties legislation offered another possibility for unity, though I knew it could not be pressed too far; right-wing groups were growing throughout the South. But there was, among Southern senators, a residue of libertarian conviction. After all, they resisted the government's domination of racial mores; they could oppose ideological conformity as well. They had voted to censure Joe McCarthy — infuriated by his attack on "their" institution, the Senate — and in the late summer of 1958, their captain dragged his feet on an issue of equal significance to hard-line conservatives at home.

The Supreme Court had upheld a Pennsylvania decision that struck a blow at local McCarthyism. Congress, said the Court, had preempted the field of antisubversive investigation, and Pennsylvania legislators were not free to pursue the likes of one Steve Nelson, a Communist organizer, for sedition against the United States. Put together with sundry other complaints about the Court and communism, and with the *Brown* school-desegregation decision, this suggested a ready-made issue for Republicans worried about revolution, and for Southerners concerned about race. Congressman Howard Smith seized the opportunity and introduced the famous H.R. 3, a deceptively simple and utterly destructive bill that read: "No Act of Congress shall be construed to indicate an intent by Congress to occupy the field in which the Act operates to the exclusion of any state laws on the same subject matter unless the Act expressly provides for that effect, or there is a direct and positive conflict between the Act and the state law so that the two cannot be reconciled or consistently stand together." It passed the House. Together with a bill of McClellan's that would simply have reversed the opinion in

Steve Nelson, and a hodgepodge of proposals by Jenner and Butler that struck at the Court from all directions, H.R. 3 arrived on the Senate Calendar. And sat there.

The Policy Committee did not discuss the bills in two meetings. As usual, we met in Skeeter Johnston's handsome office just off the Senate floor. Sirloins were served, the talk was easy and political, interrupted from time to time as Senator Johnson took a telephone call. Over dessert we went through the Calendar. I explained most of the reported bills in a few sentences, there were questions and sometimes argument, until Johnson said, "All right, can we clear it?" and unless Kerr or Russell or Magnuson or Hill said, "I'd like to look it over again, Mr. Leader," we cleared it. But not the anti-Court bills. They weren't really intended to be there; they built nothing, started nothing; they were just show. For a few weeks, I thought we might get by without bringing them up at all.

But the pressure was building. A lot of Republicans wanted them, and so advised Knowland, who went to Johnson; some Democrats wanted them too — particularly McClellan, whom it was unwise to cross. He was dogged and fierce, and had the point of vantage to be troublesome. And so the committee cleared them, one day, after a brief, almost apologetic explanation by Johnson — "I think we're going to have to give them their day on these Court bills." The way he put it gave me confidence. If he was opposed, and spoke to the Democratic powers of giving them "their" day, we would make it.

Thus when the debate began, and the Jenner-Butler bill was quickly beaten, I was at ease, glad to let them have their day, glad to vote them down in the open. The railroads and some other interstate businesses had expressed alarm about Smith's bill. They saw a chaos of state laws and regulations suddenly loosed upon them, making trouble, confusion, and expense; as often as they had complained about the regulators in Washington, they had no taste for those in the states, especially as they would vary widely in skill and purpose. McClellan and Jenner vilified the Court, and others read long, academic treatises about the Founding Fathers and states' rights. But with the Association of American Railroads and the truckers joined with liberals defending the Court, the situation was in hand. So I thought.

Hennings, in a white suit and black tie — looking the lawyer he was in St. Louis in the thirties — made the argument against the Smith bill, while Humphrey counted votes. Late in the evening of August 20, the motion was made to table the bill. It received thirty-nine votes. There were forty-six against. I gasped. So did Humphrey. There was a motion to reconsider. Wallace Bennett, a former NAM president, moved to table it. His motion carried. There was quick panic. Johnson sat there, surprised, angry, temporarily immobile. As I went to him, trying to think of something intelligent to recommend, Senator Russell leaned forward over Johnson's shoulder and said, "Lyndon, you'd better move to adjourn. They're going to pass this god-damned bill."

Russell had, of course, spoken for the Smith bill. I looked to catch his eye, delighted that he was really with us, that he knew, after all, what a benighted mess it would cause; but he had already sat back with a scowl and was busy rearranging papers in his desk. Johnson leapt to his feet and moved adjournment. Jenner objected and asked for a record vote — a rare motion, since the Senate by instinct and custom followed its leader on procedural questions. The overwhelming vote was to adjourn. Johnson walked across to Humphrey, who sat shaking his head over the disastrous tally-sheet. "Well," said Johnson, "you boys screwed it up. You thought you knew how to beat it, and you didn't." He began ticking off men upon whom the liberals had counted, foolishly counted, because they couldn't vote for the Court with an election coming up . . . He stopped and looked about him. Twenty reporters and assistants were pressing for every word. "Come on," he said to Humphrey. "Let's go upstairs. I don't know all these people." And with that he led Humphrey through the lobby, picking up Anthony Lewis of the *Times* on the way.

Next morning I heard Tony Lewis's amused and admiring account of his long evening with Johnson and Humphrey. I could sense Johnson's pleasure in describing the art of making a majority. What an opportunity: to defeat a bad bill, save the Court, and win the embarrassed thanks of the Senate liberals! It was worth doing.

That afternoon, with help from an Administration he had stirred into action, he did it. Senator Carroll, a Colorado liberal, moved to recommit the bill. The motion carried, forty-one to forty. H.R. 3 was dead. The night before, it had survived by a margin of seven. Now the conservative Democrat Lausche had switched; so, incredibly, had Malone, and Bennett of the NAM himself. Kerr and Smathers, willing to help their friend Johnson in a philosophic struggle that was of little interest to them, simply stayed away. The high-pitched voice of Senator Frear, raised against us on the night of August 20, was still on the twenty-first. As the clerk called his name, I saw him slowly disappear behind a newspaper in the cloakroom, and remain there until the issue was won.

A great victory, duly celebrated in Tony Lewis's *Times*. It produced a flood of virulent mail from Texas. I felt a fierce pride in Johnson — for fighting the kind of reaction that gripped his state, for having the power and resourcefulness to fight it successfully. Eagerly I began answers to the mail, pointing out the grave consequences that would have followed passage of the bill, which no one could abide who believed in the Constitution . . . then I realized that such answers would never be sent, and so began again, with a recital of the senator's long and unswerving commitment to states' rights and anticommunism.

It was, nevertheless, a harrowing victory, fully justifying Gerry Siegel's observation that civil liberties fared better the less they were debated in Congress.

"Unity" among Democrats did not mean unanimity. It meant keeping the conservative coalition to its irreducible minimum — thirty-eight or forty votes, in the Senate of 1957. It meant avoiding the kind of ideological blood-test that would make it impossible for Ellender, Long, Fulbright, Hill, Sparkman, Smathers, and Frear — moderates who had neither an urban base nor urban interests — to remain with the party's majority. As soon as liberal Democrats, on the Hill or in the National Committee, raised the flag of doctrine and demanded that true Democrats rally beneath it, Johnson hauled it down. The Southern moderates must not be driven away; neither they nor Dick Russell must be given the alternative of embracing urban liberalism or Everett Dirksen. At the same time, it was not enough merely to achieve unity. Progress had to be made. Legislation that was meaningful to the congeries of Democratic interest groups had to be passed.

With a narrow majority behind him, and with Southerners in command of the committees, Johnson's task was often difficult. But I thought the very strictures of his position must be satisfying to him — demanding all his skills of promotion, negotiation, and parliamentary finesse, and giving him both an excuse and a weapon. He could always tell liberals that what they desired was impossible; he could warn conservatives that unless they yielded ground, they would face a revolt. In the end, with every hope resting in him, he would pluck a moderate victory from the nettle of obstinacy, and be justly praised.

The one issue that threatened everything was race. It was pervasive, insistent, and aroused unequaled passion. FDR had avoided it wherever possible; Truman had raised it boldly, but in a hopeless climate controlled by the coalition; Stevenson had only touched it rhetorically, without dangerous conviction. But it was there. The embers still burned from the days of the Klan, the defeated antilynching bills, the white primaries. Suddenly the Court set it ablaze in the *Brown* case, and the country and its

Congress, the Democratic party and its leaders, found it inescapably before them.

The Southerners attacked first, with a "manifesto" of opposition to the *Brown* decision which Johnson, by refusing to sign, disabled. Judicial appointments were resisted where the nominee was known to be "biased" — favorably — toward civil rights. These were harassing movements, often made weaker by the lack of cohesion among Southern senators. When the motion was made to recommit the Court of Appeals nomination of Simon Sobeloff, there were critical defections — Fulbright, Gore, Holland, Johnson, Kefauver, and Smathers — which shrank the image of an aroused and mighty South.

There were ancillary struggles against statehood for Alaska and Hawaii, because it was assumed that any representatives they might send to Congress would vote for civil rights, and perhaps for reducing the cloture requirement. (Years later it was said that Bob Bartlett, Alaska's territorial representative in Congress, had assured Russell that he would be amenable to the two-thirds cloture rule as a senator, and that this had paved the way for statehood.) There was also an edge of racism, generally concealed in debate, in Southern opposition to Hawaiian statehood. But when at last it seemed inevitable, most of the Southerners yielded and permitted Johnson to rush it through in an afternoon. The appointed Republican governor — certain to be his party's candidate in the first popular election — was flying to Washington to make a last-minute, well-publicized, and wholly unnecessary plea for the bill. His plane was due in the capital at seven in the evening. It was important that the bill be passed before he landed, if he were to be denied credit for converting anybody. So lengthy Southern speeches were simply handed to the official reporters for printing in the *Record* as if read. Only Thurmond insisted on speaking, and as he read on, his colleague, Olin Johnston, grew more and more restive in the cloakroom. "Lyndon," he said, "Strom's out there speakin', and *I'm* the one who went to Hywaia last year with my committee, and we came back and recommended *unanimous* against statehood. What are my people going to say if I don't speak out now? They're going to say one of those Hywaiian girls thowed a *lei* around old Olin's neck, and *bamboozled* him!" He looked put-upon, but self-amused, in the laughter that burst around him and out into the chamber as Lyndon charged back to plead with Strom. The bill passed at six, and the Republican governor lost his chance to shine. He won the election anyway. But Hawaii had become a state.

The cloture rule was far more important to the Southerners. To break a filibuster on a civil rights bill, two-thirds of the Senate had to agree. The rule was safe from liberalizing amendment, because it was its own defense: you could not get to it to change it, without using it. With a score of sympathetic Republicans on their side — together with a number of Western Democrats who saw, in unlimited debate, political strength that their outmanned region lacked in the House and in national conventions — the Southerners were protected. They were without the votes to change what *Brown* had done, but they could stop congressional efforts to improve upon it.

On the crucial issue — the enforcement of civil rights for Negroes — Johnson was far less assertive in 1957 than he later became. I had no idea what he really thought of the *Brown* decision, except that he could not embrace it in addressing Texas voters. That would have been suicidal in the fifties. Someone less progressive than Johnson would have used it to defeat him, and he believed that he could do more to improve the economic condition of Southern Negroes by remaining in the Senate, ducking a debate on the wisdom of *Brown*, than by carrying the torch for it in a noble, educational, and losing campaign. Yet it must have troubled him. When civil rights organizations called upon Congress to support *Brown* with enforcement legislation, Johnson replied privately that a justice of the Court had told him that none was needed; better to let the Court handle the job through its own processes, than to expose the principle of desegregation to defeat or dismemberment in the Congress.

This is not to suggest that he was then totally committed to desegregation and was prevented from saying so only by the realities of Texas politics. The issue was extremely dangerous for a national-party Southerner who wanted to hold his fellow Democrats together. Far better to work for programs that benefited "all Americans, rich and poor, black and white," than to become involved in readjusting the Southern political system, setting race against race, section against section.

As a private man, Johnson was much closer to country-born Southern politicians than to those from Northern cities. His jokes, his tales, his heroes and villains, were in the broad style of the South and Southwest. He could be amused by stories in which Negroes seemed fearful, or lazy, or raffishly cunning—Stepin Fetchit or Sportin' Life stories. The growing militancy of Negro spokesmen disturbed him—as it did me. In the late fifties, I thought Roy Wilkins was unfair and impatient, because he was unwilling to let the civil rights issue be settled by compromise within the congressional Establishment.

But Johnson was not a thoroughgoing Southern apologist. He did not pretend, as many Southerners did, that Negroes "really enjoyed" the Southern way of life. He did not romanticize the fifth-class schools, the bad housing, the menial jobs, the political powerlessness. He did not expect white Southerners to make early and significant changes in their political and social system without pressure from Washington. He did not attribute Negro living conditions solely to white neglect and discrimination; but he did not deny their central role.

He was tough-minded about what he had seen; and he had seen the degradation of poverty under the hard Texas sun. Its victims in central Texas were mostly whites and Mexicans; its perpetrators were the banks, the power companies, the farm implement makers, the distant commodity markets — the whole rural economic system which depressed entire regions, without regard to race. Johnson remembered watching children in San Antonio, in the twenties, scrabble for grapefruit hulls in garbage cans. He remembered a community of tarpaper shacks in East Austin where a dozen Mexican families shared a single water spigot, and where tuberculosis was endemic. To connect their suffering to that of Southern blacks was not an exercise in abstraction for him. Born to a good family, he had nevertheless been very poor himself, and like millions of young whites and Negroes throughout the South, he had wanted out.

Years later, I listened as he and the novelist Ralph Ellison talked of the Depression. Ellison told of living in Chicago as a child; of going out in the early mornings to bakeries, in search of old bread; of traveling home to Oklahoma, after a flood on the Mississippi, and seeing snakes dead in the white branches of trees; of his ride to Tuskegee Institute on a series of freight cars, and of his elderly guide dying in St. Louis on the way; and finally of hiding in the woods while the Alabama police searched the tracks for black riders in the wake of the *Scottsboro* case. Johnson recalled driving to California in search of work, in an old car loaded with cases of pork and beans. He and his friends, with fifty dollars between them, were threatened in a small west Texas town. Their money had been seen, and it was suggested that they remain to join the weekly poker game. They drove away fast, and that night in the desert Johnson buried their cash in a hole beside him. For two hours the talk went on, Ellison remembering the kindness of people in the Depression, the help of strangers, Johnson observing that traveling poor had its pleasures as well as its fears and discomforts. There was never any mention of the special disabilities of color — of the horrific bigotry that Ellison had described in *Invisible Man*. I thought that was so not because Ellison was really "white," or because Johnson had tired of the discrimination issue; but because the two men, preeminently successful in their fields, communicated on a level of experience with poverty and hope that bound them beneath their skins.

Like most politicians, Johnson made use of his acquaintance with poverty. He told the story of the grapefruit hulls many times. The Mexican children he taught at Cotulla, Texas; the farmers in Johnson City, bewildered by the sudden collapse of prices for their stock and crops; homes without electric light, families on the dole — all were summoned up on occasion, either to make a point or to prove his humanitarian instincts. Watching him enter his limousine, knowing that he had made a great deal of money in broadcasting, I sometimes thought his talk about poverty was contrived posturing — and yet he had known, and had never entirely forgotten, the taste of it. He might not know much about the Northern ghettoes, already filling with black migrants, but he knew about the barren towns in Texas where the stores were dark and the children went hungry in winter.

He also knew about the Klan, which his father had fought in the Texas legislature, and about discrimination against national minorities. In central Texas, when Johnson was a boy, German-Americans were viewed with a deep mistrust amounting to hatred. Nearby in Fredericksburg, there were hundreds of German families, some of whom he knew as neighbors, all of whom were dangerously strange to millions of other Texans. They were German, and the country had just finished a war with Germany; they liked to drink, and the country was entering Prohibition; their ancestors, who pioneered the region, had opposed slavery and secession with a passion born in the republican revolutions of Europe. Johnson told funny stories about them, mimicking their accent and stubborn ways. But he was contemptuous of those who abused them. That was wise in one who sought to represent them politically, but it was also genuine.

Johnson was not a lawyer, and so far as I knew, never went to the Senate library to read cases in any field. But he read memoranda from lawyers, and in early 1957 he received a number of these in which the current status of civil rights law was explained to him. He had very little academic interest in the subject — or, indeed, in any other — but he knew he should be sufficiently equipped to recognize what was within the canon of existing law, and what lay outside it, when and if the Senate debated a civil rights bill.

In the light of what followed in the 1960's, the civil rights case law of the fifties reads almost like medieval scholasticism. It was unconstitutional for a policeman to eject Negroes from a privately operated swimming pool. That was "state action" in violation of the Fourteenth Amendment. But where park land given to a city automatically reverted to the grantor when Negroes used it, no state action was involved, and the reversion was therefore not unconstitutional. These and similar struggles all took place in courtrooms. They were debated in law reviews, and not on television. The Negroes involved merely grumbled when they lost, and there was little exemplary effect when they won. Progress was made, but it was the progress of a laboratory experiment — quiet, controlled, without immediate application to life outside the laboratory.

It was encouraging, nevertheless. The prospect of court-ordered racial justice was deeply satisfying to a young Southern liberal — calling up images of dignified Negro fathers leading their brilliantly clean children to unsegregated schools, of swaggering sheriffs forced to release innocent black men from jail. I imagined a succession of such verdicts removing the mark of guilt from the South, at once making it a more palatable society and relieving me of the need to establish my progressive credentials among my Northern friends.

I talked a lot about racial injustice, and generally felt better as a result. I did not notice, at the time, that I invariably used the passive voice in speaking of Negroes: they were "to be freed," "to be permitted to go to integrated schools," "to be trained," "to be given better housing." Martin Luther King's bus boycott in Montgomery was vaguely disturbing to me, though I was gratified by his insistence on nonviolence. When the sit-ins began, I was even more uneasy. I thought it might be that I was simply middle-class, property-oriented, nervous about people seeking rights in the street that they ought to obtain in court. All this was true. But I believe what really bothered me was the Negroes' assertiveness — their insistence, their use of the active voice in their own behalf. Demanding rights from the entire society, they were no longer content merely to ask for help from the well-intentioned whites within it.

In any event, by 1956 the slow progress of individual litigation was no longer enough. The *Brown* case, and the constant moral and political pressure it represented, made it certain that one day the Senate would cope with the race question — cope with it straight, stripped of parliamentary metaphors like cloture, judicial appointments, and Hawaiian statehood. I speculated that sooner or later Johnson's urge to fix problems would cause him to take it on, despite its dangers, and with Western help make a way for it between the committed men of the North and South. I believed the encounter would come later. What made it sooner was the shift of Negro votes in the 1956 elections from the party of Roosevelt to the party of Eisenhower; the obvious threat to the Democratic North if this continued; and the need for Lyndon Johnson to reveal himself as a national, and not a sectional politician, if he were to be seriously considered for President in 1960.

The Negro votes had shifted, in part, because Eisenhower sent a civil rights bill to Congress in 1956. When he sent it back again in 1957, the Southerners faced an unprecedented situation. Their traditional friends on the Republican side were under great pressure to support the bill. Most of them quickly succumbed. Thus in the showdown, it was the South against the country — the South, with its predominance in Congress, its delegate strength that, barring a disaster, would surely go for Lyndon Johnson in the 1960 convention, against a mixed company of liberals, city machine pragmatists, and Administration Republicans who saw in civil rights an opportunity for doing good while splitting the Democrats asunder.

There were many possible outcomes, most of them bad. The bill might fail, because the South was intransigent and managed to prevent cloture. Then the shift of Negro voters would continue, and among liberal whites in the North a revengeful spirit would write the South out of the party, together with its candidate, Lyndon Johnson. The bill might fail, but as a result the cloture rule might be amended. Then the Southerners, embittered and defensive, would use their control of the committees to harass the liberals and thwart their bills. Or the bill might pass, leaving Southern blood on the floor, and Eisenhower acclaimed as a second Lincoln.

Conceivably, the Democratic leader — representing a state just Western enough to permit him a little room for maneuver — might work one of his familiar miracles of compromise. Doing so would require him not only to make use of all his strategic skills, but to risk his special relationship with the Southerners. Ultimately he would have to do what no Texan had done since Reconstruction, vote for a civil rights bill.

In his twenty years in Congress, he had never strayed from Southern orthodoxy. He had voted against antilynching and anti–poll tax legislation throughout the forties and fifties. With the majority of Democrats, he had resisted "Powell amendments" — Adam Clayton Powell's many attempts to deny funds under education and housing programs to those who practiced racial discrimination. Because the passage of such amendments would have dragged useful bills down to certain defeat, Johnson regarded them as quixotic and self-destructive.

But that was not all the Johnson record. He had indicated some liberality on the racial question soon after he arrived in the Senate, in 1949. "Perhaps no prejudice is so contagious or so dangerous," he said, "as the unreasoning prejudice against men because of their birth, the color of their skin, or their ancestral background. Racial prejudice is dangerous because it is a disease of the majority endangering minority groups. . . . For those who would keep any group in our nation in bondage, I have no sympathy or tolerance. . . . My faith in my fellowman is too great to permit me to waste away my lifetime burning with hatred against any group." The spirit was right, and the phrases were artful. Only an incurable bigot could defend "unreasoning prejudice," keeping "any group in bondage," or a lifetime of "burning with hatred."

So: the *attitude* was fair; the voting record on traditional civil rights questions caused no problems in conservative Texas; after four years of his unexampled success as the Democratic leader, the confidence of his colleagues in his abilities was never stronger. He could negotiate with the Southern powers on intimate terms of trust. Many liberals had come to accept whatever he produced as the best they might expect. The struggle ahead was forbidding, but his assets were considerable.

In the end, they proved sufficient. The story of the 1957 civil rights bill has been told many times, most skillfully in the excellent *Lyndon B. Johnson: The Exercise of Power*.* It needs little repetition here. In brief, Johnson convinced the Southerners that it was in their interest to permit a bill to pass, without a filibuster, in order that the two-thirds cloture rule might be preserved. In turn, the Southerners exacted a price. First, they demanded that Title III of the bill be abandoned. This would have empowered the Attorney General to seek injunctions against those who deprived others of their civil rights. It was perfectly suited for use in desegregating schools, and the Southerners were determined to keep that issue one between parents and local school districts — without the powerful third-party assistance of the fed-

---

* By Rowland Evans and Robert Novak (New York: New American Library, 1966). See particularly Chapter VII, "The Miracle of '57."

eral government. In addition, Russell insisted on a jury trial for anyone charged with contempt of court in a civil rights case. At length Johnson secured the substance of both amendments. In the case of jury trials, he had the support of the labor unions, whose long and bitter experience with contempt citations arising out of no-strike injunctions made them sympathetic to anyone who faced summary punishment by a judge without a jury. When he sought to eliminate Title III, he received, unexpectedly, the assistance of the President, who showed little understanding or interest in the matter, and implied as much in a press conference.

Throughout the long debate, Johnson made a series of brief statements, extolling the good sense of the members. He rarely argued the issues. But as repetition is a rule of good politics, his constant description of the tone of the debate as reasonable and prudent helped to make it so. In the face of his praise for the moderation of both sides, it was difficult for those who felt passionately about the matter — Thurmond on the one hand, Douglas on the other — to attract much support for "immoderate" action.

He maintained lines of communication with all sides. Once in the cloakroom, I heard him tell Douglas, "If we're going to have any civil rights bill at all, we've got to be reasonable about this jury trial amendment"; five minutes later, at the opposite end of the room, he advised Sam Ervin to "be ready to take up the Nigra bill again" that afternoon, after an interlude of other business. Round or flat.

I watched him with fascination. Often he sat slumped in his chair, drawing on a nasal inhaler, his eyes fixed in a stare of thought. Then he would quickly rise, and hands deep in his pockets, walk over to someone who might support him, if he were careful — Margaret Chase Smith, whom he charmed with masculine attention and genuine respect, or Joe O'Mahoney, or the young Frank Church —sit down, and after a moment bring his face close, slightly above the other's eye level. He would talk rapidly and with intense commitment to his own logic; the big warty hands would span out, poking the air near the other's shoulder. Then he would sink back into the chair, his eyes wide with the injustice of his burdens, the corners of his mouth inviting pity and support. As the other prepared to give it, eager to comfort and assist this man who had taken so much on himself, whose problems made those of any ordinary senator seem trivial, Johnson would come back face to face, perhaps sensing that the other wanted to help and in that event should hear the whole story, all the demands, all the pressures and threats, as well as the glory and achievement that awaited reasonable men if they would only compromise, not on the main thing, but just on this part that the other side could never accept as it was; unless there could be some accommodation there would be nothing, the haters would take over, the Negroes would lose it all, I need your help.

Gerry Siegel was his counsel on the floor, George Reedy wrote the many paeans to reason, and Bobby Baker counted votes. I spent a lot of time in the Senate Library reading cases. Johnson used a few of my memoranda in private arguments, and to my delight, two senators delivered speeches exactly as I had written them. It was my first experience with ghostwriting. I carried around the pages from the *Record* for months afterwards. It gave me pleasure to hear the same phrases that I had written out in longhand upstairs spoken verbatim on the floor of the United States Senate, and then to see them, *mirabile dictu*, printed in the *Congressional Record* by the United States Government Printing Office. That made up for a great many hours of robo-typing.

Much of the time I simply listened to the debate. I did not quite understand, at the time, that almost no one else did. When Senator Eastland, or Senator Ervin, became especially tendentious in his use of the case law, I remonstrated with Baker, Siegel, and other staff men about the chamber — sometimes with

Johnson himself. Their response was usually polite, but hurried. Debating the meaning of old decisions was not what the big game was about. I understood this from other experiences — I often interrupted people who had practical things to do, with a newly discovered poem, or a historical insight — and for a time I compensated by trying to be even more "realistic" and hardnosed than the political actors themselves. I was uncomfortable in that role, and after a while I gave it up.

The bill passed and became law. It was no longer Eisenhower's bill. It was Johnson's. The moderate commentators in the *Times* and the *Post*, and the syndicated columnists, were effusive in their praise. A Texan had achieved what others had failed to do in eighty years. No one else had had the political instincts, the intelligence network, the credits with so many senators, the ability to negotiate with both sides, the creative energy, the stamina, and the environment — a broad public demand for action, and a President of the other party who seemed ready to capitalize on it. Unquestionably it was a triumph. When at last Johnson revealed his own feelings about the bill, and said, "So far as I am concerned, Texas has been part of the Union since Appomattox," I was ready to commit myself to him, his ambitions and purposes, for the duration.

Many others were not. The excision of Title III, the jury trial amendment, perhaps most of all the constant appeals to moderation which dulled the edge of moral outrage, left a bitter taste in many mouths. And by comparison with the civil rights laws of the sixties, the bill was very weak. A civil rights commission was created, but the heart of the bill, a voting rights provision, was encumbered with so many procedural requirements that it proved almost wholly ineffectual in securing Negro suffrage. Nothing remained that would help to desegregate the schools and guarantee other rights.

Johnson argued with a succession of journalists and liberal activists that voting was the key; all else would flow from political power. Yet he understood their concerns, and told one group, "It's just a beginning. We've shown that we can do it. We'll do it again, in a couple of years." Several friends of mine, professional lobbyists for civil liberties, accepted his promise. But for some, the compromises which had sapped an already inadequate bill were infuriating. They would have preferred no bill at all, to one purchased by trades with the benighted Southerners. Then at least the issue would have been kept alive, and indeed would have intensified. For such men, including Joseph Rauh of the Americans for Democratic Action, Johnson's triumph was so tarnished that it proved his unfitness for national leadership.

With so much praise ringing in his ears, Johnson might be thought not to have heard these complaints, but of course he did; he might have been content to use them as proof to the South that he had saved it from a worse fate, but he was not. Made proud and ebullient by his success, he was nevertheless hurt that it had not secured his acceptance by all elements of the party. His partisans rightly argued that Humphrey, for all his eloquence, could not have passed a civil rights bill. That Kennedy had voted with Johnson on the crucial amendments. That Stevenson had done nothing to promote a stronger bill. That imperfect as the final measure was, it represented progress, where before there had been only vituperation and stalemate. The Negroes had gained something, the Congress had shown itself capable of acting on the most divisive issue in the country, and the Democratic party had been saved from self-immolation. One might have expected universal gratitude for such an achievement, and it might have been forthcoming for another man — Humphrey, for example; I thought Rauh would have discerned a shrewd practicality in him, where in Johnson he saw only dark connivance. Perhaps this was the price of being a Southerner; or perhaps it reflected the mistrust people felt toward a man who could speak one way to Paul Douglas, and another way to Sam Ervin, on an issue of deep conviction to both. Though the result was a clear gain to the nation — given the circumstances in 1957, it was an astonishing gain — the maneuvering by which it was achieved was disquieting.

It troubled me as well; yet ultimately I approved of it, as I approved of Johnson himself — not only because it achieved progress, but because it reflected the ambivalence I felt about the enforcement of civil rights. The following year, after the turmoil in Little Rock, Senator Fulbright filed a brief amicus curiae in the school desegregation case of *Aaron v. Cooper*. In part it read:

The people of Arkansas endure against a background not without certain pathological aspects. They are marked in some ways by a strange disproportion inherited from the age of Negro slavery. The whites and Negroes of Arkansas are equally prisoners of their environment. No one knows what either of them might have been under other circumstances. Certainly, no one of them has ever been free with respect to racial relationship in the sense that the Vermonter, say, has been free. The society of each is conditioned by the other's presence. Each carries a catalogue of things not to be mentioned. Each moves through an intricate ritual of evasions, of make-believe, and suppressions. In Arkansas, one finds a relationship among men without counterpart on this continent, except in similar southern States. All this is the legacy of an ancient and melancholy history.

. . . We are confronted here with a problem, novel and unprecedented in the history of our country and extraordinarily complex. In our congenital optimism, we Americans believe, or affect to believe, that social questions of the greatest difficulty may be solved through the discovery and application of a sovereign remedy that will forever dispose of the problem. Yet all this flies in the face of human experience. . . .

In this general context, we must observe a constant in the affairs of men. It is this: When their ancient social convictions are profoundly violated, or when sudden change is attempted to be imposed upon attitudes or principles deeply imbedded within them by inheritance, tradition, or environment, they are likely to react almost as by involuntary reflex, and often violently . . .

[Quoting Morris R. Cohen] "The clericalist and the legalist have an undue advantage in identifying their causes with those of religion and law, causes for which humanity is always willing to make extreme sacrifices. . . . Jesus' protest that the Sabbath was made for man, and not man for the Sabbath, cuts the foundation of all legalism and clericalism. It makes us see the profound foolishness of those who, like Cato, would adhere to the law even though the Republic be thereby destroyed. Without a legal order and some ministry of religious insight, the path of anarchy and worldliness is, indeed, dangerously shortened. But without a realization of the essential limitations of legalism and clericalism there is no way of defending the free human or spiritual life from fanaticism and superstition."

I thought this was very fine — brave in its description of race relations in Arkansas, wise in its insistence that law is a part, but not the only part, of society's legitimate universe. It would take time for the races in the South to accept a new relationship based on equality. Only violence and implacable hatred would follow from the blind imposition of what Fulbright implied was the "sovereign remedy" of forced racial integration upon the "intricate ritual of evasions, of make-believe, and suppressions" that characterized Southern life. I showed the brief to my friends, urging them to understand, to take the long view. Some of them seemed persuaded, but at least one man replied in a way that brought me up short: "Hell," he said, "I didn't think anybody was trying to destroy the Republic. I just thought some colored kids were trying to go to a white school down there."

So I read the brief again, and saw that the admonition against provoking a violent reaction by "sudden change . . . imposed upon attitudes or principles deeply imbedded within [the Southern whites] by inheritance, tradition, or environment" — that this admonition was almost meaningless to Southern blacks, who had suffered countless violent reactions at the hands of the whites, all quite unprovoked by sudden change, Supreme Court decrees, mixed schools, or of other products of "legalism" and "clericalism." They might fear the hot-eyed response of whites forced to give up the "intricate ritual," but they had known fear for generations — and none before with such a promise of deliverance on the other side.

This was, in Fulbright's words, an "ancient and melancholy history." And I knew it ought to be changed as soon as men could change it. Prolonged delay, whether caused by timidity or skepticism, was unconscionable and unwise. Charles Black of the Yale Law School argued that the failure of the national government to insist upon compliance with *Brown* not only deferred justice for the blacks, but undermined those well-intentioned Southern whites who needed the threat of the federal club in order to encourage voluntary change in their communities. The majority of white Southerners were not well-intentioned about the forced integration of the races, and as their representatives in Congress spoke for the majority if they remained there to speak at all, it was up to the Judiciary, and hopefully to the Executive, to persuade, to induce, and finally to threaten unless changes were made. That is what it came down to, and appeals to Jesus' humanism did not alter it.

I found it easy to say this to Southerners — expecially when our arguments escalated, as they often did, to the level of absolute rhetorical conviction. When I visited my wife's home in Georgia, it was a little different. Then I went out on Christmas morning to a Negro community nearby, delivering presents to families whom my wife's mother had befriended for decades. I heard from them that "Miss Nelle" had gotten up at three o'clock in the morning last week, and had driven her old Dodge down to the city jail and signed a recognizance for Willie Moore, who was drunk again and fighting; that Susie Archibald had so much enjoyed Miss Nelle's reading of her stories last Thanksgiving; that George Alexander would be there to help serve Christmas dinner — and I knew that this time there would be money to pay him.

Miss Nelle was literary, she had lived in Europe, she had supported the Spanish Loyalists. But with respect to the ideology of race, she was deeply Southern-conservative. Lincoln was a vulgar politician — there was Henry Adams's book to prove it. Though her life was utterly enmeshed with those of many black people, and though she dealt with them more or less according to their deserts, she was inflexibly opposed to the language and concept of egalitarianism when it came to Negroes and whites. She loved small children, and following Rousseau, considered them divinely inspired — in many ways more sensitive, knowing, and fair than adults. But the idea that she might have been required to associate with them, in a situation in which she did not wish to do so, would have appalled her. The parallel was exact.

I did not know many liberals in Washington who had a similar range of friendships among Negroes; who would have left a warm bed at three in the morning to spring a drunken black man; or who enjoyed such a reciprocity of obligation and grace with black neighbors. With Miss Nelle, the Georgia Negroes had a relationship that included several of the necessary requirements of civilization. I did not wish to see them lost in a society made officially more just. But the relationship did not admit of maturity on the part of the Negroes, or of their standing to insist upon their rights and contend for their wishes with the white lady. Such an association would have been intolerable to me if I had been a black man. I wondered if it was possible to retain its civility and mutual concern, while encouraging black independence and assertiveness. A professor at my university said no; every tolerable society depended upon fixed relationships, with one class or group ascendant. You could have democracy or decency.

The debate is familiar. What gave it point in this period was that Lyndon Johnson, like me, was a Southern liberal, whose family history and early circumstances — and his wife's — very likely suggested the same questions to him. And it was he on whom the responsibility came to rest for guiding civil rights legislation through the Congress, and for dealing with the fevered cities, black at the core; on a Southern liberal. It is dangerous to extrapolate opinions and instincts from one man to another, but I believe that in the late fifties Johnson felt about the race question much as I did, namely, that it obsessed the South and diverted it from attending to its economic and educational problems; that it produced among white Southerners an angry defensiveness and parochialism; that there were, nevertheless, mutually rewarding relationships between many Southern whites and Negroes; and that it should be possible to remove the common guilt by federal law while preserving the private values.

This was a good attitude for one who set out to persuade the Congress, and the country, that stronger civil rights laws were needed in the interest of justice. It dealt with the race question first as one involving legal rights, and later as amenable to a kind of repair job, making up for the consequences of rights long denied. It did not encompass the staggering and complex needs of urban Negroes. It did not comprehend — perhaps I should say, *I* did not comprehend — that federal intervention, in the form of civil rights laws, would be insufficient; that the long-held dream of the Southern liberals, to free themselves and the country of guilt arising from official discrimination, was almost irrelevant to the new situation in the cities.

In the sixties, Pat Moynihan would tell me, "The worst part of the Negro problem is, it's being tended by you Southern liberals." It was a class problem, he said. "We've got a lower-class problem in the cities, and you people don't know anything about that."

He was right about me, at least. The riots that were to come would prove it. But there were things that only a Southern liberal *could* know, satisfactions that could only come to those who had shared in that "ritual of evasions, make-believe, and suppression," and to whom an increase in Negro freedom was an increase in their own. Long after the passage of the major civil rights acts for which Johnson was responsible, I went home to East Texas to speak at an annual festival. There was a parade, with a great many high school bands, elaborate floats, mounted companies of cowboys and Shriners — a vast ephemeral display that moved through thousands of farmers and working people toward a football stadium, where the queen and her court would be celebrated.

And the bands — were mixed! A Negro trombonist, next to a white cornetist; three black drummers, and a white cymbal player! And at the front of it all, black and white majorettes, in perfect unison turning their batons about their wrists and shoulders with grimly smiling concentration; step step step mark time.

The driver of our car was sleepy; he had refereed a football game the night before, and returned home late. Palestine against Woodville, two small towns not very different from those in northern Louisiana or Mississippi. Were their teams integrated? Oh, sure, about half and half on each one. How did he feel about that? It's all right with me. I was in the navy for four years, I guess it changed me. My daddy, though, if he was alive, he'd be having fits.

Alongside, the crowd quietly applauded, and some people pointed to the big sign on our car that said "Counsel to President Lyndon B. Johnson." Then we passed through a Negro section, and suddenly there were cheers, and waving, and a lot of "V" signs; an old man grinned at me and, nodding, said, "That's right, that's right."

So there had been change, so much that one could scarcely remember the thunderclap that *Brown* had loosed across the South or the careful, apprehensive steps which the Senate had taken in 1957, the struggle over Title III and jury trials, the different words for Douglas and Ervin, the praise and resentment. But it had started there, and then King and Wilkins and the rest had moved it on.

I anticipate the story. None of us knew, on that day of triumph in 1957, what grief lay ahead for both races, what awful consequences were still to follow from our invincible ignorance and neglect. All we knew was that the boil had been lanced. There was, after eighty years, a civil rights bill. It seemed possible that the architect of its passage, standing in the center aisle of the Senate and accepting the congratulations of Democrats and Republicans, Northerners and Southerners, would use it as his key to the Presidency. And that surely would be worth waiting to see.

6

Johnson for President

DATE: March 13, 1959
TO: Senator Johnson
FROM: Harry McPherson
SUBJECT: Major legislation in committee

1) Area Redevelopment (S. 722): the staff says the bill will be reported on Tuesday or Wednesday of next week. There is 389.5 million dollars in the bill, considerably more than last year's bill which the President vetoed. The House put part of the excess in the Community Facilities bill last session; that may be done again.

2) International Health Research (S.J. Res. 41): the committee has completed its hearings, but there is no clear indication of what it will do next on this resolution. It is badly drafted, and the Administration opposes part of it, although there is no controversy over the desirability of an international health program. The Administration wants to put the whole thing into ICA as a part of foreign aid.

3) Railroad Retirement (S. 226): there is some agreement on this bill in subcommittee, but the problem is getting enough Senators away from the Kennedy hearings to sit in executive session on it. Railroad labor pressure is increasing.

4) The Kennedy labor bill (S. 505): the committee has arrived at Title VI of this bill, and has adjourned until next week to consider it then. There is no way of telling how long it will take until after the next executive session.

5) International Monetary Fund (S. 1094): hearings are to be held on Tuesday, at which non-governmental witnesses are to be heard. After baiting the Secretary of the Treasury on Monday about putting this item in the 1959 Budget, Chairman Fulbright let Under Secretary

Dillon off with hardly a question on the subject. There is some feeling that it would be wise to proceed with the bill without delay, because of the Berlin situation during which the drain on the Fund may be extremely severe.

The only major legislation on the Calendar is the Education TV bill and the Clayton Act Enforcement Order bill.

INFORMATION: rumor, speculation, opinion, fact. Reports of vendettas and alliances. "Pure politics" and "on the merits." Johnson absorbed it all against the time when it might prove useful. Most men in political life, from impatience or a need to seem informed, stopped others from telling them what they already knew; but Johnson listened, like a skillful journalist, for the minor revelation which put everything into perspective.

A procedural memorandum like the one above was useful, not because it told him much about the substance of each bill, but because it gave him a sense of the pace and direction in which the Senate was moving; he could then try to force it, amend it, or tacitly declare a recess. No other senator would have cared to know even this much about matters outside his committees or interests. No one else needed a rudimentary order of battle for the coming weeks, because no one else sought to command the Senate. There was only one Leader, there was no other Leader but him, and he needed to know.

Numbers of us labored to meet the need. Gerry Siegel went off to teach at Harvard, and three lawyers replaced him: Solis Horwitz, a bright, testy, chain-smoking man from Pittsburgh; Jim Wilson, from Texas, and me. While Solis and George Reedy talked strategy upstairs, Jim and I worked the floor. We delighted in the Senate and kept a sharp watch for its eccentricities. One senator could not begin his remarks without recalling his college degrees, bar association memberships, and past offices; another got everything wrong, even if he was handed a script. Still another, an old Westerner, came in one night, stupefied by bourbon, and raised his hand for recognition; at last recognized, he stood speechless for half a minute until, hand still raised, he slowly subsided into his chair. We doubled with laughter and left the floor to avoid a rebuke. In Jim, for the first time, I had a fellow spirit in the chamber.

And he was much more than an amused observer. When Lewis Strauss's nomination as Secretary of Commerce was debated in 1959, Jim put his lawyer's skills to work on the hearing record with devastating results. Johnson, torn between Clinton Anderson's furious desire to beat Strauss and Eisenhower's equal determination to have him in his cabinet, asked us for a paper "weighing the pros and cons." We believed he had already decided to oppose the nomination, and like Anderson, we were offended by Strauss's arrogance and evasions; but we knew that a sharply biased brief would raise doubts in Johnson's mind, and be useless in persuading others. For days we read testimony, columns, and editorials, and at last composed a long and careful memorandum whose first part, the "pro," was quite persuasive — until one reached the "con." Johnson used it widely, reading the "pro" part to Strauss's opponents and the "con" to his supporters — as if to say, "And you expect me to go along with you in the light of that?" So our calculated fairness served his purpose of remaining publicly uncommitted until very near the moment of truth. Strauss was beaten, with Republican help — I heard Barry Goldwater gasp, "God . . . damn!" when Mrs. Smith voted "No." The memorandum was returned to us with an "Excellent — you get an 'A'." It was extravagant praise from one whose usual sign of satisfaction was a simple grunt.

The principal ingredient of the [Johnson] Procedure was flexibility. On any major piece of legislation, never make a commitment as to what will pass; determine in advance what is *possible* under the best of circumstances for the Senate to accept; after making this near-mathematical determination, don't reveal it; keep the leader's intentions carefully masked; then, exploiting the Johnson Network [senators and staff of both parties, committed to Johnson for one reason or another] start rounding up all detachable votes; when all is in readiness, strike quickly and pass the bill with a minimum of debate.°

With the Senate narrowly divided, this was an ideal procedure. Any appeal to ideological combat, anything that resembled take-it-or-leave-it and no compromise, would have invited a steady series of defeats. Watching Johnson win his measured victories, listening to George Reedy expound the necessary middle course, I thought the results were probably consonant with the nature of the country itself. Diverse and parochial, it could not be governed except by amelioration. There was no mandate for vigorous action with a majority of two. A leader's job was to file down the refractory edges that prevented agreement — the personal animosities, the sectional differences, the passionate commitments — so that the gears might mesh and the wheel might turn, slowly, as the nation apparently wanted it. Johnson and his supporters thought such a role "responsible." His opponents called it "expedient." To them, it was not leadership, but brokerage. To him, the political process required it.

The country divided its vote, in most elections, between 55 and 45 percent. Johnson had lost one election by a hair, and won another by eighty-seven votes. So the tolerances were fine. If you wanted progress, you worked within them, you shifted a little here and there, you avoided frontal assaults and inflexible lines of march, you took what you could get. There were no trumpets, the pennons never flew; the model was not Henry at Agincourt, but Metternich at Vienna. The "art of the possible" was a middlebrow art, practical, successful, and in the end rather dull.

Many members chafed under it. They were not content with partial advances toward totally desirable ends. They did not like being posed as bogeymen whose unreasonable tenacity compelled the other side to compromise.

But there was no alternative, if laws were to be passed. Paul

---

° Rowland Evans and Robert Novak, *Lyndon B. Johnson: The Exercise of Power* (New York: New American Library, 1966), p. 112.

Butler, the intensely partisan Democratic chairman, once devised another course for "national" Democrats suffering under the low ceilings of Congress. A Democratic Advisory Council, set up under the National Committee, would adopt positions on the merits; true Democrats would seek to enact them, and failing, "take them to the country" in the next election. It was a new version of the original Policy Committee idea, and for a time I was attracted by it. Johnson and Rayburn were not, and their contempt for Butler and all other enthusiastic losers was not the only reason. I thought they might have welcomed the chance to sit down with Mrs. Roosevelt and Adlai Stevenson and make policy; I certainly would. But on the contrary, the idea of striking bold figures in the morning downtown, and returning to the Hill and its politics of adjustment in the afternoon, had no attraction for them whatever. Perhaps by predisposition, certainly by the requirements of congressional leadership as they perceived them, they thought steady incremental gains achieved in an obstinate environment more important than preaching to the converted. When it came down to it, so did I.

There was no real choice, not with a two-vote margin in the Senate. But a deep recession hit the country in 1958. The Administration was obviously uncertain about how to end it, and the large Republican class of 1946, elected first in a spasm of opposition to Roosevelt and Truman, reelected with Ike in 1952, was exposed to restless constituents. The result was carnage. Suddenly there were more Democrats in the Senate than any time since the early New Deal. The look of the Senate changed radically in 1959: sixty-five seats and desks jammed together on the Democratic side of the aisle, making it physically difficult for Baker to reach the interior members; thirty-five others, in spacious comfort that belied the catastrophe, on the Republican side. It was exhilarating. It was also symbolic: anyone leading that mass of Democrats should be able to ram a vigorous program down the Administration's throat. No need to compromise, no need to hang back until the votes developed; they were already there. So I thought.

Not long afterward, Karl Meyer wrote a perceptive analysis of the new Democrats in *Commentary* magazine. He called it "The Triumph of the Bland." He found the 1958 class intelligent, moderately liberal, and above all reasonable. By comparison, the liberals and progressives of the thirties — Norris, LaFollette, Borah, and Wheeler — were peculiar men: excessive in action, stubborn in error, and often isolationist.

But the new liberals, Meyer thought, would never excite the public imagination as the old ones did. They would not expose the malefactors of wealth, or fight the great corporations in the public's behalf. They would vote for the right things, as these were served up in the liberal kitchen — in the universities, trade union headquarters, and foundations. But they would not embark on ardent quests of their own. They would embarrass no one. Neither would they galvanize the country by striking at the roots of whatever conned and abused it.

Perhaps Meyer was right. Yet compared to those whom they had succeeded, by and large conservative Republicans, the new Democrats were welcome. If they did not burn with reforming fire, at least they apprehended the world as it was. They spoke without grandiloquence, without the studied inflections of men who had served too long in the hermetic world of the Hill. They were fresh from the country, and they sounded like it. Instead of debating the morality of helping the unemployed, they regarded the recession as an evil to be ended; they saw its victims not as subjects of an ethical debate, but as people caught in an economic trap not of their making.

They were serious, but not solemn. And they were highly political. Most of them had served in the House, or in state or local governments. They knew that one should "go along and get along" in Congress — that famous axiom of Speaker Rayburn's aimed at his fellow Southerners and subsequently cited, by his friends and enemies, as his prescription for every member. At the same time they brought with them, and to some degree retained, a sense of independence. They acknowledged Johnson's leadership and the requirements of the committee system. But they seemed more concerned about their own opinions, and about what people back home thought of them, than about making it with the Senate powers.

It was easy to like them. Philip Hart of Michigan, Ted Moss of Utah, Gale McGee of Wyoming, Vance Hartke of Indiana, Pete Williams of New Jersey. Very different men, yet collectively a new kind of senator — "born in this century," as John Kennedy would say in 1961. I had never met a man like Hart in politics. He was intelligent and straight; he did not pretend to know the truth about every issue of the moment; and he was easy and gentle. (Staffmen are always on the lookout for amiable bosses. It relieves the tension of working under constant critical judgment of others, and provides anecdotes for one's wife and friends that magnify the staffer's own position — making him seem at ease with power, and therefore powerful himself.) With most of the older men in the Senate, I had always felt distant, separated by a generation or two, and by their stature as famous figures of my adolescence. With Hart and some of the other new men, I felt completely at ease, a contemporary.

The youngest senator of all, Frank Church, had come in two years earlier. In the beginning he spoke with all the mannerisms of a national forensics champion, as he had once been. I thought it would take a while for the formal edge to wear off, and it did; but even at the beginning, it was possible to be a friend of Church's in a way that owed more to common age and interest than to our professional roles. At sundown one evening, in the course of a long debate, my wife brought sandwiches and a Mason jar of martinis to the Capitol, and we spread them out on the balustrade that runs along the terrace above the Mall. The light was mellow gold and green. Marble buildings in the Triangle glowed with an unusual warmth. Church, taking a stroll, joined us. We shared the supper and talked of Washington, of the satisfactions and frustrations of working there. I had a keen sense of belonging to the place, as Church did. I was getting older, and a little wiser. And the men with whom I worked were getting younger.

Two blocks from the Capitol, near the row house in which we lived, there was an old brick Gothic church, St. Mark's Episcopal. Before going to college, I had thought about entering the ministry. The church was the one institution in my Texas town that concerned itself with matters beyond the marketplace. But as the years passed, it came to seem much less than transcendental, and merely irrelevant to ordinary life, especially to political life. The seminary at my university turned out two kinds of ministers: one the hail-fellow, camp-counselor variety, the other bookish and fragile. Neither seemed capable of understanding, much less assuaging, the dilemmas other men encountered in business and the professions, The Episcopal church was for older women, very young children, and the sort of man who thought he should take one or the other somewhere responsible on Sunday.

St. Mark's was different. That became clear after my first visit. William Baxter, the minister, was trying to create a community of disabused Christians who behaved sensitively, but critically, toward each other, and for whom faith was more an affirmation of life than a matter of belief. After a talk in which I expressed contempt for the church and its theology, he invited me to teach a confirmation class. I could use Kafka and Dostoevski for text, and forget the Book of Common Prayer. What was important was that men and women should "enter into their griefs" until they reached bottom, experienced helplessness, and became able to ask for help. That was, of course, very hard for middle-class Americans to do — to acknowledge that life was often too much for them; that they could not be sure of managing well enough alone; that they needed a hand—even a stranger's hand. Most churches I had known were built on Christmas and Easter. At St. Mark's there was also Good Friday, the time of unconscionable cruelty and death, when the spirit withers into its cave. If there was any "good news," most of us could hear it only there.

It was an irresistible invitation: to use the bleak insights of modern writers in the comfortable rooms of the Episcopal Church. With no idea of where we would end, we began. It was the first of many mixed experiences in the church, most of them political — in the sense that I learned something from each about people and their response to authority, power, and manipulation. I carried my confirmation class into the depths, and could offer them no means of retrieval, except that one should act, even where motives were impure and results were certain to be disappointing. Anyway, when spring came, the bishop would arrive and confirm them all as faithful soldiers in Christ's army. Then they would live like the rest of us, vaguely tormented, occasionally sustained by the tolerance of others.

I became senior warden of the vestry, because friends got out the vote on the crucial night of election against a good man who had not mastered the language of "Christian existentialism." I worked for Bill Baxter's nomination as suffragan bishop of Washington. It was a losing cause. The urban church was torn between a comfortable leader from the suburbs, where the Episcopalians lived, and a black from the inner city whose election would salve white consciences. At length the delegates chose a social Christian with strong views about race and war. Disappointed, I took the result as proof that the church cared more for correct opinions than for providing evidence that it was useful in the crises of private life.

The great political experience of my life at St. Mark's was in drama — in directing and writing plays, and acting in them. Bill

Baxter had organized a chancel drama cycle several years before. The plays of Eliot, Miller, Ionesco, and Brecht were produced before the altars of churches in the area, as part of Lenten prayer services. Afterwards there was long discussion about what they meant, their religious significance being assumed by the setting. I began as a walk-on player, and soon had the bit in my teeth. I wrote a play about the unveiling of a new intercontinental missile, and the moral predicament involved in making or refusing to make it; another about the price of giving and receiving charity. Their language was argumentative, rather than dramatic, and it was too clear that my purpose was only to prove that all decisions are ambiguous — that man is forever in a "fix" or a "box," two words from the existentialist canon. Not much actually happened. The dramatist lacked a clear point of view, just as he did on the Senate floor.

Directing those plays, and others to come, was another matter. Few of my actors had ever stepped on a stage. In the beginning, their gestures were wooden. They spoke without emphasis, often with their backs to the audience. Missed cues were so common that entire pages were sometimes skipped with no one onstage the wiser. There were tears of self-reproach in the local tavern after each night's rehearsal. People quit and others replaced them. Choosing new players was simple: I took anyone who volunteered.

Slowly, agonizingly, the shape of each play emerged. The actors yielded to their roles. They began to direct each other, to set up each other's lines with their own. Speech began to show feeling. Bodies moved in a controlled but natural way. Gestures were directed toward other people onstage, and the audience was permitted to see them. Whole paragraphs were heard at the rear of several churches.

What happened was that eight or ten people of very disparate backgrounds, educational attainments, and native abilities began to interact with one another in the service of a higher purpose —

the competent production of a play. Cooperating, they expressed a coherent artistic form in a way that gave pleasure to the audience and to themselves. The result was richer than any that might have been achieved by a single performer of greater skills. And it was infinitely more satisfying than a spontaneous discussion among the same group.

This happened as a matter of course in symphony orchestras, in professional theater, in films and ballet. It bore at least some resemblance to what went on in successful families, though a family's "purposes" were more diverse. And it had much to say about good politics in a democracy.

As the director, I was important to the group, especially in the beginning. I set its standards and schedules, bullyragged offenders, encouraged the faint-hearted, and enthusiastically demonstrated my conception of each role. I worried about props, lights, and sound effects. I counseled actors offstage as well as on, and became privy to several new love affairs and the decline of at least two marriages. As the group's leader, I was necessary to its success.

But I did not make it successful. The quality of the plays, and of the actors themselves, determined success or failure. At some point in the rehearsals for each play I felt a shift of power away from myself and onto the stage. It was only a play in a Protestant church, but it suggested the way things worked in a sensible democracy, where governing purposes were known and honored, and where leaders, having set the country's course, simply watched it fulfill them — all the while remaining on guard for backsliding and defection. Achieving a specific social goal was another matter. Usually there was agreement on desired results, but not on the means of obtaining them. What was missing, to extend the metaphor, was a script — a single concept to which everyone willingly submitted. If a social goal was to be reached, political leaders intervened constantly, revising, urging, instructing, never letting go until the momentum of change was irresistible. That, of course, might be never.

Whatever their similarities, political life had never given me the pleasure I found on the makeshift stages of the church. It would have been otherwise if I had been a principal in the Senate as I was in directing plays. But there was something beyond the mere difference in roles. One night in a suburban church, as we performed Ionesco's *Bald Soprano*, we suddenly began to lean toward each other, and then away, weaving in and out as the Budapest Quartet does when they play — when it plays — Beethoven. Our words came without effort, almost without consciousness. There was nothing between ourselves and the roles we played. Each was buoyed by the others' confidence. It was an experience almost beyond exhilaration. Later, when I read Camus's notebooks, I understood why he preferred a repertory theater to all other human companies. To relate to other men and women, in a common striving for something beyond ourselves!

Johnson, working late on a parliamentary problem, once complained, "Nobody's around when I need him. Russell's home reading Plato, and Harry's off somewhere reading the Bible." More likely Senator Russell was reading naval history, and I was excoriating the church for its pharisaical view of politics before an audience of clergy or seminary students. I was in some demand as a speaker before such groups, partly because I had ostensibly retained my faith while working in the pit of politics, and partly, I suspected, because church people enjoyed being criticized for moral shortcomings. I criticized them vigorously. Here they were — swapping votes in convention, manipulating vestries, raising funds, buying real estate, organizing schools, leading or being led by their bishops and congregations — and they thought politicians devious and corrupted! Let them acknowledge that Lord Acton's famous epigram applied to them as well as to politicians. Power must be used; its use corrupts; let the corrupted judge one another in full awareness of that.

It was not an original message. But coming from within government, it acquired an aura of originality. At least it was different from the usual Christian commentary on politics — generally very liberal, and later involving marches and vigils in behalf of civil rights and peace; and it was equally far from what most politicians said to gatherings of the clergy. For a long time I enjoyed delivering it. To be invited to belabor those whose calling was to make others feel insensitive and moderately wicked; to be applauded, the more direct hits one scored; afterwards to be regarded as a tough pol with a Christian heart. It was all very satisfying. In time I realized that it had become only an act intended to shock. I could no longer pretend to myself that I wished to educate churchmen to the moral dilemmas of politics, and to the unanswered political questions in their own lives. I wanted only to strike a blow at ecclesiastical certitudes — to seem by comparison at once more virtuous and more profound than those who held themselves out as ethical guides to me and others of their fellowmen. Too often it was like shooting fish in a barrel. And it became, on occasion, disconcerting in another way, when I met seminary professors who carried my argument to extremes and assured me that they also believed moral judgments to be inapplicable to politics. I believed nothing of the sort. Exasperated with myself and my audiences, I gave up the clergy lecture circuit, and returned with some relief to the conventional pieties of the Senate.

There Johnson was not doing very well, for reasons of mathematics. He now had enough Democrats behind him to create major expectations, but not enough to override the President's vetoes. Eisenhower had begun to use the veto power freely, striking down bill after bill that proposed heavy spending. A third of the Senate was still Republican. Almost all could be counted on to support him against motions to override, and there were always enough conservative Democrats to make up for the defectors. As a result of the Democratic triumph in 1958, the South was a relatively less formidable constraint upon liberal progress; the veto had taken its place. Johnson still faced the question of whether to reduce social spending in order to pass it, or to inflate it, invite its defeat or veto, and make an issue. Though the 1960 election was on the horizon, his natural instinct was to build a record of signed legislation, and to avoid the charge of "fiscal irresponsibility." That was consistent with the image he would offer the country if he chose to run. Kennedy and Humphrey might attack the Republicans for standing still and neglecting urgent public needs. Johnson would be the responsible Senate leader, seeking prudent progress, generally cooperating with the President while suggesting that he would do more if he could. Most of the Senate Democrats lined up behind him. Most of the active Democrats in the country looked elsewhere.

After six years of praise for his leadership, he began to hear discordant voices among his own troops. Senator Proxmire, who on his arrival in 1957 had praised Johnson almost to embarrassment (to mine, at any rate — scarcely a week passed without a tribute to the leader's skill, understanding, and persuasive powers), complained that he was, in fact, a dictator. Senator Clark took up the theme. So did Morse. There was some justification for it. Johnson's control of the machinery of the Senate was complete. When it was used to pass one's bills or to secure a choice committee assignment, it was welcome, but it was oppressive to those in opposition. His constant pressure for unanimous-consent agreements, which enabled legislation to reach a vote without exhausting delays, often came close to harassment. In terms of classical theory, his eagerness to cut off debate was undemocratic. But I could not fault him. Senators who raised objections had frequently benefited from his power. Complaints about limiting debate — usually cast in language worthy of Cicero warning against autocratic rule — often turned out to be based on the plaintiff's annoyance that he must either miss a vote or forgo a speaking engagement back home. And besides — who knew better than liberals the enervating consequences of unlimited debate?

The liberals' restlessness chiefly stemmed, I thought, from a political hangover. After the exuberant success of 1958, they awoke to find that they still lacked the power to write liberal legislation. So they wished to mount an ideological offensive that would set the terms for the coming election. As before, Johnson preferred trimming reluctantly to failing proudly. He was a "doer." Doers do not fail, even if what they are able to achieve on a given issue is modest. The country had given evidence that it rejected Republicanism in a recession. Johnson was not sure that it had embraced liberalism. Eisenhower was still popular — and when, with righteous anger, he condemned big spending and stopped it with his vetoes, he had something like a majority of the voters with him. So Johnson believed. He spoke out against the vetoes, but he remained on the prudent side of the spending line. He did not flinch from the thought of opposing Richard Nixon; taking on Ike was another matter, especially for a Texan.

Behind their tactical differences, a Presidential struggle was under way between Johnson and the liberals. Obviously, he would run as the "can-do" leader, whose negotiating skills and reasonable politics would transfer easily to the White House. Those who disliked that prospect — the labor unions, civil rights groups, Stevensonians, many big-city machines — found it appropriate to attack the very basis of his claims; that is, to make his primacy in the Senate seem less the result of statesmanship than of ruthlessness and the brokerage of power. His potential rivals — Kennedy, Humphrey, and Symington — did not criticize him directly. That would have seemed like sour grapes; in any event their personal relationships with him did not permit it. Kennedy and Humphrey would seek instead to show, in the primaries, that congressional supremacy was not important in a Presidential candidate. Symington, who was more acceptable to the liberal blocs than Johnson, would avoid the primaries and hope for a deadlock at the convention, from which he might emerge as the compromise choice.

I had no part in Johnson's Presidential planning. I was truly naïve about electoral politics; as he had said, I couldn't get elected constable. I saw groups of Texans passing into the rococo chamber in the Capitol which Johnson had wrested from the District of Columbia committee and made into his majority leader's office. Older Washington lawyers — men like Tommy Corcoran, the shrewd leprechaun of New Deal days — offered their counsel. Representatives of some of the moderate building trade and railroad unions, with whom Johnson had long been friendly, gave encouragement. But his chief reliance was upon the Congress itself, upon his and Rayburn's mastery of it. Their power in the Capitol building was an important factor in the lives of most Democratic members; if it did not persuade them to come out for Johnson, it had an inhibiting effect upon their commitment to others. For a long time I thought Johnson truly believed that senators and representatives were major political forces in their states, that having their support meant capturing their delegations at the convention. Even I knew better. Carl Hayden could be elected in Arizona against Jesus himself, but he had little to do with Arizona's national politics. It was useful, for a Presidential candidate running on his legislative record, to have his colleagues testify to his unparalleled abilities — by inference depreciating other candidates in the same body. But that was ultimately just a gimmick, not serious electioneering.

Surely Johnson knew this, and felt he had no alternative to relying upon the pressures he could bring to bear within the one institution at his command. His disabilities were numerous; he was a Southerner, even worse, a Texan; his calls for moderation and nonpartisanship, while winning "independent" support, offended the hot partisans who cast a major share of the votes at every Democratic convention — and one had to win there, before taking advantage of independent support in the country. His reputation as a master wheeler-dealer was repugnant to those who regarded the Presidency as a moral, almost a priestly office; he had made little effort, after a quarter of a century in Washington, to develop important friendships in all sections of the country; he knew very few people in the universities who might produce the ideas and speeches for a campaign; he did not perform well on television, as he was more accustomed to shouting across a courthouse square than to giving cool answers before the neutral eye of a camera; his overwhelming techniques of private persuasion — vehement, understanding, hilariously funny, combining appeals to conscience, reason, pity, patriotism, faction, and self-interest — would not carry a crowd, as he knew, and so were replaced by the hoarse declamation of platitudes. His long concentration on procedural matters, and on building majorities behind other men who had detailed views on substantive issues (Kerr knew about taxes and trade, Humphrey about farm price supports, Russell about defense, Kennedy about labor, Hill about education and health, Fulbright about foreign policy) made him seem vague and elusive under questioning outside the Senate chamber.

Most important, I believe Johnson did not think he could win the nomination. I believe he thought John Kennedy was too rich, too glamorous, too much admired by journalists, too knowledgeable about the politics of each state, to be overtaken. One afternoon on the Senate floor, I sat at Johnson's desk, looking for a memorandum among the roll-call slips and other debris of a week's work. I found a thick hardbound document labeled "Indiana." I opened it and read a detailed analysis of Indiana politics, with comments on important political figures, labor leaders, citizens' groups, and so on. The test of each man was whether he commanded votes, and whether he was with us. "Us" was Jack Kennedy. Johnson had asked him to occupy the majority leader's chair at the front of the Senate, while Kennedy managed a labor bill. He often did that in order that the manager might be easily recognized by the presiding officer. Obviously, Kennedy had left the document behind by mistake. For a moment, I considered taking it to Johnson, not in order to let him read about Indiana, but so that he might see how sophisticated and thorough the Kennedy campaign was, and emulate it. But showing him Kennedy's paper would be dirty pool, and anyway Johnson would never launch such an extensive intelligence operation. His world was embodied in the roll-call slips, the memos to senators, the reminders to speak to chairmen about bills in their committees. I called a page and sent "Indiana" back to Senator Kennedy.

For months Johnson debated whether to run. His mood varied from day to day, sometimes expansive, sometimes dour. Members from the Bible Belt assured him that a Catholic could never carry their states; an occasional city boss promised support on the second ballot; Texans led cheers; and occasionally he brought off a coup with a difficult bill, winning praise even in the *Times*. Then he seemed ready, sure that he was smarter and tougher than Kennedy, that the old masters of the party — particularly Truman — would tip the balance his way. Next day, told of the vast resources Kennedy was throwing into each primary, admonished by the *Times* that he had compromised too cheaply on vital legislation, reminded by liberal journalists that his origins, speech, and demeanor were unacceptably Southern, warned by Texans that he could not stray too far to the left without risking their censure, he was depressed and unsure.

Humphrey did not seem so, though how much of his mood was self-induced one could not say. He was, as always, full of enthusiasm for new legislation. With a liberal majority behind him, he could now put some of his ideas through the Senate — a food stamp program, a Youth Conservation Corps modeled on the CCC of New Deal days, disarmament resolutions. Though little of his work survived in the House, his success in his own body encouraged him. He entered the Wisconsin and West Virginia primaries with little but his tongue and a few devoted friends to match against the efficiency of the Kennedy organization. He knew so much, cared so much, and spoke so well! Even under the onslaught of Kennedy's personality and money, Humphrey was indomitably optimistic. I heard it said that he was a stalking-horse for Johnson, but I never believed it. He wanted the nomination.

It was, nevertheless, equally important to Johnson that Humphrey succeed in West Virginia. Unless a New Dealing Protestant could win there against a wealthy Catholic, there would be no stopping Kennedy before Los Angeles. Humphrey could not win the nomination, but he could keep it alive for Johnson.

The state had long been in Johnson's thoughts. In 1959 he had asked me for a memorandum spelling out what might be done for it under existing programs. The memo was then given to the new senator, Robert Byrd, as evidence of Johnson's concern. West Virginia seemed ideal for a politician in Johnson's position; poor, fundamentalist, mostly white, not really Southern but without the organized liberal activists who made the Eastern cities so forbidding to him. Winning there would show his strength outside the old South. He was urged to enter the primary, but refused. Humphrey was already in, and Johnson would only split the anti-Kennedy vote with him. No — he would remain in the Senate, "minding the store," winning praise — from his supporters, at least — for his dedication to the office to which he had been elected.

The morning after West Virginia, I stood beside him as he met the press, ten minutes before the Senate convened. As usual, reporters crowded around in concentric circles, straining to hear the leader's replies. It was unusually difficult that morning. Johnson's face was drawn and somber, his words low and almost inaudible. "No, it doesn't mean that Senator Kennedy has sewed up the nomination. I'm sure the delegates in convention will choose [inaudible] . . . will be the best President . . . Yes, it does show that Senator Kennedy is very popular . . . everybody knew that already . . . they put a lot into the state, I understand, though I wouldn't know. I haven't followed it closely. I've been trying to get these bills through . . ." As Alben Barkley once told me and Baker, never show it when you're hurt, raise hell when you're not.

In time he announced, symbolically before a big crowd in the Senate auditorium. The applause struck me as more dutiful than spontaneous; the leader's announcing, everybody say Hey! real loud. I was also struck by my own uncertainty about whom I wanted to become the Democratic candidate. Most of my friends were already committed to Kennedy, Stevenson, Humphrey, or Symington. Arguing with them, I was defensive about Johnson. I thought he was clearly the Best Qualified Candidate; but was he only the Best Qualified Senator? Could he win the support of liberals in his own party? His speeches were uninspiring. But so were those of Kennedy: the litany of "I think we ought to get this country moving again" was neither policy nor music. Humphrey could not quit talking; having evoked a good response with a memorable phrase, he repeated the thought four different ways until the audience squirmed with boredom. He conveyed the sense that he would rather talk than govern. Untrue, but there it was. Symington was a mystery. Everyone assumed that he would make an excellent manager in the White House, but could he excite enough people to get there? About Stevenson, I held complex and chiefly negative views. In the service, in 1953, I had run down a car's battery listening to replays of a speech he gave during his first campaign. What elegance, what simplicity, what common sense! It was different four years later, and now, in 1960, I thought him indecisive and preoccupied with the dignity of his position. He wanted the nomination to come to him, as it had in 1952. Apparently he believed he had earned it in two hopeless campaigns. But the stakes were different now, as were the issues. He would have to contend with several healthy competitors, in a climate that had changed since 1952, for a nomination that was worth having. If, on the other hand, he wanted only to be a sage, I thought he should step firmly out of the road to Los Angeles.

None of them was good enough. It came down to that. And yet any one of them might have made a good President — not a Lincoln, but one who was right most of the time, and accomplished some good for most of us. Roosevelt had done great things in office, but the figure he struck in getting there had been equally disappointing. What did it prove? That every four or eight years, Americans sighed for a savior, a very parfit knight, and failing to receive one, settled down in reasonable comfort — for a while — with the very human creature whom they had chosen to lead them.

There were no such doubts around the Johnson office. The boss had pulled the Senate Democrats together, and alone among the Democratic candidates, had negotiated on equal terms with the Republican President. His performance throughout the fifties had far exceeded that of Kennedy, Humphrey, or Symington. He knew so much about the politics of power in Washington; he must surely be able to master those of a quadrennial convention. He would "pull it off" — they did not know exactly how, any more than they knew how he had engineered the passage of beleagured legislation. But they had faith in him.

It would have to be a one-man show. There was no political staff with national experience, and no time to find one. A secretary in Walter Jenkins's office once addressed a letter to "Miss Carmine De Sapio, Tammany Hall, New York." It was caught before mailing, but it remained as a metaphor of our provincialism.

Johnson himself was a provincial. Theodore White, in his superb account of the campaign of 1960,* made the point, but I thought he got the province wrong. He said it was the South,

---

* *The Making of the President 1960* (New York: Atheneum, 1961), pp. 132–133.

and his vivid description of Johnson speaking there captures the voice that "roars like a bull's; drops to a confidential whisper as he tells grassy jokes; achieves a high-pitched Southern resonance; . . . all texts are discarded, and the flavor of the slow drawl, the snapped phrases, the smirked confidences are never recaptured in the printed text." That was Johnson's style on the Southern stump, and it was difficult to transport into other regions. Yet his true province was not the South. It was Washington. He had been there almost constantly since 1932, and even his years away from it had been spent in working for a federal program (the National Youth Administration) or in campaigning to return. Hearing the speech, watching the gestures, many people thought him "cornball," as White says. In fact Lyndon Johnson was an extremely sophisticated man, more subtle in his appreciation of power in Washington than the journalists and political opponents who derided his Texas style. In years to come, he would rage against "the Georgetown crowd," particularly those who needled him in their columns and editorials; their devotion to John Kennedy's memory made them incapable, Johnson thought, of fairness to him. But in 1940, as a second-term congressman, he had spent many black-tie evenings in Georgetown houses, making friends with William O. Douglas and Harold Ickes, with men on all sides in the wars of personality and policy that continued throughout the Roosevelt era. During the next two decades, he had known most of the major figures in the government, and in the Washington community that lives by the government — the press, the lawyers, the lobbyists. A child of the Depression and a young tribune of the New Deal, he believed that what Washington did — what the Congress passed, what the President executed — counted for more than all other cities and institutions in the land. He heard about the country and its moods through its representatives in Washington. He wanted to help the country through programs written and administered in Washington. America, to Johnson, was a vast power grid, whose dynamo was in Washington — its armature running between the Capitol and the White House.

A Southern-style Washington provincial — hanging on to his Texas mannerisms after a quarter of a century in the Capital, because they were useful back home and with old boys in the Congress who really were Southern provincials; and because he had an independent streak in him that would not be molded to suit Eastern tastes. It was that long concentration on power in Washington, at least as much as his twang, that disabled him as a national candidate against one who had sent his agents into the states to find and attract the power there.

The end came in Los Angeles as he must have known it would: beaten by handsome Jack Kennedy, the kid whom he had liked and whose grace I thought he envied, who knew so much less than he about getting things done in Washington, and so much more about the search for delegates and the building of an image. He took the Vice Presidential nomination and in the process alienated many of his supporters, to whom the Kennedys were anathema — not only Southerners, but Jews who had hated Joe Kennedy for almost two generations, and liberals who could not forget that Robert Kennedy had worked for Joe McCarthy and that his brother John had not announced his position on the censure vote. Most of the Texas staff accepted Mrs. Johnson's reason for his decision: the majority leadership was an exhausting job for one who had survived a heart attack. The Vice Presidency would give him relative peace and quiet. Others thought he had taken it out of a sense of duty: Kennedy could not beat Nixon without Johnson; to reject the offer would have been disloyal to the party.

Both explanations may have been true, both may have been rationalizations. I never knew. I believed, however, that he had accepted Kennedy's offer of the Vice Presidential nomination primarily because he did not care to be Kennedy's Senate leader. In the latter position, his role would have been to put the Kennedy program through Congress. If he had succeeded, the credit would have been Kennedy's. If he had failed, the fault would have been his. There were plenty of Kennedy advisors who would have made that clear to the press. Whether succeeding or failing, he would have had to represent the views and objections of the Southern committee chairmen to the liberals in the Administration; thus he would have remained a Southern, essentially conservative figure. It was better to be Vice President, even if the job was, as John Garner put it, not worth a bucket of warm spit, than to endure such continuous frustration. If Kennedy won, it would be, at least in part, because Johnson had carried Texas and some of the South; Johnson could make use of that; they would need him. If Kennedy lost, he would still be majority leader, with a Republican in the White House — he had seen to it that Texas law was amended to permit him to run simultaneously for reelection to the Senate and for Vice President.

Before he could run for either, he and Kennedy were required to return to the Senate for a postconvention session. This had been designed by Johnson and Rayburn in early summer, partly as pressure on the delegates, partly to give Johnson, if he could win in Los Angeles, a springboard from which to enter the climactic weeks of the campaign. It was an abysmal period. What passed the Congress had little political appeal; the major initiatives in the Democratic platform, aid to schools and medical care for the aged, were put to an early test and failed ignominiously. Nixon was already campaigning in the country. His fellow Republicans sniped away at Kennedy and made amusing references to the reversal in his and Johnson's roles; they asked Johnson if he had cleared a certain move with "your leader," with the intention of getting under his skin and provoking an embarrassing response. He knew their purpose and kept his tongue. Senator Hugh Scott, a cultivated moderate with the political instincts of a jaguar, attacked the Kennedy Foundation for transporting African refugees from Dar-es-Salaam to schools in America; it was a political move, he said, meant to preempt the Administration, which had the same thing in mind. Kennedy replied with heat. Johnson summoned a score of Democrats to the floor, and together they went after Scott. In the midst of their broadsides, I saw Johnson watching Kennedy with a kaleidoscope of emotions on his face: fondness and pride; then impatience; then a thoughtful musing, as if he had just become aware of him. Those were the emotions one might expect to see on a father's face, whose son has just announced that he intends to take over the family business. The father knows the son is right; the time has come for old techniques to give way to new; but can the son do it? What does he know about business? He has scarcely set foot in the place before now! And yet he seems very capable. But — what's to become of me?

In time it ended, this miserable session filled with partisan sandbagging. I decided that the Senate was not a good place *in* which to run for President, especially if one's intentions were known. It was at best a tolerable base *from* which to run. Kennedy flew away next day on the first leg of his cross-country campaign, relieved to be out of it. Soon thereafter Johnson left on a train through the South.

We were all requested to see him off, not at Union Station, but at his first stop in Culpepper, Virginia. It was a chilly morning. There was a crowd of several hundred, many of them old friends and employees. A country band with electric guitars mounted a baggage cart and began to play, their faces pale and puffy, most likely from a long roadhouse engagement the night before. After a while the train pulled in, gay with signs and bunting. Pretty women wearing straw hats crowded around the Johnsons on the platform of the last car. Johnson started to speak in a leisurely way. The audience was friendly, but not demonstrative. Unexpectedly the train gave a jerk and began to pull out. A look of dismay crossed Johnson's face. Clearly he had not reached this crowd. He began to shout, rapidly, that the Democrats would get things going here in Virginia, in the South, and throughout the country . . . the train was picking up speed now . . . and anyway, what's Dick Nixon ever done for Culpepper? There he stood, disappearing down the track, his question hanging in the air, his audience gaping at the spectacle and maybe wondering what anybody had ever done for Culpepper. The country band struck up "The Yellow Rose of Texas," tentatively, and then let it drop, and the crowd slowly dispersed.

That was the last time I saw him in 1960.

7

Racing in Neutral

Icy winds swept the Capitol plaza. The cardinal's interminable prayer brought God's judgment in the form of a fire on the lectern. Frost read his poem, with the wind whipping the pages, and then the new President made his speech. I thought it had been written to assuage the departing general; it called for renewed national and personal responsibility, and it was without program. Only when it announced that a new generation of Americans was taking over did it risk losing Eisenhower. The rhetoric, the ringing voice, the young leader coatless in January, were all images of a new myth — of a new Roland, his silver trumpet flashing in the sun, handsome, learned, witty, and brave. John Kennedy's ascendancy had interested many Americans in politics for the first time in years. It remained to be seen whether he could master the men in the building behind him.

I walked back into the Senate chamber, and handed Senator Mansfield a memorandum on the filibuster rule. It was like going home to mother after a weekend with a chorus girl. Outside, poetry. Inside, prose. Senators filed in: Stennis, Eastland, Ellender, Dirksen, Hickenlooper, Russell, Kerr. The same men who had been there before the New Frontier was proclaimed, and who would now determine much of its fate. Presidents have entered office with such a mandate from the people that even their dedicated opponents took care not to obstruct them openly. Kennedy had received exactly 118,574 votes more than Nixon. Whatever he was able to achieve in Congress would depend on the skillful use of his office — not on pressure from the electorate.

Mansfield had asked me to remain with the Policy Committee as its general counsel. I agreed at once. I liked him and always had. When Earle Clements was defeated and Johnson surveyed the field for a new whip, I wrote a memorandum urging Mansfield for the job. He was Western, liberal enough to satisfy the North but not so compulsive as to alienate the South. I learned that Johnson had already discussed it with him, and that Mansfield had accepted. He was not as aggressive in the role as Clements had been, but Johnson, with Baker working for him, did not need a drover. He needed a reliable man who could manage the flow of legislation in his absence.

Now, in 1961, Mansfield was the obvious choice for Democratic leader. The initiative of government had shifted to the White House, to a President who promised forward motion instead of retrenchment, progress instead of vetoes. He needed a leader in the Senate who would serve as a conduit for his programs — not an independent source of power who wished to write his own. Johnson was the ideal opposition leader; Mansfield would be the perfect team player. The Policy Committee staff and all the other paraphernalia of Johnson's leadership, swollen to serve as a shadow government in Eisenhower's time, could be reduced to a handful of mechanics: Baker to round up votes and advise Mansfield of his chances, I to prepare the program and work the floor, Pauline Moore to keep the records.

It took time for me to see that it would be this way. I was accustomed to Johnson's hyperactive leadership, his personal involvement in every bill the Senate passed, his goading and restraining, his emanations of confidence, despair, affection, and hatred that filled the air of the Capitol. That was what it was to be leader. Mansfield was an utterly different kind of man. It was against nature for him to intrude his wishes into the deliberations of committees of which he was not a member. If Mansfield threatened anyone, it was to expose him to the wrath of his colleagues — not to his own. He was not a passive man, but he was willing, as Johnson was not, to accept the consequences of other men's bad judgment. This is not to say that he was a poor politician within the Senate. On the contrary, he understood at once that the Democrats were weary of Johnson's unrelenting management of their lives. Hence his announcement, described earlier, that everyone would get home for supper and for a month in the summer.

His relations with Johnson were still good at the beginning of the new Administration. Then it was suggested that Johnson should become chairman of the Democratic caucus. There was immediate opposition to that from other members, so much that Johnson understood that his guidance was not welcome in the absence of his power. Afterwards he spent a lot of time in the presiding officer's chair, apparently in the hope of breaking the record for attendance to that menial chore of the Vice Presidency. From time to time one of his staff put out a chart showing just how much. Apparently he meant to say, you see, I'm having a fine time and outdoing all others. It was clear that he had lost his sway over the Senate. One morning, as I sat in the cloakroom with several senators, he came in from the chamber — slowly, seemingly without purpose except to chat. In previous years, his entrance had galvanized those who sat about talking or reading the paper. They had known that he wanted something, their votes or their assistance in committee, their commitment to stand fast or yield in conference with the House. Now he was just a figure around the Senate, with even less power and authority than theirs. They were courteous, but cool. No one stood up, no one asked him to sit down, the desultory conversations resumed. Perhaps there was malice in that; you've made me uncomfortable, Lyndon, now you feel some discomfort yourself. But the lesson I learned — one of the oldest lessons of American government — was that the Vice Presidency is empty of power.

Johnson is supposed to have said, upon accepting the nomination in Los Angeles, that "power is where power goes." Not so, if it goes into the Vice Presidency.

As usual, the Senate began the new Congress with a fight over Rule 22 — the cloture provision that requires the votes of two-thirds of the Senate to shut off debate. Vice President Nixon, in his last ruling before turning over the chair to Johnson, had suggested that the Senate could adopt new rules at the beginning of each Congress without regard to the two-thirds requirement. This had inflamed the Southerners, who insisted at length that the Senate, unlike the House, was a continuing body, whose rules continued with it. Liberals, encouraged by Nixon's ruling, sought to cut off debate at once, and failing that, to secure an amendment to the old rule providing for cloture by majority vote. Rather than encumber the new Administration with a donnybrook at the outset, the argument was deferred until later in the session.

The cloture rule raised several discreet but related questions, of great interest to lawyers like Ervin and Javits. Was Nixon right, and could the Senate, acting under the constitutional authority given each house to "make its own rules," escape bondage to the old cloture rule for an undetermined period in each new Congress? Were the Southerners and Westerners right in arguing that, since at any moment two-thirds of the senators were duly sworn and serving, the Senate was a continuum, its rules carrying over from Congress to Congress without a break, binding the new as they did the old, until changed in accordance with the rules themselves? Passing to the merits, was it right to give a simple majority the power to shut off debate? What kind of institution was the Senate supposed to be? How valid was the "cooling-off" argument — that senators, exercising the right to speak indefinitely, often prevented action on ill-considered legislation? Acknowledging that unlimited debate had been abused, wasn't it better to retain it for an emergency? If the country really cared for action, wouldn't two-thirds of the members vote to close debate? On violently controversial matters, didn't it make political sense to force a compromise through the threat of prolonged debate, so that the losing region or interest group was not driven to an extreme response? If cloture by a simple majority was too easy, what was the right requirement? Three-fifths? Two-thirds?

Three-fifths — sixty — seemed about right to me. It had a congressional feel to it. Every year Lister Hill took his enormous appropriations bill for health research into conference with the House. It required very little higher mathematics to reach a compromise, viz.: Item four in disagreement, National Heart Institute. Senate figure, $100 million. House figure, $80 million. Conference figure, $90 million. The same could be done with the number required for cloture. Two-thirds was reactionary. Half was radical. Three-fifths was senatorial.

When the debate resumed in late summer, I wrote a speech for Mansfield of which I was very proud. I quoted Judge Learned Hand's definition in *The Spirit of Liberty*, of "the qualities that clear the path toward truth: skepticism, tolerance, discrimination, urbanity, some — but not too much — reserve toward change, insistence upon proportion, and above all, humility before the vast unknown."

At its best moments the Senate had demonstrated those qualities. Mansfield would uphold any tradition which furthered them. Full debate was such a tradition. "Whenever a majority, incensed by a public wrong or driven by emergency, seeks to affect the lives of our people by precipitate action, a minority of Senators may rise to expose the measure on this Floor — at length. And this right of the minority is not conditioned on the 'correctness' of its view in the eyes of the majority, or even in the eye of history. It is so vital to the responsibilities of this body that few men, conscious that matters of ultimate consequence to the people *they* represent may one day be similarly challenged, have seriously disputed its wisdom." Hence "I could not endorse majority cloture."

But freedom of debate was subject to abuse. "No Senator or group of Senators has the 'right' unconscionably to prevent this body from doing the nation's business." It was difficult to say where the point of abuse lay; "I might define as 'intractability' what others would call the necessary defense of human rights." Most would agree, however, "that a time does come when the arguments, although relatively germane, have been repeated sufficiently to be heard by those who have ears to hear; when physical exhaustion, and not intellectual conversion, is the apparent goal of the debate; when privileges have been fairly extended to those seeking delay, and when the rights of those seeking passage must also be weighed in the balance. At such a time, it should be within the power of a substantial majority of the Senate to bring debate to an end, and to vote the matter up or down." Three-fifths was a reasonable coefficient of a "substantial" majority.

When Mansfield sat down, Johnson and Russell came by to congratulate him. Russell said he thought it was one of the better speeches he had heard in defense of the present rule. I remonstrated and urged him to read the second half of it again; but then it struck me that I had, in fact, greater sympathy for the moderating role of the Senate than for its conversion into a forum for quick action. Here again, I was thinking of the Senate under the spur of Johnson's leadership. If legislation needed desperately to be passed, he saw to it that it was passed. If there was great moral and political force behind a measure, but no deadline by which it must be adopted — the Civil Rights Act of 1957 was a good example — he set about to arrange the necessary compromises. Later, during his Presidency, the Senate would actually vote cloture, two-thirds requirement and all, and pass much stronger civil rights laws. The rule was an impediment, an annoyance, a constant barrier in the way of activists. But it was not impassable; and it could also be, as Morse, Proxmire, and Clark discovered, a liberal defense against bad laws. It would be better, I thought, if it took something less than twice as many senators to obtain a vote as it took to block one. But it was unlikely that John Kennedy's legislative program would fail because stopping a filibuster required sixty-seven, instead of sixty "ayes."

Debates on the Senate rules, particularly when they involved the "continuing-body" question, often seemed as remote as arguments about transubstantiation. But many men took them with bitter seriousness. In 1963, Joe Rauh and several of his fellow lobbyists for civil rights demanded of Vice President Johnson that he summarily cut off debate on the filibuster rule and call for a vote. I sent Johnson a memorandum arguing that he had no right to do that; he was not the leader of a junta, but the presiding officer of a body in which he had no vote, except in case of a tie; if he intervened on the theory that he was empowered by his interpretation of the Constitution to do so, I thought Russell, old as he was, might climb right over Charlie Watkins's wispy head and seek to throttle him. The Senate did not operate free-form, except by unanimous consent. Johnson needed to be told none of this, but he made use of the metaphors, usually prefaced by "my lawyer tells me . . ." Joe Rauh promptly accused him of siding with the racists.

In the end, the argument was academic, if emotional. It required only thirty-four men to resist cloture on the motion to cut off debate on the motion to change the cloture rule. The Southerners, the conservative Republicans, and a number of Western Democrats were more than enough for that.

Each weekday morning, Capitol guides passed by outside my office, lecturing to packs of tourists on the history of the building. Every guide had a spiel, and repeated it with little variation to visiting crowds of teachers, bus-loads of union men, and gum-chewing, chubby girls in curlers and tight shorts who invested the galleries in summer. I liked especially the routine of a thin-faced man whose hard, driving voice sounded as if it had been trained in a carnival. Sometimes I got up and joined his audience, and more than once I heard him say — as we stopped to contemplate the birds, animals, and airplanes with which the halls of the Senate wing are painted — "Art critics have told me, folks, that the paintings on this wall may be favorably compared to the works of the Eyetalian master Michelangelo."

There was similar hyperbole in the way apologists for the new Administration described the 1961 legislative program. In truth it was not a bad program; it had the great virtue of familiarity; but after Kennedy's high C at the inauguration, it seemed pedestrian. Manpower training; aid to education; increased coverage under the minimum wage; Medicare; aid to depressed areas. Eisenhower's vetoes had left the Democrats a ready-made list of bills. There was nothing remarkable about proposing them again. Kennedy was "getting the country moving" by sending back to Congress legislation that had been debated many times, in some cases for decades. The composition of Congress had not changed much, surely not enough to assure the success of what had failed before; the only difference was that someone friendly to the legislation now sat in the White House and urged its enactment in better language than we had heard in the fifties. Such were the innovations of the New Frontier, as seen from Capitol Hill.

Some of the bills passed, though after so many compromises that liberals were dismayed. Tom Wicker has written of the early struggles in the House,* in which misjudgment and underestimation of conservative power broke the new Administration's thrust almost before it began. I thought it curious that a group of *wunderkind*, who had captured the nomination against so many entrenched professionals, could not outmaneuver the unsophisticated men of Congress. But this was the obverse of Kennedy's dedication to national, as against congressional politics. He had

---
* *JFK and LBJ* (New York: Morrow, 1968).

spent a dozen years on the Hill, and so he was accustomed to trading; but he had little taste for the mundane courtship by which Presidents succeed with Congresses—for the attention to minutiae, the routine indulgences, the tolerance for banalities that pass for opinions. Some of his staff members celebrated that, and made him appear nobly beleaguered, a prince among merchants; others, like Larry O'Brien, tried to master a world in which power inhered in position and personality, and not in masses of votes. Perhaps the chief problem was that throughout his years in Congress, Kennedy had relied (as had most of his colleagues) on Sam Rayburn and Lyndon Johnson to negotiate with the conservatives for such progress as could be made. Rayburn died within a year of Kennedy's accession to the White House. Johnson, while Vice President, was rarely asked to transact legislative business for the Administration.

There were plenty of reasons for that. Fear that he might seek to dominate the new Administration's legislative politics, by emerging as the vital intermediary between White House liberals and Senate conservatives. Sensitivity to Mansfield's feelings if Johnson became *de jure* leader of the Senate Democrats. Apprehension that those who had begun to attack Johnson in the previous Congress — Proxmire, Clark, Pat McNamara — and the organizations which supported them, the UAW and ADA, would turn their fire on the President if he yielded his legislative responsibilities to the king of the old regime. All good reasons, but the result was that Kennedy found himself, as Johnson said, with the minnows, and with a Senate leader — Mansfield — whose deference to the Senate's prerogatives made him reluctant to use his position as a compelling force for Kennedy's program. Some of the Johnson staff argued that the President was only hurting himself by disarming the Vice President in a field of which he was the undisputed master. But Kennedy did not disarm Johnson. There were no Vice Presidential powers of which he might have been deprived. He simply chose not to court trouble by vesting in Johnson responsibilities which Vice Presidents had rarely, if ever, borne.

Johnson tried to keep busy, and as that is usually easy for any official in government or business, he succeeded. There were advisory commissions whose intelligent, futile recommendations should be amended or approved. There were *ex officio* duties to perform; I once met him on the elevator as he returned from a meeting of the Smithsonian Board, where he had found a discussion of the National Zoo — the Zoo! Johnson! — fascinating.

There were speeches to be made, often as a substitute for the President; foreign trips to be taken, White House meetings to be attended. I learned very little about the substance of those meetings, though I caught some of their emotional fallout. In 1962 and 1963, Johnson occasionally complained about the President's failure, and that of his brother and staff, to come to grips with the congressional problem; and he reported (what I also heard from my father in Texas) the disaffection of middle-class Democrats in the country, who were put off by stories of high living, midnight plunges into the pool at Robert Kennedy's home in Virginia, and so forth. But he reserved such comments, at least in my hearing, for private sessions around his chair on the Senate rostrum. And often he would conclude them with an expression of real concern for the President's burdens. One day I sat beside him and listened as several senators pontificated on the latest foreign crisis. "None of them knows how hard it is," he said. "That one there" — pointing to a particularly voluble and self-assured member — "would have a fit if he had to do more than talk, if he had to decide."

He was restive in his no-man's-land. He resented his powerlessness and the condescension or cool hostility with which several members of the Kennedy entourage — not including the President himself — treated him. But he was gaining a deeper appreciation of the pressures on the Executive, and in public speeches, as in conversations with journalists, he was strictly faithful.

When I saw people from the Administration, it was usually in Mansfield's office near the Senate floor, and almost always in an atmosphere of crisis. Some major element of Kennedy's program was in trouble, and the first fact to be determined was whether its prospects were hopeless, or only doubtful. The Kennedy men had discussed language changes with senior committee members, and advised us which were acceptable and which would gut the bill. Baker estimated votes, relying heavily on conversations with a few whales; I suggested amendments and added whatever intelligence I had picked up in the cloakroom, on the floor, or from committee staffs. There were calls to check facts with departments downtown, and sometimes to Kennedy himself, to determine the degree of his interest.

These early meetings were largely speculative. Sometimes a few senators and government experts would join us to talk about the merits of what the Administration proposed. But as the vote came closer, there was very little philosophizing about "ideal" legislation. We were concerned with winning the support of particular men on the issue as it emerged. Senator A might come with us, if Senator B, an admired friend, could be persuaded to talk to him. Senator C wanted a major project out of Chairman D's committee; maybe D, a supporter of our bill, would release it in exchange for C's commitment. Senator E might be reached through people in his home state. If Senator F could not vote with us on final passage, could he support us on key amendments? Could G take a trip? Would the President call Senator H? I had an almost mystical faith in Presidential intervention, having seen it work in several cases; O'Brien and his assistants were inclined to conserve his efforts, perhaps believing that his influence would be spoiled by overuse — perhaps only reluctant to impose chores upon him with which they knew he was impatient.

Often we failed. We met for several evenings in 1962, trying to work out, with O'Brien, Burke Marshall, Nick Katzenbach, and Harold Reis, the language of a bill establishing that persons with a sixth-grade education met literacy test standards for voting. This was a much simpler proposal than those the Congress had adopted in 1957 and 1960, and it gave promise of being more effective. But because it invaded, to some degree, the states' constitutional powers to set voter qualifications, it gave those whose enthusiasm for civil rights had never been very great a highminded excuse for opposing it. (With the departure of Eisenhower, Republican interest in the black vote had waned, and the Kennedy people seemed unwilling to push in their stack behind new civil rights laws. Indeed, Kennedy's success among Negroes in 1960 had surprised me. He had never been outspoken about civil rights, and Nixon, with his progressive rulings during the filibuster debates and his chairmanship of a government fair-employment committee, was at least an equal friend to black aspirations. A bright Negro woman, teaching at Howard University, told me I had missed the point. "Those cats," she said, meaning younger black voters, "will come out of the house on election morning, and say, 'Man, that Jack Kennedy's got more bread than anybody. If I vote for him, when he's President, he's going to buy me a big lavender Cadillac.' Nixon can't do that." She may have been right: many Negroes may have inferred that Kennedy's wealth and style would translate into liberality toward their needs. But the last-minute suggestion that the Kennedys should seek the release of Martin Luther King from jail in Georgia must have been equally important. It was proposed by Harris Wofford — an imaginative social activist with whom I had argued heatedly during the preconvention campaign, and who was entitled, by an irony of Presidential politics, to share with Johnson some of the credit for Kennedy's victory.)

The literacy-test ran into a filibuster, and Mansfield was unwilling to force the Senate into round-the-clock sessions in order to break it. Johnson thought that was a mistake. He had tried it in 1960, and Congress had passed a civil rights bill. Q.E.D. There was some question about the cause and effect, however; with an election coming up that year, both parties — and the Democratic leader — needed to get something through. There was no such pressure in 1962. In any event, the sheer brutality of all-night sessions — in which the aim of each side was simply to exhaust the physical stamina of the other — was distasteful to Mansfield, as it was to most senators. I could not imagine Mansfield slipping into the chamber at midnight, as I had seen Johnson do, to confront Russell emerging from another door, both of them on the alert for parliamentary tricks.

Whether civil rights bills might have fared better in Congress if the Administration had put its full weight behind them is an open question. But there is no doubt that neither the President nor the Attorney General spent much political capital on them. Rumors circulated that Robert Kennedy had "made a deal" with Eastland: approve our judicial appointments and we'll lay off civil rights. A formal agreement seemed most unlikely. Yet there was a feeling, in the Congress, that the Administration considered its principal obligations satisfied upon sending up legislation and an accompanying message. And as all was political-rhetorical, there was no inconsistency in sponsoring a comprehensive bill in 1963, after failing to secure a much more limited voting law in 1962. The hope that Congress, having declined to protect Negroes against the misuse of literacy tests in federal elections, would insist upon equal treatment in private hotels and restaurants seemed preposterous. I sat beside Johnson as he presided over the Senate soon after the bill was introduced. "Not a chance," he said. "And yet, you know, it really ought to pass. I was talking to some of them [the Southerners] about my cook. I said she and her husband had driven my car down through Alabama and Mississippi and Louisiana on their way to the ranch.

And when they got hungry, what would they do? Here were these two educated black people, driving the car of the Vice President of the United States down through the South, and when they wanted to eat they had to stop at one of those country grocery stores and buy 'em some beans and Vienna sausage. And when they had to go, they would go by the side of the road. Two people who worked for the Vice President of the United States, peeing in a ditch. I said, that's not right. It ought not to be that way. One of them looked at me and then down at his shoes and stammered out, 'Well, Lyndon, our people will need a lot of time to make these changes,' or something like that. This bill ought to pass, but there's not a chance."

True enough, in 1963. By 1964 the world had turned around, and a public accommodations bill did pass. It was sufficiently observed that, at least in the urban South, Negroes were no longer forced to travel like refugees in their own country.

An aid-to-education bill passed the Senate, brilliantly guided by Wayne Morse. Given that responsibility, he was *pari passu* transformed from an irritating, often impractical critic to a resourceful politician. He beat back an effort by Thurmond to prohibit the withholding of funds from segregated school districts, and then, determined to leave the race issue thoroughly ambiguous, defeated a Powell-type amendment which would have imposed a strict requirement to desegregate. The latter attracted a number of conservative votes, as it always did — spoiler votes, intended to provoke a filibuster which would defeat the underlying bill. Goldwater proposed loans to private schools, and many liberal senators from heavily Catholic areas supported him. Morse, fearful of the constitutional issue, resisted and won. The bill went to the House suffused with triumph and hope. I thought the millennium had arrived. We were to have aid to education. We had prevailed on what I thought were the two principal issues involved, states' rights and race.

But there was a third issue, to which, as a Protestant Southerner, I was blind. Bishops of the Roman Catholic Church lashed out at the bill because it failed to give any relief to parochial schools. Cardinal Spellman would not have it. That was enough to persuade an otherwise tractable New Yorker, Congressman Delaney, to join with Howard Smith and his fellow conservatives in killing the measure in the Rules Committee. Aid to education could not pass until some form of aid was provided the Catholics. Kennedy apparently believed that, as the nation's first Catholic President, he could not propose it. It remained for Johnson to work out a formula by which parochial schools might receive public funds. That freed the big-city delegates to support it, and it became law. The lesson seemed to be that reasonable things could be done best by those whose heritage required that they oppose them. Johnson, a Southerner, could get away with advocating civil rights. As a Protestant, he could urge help to the Catholic schools. Eisenhower, a general and a member of the Taft-McCarthy party, could recommend peaceful coexistence with Russian Communists. As the leader of America's business party, his antitrust chief could be active in opposing the combinations of great industry. Where there was no such natural camouflage for change, it was best to construct one. Kennedy's hard line on Cuba, and his dedication to counterinsurgency and the Green Berets, offset his nuclear testing agreement with the Russians; Johnson was to turn out the lights in the White House, and pay exaggerated attention to Harry Byrd, before setting the country on a course of heavy public spending.

A trade bill passed the Congress. Its purpose was to give the President flexibility in adjusting tariffs, so that America might deal effectively with the emerging European Common Market. Everyone—except Molly Malone and a few protectionist lobbies — deferred to the principle of free international trade; but the principle had as many exceptions as there were industries challenged by cheaper foreign goods. The South was the traditional bastion of free trade, out of its concern for the flow of cotton exports. Asian competition changed that, and the Administration wisely secured an agreement in Geneva limiting imports of cotton textiles before seeking a general law. There were other endangered species — chemicals, rubber shoes and boots, carpets, watches, a whole gamut of industries and workers — which needed attention and got it. Peter Jones, a lively ex–Wall Street lawyer with the convictions of a Missouri Democrat, spoke to crowds of senators in Mansfield's office, assuring them that their concerns were understood by those who would negotiate for us with the Europeans. A Philadelphia banker came down to organize friendly industries into a coherent political force. Bright men like Monroney's Tom Finney and Mike Rashish, an economist with an amused, spacious mind, provided the substantive arguments. Nothing would have happened, however, without Senator Kerr. I had no idea why he had chosen to lead the fight. I had heard a good story about Kennedy's bargaining with Kerr over the Administration's tax bill, which had been bottled up in the Finance Committee. The President, so the story went, made the case for an investment incentive, as a means of bringing the country out of a recession. Kerr responded by asking why the Budget Bureau opposed his Arkansas River project. So it went, tax bill versus Oklahoma pork. At last Kerr put it simply: he could not imagine releasing the one without assurances about the other. Kennedy smiled and said, "You know, Bob, I never really understood that Arkansas River bill before today." Whether Kerr received a similar tribute of danegeld before agreeing to manage the trade bill, I never knew. But the results were equally dramatic. He mastered its intricacies and outargued, when he did not simply intimidate, those who sought to limit the President's discretion at Geneva.

(Friendship also played a great part in passing a good trade bill. A "peril-point" amendment, which would have vitiated much of the bill's purpose, came within a hair of adoption. The textile industry supported it, and Senator Everett Jordan, himself a mill owner, first voted for, and then against it. Afterwards Peter Jones thanked him and began to discuss the dangers of the amendment. "I didn't do it because of the dangers, Peter," Jordan said. "I did it for Luther" — Luther Hodges, his fellow North Carolinian and the Secretary of Commerce, whom Kennedy had charged with responsibility for getting the bill through.)

A manpower training program passed the Congress. So did a farm subsidy bill, heralded as an analogue of the "new economics" as practiced in the White House. Defense spending rose to record levels, though the missile gap of which Kennedy had warned in the campaign proved to be nonexistent. Foreign aid was reorganized, as it had been many times since 1947. The Administration undertook two new programs on the "soft" side of foreign policy: the Arms Control and Disarmament Agency, and the Peace Corps. Humphrey was their spiritual father and managed both on the floor. He had become the Democratic whip, and when emotionally committed, as he was to these measures, he was exciting to watch. All his great energy and goodwill were channeled into hustling votes, amending, rewriting, yielding on one point to gain support on another. Many people thought he "just talked" for the pleasure of exercising his glands, and sometimes I thought so too; but when he had a specific purpose in mind — and (like Morse) when he bore the main responsibility for achieving it — he was extremely effective.

Other useful bills passed the Congress. But the big ones did not: civil rights, aid to education, medical care for the aged, a massive effort to stop the decay of the cities, protection of the environment. I grew restless. I did not wish to spend my life as a legislative mechanic, tinkering with bills whose effect I would never see. The glamour of the Senate was fading. The old whales were not as active as they had once been, and new prospects were slow in developing. Of those who had entered the Senate after 1956, I thought only two — Eugene McCarthy and Edmund

Muskie — were likely to enter the "club" of the Senate powers, and said as much in a university speech in 1961. How wrong I was! Both had claims on the Senate's attention. McCarthy was the wittiest man in Congress. He was a realist in dealing with the prevailing congressional system, and still he conveyed the impression of one who would prefer a better system if it were available. Muskie was easy, but very straight; his integrity and careful intelligence were widely admired. Both often voted with the club on critical issues. McCarthy was regarded as "safe" in the Finance Committee, Muskie had no apparent desire to embarrass anyone. Both understood the Congress.

But neither seemed willing to make an ultimate commitment to it. Neither was driven to lead a faction, much less the Senate itself. McCarthy spent a lot of time in the Senate restaurant, delivering bons mots about the political situation to infatuated reporters; Muskie became an expert in such arcane matters as intergovernmental relations and water pollution. In time, both men would become nationally famous, even household words. But neither would become a formidable Senate power, whom other senators must propitiate. I thought of Humphrey, sweating and smiling his way to an agreement upstairs, while McCarthy concentrated on what Hesse calls "feuilleton," absorbing trivia, in the first-floor coffee shop. If one were writing a political column, there was no doubt about which Minnesota senator one would seek out. But if one were a Minnesotan, or an outlander interested in liberal legislation, one would surely go to Humphrey. I thought something more would come of Muskie. How much, and why, I did not foresee.

Esquire did a story called "Who's Minding the Country." Gene Lichtenstein, a friend of many social evenings, wrote it, and his choice of eight young men who qualified for the title suggested much about New York political journalism — idiosyncratic, but not to be challenged by readers (or editors) who knew little about Washington. Baker and I represented the Congress. Peter

Jones was included, as was Bill Moyers—an extraordinary man whom I had just come to know, though he had been associated with Johnson almost as long as I had. All of us were involved in useful work, but with the Congress in the doldrums, I thought some of the young tyros whom Kennedy had attracted to Washington, especially to Defense, Justice, and State, were more likely "minding the country" than were Baker and I.

Anyway, Baker was on the verge of serious legal trouble. He had thought about quitting the Senate in order to devote more time to his business affairs. Johnson told him he should; Kerr and Mansfield both said no — he had become indispensable to them, and to the Senate itself. When his troubles came crashing down upon him, not many senators rose to defend him, or even to acknowledge his ubiquitous assistance. Morse did, though Baker had often rounded up votes against him. For most of the others, he was too hot. The press usually described him as "Johnson's protégé." But he was also Kerr's, and Mansfield's, and a score of others'. Most of all, he was the raffish projection of a dream deriving from his friends Smathers and Kennedy. In the dream he was, as they were, suave, rich, influential, and progressive. Neither Johnson nor Mansfield, I believe, knew much about his enterprises. No doubt they should have tried to know; politicians are willfully obtuse about such things where a valuable friend is involved. I had heard rumors about him, but I was no less determined to be ignorant, especially as the rumors came from people — on his own staff and Johnson's — who were jealous of him.

Baker's problems were symptomatic of a general malaise. In the late summer of 1963, Johnson had grown heavy and looked miserable. The Administration's program was moribund. If Kennedy hoped, as Arthur Schlesinger wrote,* to "redeem American politics by releasing American life from its various bondages to orthodoxy," he was light-years away from achieving it.

One day, as I sat fiddling with an unpromising tally sheet, Sec-

---

* *A Thousand Days* (Boston: Houghton Mifflin, 1965), p. 115.

retary of the Army Cyrus Vance called to ask whether I would like to work in his office at the Pentagon. I had known and admired Cy Vance since Johnson's hearings on the space program, in 1957, during which I had worked for him and his partner, Edwin Weisl. I had never heard of the job he described — "Deputy Under Secretary of the Army for International Affairs." It had to do with the Panama Canal Zone, Okinawa, and in some ambiguous way with the Special Forces. It was obscure, but it was different from handling a legislative program that had become almost inconsequential. I thought it would be fine to manage an office in the Pentagon, no matter how small, and so to become part of the virile community of effective men whom Robert McNamara had attracted there. But it meant moving from a situation in which I felt secure, confident, and widely known, to near anonymity. I thought it wise to seek Johnson's advice.

I found him in his office in mid-afternoon. When I explained Vance's offer, he replied firmly that I should not accept it. I had a place here, useful to Mansfield and the Senate Democrats, and with Baker's problems mounting I would find it increasingly important to them, and satisfying to myself. I complained about the tedium of the place during the past year. I thought I had learned all that I was likely to learn from it. It was time to explore something new.

As I talked, his heavy eyes narrowed, and he sank farther into his chair. I thought he was going to sleep. I stopped, and we sat in silence for a minute. Suddenly he asked me, his eyes still low, "What do you *want?*" I knew what he meant. Not which do you choose between what is offered you, between A and B, but what do you want, what are you after?

I did not know. In the winter of 1960, I had visited the transition headquarters of the new Administration, and tentatively announced to my friend Ralph Dungan that I might be interested in leaving the Hill. Fine, he said, what do you want? I had hoped he might say, what about doing this, or that? Very sensibly, as I had no experience as an administrator, nor any background as a specialist, he left the choice to me. And I didn't know.

Johnson would have been clear about it if someone had put the same question to him. Power. One could not say such a thing, of course, even to oneself. One had to clothe it with fine purposes. In Johnson's case, I believe it was purposeful, to a considerable degree. He really did want to use power to improve the way people lived. And of course he also wanted it for itself.

In the end, I replied tactically, not with the seriousness his question demanded. I wanted to run an executive office, to be responsible for decisions, and so on. He said he understood. If that was what I wanted, so be it. I had the feeling that he did not wish to argue. I was, after all, no longer necessary to him; if I left, that was Mansfield's problem.

During the next few weeks I thought a lot about the Senate, and what I had learned in the past seven years.

I had come to few conclusions about the institutional issues that had always vexed the political scientists. I did not even know whether the idea of the Senate made sense — two members from every state, regardless of population, some of them representing deserts and plains dissected by imaginary lines. I knew the faults of the seniority system, but no alternative gave me confidence that it would be an improvement. Some Americans were better treated than others because the senators who spoke for them were more powerful, or energetic, or simply better liked; I knew no way to equalize that.

I had radically changed my mind about senators as a group. They were, on the whole, much more intelligent than I had expected them to be. And they were at least as ethical as most private citizens, if one considers the pressures on them; certainly as ethical as most of the doctors, lawyers, social workers, students, and businessmen whom I had known. They were (again, generalizing) also more interesting.

That had much to do with the questions they faced — most of them important to their fellow citizens, few of them susceptible of being answered with assurance. The least interesting members were those "men of conviction" who told you what was right almost before the question was asked. I liked best those who troubled over the merits of issues, and over the political consequences of voting one way or the other. Should public spending be increased in a recession, or taxes cut? Should a minimum wage be required for agricultural workers, or would that, together with mechanization, drive people off the farm? Should vast quantities of drugs and medicines be shipped to India, as Humphrey wanted, or as Fulbright said, would cutting the death rate compound the Indian population problem, and in the absence of economic development, make its survival impossible? As Congressman Clem Miller had written, one could not vote "yes, but" or "no, but" about such things, but yes or no. It was the pressure to decide ambivalent questions that gave the most interesting men the saving vulnerability by which they became more than merely smooth and successful.

I thought of the constant struggle between personality and issues — how some men could not pass a resolution honoring Mother's Day, while others had an almost automatic majority behind them on most issues. As in most human situations, relationships counted as much as facts and opinions.

I thought of the closing nights of each Congress, when the liquor flowed and we waited through long hours for a House-Senate conference committee to resolve its differences. Johnson would motion up an impossibly controversial bill to kill time. Once it was the Lake Michigan water diversion bill, meant to let Chicago clean its river by tapping the lake; the other littoral states thought it would hurt shipping by reducing the lake's water level, and filibustered it. Wisconsin's Proxmire began reading a thousand-page hearing record. A Republican, in his cups, interrupted him. "How long Sen'tor going talk?" "Oh," Proxmire said. "I think the Senate should have the full benefit of this record . . ." "Well, Sen'tor needs me for anything, number's Republic 7–50 . . ." The last digits were lost in a whoop of laughter. Soon it was over, and after the ritual motions. the Senate quit for the year. Johnson stood by his desk, accepting praise, and Frank Lausche came up and hugged him, his frizzled hair tickling Johnson's chin until Johnson patted it down with one hand, forbearing the embrace, while with his other he waved to someone over Lausche's head.

I thought of veteran staff members, sleepily piling out of the Capitol into the dawn air; and of reporters, their *Front Page* cynicism melted away in weariness, waiting to ask the last inevitable questions about how productive or "political" the session had been. I thought of Mansfield, pipe in mouth, nodding and answering briefly before walking into the faint morning light, and of Humphrey, standing expansively on the steps, calling to friends, still gregarious, marking the hour.

It was like a second home. But I was ready to leave it. The time was early fall, 1963.

8
Army and State

You have this dacron suit on, a blue shirt and a striped tie, and you are walking down a long corridor on both sides of which are paintings of furious battles, or of men waiting for battle. You pass a display of streamers, each one bearing the name of a famous military campaign. Beyond, under glass, are the medals — the Silver Star, the Distinguished Service Cross, and depending from a pale blue ribbon, the Medal of Honor. Two generals, their tunics covered with ribbons and paratroop wings, come out of an office and head your way for lunch. A colonel, no less adorned, runs up behind you and reminds you, sir, that you have a two o'clock meeting, and asks if you have any instructions. You think of something and he says yes, sir, it will be done, and you know it will. Then you turn left off the "E" ring, the outermost ring of the Pentagon, and duck into a superb little restaurant, the General Officers' Mess Number One.

Twelve years ago you were a corporal in the Air Force. You rarely saw a general; majors had the power to terrify you; you lived in fear of a sergeant finding your barracks in disorder. Now you are sitting across from a major general who survived the Bataan Death March. You make conversation. To him, you are a young political appointee whom his sense of discipline and self-preservation requires that he treat with outward respect. To you, he embodies the military virtues of stamina, courage, allegiance to country. His interests appear to be almost entirely professional. But then another general joins the table, and the two of them laugh about an evening of hard drinking at the Army-Navy Club, and a bad round of golf the next morning. You leave a question about Bataan hanging in the air.

How many in the civilian secretariat felt this disparity between their own military careers and those of the men over whom they had final authority, I never knew. But for a while it affected me profoundly, and I thought it had great significance for the principle of civilian supremacy. It seemed unlikely that former corporals and lieutenants would overrule generals in matters of "Army policy" — that men who had commanded brigades in combat would finally yield to those who had worried about turning the wrong way on a drill field.

Civilian specialists were another breed altogether. Even national heroes were no match for economists and statisticians when it came to planning for a modern military force. Lawyers and politicians had no such intimidating expertise.

In time, as I learned my way around the Pentagon, the disparity became less important to me. Everyone had a job to do. The generals commanded large staffs, "spoke up for the Army's interests," and presented detailed papers to the lawyers. The lawyers often adopted the generals' positions, with amendments; bargained for them with civilians representing other services, and with the McNamara staff; and occasionally made "political judgments" — that is, decided not to do something the generals thought it necessary to do, but which would, the lawyers believed, stir up the Congress, the press, or the public.

In my office were six colonels, each a decorated veteran of the Second War. In peacetime they had commanded armored units or infantry battalions in those steaming Georgia and Texas camps where millions of Northern conscripts had learned to hate the South. Most of them were products of West Point; most had done graduate work in international affairs, obtaining the M.A.

degrees which, they hoped, would lead to advancement in the new army. Each wished to be a general. Assignment to my office — far from the shooting army or from talk about logistics, force levels, and forward strategy — would not help them in that endeavor. Nevertheless they were loyal to their tasks, and superbly competent; if they resented the assignment, they did not show it. They mastered policy in detail. They stood straight. They were unfailingly responsible. If I could have promoted them all to brigadier, I would have done it. But their fates were in the hands of a promotion board, whose mysterious decisions were impenetrable by civilians.

Their job, and mine, was to help the Secretary of the Army administer the Panama Canal Zone and Okinawa. The Army had run the canal since its opening in 1914, primarily because it was a civil works project; responsibility for Okinawa, a prize of the war against Japan, had been delegated by the Secretary of Defense. The problems I encountered were similar to those of a military government, with the important exception that in the Canal Zone the intransigent population was American.

Soon after I settled in the Pentagon, I flew down to the Zone on an orientation tour. I put up in the Tivoli Hotel, a well-preserved, wickery old outpost of the colonial past. I saw the thing itself, the great canal, and marveled at the liquid simplicity of its gears and gauges — Northern technology triumphant in the jungle, kept running by Northern engineers, protected by Northern arms. I came to know General Robert Fleming, governor of the Zone, a small, combative man who had become friendly with the Panamanians and was correspondingly mistrusted by the resident Americans. The latter — known as "Zonians" — were mostly craftsmen and technicians, proud of their skills, living standards, and citizenship. Like the English of the Indian Empire, they were more aggressively patriotic than their countrymen back home. Fleming had worked to increase the number of Panamanians holding desirable jobs in the Zone. That was established

American policy, but as he was its local administrator, he became the target of contumely. A minor official wrote,

> *He dampens civic powder,*
> *Muzzles Union guns,*
> *Recruits the foreign nationals,*
> *Rejects the native sons* °

and was fired for his trouble. The official became a hero among the Zonians, and inspired caterwauls of sympathy from the only congressman who thought continuously about the canal — Representative Daniel Flood of Pennsylvania. Flood was an extravagant personality whose spiky moustache seemed to have been patterned after those on the French engineers who failed at the Isthmus in the nineteenth century. Ordinarily he voted with the liberals on domestic issues, but he held passionate opinions about American hegemony in the Canal Zone, and harassed the Army each time it moved to accommodate the Panamanians. The Army did not retreat before him, but advanced more slowly because of him. Such is the power of a single man obsessed with an idea.

The Zone was clean and tidy, an American army town in the tropics. Its housewives were occupied with fighting off mildew, its men with keeping the vital locks in service. There were supermarkets and milkshakes. There was no need to cross over into Panama City or Colón, and some of the Zonians never did, except to take a family member to the airport for a trip to the states. Others, more adventurous, went up-country into the cool green mountains near the Costa Rican border. There they made friends with the Swiss, Germans, and English who grew coffee and bred cattle and lived in chalets beneath the constantly dripping oaks and alders.

That was a different Panama. What one usually saw of the

° From "In Canal Waters," by A. C. Payne, printed in the *Congressional Record* (1964), p. 3919.

country was its capital city, old, tired, squalid under gray clouds and sweltering heat. Most of its people were crowded into the narrow streets of a Spanish entrepôt. The rest lived in tall, peeling apartment houses, or in villas along the Pacific. Wealthy families were interlocked by marriage, and together they controlled banking, trade, television, and the numberless radio stations that blared in every taxi and cantina. There was little apparent sense of social responsibility among them. When they were politically pressed, it was easy to finger the United States as the sole cause of Panama's trouble — Panama's share of the tolls was insufficient (true), its people were denied the best jobs in the Zone (true again), America's dominion was a living insult to Panama's honor. It was rarely acknowledged that one-fifth of Panama's GNP derived from employment in the Zone and services supplied to it — or that the *oligarchia* had always been insufficiently sensitive to the needs of the poor.

On the Atlantic side at Colón, the scene was even more depressing. Two blocks from the Zone's efficient wharves were slums that sank the heart. East Indians owned the shops where tourists on cruise bought lace and perfume; the Americans owned the canal; the Panamanians owned permanent crap games beneath sagging tin roofs. Not far away was a Special Forces center, where crew-cut soldiers in shorts and berets conducted jungle warfare training. Superboys, proud of their ability to handle weapons, eat snakes, and ford rivers, they taught other Americans and officers from Latin American armies how to put down guerrilla insurgencies.

There were several reasons why the United States remained in Panama, despite the abrasions that followed inevitably from occupying part of a poor country. The generals wanted their training center and the contacts it gave them with Latin American officers. They wanted a regional headquarters for the Southern Command — a United States presence, not heavily armed, but near the scene of potential trouble. Both these operations might have been moved elsewhere — to Puerto Rico, for example. But the canal could not be moved. And it needed protection.

Because of its peculiar construction, it was vulnerable to sabotage. On each side the locks led up, like a flight of stairs, to Gatun Lake, eighty-five feet above sea level. The lake was dammed near the Atlantic locks. Well-placed bombs could blow the dam and send Gatun Lake crashing down the Chagres River to the ocean. That would knock out the canal for an extended period, impair world trade, and make it difficult to move the navy from ocean to ocean. As long as the canal required locks, it required a reliable force to guard it. Eliminating the locks and creating a sea-level canal meant spending billions to dig a passage through the lake bed, or through some other region of Central America. Stephen Ailes, who succeeded Cy Vance as Secretary of the Army, was convinced that it should be done. A sea-level canal, having no locks, would be far more secure, the Americans could go home, the political irritant would disappear. Until it was done, geography and terrain would bind the United States and Panama in a bitter but necessary embrace. Questions of sovereignty, of Panamanian rights and American security, would continue to plague us. Before I returned to Washington, I listened wearily to an argument about where the flags of the two countries should be flown side by side in the Zone, as President Kennedy had agreed they should be. Good God! I thought. That men should spend their time fighting about flags!

In mid-November 1963, I set out with an aide for the other pole of my responsibility — Okinawa. We landed in Tokyo after midnight, and were shuttled into a hotel for a few hours' rest. Sore from the flight, I did a deep knee bend, and split the rear of my trousers from crotch to belt. Replacements were locked on the plane.

So it was, that as I stepped off in Okinawa at noon that day — the new praetor, come to look at his province — and found a military band, an honor guard, a dozen photographers from the local press, and two or three generals standing at attention in the broiling sun, I wore a heavy trench coat, and continued to wear it as I took the salute. The band played "The Star Spangled Banner," "The Caissons Go Rolling Along," and was midway through the "Washington Post March" when the general in charge led me, perspiring, to a staff car. McPherson, I thought, you are a terrible colonial.

We drove through Naha, the capital, on our way to the heights where the American commander had his headquarters. It was much like Panama City, tawdry and hot. But the GI influence was much stronger. Used-car and motorbike shops, garish signs, movies, bars, all the ugly alluring gratifications that beckon servicemen from Honolulu to Saigon to Bad Gastein. Hair slicked down, sport shirt on, lots of cologne, five hours of freedom, see the sights in Naha, Okinawa.

I showered and changed clothes, and felt much more like a Senior American Official. I walked out on a terrace and looked at the East China Sea, bright in the afternoon sun. A few thunderheads were piling up. Later there would be a spectacular sunset, and white-red clouds would float like granite sloops above the sea. It was almost enough to justify building an empire, to see clouds like that from your own terrace.

That night at dinner I met General Paul Caraway, the high commissioner. He was an intense, tiny man, whose father and mother had both represented Arkansas in the Congress. Depending on your point of view, he was an opinionated martinet or a wise and benevolent despot. In either case, he drove his officers and civilians tenaciously. He was proud of the industrial growth he had stimulated on the island, proud of its factories and power plant, proud of the obeisant locals who ran them. He was determined to impede the return of Japanese tourists and businessmen to Okinawa. That embarrassed the American ambassador in Tokyo, but Caraway was sublimely confident of his course.

The Japanese had always given Okinawa prefecture hind tit; now they only wanted to stir up demands for reversion, and he would not have it. The ranking civilian on the island, Shannon McCune, winced. A missionary's son, raised in prewar Korea, he was sympathetic to the Okinawans and had absorbed their history and culture. But Caraway was high commissioner and the island's military commander, and when he and McCune clashed over policy, the general won — at least the first rounds; he was always suspicious that McCune would finally prevail because other soft-minded civilians supported him back in the Pentagon. Several old hands told me that Caraway was just what Okinawa needed: tough, insistent on protocol, but a good showman when there were schools to open or roads to dedicate. I liked his fierce sense of responsibility, but I thought he conveyed a contempt for Asian sensibilities that would haunt us when the Western Pacific was no longer *mare nostrum.*

We would not have been there at all if we had not believed our security required it. Similarly, we would not have occupied Panama, but for the canal; nor entered the war in Vietnam, except that we thought our position in the world would suffer if we reneged. We brought no continuing sense of mission to these places, so far as the local population was concerned. We had a temporary job to do, and would leave when it was done or circumstances changed. The British had seized India, Africa, and parts of the Near East and Asia for reasons of trade. But they had also established systems of civil administration and justice, organized economies, and stopped much of the fighting between tribes and religious factions. They had introduced thousands of Asians and Africans to Western civilization, and some Englishmen to those of the East. They had learned Swahili and Urdu and Chinese. They were there to stay, or so they thought. The United States, on the other hand, took pride in its contingent role. We abhorred colonialism. We wished only to achieve certain foreign policy goals, which were unrelated to the people whose land we occupied. (We did not intend to become involved in the politics of Vietnam, Kennedy had said, we only wanted to get on with the war.) We did not attempt to master local languages, or to open ourselves to indigenous cultures. We were businesslike — authoritative, yet remote. Our traditions would not permit us to become honest imperialists; neither did they compel us to learn much about people who, poor and weak as they were, would come to have a profound effect on our lives.

I flew back to Tokyo on the morning of November 22, 1963, Japan time. I had lunch with Ambassador Reischauer, in the great mansion known as "Hoover's Folly." We talked about Okinawa and the insuperable difficulty, for a Westerner, of speaking correct Japanese. My aide — a straight-backed colonel named John Sitterson — took me to a Japanese bath. Afterwards, I fell into bed exhausted, ready for the flight home next day.

Long before dawn, the hotel phone rang. It was Sitterson. "I'm sorry to wake you with terrible news. But I thought you would wish to know. The President has just been shot in your state — in Dallas." I lay in the dark, wondering where I was, anxious to believe I was dreaming. "What, John?" Again. I hung up. Insane city, insane wide-eyed bigoted Dallas bastards. Texans! "In your state." No, by God, I'm not one of them!

I put on a robe, and walked into the hall. Several people were already there, standing apart in pajamas, or leaning against the walls. Transistors in the rooms were tuned to the American station. President Kennedy was dead. At Parkland Hospital, in Dallas, where years ago I had seen friends — I suddenly realized that Johnson was President. "Lyndon B. Johnson has been sworn in as President aboard Air Force One." A Texan becomes President after Kennedy is killed in Texas. There would be perilous suspicions. What could I do for Johnson? Nothing from here. What would this mean for my career? Selfish Texas bastard, the President is dead.

In the lobby no one spoke. People were scattered apart, as if blasted by the radio. Maybe it is worse to hear such things thousands of miles from home. You feel like a child, very dependent on the "boss" who sent you out there. Suddenly he was your father, no matter how young he was. And he is dead. You wait for the shock of it to hit you, to deprive you of some essential power. In a cavernous chair an old colonel sat, wide-eyed, like a little boy.

What to do? Plane time was late afternoon. I decided to buy some prints and scrolls. Caraway had told me about a Buddhist shrine and school, where there was a good collection. We went there. It sat in a wood, walled off from the turbulent, driven city. A stout lady wearing round spectacles welcomed us. She had the students bring scrolls and hang them from blackboards in a classroom. Samurai swordsmen, knightly ceremonies, bamboo and hillsides. Tea was produced. It steamed on the sill in the cold bright air. She bowed a little. "Very sorry about your President." The steam from the tea, her spectacles, Sitterson's big face, the pine branches outside, all were vivid, as John Kennedy had been, parts of life he would never see. Tears came at last.

And came again, two days later at St. Mark's in Washington. The Johnsons were there because Bill Baxter's ministry had attracted Mrs. Johnson and Mary Margaret Valenti, a lovely woman who had served Johnson as secretary and confidante. The Book of Common Prayer was as adequate as words could be at such a time — strong, well remembered, a means of corporate grief. Paul Tillich described true prayer as "sighs too deep for words"; but something more than a sigh was needed that day for the nation and its new leader. The sermon hymn was "America," and I saw Johnson take out his handkerchief and wipe away his tears in great sweeps of his hand. Bill said we should remember this moment, when the country was united in its shock. Soon that would pass, and we would be divided again, selfish again, we would lose sight of our common humanity and what we might achieve together. But we should mark what we felt now for what it told us of ourselves and what we might be. And pray for Lyndon Johnson.

Afterwards in the parish hall, the congregation milled about, excited and afraid. Secret Service agents crowded Johnson on both sides, the muscles in their jaws and temples working furiously. For a long time Johnson and I stood talking, I forget about what; then he said, "Come on," and we walked back through the dark empty church. Agents lined the walls. I thought that this was what churches were for, a place, perhaps the only place, to which people might come together in the elemental moments of their lives. We reached the front door and saw a crowd outside. Cameramen pushed their way to the steps. I took a hard blow in the stomach. A foot stamped on my foot, stopping me. Agents. Johnson turned, surprised; then they pushed him and his wife out fast, across ten feet of pavement. Their faces were sharp and intense. They had just failed the only responsibility they had, and they were not going to fail again. For the moment, they owned Johnson. He was their prisoner, and that of the fears against which they shielded him. Federal marksmen with rifles stood on the roof of the Library of Congress annex. It was like Latin America. Like Dallas, only these were ours.

I saw him the following week, again at St. Mark's. This time I rode back with him to the White House. In the car he was the old Johnson, running through the list of those whom he had picked to serve on a commission of investigation. He had persuaded a reluctant Chief Justice Warren to be its chairman, by reminding him that when his country needed him in the First War, he had put on the uniform of a soldier. Now, when the need was far more desperate, he could not refuse. Johnson's face, stark the week before, was flushed with excitement and pride. We went into the Oval Office, where a rocking chair summoned up John Kennedy's memory in the austere December light. Jim Rowe was ushered in. A legendary Washington lawyer and politician, he had once been very close to Johnson. But his professional sensibilities had been offended by Johnson's willfully chaotic scheduling in the 1960 campaign, and he had told him so. They had parted angrily and had scarcely spoken in the three years. Now Johnson offered his apologies to Rowe, and said he needed his support and counsel. Rowe protested that their estrangement had been his fault, not Johnson's, but Johnson stopped him by asking, "Damn it, can't you be content to be the first man the thirty-sixth President of the United States has apologized to?"

Rowe was the first, but far from the only man with whom Johnson made peace in these early weeks of his Presidency. He invited many of his old enemies — men like Joe Rauh and Charlie Halleck — to the White House, and asked them to forget the past and work with him for the country's sake. In a time of national trauma, the appeal was irresistible. Hearing of it, seeing pictures of the President smilingly shaking hands with someone I knew he had fought for years, I thought of that time on the Senate floor when he had gone over to the petulant John Williams and talked him out of his objection to a vote. Swallow your feelings, remember what is important. Smile if it hurts.

Before I left that Sunday, McGeorge Bundy came in with several cables and memoranda. They were not urgent, but the President should see them before evening. Johnson was extremely deferential. He said, "Whenever you need me, let me know." Bundy replied, "Oh, Mr. President, you let *me* know when you need *me*." That made sense; Presidents pushed the button to summon aides, not the reverse. But I wondered if there was, in his correct, fluid response, the tone of a professor gently chiding a student who'd got it wrong.

One morning in early January 1964, Governor Fleming called from the Canal Zone with an annoying tale. It was about the flags. He had put Panama's on a pole next to ours at seventeen locations in the Zone. At other places, where the sight of a Panamanian flag might have stirred the Zonians to anger, he had ordered the American flag taken down. Neither should be flown in the absence of the other. Our flag at Balboa High School was lowered. A group of students managed to run it up again. Encouraged by their parents, they camped overnight around the flagpole, protecting it from Fleming's men. He wondered what we thought he should do. He was inclined to avoid a confrontation.

The Panamanian radio stations were talking of nothing else. Who was master of the Canal Zone? The President, whose predecessor had agreed to the two-flag policy; his agent, Governor Fleming; or the jingo Zonians? The question was buried in wild, irrelevant rhetoric, but it was still a good question.

On the other hand, how would Congress and the public respond to pictures of cops battling their way through American high school students to take down the American flag?

I thought the governor should hold his fire, seek to persuade the students and their parents to abandon the fight, and if that failed, warn them that they faced disciplinary action. Vance and Ailes agreed. In retrospect, it appeared that we had recommended a modified Micawberism, a little more aggressive than the model; at the time, it seemed the only prudent course. No sense stirring up the Congress. Perhaps Vance or Ailes worried whether Panamanian rage would break out in violence unless both flags, or none, went up before Balboa High School. I did not. Panamanians could protest. Congress could hurt.

Fleming left two days later for the States. That afternoon his deputy, an efficient colonel named Dave Parker, called to report that about two hundred Panamanian students, carrying their flag, were marching into the Zone. Apparently they were headed for Balboa High School. He would have police on the scene to avoid a fight with the American students. O.K. I went off to play squash. When I came back, Parker was on the phone again.

There had been trouble at Balboa High, whose fault he didn't know, and the Panamanians were yelling and smashing car windows on their way out of the Zone, pushed along by the police. Parker had instructed his men not to break heads. He thought the worst was over. He would call again that night if there was more to report.

I went home and found my wife ill with mumps and burning with fever. I began shuttling cool cloths back and forth, called the doctor, and had started out the door for the pharmacy when the phone rang. Parker said it was very bad. When the students arrived at Fourth of July Avenue — the street that divides the Zone and Panama City — hundreds of other Panamanians were waiting to join them, ready for a fight. Cars had been set afire. Offices on the avenue, many of them owned by United States firms, had been looted. Rocks had been thrown at the Tivoli. There had been a rush on the Ancón laundry. Wait — he had a report on the other phone — somebody said there'd been firing. Somebody else said the police were hard-pressed. He thought he should call General Andrew O'Meara, the C.G. of the Southern Command, and ask for troops. Did I have any advice or instructions? No, no, you go ahead. Wife's got the mumps. I hung up and called Ailes. He said it was important that we get back to the Pentagon. Where's Vance? Out for the evening. Better find him. I wrote phone numbers next to the antimumps prescription and ran out to get the pills. Half an hour later, while I waited to take the thermometer out, Parker called again. O'Meara's troops were positioned near the avenue. The Panamanian government had protested an unwarranted assault on its students. Radios summoned everyone to join the great patriotic demonstration and fight against the *norteamericanos*. They said dozens of Panamanians had been killed and hundreds wounded by machine gun fire. Parker thought this was untrue, but couldn't be sure. I changed the cloth on my wife's forehead and left for the Pentagon.

I met Ailes in the Army war room. Very efficient. There were varicolored phones and blinking lights. Cy Vance came in, in a tux, and we got Parker and then O'Meara on the phone. The canal was safe, there was no question about the troops' ability to hold it against the mob. Rioting continued along the avenue, and across the Isthmus at Colón. Castroites were thought to be leading it. The government of Panama had protested once again. Rumors were everywhere in the flames and tear gas.

It was suggested that someone should find out what had really happened, and prepare a chronology for the President. Our embassy would normally have done that, but it was twenty blocks away in Panama City, cut off from the Zone. So the Army's general counsel, Joe Califano, and I sat down and began to question Parker. We finished a long memorandum shortly before dawn. Vance took it to the White House. It was all Johnson had to go on.

I went home and slept until ten. My wife's fever had broken, and I returned to the Pentagon to hear that the President wanted a team to leave at once for the Zone and establish contact with the Panamanian government. Vance, Tom Mann, the assistant secretary of state for Inter-American Affairs, Ed Martin, his predecessor, Bob Manning, the assistant secretary for Public Affairs, Ralph Dungan, still working in the White House, and I took off in a helicopter for Andrews. First we veered west along the river and put down on the CIA lawn at Langley. A portly, bespectacled man named King, said to know much about Central America, boarded the chopper. Then we were off.

We landed in the Zone, and at once were enfolded in the military's efficient arms. O'Meara, cool and tough, had his operations room in full gear. Officers hustled about, carrying messages, checking lines to Washington, helping us find razors and toothbrushes. Vance and Mann went off through dark streets to the Presidential palace. By candlelight in a small house Dungan and I talked to an Irish-Panamanian monsignor, a friend of his and one of the Catholic liberals who were building a Christian Democratic network throughout Latin America. Quietly the priest denounced both sides in the shooting that continued sporadically a half-mile away. Some other way had to be found for Americans and Panamanians to live together.

At midnight our group decided to visit the command post in the Tivoli. We drove without lights and parked behind a warehouse a hundred yards from the hotel. In single file, ten yards or so apart, we covered the ground between. Panamanian snipers were shooting away from a high-rise office building that by day housed the national legislature. It occurred to me that we might be seen and hit. I turned my collar up to hide my shirt, and looked back at Dungan to recommend the same precaution. He was smoking a cigar. Its red tip made arcs in the black air as he walked. That was all right for him, but he was too close to me for my safety. I asked him urgently to cup it. At last, tripping over cables, we entered the building. The dark lobby was littered with military equipment. A two-way radio emitted rasping sounds, like pebbles on a shallow beach. The popping of small-caliber rifles and pistols continued across the avenue. Our soldiers had been instructed to return it only with shotguns. O'Meara was keeping them on a tight rein. He did not want them opening up, as the frightened Zone police had done. The army was self-restrained. The record would show it. Next day sharpshooters were brought in, and hit the snipers and several other people. The record also showed that, in time.

During the first days of the riots, the American reporters who had flown down to cover the story divided into two camps: those who accepted the Army's estimates of casualties and their causes, and those who wrote qualified versions of the Panamanian. Wire-service men generally stuck with the Army. Magazine reporters, and a man from the *Washington Post* named Kurzman, held *a priori* convictions about United States brutality toward

Latin Americans. It seemed very natural to them that we should have used tanks and machine guns on groups of Panamanians. There were in fact no tanks in the Zone, and machine guns were not used; most of the Panamanian deaths were caused by collapsing buildings, looters, and stray fire from unknown guns. Such was the later judgment of an investigating committee of the International Commission of Jurists. But to a reporter who "knew" Latin America, and believed that its troubles stemmed mainly from exploitation by United States interests, nothing that a crisp general might say could exonerate his troops. That the whole affair had its roots in the chauvinism of the Zonians completed the picture. Kurzman wrote an impressionistic account for the *Post*, perfectly designed to agitate his readers. Bob Manning, himself an ex-reporter, braced him for it the following day. Kurzman pleaded lack of time to weigh the Army's evidence. He would write a factual piece later. Manning thumped him on the chest and said that he would wait to see it.

The shooting stopped in a few days. Eighteen Panamanians and six or seven soldiers were dead. Colón looked worse than ever; there, and along the avenue in Panama City, the Molotov cocktails had done their work. The Pan Am building, owned by Panamanians, was a charred wreck. Hundreds of bullet holes pocked the Tivoli. Nothing basic had changed. Americans still operated the locks — proud that delays to shipping had been minimized — and Panamanian orators called for a new national militance. We flew home, talking about a sea-level canal.

Shortly afterwards I went back, with Joe Califano and a friend named Owen Smith, to brief our case before the Jurists' Commission. We worked for three days and nights without sleeping, Califano driving colonels and secretaries as if they were nails. We interviewed the police at length. The chief said he had negotiated an agreement with the two hundred marchers as they approached Balboa High. Five of them were to be permitted to stand before the flagpole, holding the Panamanian flag. The Panamanians apparently thought they were to raise it; when the American students shouted in protest, the chief tried to explain, and then — who knows exactly what? The Panamanians remonstrated, the police tried to move them back, someone fell down, the flag was torn, and the police, whose boss, the governor, had considered forcing the Americans to behave, were now chasing the Panamanians. While the American students cheered, the five Panamanians rushed back to their fellows and showed them the torn flag, and it was on.

So: President Kennedy, in order to improve relations with Panama and hence Central America, had agreed to hoist the two flags in the Canal Zone, as a mark of Panama's "residual sovereignty." The agreement had been partially annulled by the opposition of five thousand American workers and their families. The political problem this raised was regarded as fundamentally domestic — that is, carrying out Kennedy's policy would have required quick and effective action, which would, it was thought, set off howls in Congress. So the Army temporized. Then, at the critical moment, police officers employed by the Zone government responded tribally, as Americans, unable to persuade other Americans to make way for Panamanians. Together with a frenetic mob in Panama City, whose government did not commit its own police to action for three days, we — the Army staff, the Zone government, the police, the Balboa High School students and their parents — made a wreck of what must have seemed, in 1962, an inexpensive way to improve our "posture" in Panama.

The ships kept going through Miraflores Locks, into the Gaillard Cut, and across Gatun Lake, headed for Europe. That was the main thing. If we were ever to cure the rest of it, we would need to dig a canal no one could destroy. Then we could get out.

But that was at least a decade in the future. In the meantime there would have to be some way to ameliorate the anger both sides would feel when the next round of demands and denials produced no fundamental change. Later that year I had lunch with Jack Vaughn, our ambassador, and the new Panamanian foreign minister, a suave American-schooled entrepreneur named Fernando Eleta. The talk was about the two countries, but the language was sexual and familial. "We just want a little better treatment, Jack," Eleta said. "We've been a good mistress, very faithful, always ready for love when you needed us. But now we're getting old. We need a place to stay, some nice clothes, maybe somebody to cook for us. You know, we don't want the big house. We don't want you to leave your wife. We just want a little something for old times' sake." We laughed, but then Eleta began getting specific about a little something, and we said that would have to wait for a new treaty.

I never went to Panama without feeling an exultant admiration for the canal itself, and for the skill and bravery of those who built it. I never failed to leave it without a sense of foreboding. Our two peoples would never be at peace, so long as we occupied part of Panama's land, so long as the machines worked well and the grass was cut close only on one side of the avenue. Three years later, in a light plane several thousand feet above the road from Saigon to Danang, I remembered Panama. Below were artillery, trucks, aircraft, camps, and revetments, the brilliant array of American technology that pacified all within range; beyond, in the green hills, was strangeness and hostility, and always would be.

Joe Califano left the Army and succeeded Adam Yarmolinsky as special assistant to McNamara — an all-purpose job that required finesse and consummate *chutzpah*. One of his Army assignments, overseeing the Corps of Engineers, fell to me. My title became one of the longest in government: Deputy Under Secretary of the Army for International Affairs and Special Assistant to the Secretary for Civil Functions. My office was the size of a small basketball court — "to include," as the wretched military jargon would have it, a private bathroom.

The Corps took it calmly. One more civilian to be flown around the country looking at dams, levees, sluices, and canals. To be put down softly, in an amphibian, on the Mississippi. To be commissioned an honorary navigator of the M/V *Lipscomb*. To be shown how the Corps tames nature, straightens rivers, protects farmlands, and provides tens of millions of Americans with water recreation — more than enjoy the national parks and forests, more than voted in the last election. To be entertained in the delta towns, where riparian plantation owners were members of the River Commission and recommended whether to spend more to contain its flow. To be invited to dedicate a dam in New Hampshire, to be taken up to Passamaquoddy, in Maine, where the old Rooseveltian dream of capturing the tides for power still lives in a worn plaster model, desolate, fantastic, possible. America the always building, fixing, planning, America the can-do country.

Overseeing the Corps of Engineers, from an outpost in the Pentagon, was an exercise in amiable futility. The Corps, like all other uniformed military organizations, was under civilian control. But in its case the controlling civilians were on the Hill. The Budget Bureau could force changes in its annual spending program; the President could stop it altogether, to reduce the deficit; the Secretary of the Army could insist that certain policies be enforced or abandoned. But the Public Works and Appropriations Committees decided what creeks should be studied, what reservoirs should be planned, what dams should be built and how quickly. There was an intimate conspiracy between the Engineers and the Congress, based on their conviction that public building was *prima facie* in the public interest, and that bureaucrats, city congressmen, and editorial writers who complained about waste should not be permitted to subvert the long-term common good. Of course, the country needed other things besides dams and reservoirs. But concrete visibly endured, in a way that welfare payments and scholarships did not. It was always a sufficient answer, when we questioned the Corps about a project, that the Congress wanted it that way; so, usually, did the Corps. "We are Congress's Engineers," a general of the Corps once told me, as the doorman of a men's club might say to a stranger, "Members Only."

They were bright men, said to be the cream of their West Point classes. They were proficient with slide rules, and unlike many civilian scientists and engineers, they were not ungainly as social beings; long exposure to local business interests, contractors, and politicians had given them an easy confidence of manner, without reducing them to smugness. If they were deficient in any respect, it was in a lack of imagination about things that could not be measured with a slide rule. Environmental issues were beginning to interest many people. The Engineers saw them as important only to "nature freaks" like the Sierra Club and the Wildlife Federation. Race, too, was an inconvenience. One torrid summer day in 1964 I visited several reservoirs built by the Corps in Mississippi. Dozens of Negro and white fishermen lined the banks along the spillways, side by side pulling in fat bream and perch. Families of both races picnicked under the trees, the women frying fish, the men cutting watermelons open to the squeals of their children. But up in the lodges and restaurants, which the Corps had leased to private operators, Negroes were not welcome. That was just the way it was in Mississippi. When I objected over lunch and said it would obviously have to change, everyone fell silent — engineers as well as our Mississippi hosts. I wondered if those Northern soldiers, with the crenellated insignias on their lapels, were as bigoted as the open-shirted countrymen beside them? Probably not. It was the *intrusion* of the race issue into an agreeable and cooperative — Senator Stennis would say, a *ver' fahn* — working relationship between Army and townspeople, that distressed them. They had nothing against blacks; they had nothing against trees, and birds, and mushrooms, and shellfish, or anything in nature; it was just that they had a job to do, assigned by Congress, and that was to plan, build, and operate public works projects. And get along.

Back in Washington, I called a meeting of the District engineers. We must prohibit racial discrimination in all our facilities, those we operate and those we lease. The meeting was rather grim, until I pointed out that Congress would probably soon adopt a civil rights bill that would end such discrimination by law. This had a magical effect. The same Lord who told them what to build would tell them how to manage it. That made it all right, as well as mandatory. I had no doubt that they would do what they were required to do. It was a Corps tradition.

A few weeks later my old friend Ben Read, who had become executive secretary of the State Department, sounded me out about taking a job with a title almost as long as the one I had. It was "Assistant Secretary of State for Educational and Cultural Affairs." I talked with Lucius Battle, the incumbent, who was leaving for the embassy in Cairo. I found it an attractive proposition — not because I knew very much about educational and cultural exchange, but because I would become, at thirty-four or -five, an assistant secretary of state.

Califano reported that McNamara thought it was absurd to move from an active, responsible role in the Pentagon to a "backwater" in State. In systems-analytic terms it may have seemed so. But the values I weighed were (on the one side) the excitement of helping to govern the Zone and Okinawa, planning a sea-level canal and a new treaty with Panama, jousting with the Corps of Engineers and the Congress; and (on the other) higher office. The choice was easy. Some things are immune to systems analysis.

Still I disliked leaving the Army. I had become accustomed to the generals and no longer felt intimidated by their prestige as warriors. Most of them had been in the Pentagon for years, and had more in common with corporate vice presidents than with

George Patton. The men I would really miss were the colonels who worked in my office. Magnus Smith, from Bogalusa, Louisiana, who parachuted into Corregidor in 1944. Who worked in Latin America, developing antiguerrilla teams, and then acquired scholarly language by which to describe his experience: "I saw that it was necessary to develop an ambience in which our long-term purposes might be achieved, and I done it." Calvin Hannum, shot from a tank in Europe and left for dead on a convent's steps, cool, practical, a man of immense integrity. Strapping, handsome John Sheffey, whose knowledge of the Zone was exhaustive, and whose perseverance had no limits. Sitterson, my counselor for Okinawa. None of these men quite understood the nuances of the political process. All had, to some degree, tunnel vision about America's position and goals in the world. "Politicians see all these shadings," Sheffey said. "Soldiers see only the national interest we are supposed to serve." I would not have chosen any of them to help me draft a message urging greater powers on the United Nations. But in time of war or personal danger, I would gladly have entrusted my life to them; not only because they were professional leaders and fighters, but because they were capable of unbending loyalty and would not fail any responsibility which events placed upon them. Of course these qualities existed outside the military as well as within; yet the military was one of the few institutions in which they were formally cultivated and regarded as essential to the survival of the institution and the nation. I did not wish to live or work in a place where loyalty and responsibility were regarded as the only paramount virtues — nor where they were patronized or otherwise debased. On balance, I thought the Army had rated them about right.

I could not foresee a time when the loyalty and responsibility of American soldiers would provoke agonies of doubt in them and their fellow citizens; a time when many Americans would vomit up Vietnam, and military values along with it.

What pure pleasure, to be sworn into high office on your thirty-fifth birthday. Secretary Rusk presided and told a good story. People from the Army were there, and so were many of the four hundred men and women who were assigned to the Bureau of Educational and Cultural Affairs. I knew almost nothing about what they did. They knew almost nothing about me, except that I had come from the Pentagon, which was suspect, and that I had some kind of relationship to President Johnson, which was potentially helpful. I was a politician and a Texan, and so could be expected to know very little about intellectual affairs or the performing arts. I was confident that I would surprise them. It was a happy day. In Atlantic City that night, the Democratic convention would learn that Johnson, after appearing to consider Tom Dodd, had chosen Hubert Humphrey to be his running mate.

The bureau arranged for thousands of young foreigners to study in American universities, and for American graduate students to continue their work abroad. It brought groups of leaders — parliamentarians, bureaucrats, scientists, tribal chieftains — to see America in whirlwind visits. It sent painters, musicians, educators, lawyers, and writers to live in foreign capitals, demonstrating their art, teaching and advising, making friends. It subsidized orchestras and dance companies in their travels to remote continents, or to festivals in Europe and Russia. It helped to support overseas American schools.

Senator Fulbright was its congressional father. He had been a Rhodes scholar, and his encounter with Oxford had made a great difference in his life. As America emerged from the Second War and for the first time became deeply and constantly involved in the affairs of a world at peace, Fulbright thought we should encourage American students — the Arkansans of a new generation — to learn something about other nations and peoples. Foreigners, in turn, should see us as we are, encapsulated neither in uniform nor in the special circumstances of the tourist. Shared intellectual interests would be the bridge on which people would meet and come to understand one another.

By the time I arrived, the U.S.–European element of the program was only a minor part of a worldwide "exchange," in which thousands of African, Asian, Middle Eastern, and Latin American students were brought to the United States, and a few hundred (increasingly difficult to find and persuade) American professors were dispatched to lecture in the less-developed countries. Educational exchange had become a kind of foreign aid program. Senator Fulbright retained his paternal interest, but he must have found it disappointing that a program meant to make Americans more sophisticated world citizens had become a means for instructing Africans and Asians in skills for which there was often little demand back home.

The transformation was costly in other ways. Teaching others and never being taught in turn (except as one is "taught" by a travel film) confirmed the image of America's omnipotence. We wished only to help less fortunate nations become prosperous, enlightened, and free; that they often resented our good intentions, as they did our power, was inevitable. The instructor's role also bemused us, by helping us forget that we were only one part of a diverse civilization in which our pragmatic values were admired for their results more often than they were adopted. Compared with the poor nations' needs for improved literacy and production, these were, or seemed to me, attenuated concerns. Still I could not get rid of the feeling that we ignored them at our peril. It was hard to describe, to practical men, what America needed from foreign intellectuals, or why it was so important that we should transport our own scholars abroad. One could only suggest that the miniaturist we sent to Belgium, and the logical positivist we brought to Minnesota, might prove, in the end, the cement that held all else together.

In the beginning I did not spend much time thinking about

such questions. The accreted minutiae of a bureaucrat's life fills as much of his time as he is willing to let it, and until he is certain about what he is doing, he is inclined to attend to everything that crosses his desk. It takes experience to distinguish between necessary expertise and the careful exposition of trivia. I attended scores of meetings, sitting in ignorance at a conference table while those who knew what the hell was at stake, and cared, puffed on pipes in chairs behind me. I listened to forlorn discussions about crisis that would pass within twenty-four hours, without anyone doing anything about them. (It is not only the military who deal in worst-case thinking. Looming emergencies are the stuff and justification of all bureaucratic life.) I wasted a lot of time.

But I was let alone. I met with Rusk, briefly, and again with Under Secretary George Ball. Both men were well disposed toward me and the exchange program. Yet both were involved in the escalating anxieties of the Vietnam war, in designing multilateral forces, in helping to pacify the Congo and feed India. I felt that the less I troubled them about bilateral Fulbright commissions, the better.

Three mornings a week Rusk had a staff meeting of assistant secretaries. To my surprise he seemed equally interested in a coup d'etat in Togo and in the latest developments in Southeast Asia. Certainly he would not discuss Vietnam — what the Joint Chiefs of Staff had recommended, what McNamara and Bundy and the President had said the day before — with a heterogeneous collection of men whose responsibilities ran to trade, Latin America, or educational and cultural affairs. And no doubt (as a former assistant secretary) he wished to encourage the expression of less apocalyptic concerns. Still he appeared almost indiscriminately willing, even eager, to hear what everybody had to say. He reminded me of someone plugged into a twenty-four-hour radio news station, listening contentedly to seriatim descriptions of hijackings, city council debates, war threats, ball scores, and the Pope's latest encyclical. I did not contribute to these sessions. I felt like an industrious and slightly mad uncle, rummaging around in the attic while the family quarreled and loved and argued over bills downstairs. But if my program seemed almost irrelevant amid talk of juntas, expropriations, and Soviet pressures, and if the department treated it (in a phrase later to become famous) with benign neglect, I was correspondingly free to run it as I wished.

The bureau's people were generally competent; though many of them had been stuck there for years — like my colonels, far from the action — they took pleasure in the hope that their work would benefit the country for generations to come. Few of them fitted the mold of the "State Department type." If indeed there was such a type. There were a few white-shoe men around the building, snobs who talked through clenched teeth and viewed international relations as a private domain. But there were many more ordinary citizens who worked and spoke without pretension. I was blessed with three men, Arthur Hummel, Fred Irving, and Harold Howland, whose good sense and capacity for work equaled those of any associates I had ever had.

But there was a distinct difference between the atmospheres at State and Defense. I thought it derived from money. At Defense, there was always a car and a driver to take a deputy under secretary of the Army to the Capitol. At State, an assistant secretary, much higher on the protocol list, often had to hitch a ride. At Defense, one could requisition an airplane for a trip to a military base; at State, one thought twice before sending a letter special delivery. In the Army General Officers' Mess, one had sherry before mandarin duck. At State one settled for a tasteless ragout. Little things, but pervasive. Money power — together with their sense of discipline — had much to do, I believed, with the fact that military men regularly arrived for meetings with State's representatives far better prepared for business than were their civilian counterparts. Some people thought that was because America had become a fortress — that the power of decision in all matters of foreign policy had shifted ineffably from the embassies to the war rooms. I thought it was because they lived better over there in the Pentagon.

There were external constraints on my freedom of administration, principally the academic world and the Congress. By law the selection of American scholars was left up to a Board of Foreign Scholarships, a group of distinguished professors who would, it was thought, keep the program out of politics. They did. Overseas there were dozens of bilateral commissions, composed, on the local side, of other professors and educationists. They chose the foreign students. I recognized that this arrangement gave the program stability and prestige. It also soaked up most of our funds. When we wished to bring a dozen influential journalists to America for a meeting with their peers, we often found that our allocation for their country was already committed to sustaining a few "pure" scholars. I did not subscribe to the hard-sell propagandist view of educational exchange, and I thought Charles Frankel was probably right in wishing to divorce the Fulbright program from the Information Agency. But there were many days in which I wished that professors were not quite so assertive of the pristine claims of scholarship. I could have used the money.

Fundamentally there were two ways of looking at Congress from an executive department. 1. As a blind and stupid monster, capable of lashing out to destroy the most useful arrangements; those who saw it that way naturally tried to guard what they did from its reach. 2. As an assembly of reasonably enlightened men and women, who could, if properly informed and treated with a little deference, be helpful and even creative. I found it best to adopt a little of each view.

My predecessor, Luke Battle, had immeasurably improved the bureau's relations with Congress. On the one hand, he had always leveled with Senator Fulbright and with Congressman John

Rooney, the chairman of our House Appropriations Subcommittee. Thus I inherited a fund of trust which proved invulnerable to the distaste both members felt for one another. On the other hand, Battle had removed the choice of American performing arts groups from political control — his own, or Congress's. He had created an advisory board, from which men like Roy Larsen of Time-Life and Peter Mennin of the Juilliard School picked singers and dancers and players to represent us abroad. There were no more endless and threatening phone calls from the Hill, demanding that the East Fredonia Boys' Choir be permitted to tour Europe at government expense. That was a relief for everyone concerned. I could refer my callers to the advisory board, the board could say that Robert Shaw had already been chosen, and the congressmen could avoid a test of their political pull.

Battle could not protect the program from the misbehavior of individual grantees, nor from the bursts of congressional outrage that usually followed. That was impossible, given the inherent risks in sponsoring scholars and artists abroad. Some people made expensive fools of themselves; others joined dissident groups in attacks on American embassies; a few were hostile to their host governments, and became the subjects of rough comment in the local newspapers. The assistant secretary was sure to hear about such events at the Appropriations hearings. Battle thought it wise to visit the chairmen beforehand, make a clean breast of it, and promise some form of remedial action. I followed his lead. One could not, by that, escape a challenge at the hearings, but one could keep a few sour notes from spoiling all the music.

I had amiable conversations with Senator Fulbright, who said it was sad that the government spent so much for defense and quibbled about education. He volunteered to help in any way he could. But he knew, and so did I, that the thumbs on my neck belonged to Congressman Rooney. And there was nothing he could do about Rooney.

The very name summoned up, for most foreign service officers, all that was odious and wrong about congressional oversight of the Executive. Rooney attacked, ridiculed, and purposefully misunderstood senior officials of the department; what was worse, he was a law unto himself. He could depend on the acquiescence of a majority in the House, no matter what he did to State. The department assigned several men to cater to him. Most of them came to agree with his criticism, or told him so. That made their colleagues even more furious, especially as the results of their toadying did not seem to last.

The problem was, of course, that the power to appropriate is the only consistent leverage which the Congress has on the processes of government. Ergo it must be fully exercised. The chairmen of the Appropriations subcommittees and their staffs must pursue (or seem to pursue) every expenditure by the Executive, and they must find evidence of waste. Otherwise the Congress is in no position to threaten cuts in the budget, which in turn gives it influence in Executive decision-making. Without the Appropriations committees and their badgering, Congress would be only a debating society.

So Rooney kept the pressure on. He was particularly hard on State (whose striped-pants cookie-pushers had few admirers in the largely Southern and big-city hierarchy of the House) and the courts (which shared State's enemies, for different reasons). For two months before my hearing, I heard a succession of horror stories about his mistreatment of Battle's predecessor, Philip Coombs. I became nervous. I worked hard and mastered a lot of figures. I knew it was important to the exchange program, to the people in the bureau, and to my authority as leader — not necessarily in that order — that I do well. I was not defenseless; Battle had left the bureau in good standing, and a priest friend of Rooney's had interceded in my behalf. And as I walked into the hearing room, thick briefing books under each arm, I suddenly realized, hell, I knew Mr. Rooney, he was an Irish politician from Brooklyn. A congressman. I knew about congressmen.

Before I sat down, Rooney asked, "Is this one of the ones that's going to be cut?" I blinked. "Sir?" "I said, is this one going to be cut?" No response. "Does anybody know the answer to my question?" Someone at the back of the room said, "No, Mr. Chairman. The Secretary excluded this one." "Do you know why?" "No sir." I heard later that Rusk had voluntarily reduced his various budget requests in testimony the day before. Rooney growled. There was a long pause. "Very well, sit down and tell us your name and background for the record." I felt like a fighter who had been surprised in his corner before the bell by a terrific running right cross. I began rather shakily. ". . . I was counsel of the Democratic Policy Committee . . ." "Are you bringing politics into this?" Ho, ho. "Mr. Chairman, it was already here." Ho, ho, ha, ha, ho. It was going to be all right. I had never talked to Johnson about the exchange program, but Rooney knew that I was one of his boys, and this was the heyday of Johnson's relations with the Congress. I was going to get through it. Rooney would find a few shocking examples of our profligacy, he would refuse, once again, to approve travel allowances for the families of American professors who went abroad to teach, and then he would give us about what we needed — cutting just below the padding we had added for the occasion. He represented a poor district in which the average educational attainment was the eighth grade, and we were asking fifty million dollars for postgraduate studies and traveling artists, and he would give it to us and defend it against attacks on the House floor.

I went back to the bureau tired and happy, feeling like a homesteader who had shot a bear in dangerous country.

A few weeks before the hearing, Bill Moyers asked me to see him in the White House. Mike Feldman, one of the last of the Kennedy staff, would soon be leaving. His successor as special counsel was to be Lee White. The President wanted to know if I would like to understudy Lee, who would be moving on himself in a year or so. I said I would. Moyers professed surprise that I would willingly leave a "great" job like the one in State, where I was relatively independent, for the "White House rat race." We both laughed. Neither of us had to say that for ambitious young men there was no comparison.

I asked for a little delay, so that I might confront Mr. Rooney. Art Hummel, my deputy, could have substituted for me, but then I would have trained for a race I did not run; besides, I wanted to be able to say "*I've* testified before Rooney."

By the end of February 1965, the hearing was behind me. I cleaned out my desk at State. I had been there a little more than six months. Now that I knew what I was doing, I was leaving. Francis Pickens Miller came in to say goodbye. He had been Luke Battle's special assistant, and then mine. A Virginia patrician of great character and experience, he had challenged the Byrd machine and fought for a hundred progressive causes. He was glad to see Johnson follow a liberal course, though because of the President's old relationship to Harry Byrd, Miller could not quite trust him. I asked him playfully whether he had any words of wisdom. "It's going to be very hard," he said. "Try to do right." I looked at his face. It was deeply serious. I nodded and walked out to the elevator.

Right: Being sworn in as Assistant Secretary of State for Educational and Cultural Affairs, 1964. Secretary of State Dean Rusk attending. Department of State photograph by Herbert J. Meyle.

Above: The author mimicking LBJ. Left to right: Joe Califano, Douglass Cater, Larry Temple, George Christian, the author, Loyd Hackler, Tom Johnson, and John Robson.

Top: On the carrier *Constellation*. Photograph by Frank Wolfe.

Above: In the "Lincoln bedroom," July 26, 1968.

Top: With LBJ and Rep. Wilbur Mills.

Above: The author, Joe Califano, LBJ, Jim Jones (Appointments Secretary), Marvin Watson (Postmaster General), Clark Clifford (Secretary of Defense), George Christian (Press Secretary).

Top: Drafting the State of the Union address, 1968. Larry Levinson, Douglass Cater (seated), Joe Califano (on phone at rear), and the author.

Above: The author working on State of the Union, 1968.

Above: Talking with the President about the State of the Union address, 1968. Douglass Cater in background.

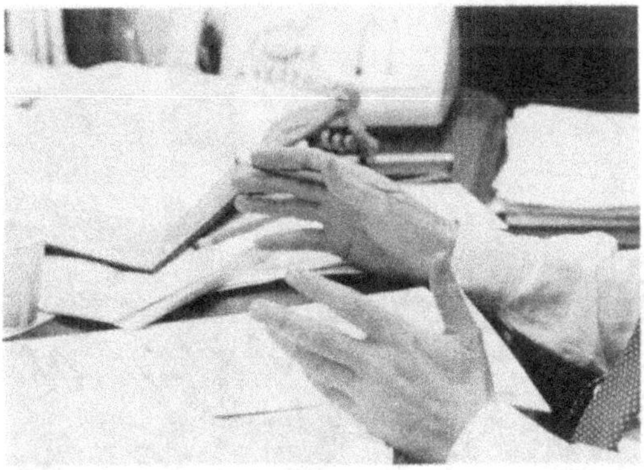

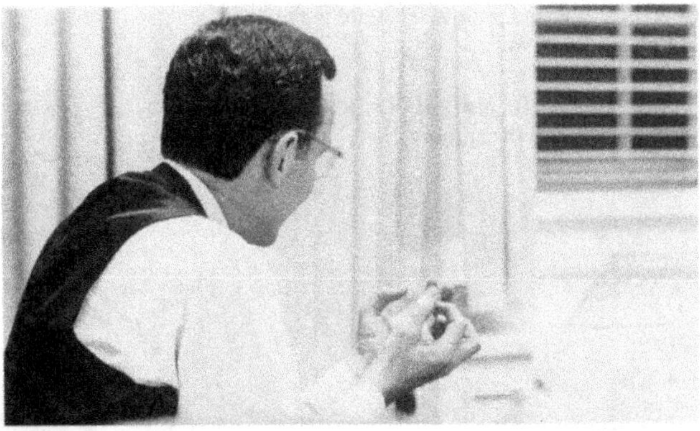

Top: With LBJ and Joe Califano prior to the State of the Union. Photograph by Frank Wolfe.

Above: LBJ, Robert Weaver (Secretary HUD), Ramsey Clark (Attorney General), and the author.

Top: With LBJ as he prepares to speak to the nation on October 31, 1968, announcing the end of the bombing of North Vietnam.

Above: With Joe Califano, LBJ, Mrs. Johnson. Photograph by Frank Wolfe.

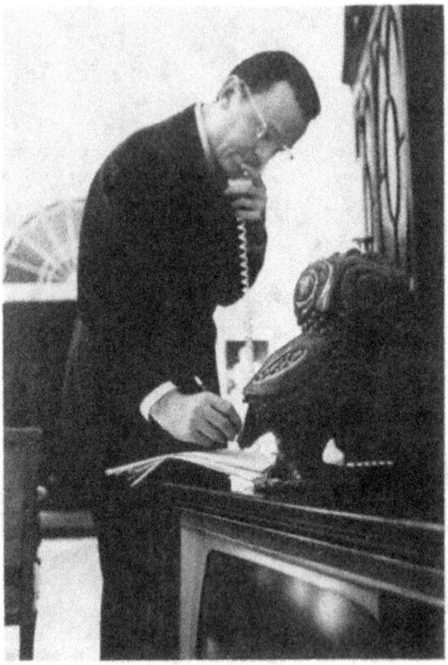

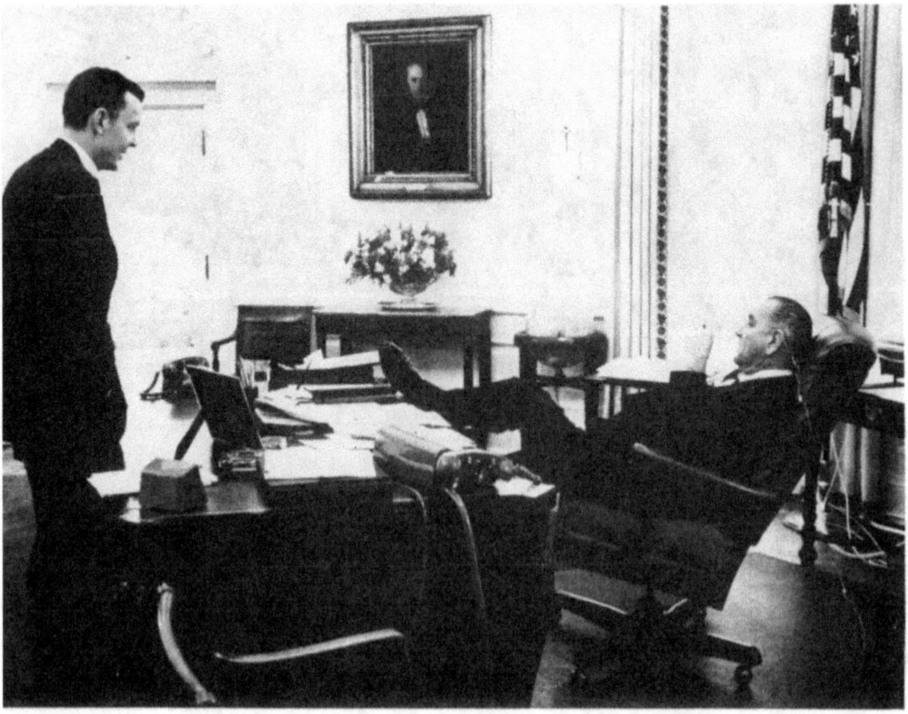

9

White House

> *—but what is heroic death compared to eternal*
>   *watching*
> *with a cold apple in one's hand on a narrow*
>   *chair*
> *with a view of the ant-hill and the clock's dial*
>
> *Adieu prince I have tasks a sewer project*
> *and a decree on prostitutes and beggars*
> *I must also elaborate a better system of prisons*
> *since as you justly said Denmark is a prison*
> *I go to my affairs*
>   —Zbigniew Herbert, "Elegy of Fortinbras"

IN 1965 one could still feel John Kennedy's presence in the White House. I walked out of the mansion one cold, starry night, headed for my office in the West Wing, and imagined I saw that lithe figure standing in the Oval Office, his back to the window; but it was only an aide.

I missed him. I missed his wry humor, his detachment about himself, his rejection of all that was mawkish and banal in politics. I missed his sense of history, that was as reassuring as Eisenhower's complacency had been disturbing. If he had not generated widespread public sentiment for social change, he had helped the nation gain a perspective on its problems in which reason played a greater part than passion.

Still I wished for, and did not see in him, a driving determination to rally the nation behind his purposes. One week before the assassination, James Reston wrote:

There is a vague feeling of doubt and disappointment about President Kennedy's first term. . . . He has touched the intellect of the country, but not its heart. He has informed but not inspired the nation. He is the most popular figure, but he has been lucky in his competition.
    Kennedy . . . makes the news. He has the headlines. He is on television more than all his opponents combined, and while there is clearly some opposition to his civil rights program in the North . . . it would probably be wrong to talk about this as a "revolt" that might cost him the election. Accordingly, his problem is probably not how to get elected but how to govern . . . he is simply better known than anybody else, and this will probably be enough to assure his re-election, but it is a far cry from the atmosphere he promised when he ran for the Presidency in 1960.°

This squared with my impressions in the early fall of 1963, and with what I heard from members of Congress — those uncertain barometers who registered public opinion through the screen of their own preconceptions and acquaintanceships, but nevertheless listened hard for evidence of how the President stood in their states in order that they might know how to treat with him.

What it did not say — what could not have been said, except in retrospect — was that in a thousand days Kennedy had changed American politics for the next decade. He had attracted many energetic and tough-minded men to government, who shared his insistence on performance and the dispassionate search for right answers. He had encouraged systematic approaches to problems of the economy, national defense, agriculture, trade, and poverty. He had helped us to see that we could reach useful agreements with the Russians without disabling ourselves. He had created a style which politicians in every state would seek to emulate — graceful, understated, contemptuous of grandstand plays to the voters' fears and prejudices.

° *New York Times*, November 15, 1963.

At the end much was left undone, so much that many people spoke only of his "potential." That missed the truth on at least two counts. Part of what he wished to do — especially in the Congress — he might never have been able to do, even with the massive liberal majority elected to Congress in 1964 as Senator Goldwater's contribution to the welfare state. His performance with the evenly divided Congresses of 1961–1963 was not encouraging. Yet he had also achieved much; not in terms of laws passed and programs begun, but in improving the tone and quality of government.

As a personality, he did not inspire the country, as Reston said — in the sense that FDR inspired it in 1933 — but he interested it. He was good copy in the *Harvard Business Review*, the *New York Review of Books*, *Time*, and *Silver Screen*. His cool glamour attracted the young; his amused skepticism attracted professors, journalists, and millions of people, like me, who thought a lot about politics and wished to hear political issues discussed without puffing. That left a vast unattracted multitude of citizens whose lethargy about, or resistance to, the New Frontier and its leader was reflected in the votes of their representatives in Congress. One of the many terrible ironies of the sixties was that the shock of Kennedy's death was a more powerful stimulus to congressional action than was his Presidency.

Another irony lay in the response many of his partisans made to Johnson. To the most passionate of these Johnson was simply a usurper. The Presidency had passed from Hyperion to a satyr. To others he was a parvenu, and always would be. His accent was the occasion for scorn among people who had regarded Kennedy's way of saying "Cuber" as picturesque. I could understand the heartache that made it hard to forgive anyone who sat in the President's chair while John Kennedy lay dead in Arlington. But I knew that Kennedy would not have permitted himself such corrosive contempt for a man whom he considered well qualified for the political tasks of the Presidency.

I thought Johnson had unquestionably proved, during his first year in office, that he could govern. I hoped that as he put through the liberal program, he would be affirmed by the liberal Establishment—that he might acquire, in its eyes, legitimacy through performance. That would in turn legitimate all who worked for him, all who had remained loyal to him when he was called a bumptious wheeler-dealer and mocked for his whoops in the Taj Mahal.

So there was self-interest in the attempts we made to win support for him in the university faculties, in the editorial boardrooms, at Georgetown dinner parties. Yet we also believed he deserved support, and when it was not forthcoming we found it easy to be bitter, not only toward those who denied it, but toward the Kennedys, with whom he was unfavorably compared. For me there was further irony in that — to find myself denigrating the former President and his brothers, men whom I had admired and defended within the Johnson ranks, because *their* supporters were stingy in acknowledging Johnson's real achievements.

The press, to be sure, recorded those achievements with dutiful appreciation, but as Grand Prix drivers might appreciate a good tractor. An inimitable part of the fun was gone. A distinguished reporter told me, "I don't hate Johnson. I just hate the fact that all the grace and wit has gone from what the American President says." I said that I found it difficult, reading his commentary, to make the distinction. I did not say that I could understand how reporters might have enjoyed Kennedy's deft banter more than three hours of self-justifying stream-of-consciousness by Johnson. It was hard to be fair in a climate spoiled by hurt feelings.

Other reporters and columnists enjoyed some of Johnson's performances as much as I did, but found it impossible to write about them without using clichés. That had much to do with

Johnson's peculiar style, which invited caricature. It was foreign not only to the Northern media, but to the new middle class in the South and West. And it was as various as it was strange. Sometimes it took off into the clouds, driven by the populist energies of his youth; sometimes it was as grave as a bishop's; sometimes it was impatient, quick with the hustle of a man who had much to do in a little time.

Soon after I joined the staff I went over to hear him speak to a group of educators about the school-aid bill then pending in Congress. His purpose was to fire them up and send them zealously to the Capitol to lobby for the bill. He had a brief text, but he was not content to rest with it on such an occasion. Most of the following is extemporaneous Johnson:

Now you can keep your blood pressure down if you want to. You can sit in your rocking chair and talk about the days gone by if you choose. But as far as I am concerned, I am going to use every rostrum and every forum and every searchlight I can to tell the people of this country that we can no longer afford overcrowded classrooms and half-day sessions. We just must not, we just cannot afford the great waste that comes from the neglect of a single child.

. . . The education bill we picked out can be improved. The T-Model Ford could be improved and has been. The first train that ran from Fredericksburg, a little town I lived close to, went to San Antonio — it has been improved a great deal. But I remember the story that they told about it the day it took off — from one of the founding fathers. He said, "Well, they will never get her started, and if they do they will never get her stopped."

. . . Now some of them are going to say if it is a billion two hundred million this year, it will be more next year. Well, it will be! Because I am not going to be proud to be the President of the richest nation in the world when there are hundreds of thousands and millions of children that can't read and write.

. . . When you go back home, those of you who have families, children (those of you that don't have mothers and fathers, those of you that don't have either have kinfolks) . . . I think you can truly say in the years to come, that on this March the 1st, I sat in the White House at 6:10 and along with my colleagues from all over the nation,

I participated in the meeting and in the conference that gave America leadership in preparing the minds of her little ones. And we inaugurated, we were there to see this first train that would never get started, and if it did we'd never get it stopped.

Well, we are going to get it started, but we are not ever going to stop it.

The educators were left wide-eyed and smiling, as if unsure what to make of this torrential display, but relieved that its producer was on their side. One reporter said, "Tremendous, just tremendous." Another growled, "Pure hokum." I thought it was both; tremendous hokum, all the more effective because Johnson believed it, believed in teaching poor children to read and write and to become good citizens; believed, too, in the idea of himself as a revered humanitarian, the first to break through the walls of church and conservative opposition, the can-do dreamer. It was an indispensable combination for productive leadership.

At the very moment when he spoke to the educators, he was wrestling with the question of committing American divisions to Vietnam. But that was another world, far removed from the tough, joyous work of enacting an aid-to-education bill, a Medicare bill, an antipoverty bill, a voting rights bill. So at least he hoped.

Months passed before I felt fully employed at the White House. That disturbed me. One was supposed to be frantic with pressure, pursued by the President, cabinet officers, bureaucrats, interest groups, and the press, turned haunted-gray by late hours and fateful decisions — and correspondingly ennobled by suffering in the public's service. It was the apotheosis of the Protestant work ethic. And it was not happening to me. I went home at seven in the evening, wondering if I had been wrong to give up my "backwater" in State.

In time the paper flow started to move my way. I became a necessary part of the staff, as pale and tired as anybody. During the intermission I got a look at what others were doing around the building.

Special Assistants to the President were relatively new in government; aides were not. Lincoln and Wilson and all the others had aides. Franklin Roosevelt was the first to institutionalize them in law — describing them as men with a "passion for anonymity" whose task was to help the President cope with the increasingly complex problems that wound up in his office.

The President required someone outside his office who knew whom he knew and whom he wished to see or avoid, someone who could be gracious and cold-blooded in turn. An appointments secretary. It was an excruciatingly difficult job, particularly with a volatile man like Johnson. Each day Marvin Watson was advised by a dozen well-meaning people that if the President would see X and Y, he would assure himself not only of their support, but of the powerful interests or voting groups they represented. Other people warned that unless A or B was given half an hour in the Oval Office, there would be hell to pay. Senators, congressmen, cabinet officers, governors, mayors, civil rights leaders, a few banking and foundation officers had special claims on the President's attention. Virtually all had requests to make; many had decisions to put before him; some brought him premonitory information about trends in the economy, race relations, politics, and technological change. There was no time for them all. Watson had to guess about whom the President should be pressed to see, and who could be shunted to an assistant. Having proposed a schedule, he often found it rejected or hopelessly amended. Just as often he commiserated with the six o'clock appointee while the five o'clock meeting stretched on past seven.

When he came to Washington, Watson was relatively innocent about the federal Establishment, and about men who had been active in urban politics, education, labor, and cultural life for decades. He had little appreciation for shades of opinion between liberal pink and Red. He was a provincial, and for a time he used that as a shield, saying that he was just an old boy from Daingerfield, Texas, who could not be expected to know better. That irritated me and many others who believed him to be a tough and canny operator. So far as I knew, he did not press his ideological views on the President. He had one purpose, and he pursued it unswervingly. It did not matter to him in the slightest whether newspaper columnists called him reactionary, or whether complaints that he paid insufficient attention to certain liberal politicians surfaced in the press. So long as Lyndon Johnson was satisfied with his performance, so long as the political loyalties of senior officials in the government — particularly with respect to the Kennedys — were fixed and clear in his mind, he was content. (If you changed "Lyndon Johnson" in that sentence to "John Kennedy," you had a perfect description of Kenneth O'Donnell.) Watson was well suited for his role, and became increasingly effective as his sharp mind picked up whatever was useful in serving his President.

The President needed someone to manage the preparation of the coming year's legislative program, and to serve as his principal conduit to the departments and agencies. If there was a key position in the Presidential management of domestic affairs, it was this. Ted Sorensen occupied it in the Kennedy Administration, Bill Moyers and later Joe Califano in Johnson's. What they did with the job depended on their native abilities and their relationship to their Presidents. Sorensen and Moyers were writers as well as task-force managers. Califano dealt almost as often with business leaders as with senior men in government.

I knew Sorensen's work only by reputation, and by reading his elegant, eighteenth-century sentences, with their antipodal phrases balanced in the air of rhetorical liberalism. Moyers was the brightest man of his years I had ever met. He was extremely ambitious, and yet he was capable of drawing away from power far enough to see its terrifying possibilities, in the President and in himself. When I arrived he was very close to Johnson. He was quick, and Johnson needed things done quickly if he was to perpetuate the image of the man of action; he had good relations with the Kennedys, at a time when that was particularly important; he was attractive to other young men in government, especially to those who dissented from prevailing foreign policies; and he was warmly regarded by many members of the press, while Johnson's stock as a credible leader was falling. He was as liberal as Watson was conservative, and as he pressed Johnson toward the left he came under increasing fire from the Texas organization led by Governor Connally. (This was a dilemma for Johnson. Throughout his Senate career he had been anxious to placate the essentially conservative Texas party, as its support was critical to his national ambitions. Now, as President, he needed constantly to reassure the essentially liberal national party that he was sympathetic to interests which were alien to Connally — organized labor, minorities, all who demanded big spending for social purposes. Johnson tried to serve both of his constituencies, or at least to serve one in a way that did not estrange the other; he thought he could not lose his Texas base without severe damage to his national leadership.)

The Johnson-Moyers relationship was essentially father-son. As such it held the potential, for Moyers, of a substantial political inheritance — and the danger that as he became his own man, he would risk Johnson's anger if he strayed from him, submersion by that powerful personality if he stayed with him, the loss of self-respect if he promoted policies in which he did not believe, and a reputation for disloyalty if he attacked those policies in public or private. To some degree all of us faced this danger, but to none of us was it so immediate as it was to Moyers. No one else was so close. No one else, I believed, made Johnson think of himself when young.

Bill Moyers grew up relatively poor in Marshall, Texas, and made his way by his wits and drive. He, Watson, Jake Jacobsen, and I came to the White House after years of association with

Johnson in the Senate or in Texas. Joe Califano came from middle-class Brooklyn, Harvard Law School, and a Wall Street law firm. He had never known Johnson until, as McNamara's special assistant, he became the point of contact for the White House in Defense. Thereafter Johnson wrestled McNamara for him and won. He was smart, indefatigable, unafraid of responsibility or of making demands upon highly placed men in government and industry. He was not abrasive, but the messages he conveyed to such men — do this, stop doing that — often made him seem so; though they came straight from the President, whatever offense they gave was attributed to Califano. That was part of the job — getting the President's message across while exposing him to as little personal and political cost as possible.

Califano elaborated the task-force network until there were groups — some made up of outside experts, some of government men, some mixed — working on a spectacular range of national problems. He made use of the new programming-planning-budgeting system which McNamara had introduced at Defense, and which Johnson, mesmerized by tales of its efficiency, had then extended to the rest of the government. It was intended to force each agency to set goals for several years hence, and then to direct its programs toward achieving them. Management would be simplified, programs which did not contribute directly to the goals would be abandoned, money would be saved. A rational concept, but difficult in practice. Congress, for example, did not take to the idea that there should be only one program for subsidizing sewage treatment plants, and not four or five under the patronage of as many congressional committees.

By necessity Califano learned to deal with Southern potentates on the Hill, to whom his managerial efficiencies and personal liberalism were peculiar, if not threatening. A few days after he arrived, Hayes Redmon, Moyers's assistant, called him and announced in a thick Mississippi voice that he was "Chaihman

Whicken" — Representative Jamie Whitten — and wanted to "talk cotton" with him. Califano swallowed and said he knew nothing about cotton. "What? Lynnon Johnson 'point somebody to run his prog'ams don't know anything about *cotton?*" He told Califano that he would meet him in an hour for lunch in the White House mess. "I'll teach you somethin' 'bout cotton, boy." Desperately Califano called around the building, asking for advice. I had inherited Mike Feldman's portfolio for agriculture, but I knew almost as little as Califano about middling lengths and skip-row planting. I volunteered to share the ordeal with him. No, he'd better do it alone. "Then call Orville Freeman. Surely he knows." O.K. An hour later, sweating, but full of statistics, he stood at the basement entrance, waiting for Whitten. After a while, Redmon came by and whispered, "Tell you, boy, Chaihman Whickens' goan have yo' *aiss!*"

It was a good introduction to the White House. One had to learn to distinguish between ersatz pressure and the real thing — to know when politicians were serving *pro forma* interests and when it really mattered. More importantly, when it really mattered to us. One could never be sure.

Developing a new program was a long process, culminating in sessions with cabinet officers and with White House and Budget Bureau staff in Califano's office. We narrowed the discussion to details of administration, then widened it to policy alternatives, narrowed and widened it again. Califano had a sensible means of resolving the debate. At eight or nine in the evening, he would announce that the President wanted an agreed-upon program by ten the next morning. Therefore Califano needed it by nine. (Groans. Impossible. We'll have to work all night. I'm sorry, but you know the President.) Some of us suspected that the President had been told there would be a program on his desk by that hour, and had said all right; but who could tell? Even if it was

Califano's initiative, Johnson now expected it and would ask why it wasn't there, who was making problems and otherwise refusing to cooperate. Tactics like that were worth remembering.

In the basement of the West Wing fifteen or twenty analysts and cryptographers were crowded into a few narrow rooms, in one of which the Special Assistant for National Security Affairs had his office. There McGeorge Bundy worked, and later Walt Rostow.

People still debated the proper scope of the job. Obviously the President needed someone to sift through each day's mountain of intelligence cables, the product of a hundred embassies and consular offices, military units, the CIA, electronic and satellite surveillance, and so on; and to send him, with analyses that put it in context, the important parts of it, with alternative responses, if a response was required, and the recommendations of his principal institutional advisors — Rusk, McNamara, McCone/Raborn/ Helms and their subordinates. Then to tell the lot what the President wished to know or do.

The debatable questions were (1) to what extent the Special Assistant should press his independent judgments; (2) whether he should develop private relationships with foreign ambassadors and ministers; (3) whether he should impose his own intelligence and policy requirements on the departments; (4) to what extent he spoke for the President in interdepartmental meetings; (5) whether the United States needed, thirty yards from the Oval Office, a combined Secretary of State and Defense — Director of Central Intelligence — Chairman of the Joint Chiefs, a funnel and penultimate judge; and (6) if the exigencies of our times required us to have such an official, whether his views and performance should be examined by representatives of the people? If a Secretary of Defense believed in the inevitability of a worldwide race war and instructed his department to prepare for preventive strikes on colored nations, clearly that fact should be made known to Congress. But if a special assistant held such views and urged them on the President, the need to assure confidentiality between the President and his staff required that the Congress be denied the right to question him. In practice, the conundrum was resolved by the self-restraint of men like Bundy and Rostow. Yet the possibility of mischief was always there.

In shaping foreign policy, there were, to be sure, built-in advantages for the Secretaries; they had enormous staffs and intelligence resources, the Special Assistant had few. But he had proximity to the only man in whom the Constitution vests responsibility for the conduct of foreign policy. All that was needed to give his views absolute authority were the words, "The President wishes . . ." and a certain amount of passivity on the part of the bureaucracy.

McGeorge Bundy — the name was difficult for many people; even in the days of his eminence, many senators referred to him as "George McBundy" — was a brilliant executive, thoroughly schooled in twentieth-century foreign policy, almost antiseptically clear in his views. He had the capacity to intimidate, and often did. One felt that behind his "That won't do" lay decades of experience in affairs of state, a New England devotion to country, a Brahmin impatience with messy thinking. He had worked and written for Stimson. He was related to Dean Acheson by marriage. He was a Harvard dean. John Kennedy, like Lyndon Johnson, had depended on him. He could put a meeting back on track by posing, with structural simplicity, three or four questions which must be answered and could be. He could expose a weak argument, and pluck a good one out of another man's cloudy attempts; when he said, "What you're contending, I believe, and it's very much worth consideration, is . . ." he made a grateful ally. I thought his only conceivable limitation was that he would find it hard to reverse field — to accept evidence that a certain policy in which he believed and on which he had acted in the past was actually misguided.

His successor, Walt Rostow, was of a very different temper — not so much an analyst as a theoretician. He was as benign toward amateur contributions as Bundy was severe. His passion was the construction of general principles from masses of data; it was his memoranda to Johnson from the Policy Planning staff in State, in which Johnson's activities in foreign affairs were seen as elements in a great and beneficent design, that attracted the President to him and led to his appointment when Bundy left. Rostow thought a lot about "regionalism." He believed that poor nations in Asia, Africa, and Latin America were beginning to pool their resources and to commit themselves to the common defense of their regions. This he thought would relieve the economic and military aid pressures upon the United States. It seemed plausible and therefore hopeful. But it was based on several shaky premises: that the frail regional organizations based in Bangkok or Addis Ababa represented something more than ideas, and could actually commit the governments of their regions to common action; that the primordial animosities of race and religion, and the new demands of national pride, would yield to unproved theories of economic and political cooperation; that there was, in the end, any substitute for the massive transfer of resources from the northern developed nations to the poor and disorganized ones of the south. For me, and I believed for the President, Rostow's most useful ability was in demonstrating grounds for optimism. After all, neither developments in the world since 1945 nor American foreign policy decisions had been an unmitigated series of disasters and mistakes. To regard them as such was to become despairing and therefore impotent. The obverse of this ability was a panglossian determination to see every event as part of an upward trend. I speculated that Rostow would advise the President, upon learning of a nuclear attack on Manhattan, that the first phase of the island's urban renewal had been accomplished in a flash and at no expense to the Treasury.

Both Bundy and Rostow believed in the need to prevent North

Vietnam and the Viet Cong from seizing power in South Vietnam by force. So did I. Both believed in the ability of the United States to meet that need. Though he had vigorously recommended it, I did not know how much faith Bundy really put in the air bombardment of North Vietnam as a means of slowing the invasion of the South or producing negotiations; Rostow had great faith in it, and faulted every assessment that suggested otherwise. Both believed that the corruption and ineffectiveness of the South Vietnamese government were neither so intractable nor so debilitating that they would cancel out America's efforts. They were not insensitive to the growing resistance to the war at home, particularly in the university environment from which they came. But they believed that containing North Vietnam and China was in America's long-term interest (which included the long-term interest of the dissenting professors and students) and should be pursued in the face of teach-ins and demonstrations. Rostow had been a Rhodes scholar in the late thirties, about the time the Oxford Union resolved not to fight for king and country — and moments before Munich and the conquest of Europe. The experience of those years was a vital piece of the argument, which I accepted as completely as any man in the White House, that what we were doing in Vietnam might help to forestall the cataclysm of another major war.

The President needed someone to deal with the press. To make sure they were provided with buses, planes, cars, food and drink, hotel rooms, telephones, wall plugs, cables, desks, chairs, reports, advance texts, schedules, and time to file. To answer inconsequential and even demeaning questions, and to make announcements that rocked the stock market and set nations to quarreling. To leak certain stories and deny others. To report that the President was fit, working hard, or going to the hospital for minor surgery. To plead ignorance, buy time, dodge, duck, become righteously angry, temper unpleasant news, and emphasize the positive. To prepare the President for press conferences. To be certain the Teleprompter worked and the camera distance was right. To arrange meetings with writers in which, it was hoped, the President would project the image of a tolerant, dedicated, hard-pressed but masterful leader. To maintain his confidence, and theirs, when great issues were being fought out behind closed doors, and about which nothing could be reported. To discover what reporters were after from the White House staff, the departments, and Congress. To tell the President when he had performed badly. To be his friend and radar screen, his public apologist, his private critic and goad.

Was there another country whose leader was under such unremitting surveillance? Was there another president, or a premier, king, dictator, party secretary, chieftain or chairman whose every action and statement were reported? Whose weight, color, clothes, favorite foods, family, friends, handwriting, voice, tics, cuts, blemishes, and stumbles were examined and debated as if they were the droppings of eagles, auguries of the country's future? Did other leaders work so hard to dominate the news? Were journalists in other countries so indulged? Did Mrs. Gandhi's press secretary, or Kosygin's, or Harold Wilson's, combine the roles of informant, baggage master, electrician, and wet nurse? Did they worry about whether to preempt the time of a favorite television show in order that their leaders might explain their policies?

Answer "probably not" to all the above. In fact it was hard to imagine any other human relationship like that between America's President and the press.

In good times it could be mutually rewarding; but the potential for trouble was always there. Their common dependency was grating. To succeed with the public, the President needed favorable attention from the press; to do its job the press needed news from the President. That they depended on, and yet constantly failed each other, made for mutual resentment.

A President was by nature an actor, scornful of those who only kibitzed. ("It's not the critic who counts," Theodore Roosevelt said, "not the man who points out how the strongman stumbles. . . . The credit belongs to the man who is actually in the arena, whose face is marred by dust and sweat and blood . . . who spends himself in a worthy cause.") That a President should have to struggle for understanding, for sympathy in his plight, when (he thought) that should come naturally from fair-minded men, was distasteful — a terrible waste of time when there was so much else to do. But the press, like most critics, would not commit itself in advance. Generally it was willing to be fair, but not to withhold judgment in order that the President might write his own reviews. The actor wanted time to work out his routine. He wanted to "preserve his options" until the circumstances for action were right. The critics could not wait. They met a deadline every day. He wanted them to transcribe his best intentions. They were required to report all he did and all that happened to him.

Kennedy had his trouble with the press. His Administration was accused of "managing the news." Pierre Salinger defended the practice as part of the natural competition of motives between government and press. This had an appealing candor, but it provoked violent editorial complaints. It was unwise to engage the press directly on an issue that could only be debated on its turf. Once in the Senate I had urged Russell to respond to a newspaper's particularly egregious account of his position. "No," he said. "I never get into a pissing contest with a polecat."

Johnson's problems were more deeply rooted than Kennedy's. He had no physical glamour to carry him through when the news was bad. He was a high-pressure salesman, always trying to get his foot in the door, frequently arousing — in professionally skeptical men who had spent their working lives listening to the apologies of politicians — an incredulous resistance. Worst of all, he was a chief of government.

In the summer of 1966 I went off to Rhode Island for a vacation. As I left town, Johnson was working furiously to end a strike that had grounded the airlines. A wage settlement that would break the Administration's guidelines seemed the only solution. I thought I might hear complaints about that on the Rhode Island coast — if not from the Democratic natives, then from the Republican vacationers. I heard something very different from both. A gas station manager, a local real estate operator, and a New York banker offered identical judgments. What was wrong, they thought, was that nobody in Washington was really trying to stop the strike. Nobody in Washington cared, because everybody there had his own airplane.

It was ludicrous, but it grew out of deep feelings of mistrust for government — for "politicians" who looked after themselves and couldn't care less about the people. That was the residual image, and all of Adlai Stevenson's speeches about the high calling of politics hadn't changed it. It had much to do with the way the public regarded Johnson as President. Looking back over three years, you could see how his virtues had come to haunt him.

In the fall of 1963, the machinery of government was badly stalled. Congress would not pass on the President's proposals. A sense of listlessness, almost of desuetude, pervaded many of the departments of government. Then the President, in whom hopes still resided, was murdered.

The train had quit, the engineer was dead. Dangers abounded on all sides. The big man with the inverted "v"'s on his forehead, like John Wayne's, left his seat and walked forward to the engine. Sounds of his tinkering and adjusting drifted back to the cars. He hollered and pleaded. He mimicked those who stood by watching. He requested that a bipartisan delegation come forward to observe him at work. He offered words of praise for the fortitude of the passengers, and a tribute to the fallen engineer. He wheeled and dealed, the object of all hope. Suddenly the train jerked forward and started to roll. The passengers cheered. Stories quickly circulated about how he had talked one recalcitrant into oiling the drive shaft, another into firing the boiler. His craftiness became a legend. He was lionized. He was just what the country needed. Everyone settled back for the ride — and in time took it for granted that the train should be running. People started talking about his big nose. They remembered him pulling up a dog by the ears, and showing off his abdominal scar. Good Lord, they thought, he's just a fixer, not a leader; an uncouth politician, not a statesman.

A fantasy, but something like what happened. Johnson was a master craftsman of politics, someone who knew where the power was, and how to use it — within the mistrusted world of Washington. He was, using a distinction I had heard Solis Horwitz make in Senate days, a chief of government, not a chief of state. People suspected the former and admired the latter. Ike had been a chief of state — the engineer who rarely examined his machine, but who cheered us on by his trust in our good purposes. Kennedy, faced with the threat of Soviet missiles, had been a chief of state. In a sudden crisis, the nation always saw its leader that way and rallied behind him — as it rallied behind Johnson in the early months after the assassination, when he made a stalled and shaken country move again.

Then the crisis passed, and he was still there, tinkering, bargaining, propagandizing. He was sensationally successful; each legislative achievement topped the last. But his attention seemed to be riveted on the machinery itself, on making it work and afterwards talking about how he had done it. He resisted inquiries about the alternatives he was considering. He wanted no stories that might get somebody mad, or somebody else's hopes up when he might change his mind. He wanted no sermonizing about the right thing to do, when circumstances might force him to do something else. He wanted, it seemed, not so much to surprise as to be free of pressure — to fix the machine in his own time, without people standing in his light. That was his way in the Senate, and he did not change in the White House.

His secretiveness magnified the skepticism which the press felt toward all Presidents. Skepticism became bitterness as he turned off the news — denying this story, shifting the lens on that one until the picture was thrown hopelessly out of focus, giving out homilies in place of views. As the reporters' hostility became evident, a sense of being hounded grew in him. He came to believe, as John Kennedy did, that almost nobody in government could keep a confidence. Kennedy had scolded the State Department's upper echelon for its loose tongues. He was narrowly dissuaded from requiring desk officers to report verbatim every conversation with a journalist. Johnson scolded his staff for seeing the press at all. Like Kennedy, he confided in a few trusted reporters, hoping to get his story across while inflicting pain on the others, leaving them without access to the fountain of news. That made it worse. Some of the trusted men were embarrassed to be given special treatment, with its implicit obligation to repay in kind. The untrusted ones were confirmed in their suspicions.

Events made a naturally unhappy situation worse. For the first two years there was almost too much to report. Most of it was favorable, and wrote itself — the transition, the campaign against Goldwater, the Southern champion of civil rights, the tide of new laws. Then Vietnam, city riots, violent demonstrations, and imprisonment in the White House. The President still traveled about the country, but from military bases to Legion and farm conventions, using these like stepping-stones in a torrent. Congress became stubborn; his very success with it had emptied the bag of programs for which the country cared very much. If he had set his sights low at the beginning, the contrast would have been less vivid. If he had not staked his claim to greatness on his demonstrable achievements — his coonskins on the wall — he would not have fallen so far when the achievements became rare. If he had been a charismatic entertainer, he might have taken to television, thumbed his nose at his critics in the Congress and the press, and appealed directly and successfully to the public. If, if.

His problems with public opinion were too deep, and too complex, to be cured by a press secretary. Bill Moyers tried, and the admiration many reporters felt for him was translated, for a while, into tolerance for his principal. But in time that became just another disability for Johnson. The notion developed that Moyers was a beleaguered voice of reason and trustworthiness in a sick environment, that the sensible and compassionate views he had ascribed to Johnson were in fact only his own. Relations between them became increasingly tense, and in 1966 Moyers left the White House. It was a melancholy denouement to a long and valuable friendship, and for me it was a painful loss.

His successor, George Christian, had an altogether different concept of his responsibilities. Laconic, highly intelligent, he understood that his first duty was to convey, as accurately as possible, what the President thought, did, and intended to do. He was an instrument who played Johnson's music, not a composer. Privately he was as critical an advisor to Johnson as Moyers had been; but he gave no hint that he disagreed with him in any respect. He was thoroughly professional. With Tom Johnson, a bright young man whom Moyers had discovered, he met the reporters' need for hard news. In a bad time, Christian won the respect of both antagonists, President and press.

The rest of us talked with a good many reporters and columnists each week. The President complained about that, especially when what he read and saw was unfavorable. (And he read and saw almost everything — papers, magazines, news tickers, all three networks at once. As the commentary got worse, I wondered if his insatiable desire to see it reflected a kind of masochism, a need to prove to himself how unfair the bastards of the media really were, or simply a political interest in what the voters were being told? Maybe all three.) But his complaints about consorting with the enemy were not nearly so forbidding as they were reported to be. They never amounted to an outright prohibition. Perhaps he knew that to the extent we were regarded as sensible and candid, we helped his cause. And he retained, even in the worst days, a kind of grudging affection for many members of the White House press corps.

That "corps" was in fact a heterogeneous array of personalities, intentions, and talents, united only by their need to produce copy, and their annoyance with whatever made that difficult. It included old pros, men who had worked police desks, city halls, the Congress, and the Eisenhower and Kennedy White House; young tyros, graduates of schools of journalism and political science, who were as a rule ideological and given to inductive reasoning; heavy thinkers, men who did not so much report the activities of government as issue moral tracts intended to improve the behavior of its officials; light thinkers, to whom an insurrection, a White House wedding, a political convention, and a litter of beagle pups were equally "newsworthy," and who gathered facts about them all with the same contented industry; wire-service men and women, whose god was speed; television men, who reduced highly complex events and policies to a minute on the tube; economic specialists, military specialists, diplomatic, political and society specialists, people who wrote for trade papers, labor papers, Great Gray Papers, syndicates, chains, tabloids, the slicks, the liberal and conservative weeklies, the *Economist*, *France-Soir*, Tass, and *Asahi Shinbun*. In the main they struck me as intelligent and reasonably assiduous, more opinionated than most people, and also more knowledgeable, interested, and therefore interesting.

They were required by their trade to seek out conflict and controversy. Once I heard Johnson protest to Henry Luce about this. So many encouraging things were happening in the country, he said, and still the press concentrated on friction, expressions of mistrust and doubt, violence, and the gap between what the government desired or claimed and what some malcontent said was actually happening. "But, Mr. President," Luce replied, "good news is no news. Bad news is news." Johnson stared at him for a long time, thinking about that, and finally nodded and changed the subject.

The President needed a legislative staff to work the Hill. Theirs was largely a transmitting job — relaying the members' hopes, dilemmas, and complaints to the President, explaining to the members what the President wanted. Often they took part in our discussions about new programs, and provided a sense of the possible in talks that by and large concentrated on the desirable. They put the pressure on when the votes looked tight, reported offers of compromise, and took soundings as best they could. Like many of our ambassadors abroad, they represented the needs and views of the principality to which they were accredited more often, if not more urgently, than they did ours to it. No doubt that was necessary for effective representation, and Larry O'Brien, Henry Wilson, and Mike Manatos were very effective. They were trusted on the Hill, and that was the main requirement.

Johnson, of course, was the recognized authority on dealing with Congress. As the war, the economy, and problems in the cities began to absorb his time, he gave less attention to his legislative program. But he was still something to watch when, on the eve of a close vote, he made two or three dozen calls to wavering members. In 1965, as the most productive session in many years came to an end, he worked seven days a week, trying to turn a spectacular score into a perfect one. He took on the District of Columbia home-rule bill as a personal challenge. Several Presidents had tried to put it through and failed. There was, as always, deep Southern resistance to letting a Negro majority run the capital city. Republicans were not eager to establish a new big-city Democratic machine. Even moderates, who had voted with us consistently throughout the session, were reserved about home rule for Washington. "This is the federal city," one of them told me when I called to remind him of the upcoming vote. "I want my constituents to enjoy it when they visit here. They own a piece of it."

Johnson worked almost round the clock, and lost. Several commentators clucked that he had pushed his luck too far, that the Congress was exhausted and bitter about being forced to take on one more contentious issue. I asked Johnson if he now agreed. "I agreed before I started," he said. "But I wanted to pass it, and I knew this was the only chance I would have." Why was that? Why hadn't he waited until the next year, when the same liberal majority would be back? "Because they'll all be thinking about their reelections. I'll have made mistakes, my polls will be down, and they'll be trying to put some distance between themselves and me. They won't want to go into the fall with their opponents calling 'em Lyndon Johnson's rubber stamps. Not on something like letting the Negroes run Washington.

"You've got to give it all you can, that first year," he said. "Doesn't matter what kind of majority you come in with. You've got just one year when they treat you right, and before they start worrying about themselves. The third year, you lose votes; if this war goes on, I'll lose a lot of 'em. A lot of our people don't belong here, they're in Republican seats, and the Republicans will get them back. The fourth year's all politics. You can't put anything through when half the Congress is thinking how to beat you. So you've got one year. That's why I tried. Well, we gave it a hell of a lick, didn't we?"

The President needed specialists, men who understood the substance of particular issues and knew where to go for objective judgments of his programs.

The Council of Economic Advisors — composed of three such men — was one of the wise inventions of the postwar years. A succession of academics remained there long enough to make the essential connection between the economy and specific government programs, and to give the President the best advice modern economics could provide; and then left before they lost their cutting edge.

Economics is called the "dismal science"; but there was nothing dismal about the minds or writing styles of Walter Heller, Gardner Ackley, and Arthur Okun. By general consent, the policies they recommended helped to bring about the longest streak of prosperity the nation had ever known. In time the war and increasing deficits began to pull it apart. The apparent lesson from that was that Keynesian economics worked only so long as there were no inflexible constraints upon the government. If the nation became involved in a war, and political considerations (reluctance in the Congress to raise the taxes to pay for it, reluctance in the President to force the issue, to say that we could not simultaneously make a Great Society and limited war without new taxes) — if such considerations rendered it impossible to take the appropriate countervailing steps, there could only be trouble. In a metaphor of the day, that was like driving a car without brakes.

I thought that if one special assistant would be identified with what would endure from the Johnson years, it would be Douglass Cater. His fields were education and health. He had an acute sense of history, a gift for clear prose, and excellent contacts in the universities, education associations, medical schools, foundations, and Congress. He helped to draw up and put through most of Johnson's programs for aid to education and better medical care. For some reason — perhaps having to do with their roles as critics and their preoccupation with day-to-day events — journalists seldom joined the government and took responsibility for developing long-term policies. Cater, a former editor of *The Reporter*, did so out of concern for the country's needs and a long affection for Johnson. He was always open to new proposals, and he made no public complaint when it became difficult to finance the old ones — those which he had helped to draft, and in which his hopes and pride were deeply invested.

The President needed a generalist, a man who could put out a fire in Congress, write a speech, plan a trip, talk to political supporters, arrange a television interview, share his griefs and victories, and convey the impression of one who was authorized to speak for, but was not himself, the President. A Jack Valenti. He was a true believer — his "I sleep better at night knowing Lyndon Johnson is my President" had demonstrated that. But he was much more than an uncritical admirer. His ripe language — the product of extensive reading of eighteenth- and nineteenth-century British historians — amused people who would have regarded similar praise from another man's assistant (Sorensen or Schlesinger, for example) as perfectly natural.

Valenti was expected to be ready and creative at all times, and generally he succeeded. He had been a public relations man and a newspaper columnist. He was accustomed to a world where the premium was on a fast and superficially attractive response to any emergency. Yet behind his quick affability was a questing mind and an unusual generosity toward his fellow workers. He, Moyers, and later Christian were under the basket for the rest of us, tapping in our shots: they were there early and late, when the President read our memoranda and suggestions, and they often persuaded him to take another look at what we proposed and maybe to agree. Every President needs a man like Jack Valenti — a resourceful friend to whom he can turn with any political problem and know that the skies will fall before he quits trying to resolve it.

The President needed, I supposed, a resident intellectual, though after Professor Goldman's efforts with the White House Festival of the Arts I could not be sure. What he got when he acquired John Roche was something very different from a conventional academic. I had read many of Roche's articles over the years, and thought they were original and penetrating. But when he arrived in the White House, sporting a Pedro Armendariz moustache and griping about Jimmy Breslin's use of some off-the-cuff remarks, I was nonplussed. He did not fit the image of a gentle professor, patiently presiding over a babble of views. He was opinionated, in the manner of one whose opinions have been subjected to passionate dispute. He bore the scars of his prewar pacifism — he had been bloodied in a picket line when he protested our aid to Britain — and of his postwar anticommunism. He had fought the Communists in the American Veterans Committee, and then fought to keep the ADA, of which he was once national chairman, from easing its stand against Communist aggression anywhere. A cold-war liberal, a Brooklyn Irishman whose oldest friendships were with Jewish trade unionists, a respected historian with the instincts of a ward politician, Roche was one of the most honorable men I had ever known.

We shared a suite of offices for almost three years. At the beginning I thought his job was to "relate" to the intellectual community, as Schlesinger had done for Kennedy. As the war grew and university protests grew with it, that became increasingly difficult. Poets and literary critics took to the *New York Review of Books* to denounce Johnson as a preternatural villain, a monster who had seized on domestic liberalism as a cover for his stupid (or cunning, depending on the writer's needs) intervention in Vietnam. History became psychopathology. Roche had little use for literary critics as grand strategists — most precisely, he thought it was futile to try to win them over to a view of history that had more to do with power politics than with Freudian analysis. I was more hopeful. I thought we might "bring them around" if we explained the dilemma we faced, listened sympathetically to their concerns, and pointed out that despite the war we were making inroads against poverty and discrimination at home. As the climate grew steadily worse, I gave up. Intellectuals — men who in their own fields resisted loose reasoning and specious analogies — began to accept the most extreme assessments of the country and of those who governed it. The more savage the analysis, the more appropriate they found it; the more violent the proposed response, the more condign. It was hard for any man whose livelihood and reputation depended on his relationship to this literary-academic world to take positions directly opposed to its hysterical *weltanschauung*. Roche did, and with combative zest.

The more closely he observed the President, the more certain he became that governing was neither a game nor a morality play. It was serious bargaining between competing imperatives. He believed Lyndon Johnson was in the mainstream of democratic liberalism; that through persuasion, maneuver, and guile he was bringing the country closer to its ideal of social justice; that he was a civil libertarian who understood the deep divisions of opinion in the country, but did not shrink from the obligations of power. Roche was born outside what some of his faculty colleagues called "the ruling class in America." So was Johnson. The road to achievement for both of them was pocked with failure and obloquy. Both had to sweat for what they got. Roche had loved and enjoyed John Kennedy — particularly the Boston Irish politican in him; he felt kin to Lyndon Johnson.

Roche believed in the war's purposes — the human, as well as geopolitical ones. He despised police states, and he believed that democracies could not in conscience permit them to dominate others. He had no desire to bring on a final confrontation with the Soviets and the Chinese. But he thought they should not be allowed — as a moral matter — to extend their power. Kennedy's words — "we shall pay any price, bear any burden, meet any hardships, support any friend, oppose any foe to assure the survival and the success of liberty" — were more than just rhetoric to John Roche; they expressed what democrats should feel and be prepared to live by. In time I came to doubt the practicality of that position — which had been Democratic dogma since the late 1940's — but to the end I respected Roche for holding it.

Still, he thought the campaign in Vietnam had been badly managed, particularly in its reliance on air power. The most serious error, he believed, had been our failure to move swiftly to train the South Vietnamese and arm them with modern weapons. He admired McNamara and his systems analysts, but he thought their computers and productive efficiencies had obscured the fact that an AK-47 shoots much faster than an M-1. When claims were made for the effectiveness of our bombing, and still the ARVN went without M-16's, Roche bit into a black cigar and rapped out an acerbic memorandum to the President. It was an unexpected role for the "resident intellectual," whose predecessor had been more concerned with providing friendly academics with arguments for the faculty lounge.

The President needed a Special Counsel. Clark Clifford and Charles Murphy had held the job in Truman's day, Sorensen and Mike Feldman in Kennedy's, Lee White and then I in Johnson's. Each performed a few of the same chores, and some that were unique to his skills and experience. The following examples give an idea of what it was in my time, to "counsel the President."

LEGISLATION: TO SIGN OR NOT SIGN

After a bill passed Congress, it was delivered to the Bureau of the Budget, and thence to the departments concerned with it. Usually they had no objection to the President signing it. Sometimes they suggested a statement expressing his satisfaction with it, or his intent to sign it and seek a later modification. From time to time they recommended a veto. Budget received these views, added its own, and sent them all to the President. I saw them first and gave him my judgment.

The departments were inclined to recommend approval of borderline legislation. That made life easier with the congressional committees which oversaw their affairs and had most likely written the bill in question. It also pleased their constituencies — the businessmen, labor unions, farmers, contractors, or developers with whom they dealt, and who would gain from the proposed relaxation of standards or federal subsidy. Budget, on the other hand, was almost primly righteous. If a bill did not square with the President's program, was too expensive, or set a bad precedent, Budget was for veto. Cabinet and subcabinet officers often argued that a bill was "not really very far from what we wanted," and besides, important members of Congress favored it. Budget replied that seen objectively, it was unwise or positively harmful. Political considerations were not in its territory; if the President felt it was necessary to yield to them, so be it. Budget's analyses of the issues were more detached than those of the departments, though its staff, in pursuit of a point, could bend an argument with the best of them. Ordinarily I started with its hard-line position and then tried to weigh the importance of political considerations, as I understood them. Here is a typical memorandum:

6:45 p.m., Tuesday
November 8, 1966

FOR THE PRESIDENT

This bill concerns the development of geothermal steam — steam generated within the earth — as a power source. It is a bad bill and I believe you should veto it.

Geothermal steam springs are known to exist in four States — California, Nevada, Oregon, and New Mexico. Most of them are on Federal lands. One of them is now producing enough electricity to serve a community of 50,000 people. Nobody knows how extensive or how valuable these springs are. Electricity is probably their most valuable product, but there are brines in some springs that contain lithium, gold and silver. What is most important is that they may well prove to be an inexhaustible source of energy. They ought to be developed.

After four years of considering the matter, Congress has passed a bill designed to encourage private development of the springs. In seven respects the bill violates sound public policy.

(1) It provides for perpetual leases — as long as there is production in commercial quantities. As [FPC Chairman] Lee White says in

his letter on the bill, it would "relinquish the stake of future generations of Americans in the formulation of appropriate public policies for an apparently inexhaustible natural resource whose significance to America's energy needs we can only begin to grasp today." Interior had recommended a maximum lease extension of 90 years. That gives the public some protection.

(2) It provides unconscionable grandfather rights — giving those who held valid *mineral* leases or mining claims on September 7, 1965 the right to convert them into geothermal leases. Interior told the Committee:

> Had it been made known to the Department at the time of application that the real purpose and intent of any applicant for an oil and gas lease was not to develop the lands for oil and gas, but . . . for geothermal steam, we would not have issued the lease . . . the holder of a mineral lease has received exactly what he bargained for . . . to give him another right [to convert these mineral leases into geothermal leases] is to confer on him a new benefit amounting to a gratuity from the Government. The public would lose the advantage of competitive bidding in the best potential areas. . . .

(3) It provides no authority for renegotiating the terms, conditions, rents or royalties of the leases at five-year intervals. Interior, which asked for this authority, now suggests that it may have it, although it wrote to Budget in mid-October that "the legislative history being what it is (several members of the House committee having strongly opposed renegotiation authority, and succeeded in striking it) we doubt the practicability of attempting to accomplish renegotiation administratively."

(4) It provides for competitive bidding *only* in "known geothermal resources areas." This follows the Mineral Leasing Act of 1920 provision. Nevertheless our general policy in recent years has been to encourage competitive bidding for resources everywhere, not to exempt certain areas.

(5) It provides that royalties are payable only on steam *sold or utilized*. All agencies agree that this encourages waste for no economic purpose and to the detriment of conservation.

(6) It provides a primary lease term of 15 years—even without production. This is too long.

(7) It provides a maximum lease of 51,200 acres, as against Interior's recommendation of 10,240 acres.

Agency recommendations:

FPC, *Budget,* and *CEA* vigorously against. *Agriculture* does not object.

Interior is for signing, primarily because the bill does provide a way to get geothermal steam development going. In my opinion Interior has folded, after being beaten down on every issue of consequence.

This matter has been in Congress for four years. It can wait another year.

Two Senators have called me about it, both before the bill reached my desk. [   ] said "I've called; I've done my duty; you do what's best." Clearly he has no heavy stake in it, but is only serving some of his constitutents. The bill's sponsor, [   ], called last week to say he hoped there was no problem with it. As I had never heard of the bill I could tell him nothing. If you decide to veto it, I should probably give him a call before it is announced.

Johnson vetoed it, though its sponsor was an old friend and supporter.

Frequently a bill trespassed upon the President's executive powers and duties. For example: Congress, or one of its committees, sometimes demanded the right to a final say about specific projects, previously authorized by general legislation, before they were launched. If this amounted only to requiring that a department provide notice of what it proposed to build or do — giving Congress time to stop it if it chose — that was tolerated. But if the department was forbidden to proceed until Congress or the committee authorized it to do so, or if the reporting period was so long as to tie up the department for many months, that was regarded as repugnant to the principle of separation of powers. Chairman Rivers of the House Armed Services Committee often ran afoul of this distinction.

9:15 a.m., Friday
September 9, 1966

FOR THE PRESIDENT

The Military Construction Authorization bill has a serious problem involving the reporting requirement for military base closures. You vetoed a bill last year requiring 120 days' notice before closing could be effectuated, and providing that notices of closings could only be made between January 1 and April 30 of each year.

Subsequently you approved a bill containing a simple requirement that the relevant *committees* be notified 30 days before a closing took effect.

This bill requires 30 days of "continuous session" with the report going to *Congress* rather than *committees*. The result of the change is to preclude base closures up to 30 days before Congress adjourns, during the entire time it is out of session, and for at least 30 days after it returns.

Congress' arguments for this change are:

(a) If Congress is to have a real opportunity to act on a proposed base closure, it must be in session.

(b) The "continuous session" requirement is in other laws, including the Water Resources Research Act which you approved in April.

(c) Congressional sessions now run so late into the Fall that as a practical matter there will be little delay.

Arguments against the bill are:

(a) There is a serious question as to whether the new requirement meets the test of a "reasonable waiting period." If Congress adjourns on October 15, the waiting period would be four months. If it ever adjourns on July 31, the waiting period would be seven months.

(b) As Justice says, the ability of the executive to act is conditioned on a purely legislative action — adjournment.

(c) While there are recent precedents, these did not relate to Defense programs where you are involved as Commander-in-Chief. The recent precedents also involved the *initiation* of programs, not their *discontinuance*.

Defense does not like the restriction, but it says it will not adversely affect its base closing program. It is well to remember that Defense also did not object on program grounds to the bill you vetoed last year.

Justice says that if you think the continuous session requirement makes the waiting period unreasonable, a veto could be supported on Constitutional grounds. If you think the waiting period does not impede your Defense program, then "we do not believe that the Constitutional question calls for a veto."

I believe you should sign the bill with either the Budget statement or a stronger one if you prefer. I think it would be very hard to explain the basis of your veto to the country, or to sell it to Congress. After all, it does seem "reasonable" to require, as a condition for fair notice to Congress, that Congress be in session to receive the notice.

The President, as a former member of Congress, was sensitive to its desire for a role in deciding what should be built, maintained, or closed; but he was even more sensitive about preserving the legitimate powers of the Presidency. He was unsuccessful in persuading several tough committee chairmen, jealous of what they conceived to be congressional prerogatives, to repeal offensive reporting requirements. But he vetoed several new ones, and by holding up work on a number of desirable projects, gained a measure of cooperation from the chairmen that he could have achieved in no other way.

The veto is the most dramatic expression of division between the branches of government. Presidents, cabinet secretaries, and ordinary bureaucrats may thwart the will of Congress, either by refusing to carry out its instructions as embodied in law (because these are regarded as repugnant to the Constitution) or by simple inattention. Congress may conduct guerrilla war on the Executive, delaying action on its requests, cutting its appropriations, refusing to cooperate with a particular official, and so on. But the veto symbolizes what these only suggest. Congress, with its constitutional authority to "make laws," is stopped cold by a single official whose principal responsibility is to execute those laws, and can have its way only by a two-to-one vote. In this sense, vetoes put the representative system on trial.

And they are seldom without political danger for the President. (I am talking, of course, about the veto of significant measures. Vetoing private relief bills disappoints nobody but the intended beneficiary, and occasionally the sponsoring congressman. FDR sometimes instructed his staff to "find me a few bills to veto," just to remind Congress that he was there and watching what it did.) Eisenhower made brilliant offensive use of the veto, on the spending issue; ° usually the veto offers very little political gain for the President to compensate for the danger. For example: in 1966, Johnson pocket-vetoed the so-called "District of Columbia Crime Bill" because it "would add endless complications and confusion to an already complex situation. It would make the job of the policeman on the beat and the public prosecutor much more difficult." This was art; what really troubled him was that the bill tipped the balance between police and suspect in a dangerously authoritarian way. His veto was an act of considerable courage. The *Washington Post* editorial writers much admired it. Those of the *Washington Star* did not, and neither, I suspected, did the great majority of citizens in Washington and elsewhere who heard about it. To put the question as Johnson might have done for his old debating class, "*Resolved:* That permitting criminals to run loose on the streets because of procedural restrictions on the police is a good thing for you and your wife." Because Congress was out of session, that issue was not immediately joined. A better bill passed the next year and Johnson signed it.

He signed the Safe Streets Act in the early summer of 1968, too, though it contained several provisions that were as obnoxious as those in the vetoed District bill. It also contained a lot of money for police departments around the country, for training, modernization, and the like. Safe Streets had started out as Johnson's bill, and then Congress had taken it away from him and returned it misshapen and abused. In an off year, Johnson might have risked a veto. In an election year, he faced the probability that Congress would override him, and the certainty that the Democratic nominee would hear about it all through the campaign.

───────────
° See pp. 168–169.

6:50 p.m., Friday
June 14, 1968

FOR THE PRESIDENT

I recognize that you must sign this bill.

But it is the worst bill you will have signed since you took office. Title III, the wiretapping-eavesdropping provision, is extremely dangerous. It can turn any given town or state into a little soviet. All that is needed is the will of the D.A. and permissiveness on the part of the judge.

I think Title II is manageable. As it applies only to the Federal system, Federal officers can be instructed not to follow the procedures that it purports to make legitimate.

If you choose to veto this bill and to take half an hour of TV time to explain why, I will work around the clock to produce a statement.

If — as I think you must — you sign it, I hope the signing statement will blast those provisions of the bill (and there are many) which are obnoxious, and resolve to seek their repeal — treating them as continuing questions of public policy. I hope you will also attack the weakness of the gun provision.

He made such a statement. It cheered me, though I recognized that it would be about as effective as a panegyric on celibacy by a pregnant lady.

Writing a memo urging a veto was not the end of the matter. If you succeeded, and the President decided to veto, it was your job to call the bill's sponsor and warn him of what was coming. (This gave the member time to call the President, if he felt strongly about it; that in turn put the President into a strong bargaining position.) One evening in 1968, I recommended vetoing a bill of Senator Hayden's, involving land claims along a shifting river between Arizona and California. Johnson had vetoed a related bill two years before, but obviously he disliked the notion of parting with Carl Hayden — who, like himself, was retiring — on the heels of a veto. But he agreed that it was a bad bill. "Call Hayden and tell him I've got no alternative." That came at 10:30 p.m. — on the last day before the bill would have become law without the President's signature. Hayden lived at the Methodist House, across from the Capitol. I assumed that he had survived so long in part because he went to bed early. "Surely Hayden is asleep, Mr. President?" "Wake him up," he said. "I don't want to do this to him without warning." I thought about suggesting that he might have done it to him in any manner he chose, earlier in the day, but let it go. The phone rang a long time. The old man's voice came on, and after a few minutes he had it straight who I was and why I was calling. "Vetoing the bill, is he?" Yes sir, must. "Well, O.K. Tell him that's O.K. I thought it was a pretty good bill, had the problems worked out with Udall. But if he can't sign it, he can't. Thanks for calling." He hung up. I breathed out slowly, reflecting that Arizona had known what it was doing for fifty-six years in returning Carl Hayden to Congress.

DEALING WITH CONGRESS: PICKING OUT THE BURRS

Shortly after I arrived, I was given responsibility for straightening out the Great Veterans' Hospital Caper. Encouraged by his landslide victory in 1964 and egged on by the Budget Bureau, Johnson had announced the closing of eleven veterans' hospitals where standards of care were poor, buildings were outmoded, or the patient load was small. It made sense in terms of managerial efficiency. But it enraged the Congress. Even Mansfield, in whose state one of the hospitals was located, made threatening speeches. The veterans' organizations were, of course, livid. All this had happened before I came. My job was to figure out what to do next. I proposed a committee of experts, most of them chosen from the medical profession. The committee would, I assumed, make findings that not only supported the President's decision but inspired the public to demand closing the hospitals as health hazards. The President agreed — though he amended my proposed statement to say, "Hearings in the Congress have produced conflicting statements of fact. I have been reading the reports of these hearings very carefully, and I must say they have raised some doubts in my mind about some facilities included in the original order." If I had been more alert, I would have seen in that the signs of a man very carefully stepping away from a precipice to which his advisors had led him.

Barrett Prettyman, a retired Court of Appeals judge, was our chairman. The administrators of the Johns Hopkins Hospital and the Mayo Clinic and a famous internist joined the committee, as did a former VA administrator and General Gruenther of the Red Cross. So far so good. The President thought it wise to include several members of Congress — Senator Long, Chairman "Tiger" Teague of the House Veterans' Affairs Committee, and Congressman Adair, the committee's ranking Republican. That was all right; if things went well, we would still have a 5–4 or even a 6–3 edge. So I thought.

The committee made several field trips and held a series of meetings in Washington. What specifically happened in those meetings, I never knew, except that "Tiger" Teague took us to the cleaners. The committee decided that nine of the eleven hospitals were worth keeping open, and indeed expanding and improving. The President accepted its findings and the crisis passed. One day he laughed and said, "Tell your boys with the computers that they ought to study up on the Congress sometime." For a moment the idea crossed my mind that he had sent word to the committee to fold, as the best means of getting himself out of an insignificant but embittering contest with Congress. Anyway, it was clear that he welcomed the outcome.

Special counsels, like special assistants, often went to the Hill to explain the President's policies, seek support, or negotiate a compromise. Sometimes the President called all the shots; sometimes we acted before he knew about the problem.

WHITE HOUSE 283

1:45 p.m., Saturday
May 14, 1966

FOR THE PRESIDENT

The Land and Water Conservation Fund Act of last year calls for user fees on Federal recreation areas. The Corps of Engineers, alone among Federal agencies, took it literally and announced that they would require the fees at *all sites* on those Corps projects (95 out 295) where there was recreational development. This meant that on some dirt roads leading to unimproved sites on the water's edge, signs went up saying fees were necessary for use by the public — the criterion being that somewhere in the project, miles away perhaps, there was improvement for recreation.

Wilbur Mills introduced a bill providing that the Corps should not charge for the use of unimproved sites. Ed Edmondson and Carl Albert took up the fight for the bill; between them they have nine corps projects where the fees would be charged, and by and large these are in very poor areas.

Interior and Budget are opposed to the bill, because they anticipate it would lead to further chipping away at the user-fee principle of the Act — on reclamation projects and Forest Service lands, for example.

House Public Works reported the bill, and it is on the suspense calendar for Monday. Last night on John Dingell's request Milt Semer, Sam Hughes and I went up to see him and Edmondson. (Dingell is against the bill and is prepared to fight it Monday if necessary.) We decided we would try to get the Corps to amend its practice administratively, and thus avoid a confrontation on the bill.

This morning I met with the Corps and they have agreed
1) to take down the signs on unimproved sites
2) to change their criteria and charge only where there has been improvement
3) to get their Oklahoma man up here for a meeting with Albert and Edmondson on Monday. He will show them where fees would be charged under the new criteria.

If this satisfies Albert and Edmondson, as I believe it will, they will not press the bill. I am informing you of this because the *Times* has editorialized against any change in the Conservation Fund, and against the Edmondson bill; they may say we have caved by chang-

284 A POLITICAL EDUCATION

ing our regulations. I think what we have done makes sense and brings the Corps into line with Interior and Agriculture.

In many cases, other executive departments were involved, as well as the Congress. Then it was like a chess game.

6:30 p.m., Wednesday
October 5, 1966

FOR THE PRESIDENT

We have had to put together a double legislative package in order to get the Hirshhorn Gallery bill through.

Rep. Ken Gray told us (and we have evidence to believe it is so) that we could not pass the Hirshhorn bill unless we took care of the armed forces pathologists, whose museum-laboratory the Hirshhorn gallery would replace on Independence and 7th. We had made progressively more generous offers to the pathologists, including three buildings at the Bureau of Standards; but they had set under way a wave of protests among doctors throughout the country. Reps. Fogarty, Kirwan and Cramer all told Gray that Hirshhorn would not make it unless the pathologists were given a new building of their own.

We then asked Defense if it could support an authorization bill for a new museum-laboratory at Walter Reed. This had been part of the long-range plan for Walter Reed anyway. The question was, could Defense support it this year, in view of the go-slow attitude on construction projects?

McNamara felt he could support an authorization bill, so long as he was not tied to an appropriation schedule. Gray therefore introduced a pathologist museum-laboratory bill. It was referred to House Armed Services. Chairman Rivers, with a favorable report from Defense, reported it out at once.

This we believe clears the way for the Hirshhorn bill, which has already passed the Senate. The arithmetic is, that in exchange for a $30–45 million art collection, we build a $10–12 million gallery, and a $7.5 million museum-laboratory at Walter Reed that we would have in any event constructed in a few years. This was necessary to get the Hirshhorn bill through and I believe it was justified.

In every case, the special counsel or assistant carried with him the contingent authority of the President. He needed that authority to accomplish anything at all, as the law gave him none of his own. And it was necessarily contingent; the President had to be free to repudiate his assistants' views and apparent commitments. The counsel-assistant's position was almost exactly opposite that of the Vice President. The Vice President was powerless, but he was only a moment away from holding enormous power; the special assistant had power, which might be withdrawn just as suddenly. Working for Lyndon Johnson, an assistant did not easily forget that he carried his authority on sufferance.

DEALING WITH THE OUTSIDE WORLD: HUFFING AND PUFFING

No idea was more widely accepted in the political science faculties than that of Presidential supremacy. An "activist" President was thought to have almost mystical powers of shaping corporate as well as governmental decisions. Even Richard Neustadt's extraordinary essay, "Presidential Power," had not changed that assumption. Neustadt had shown that in order to have any continuing effect on the departments, the President had constantly to lobby for his goals, using persuasion more often than fiat. Otherwise his pressure was only one of many in the conference rooms where bureaucrats met to make policy.

Outside the government, his influence was even more tenuous. The President had certain apparent advantages—billions to spend or withhold, quantities of raw materials in the national stockpile that could be dumped when prices rose, an unparalleled ability to make news—and others that were assumed, but rarely seen. It was believed that he could turn the heat on a recalcitrant city, state, industry, or group through the government's regulatory and investigative agencies. In fact his ability to make use of these tools was sharply limited. Congress decided how much he could spend, and for what. Procurement procedures made it difficult to benefit only his friends (if, indeed, he wished to do so; Johnson was sensitive to the dangers of influencing procurement, and on several occasions warned the staff that he would fire any of us who tried). The adversary system in the regulatory agencies, and the right to appeal their orders in court, protected against their misuse. The press was always watchful. So was the opposition party.

Still the idea persisted. The President, and vicariously his staff, were thought to vibrate power. People would do what they asked out of respect, ambition, or fear. The enormous panoply of office that surrounded us — the jets and helicopters, the limousines, the communications systems, the ubiquitous guards, the train of press — all contributed to the idea.

It was exaggerated. I never tested it without discovering that anew.

Soon after I joined the staff, John Sweeney, the director of the new Appalachian Commission, and Pat Moynihan came by with a problem that seemed almost ridiculously easy for a White House man. Ten hospitals, built by the United Mine Workers to serve the miners in West Virginia, Kentucky, and western Virginia, were in trouble. A million-dollar note on them was coming due on June 1. They could not meet it. The note-holder was threatening to put them up for auction. This would almost certainly mean that men suffering from black-lung disease, or otherwise crippled by their work, would be turned away. The new proprietors could not afford to care for them at a loss. All right. Who held the note? The mine worker's welfare and pension fund. Surely the management of the fund was sympathetic to sick miners? The management of the fund — specifically Miss Josephine Roach, an estimable lady who had run it for many years — was principally concerned about maintaining its solvency. Conceivably, however, she could be persuaded to extend the note for a year — giving a committee of industrialists and churchmen time to raise the necessary funds — if the White House showed its interest.

We made an appointment with Miss Roach at her headquarters, a narrow old building facing McPherson Square. Two lawyers — both of them pale and slightly trembling — greeted us and explained the difficulty. The note had been extended before. It would be hard to extend it again without jeopardizing the fund. Miss Roach came in. A slender septuagenarian, she listened as I related, in my best White House manner, the President's deep concerns about medical care for the poor. All we were asking was a little time . . . "No! No! They won't pay!" she said. "We let them off before. They said they could raise it. They haven't. This time we're selling them. I've got my fund to think about!" She rapped white knuckles on her knees. I started to say something un-Presidential, but Sweeney cut in and suggested that we leave. We had exercised enough White House power for one day.

Maybe John L. Lewis could help. He'd built the bloody hospitals. We drove out next day to his house in Alexandria. It was a benign spring afternoon, but there were fires throughout the house and Lewis wore a shawl. I was excited to be talking with John L. Lewis. I asked him about old strikes and organizing campaigns, and about his relations with Roosevelt. He talked expansively, colorfully, in a great rumbling voice. An hour went by, and most of a second. Then I explained our mission. Could he persuade Miss Roach to spare his hospitals? His voice faltered. He looked at his shoes. "Miss Roach is a very fine woman," he said. "A very independent woman. The fund is also independent. We set it up that way." He spoke of its beginnings, and of all the miners and their wives whom it had made secure in their old age. "I'm not sure I'll be able to help, but I'll try," he said, rather wistfully. We went back to the White House, feeling frustrated and low.

In time the President asked his old friend Donald Cook, the chairman of a power company serving Appalachia, to work with the Presbyterian church in raising money for the hospitals. Cook agreed, the money was raised, and the emergency was put off for a while. Obviously Presidential power was more effective with the President's gentleman friends than with very fine and independent women.

Even when he wished to act, the President was restricted by his own notions of what was appropriate. He was fond of George Meany, and he knew what labor had done for his program on the Hill and for the Democratic party in past elections. Repaying that debt, however, could be difficult.

> 5:20 p.m., Wednesday
> April 19, 1967

FOR THE PRESIDENT

We have met twice now on the problem the AFL-CIO raised with you last month — concerning firms who persistently and flagrantly violate the labor laws, and yet continue to receive Defense and other government contracts.

As you remember, the union wanted you to consider issuing an Executive Order prohibiting this. You said you had grave doubts about the wisdom of acting in this manner, particularly when the main argument for issuing an executive order was the difficulty of getting Congress to pass a law. You asked us to explore the matter.

Here are some of our tentative findings:

1) The only major offender we have been able to discover — the only firm that persistently and flagrantly violated the Labor Relations Act, and still receives major government contracts — is the J. P. Stevens textile company.

Other firms doing business with Defense have been accused of unfair labor practices, but these have been relatively routine. Only Stevens has "outraged" the NLRB, as well as labor.

2) Stevens did about $75 million in Defense work in fiscal year 1966 and will do about $42 million this year. Its gross sales are over $800 million. So this year Defense work will amount to about 5% of its gross business.

(Incidentally, in FY 1966 Stevens took the lead in getting the textile industry to respond to DOD's large Vietnam requirements. The industry had near-capacity civilian business, and was reluctant to meet sudden one-shot Defense orders. Stevens not only responded, but rallied others to do so.)

3) Defense would be hurt if it had to quit doing business with Stevens today. Stevens is the sole supplier of some textiles. Defense estimates the dollar cost to it of cutting off Stevens to be $10 million.

4) There is no question about Stevens' labor practices. They are Neanderthal. More enlightened business leaders have privately described Stevens as embarrassing to them.

5) It would be legally possible (although the Government Accounting Office questions this) to issue an Executive Order instructing procurement agencies to require contractors to adopt or maintain fair labor practices, and to refrain from doing business with those who persistently and flagrantly violate the labor laws.

There are, however, several major problems with doing this:

a) Determining who is guilty of such violations. Should an NLRB finding of unfair practices in a particular case be sufficient? What if that finding is appealed? At what stage of the legal process should the procurement agency decide that it should act? How many violations does it take to amount to "persistent and flagrant" behavior?

b) The established means of combating unfair labor practices is through the NLRB. Ordinarily we do not transfer that responsibility to procurement agencies without some Congressional authorization to do so.

c) An Executive Order is an expensive instrument to use on a single offender.

d) If we adopt this practice in the case of unfair labor practices, it is hard to say why we should not expand it to include anti-trust violations, tax delinquencies, and other wrongs. Soon procurement would be loaded down with social policy requirements, encumbering the government's business and creating the possibility of real inequities.

e) Until the first Stevens case is decided by the Court of Appeals, any kind of action, even if desirable, would be premature. We do not know when that will be.

f) Since only 5% of Stevens' business is with the government, there is room for doubt whether an order of this kind would be effective in improving its labor practices.

g) There is almost no chance that legislation in this field could pass the Congress. Amendments to the Defense Procurement Act would go to Armed Services — to Russell and Rivers.

Also, there is great fear that opening up the legislative box will start a general debate on labor law, with labor coming out second best.

Our recommendation is to tell the AFL-CIO that there are too many problems with this now to make executive action feasible (certainly until the Court of Appeals decides the case); and that we will ask the Labor-Management Advisory Committee to examine the question and give us its best judgment on what could and should be done.

Beyond question, Congress had given the President authority to act in the field of international trade. During my first years in the White House I spent a lot of time worrying about imports of textiles, meat, watches, carpets, glass, and foreign airplanes.

The range and depth of political support for the domestic textile industry, and against foreign imports, were astonishing. It included the manufacturers, the unions, the apparel industry, and dozens of Southern and New England senators and congressmen. The Agriculture Department supported the industry in the interest of the cotton farmers; the Treasury, because of the balance of payments. But its greatest friend was the Commerce Department, in which it had an intelligence network equal to the British MI 5. I represented the President on a cabinet-level textile committee. Ordinarily we met in the Commerce building, just across the Ellipse from the White House. We decided, according to the state of the domestic industry and the current level of textile prices, whether to restrict or expand the level of imports. I often walked back to my office after the meeting — that took about ten minutes — to find that a representative of the industry had already called to complain about our decision.

Johnson, like most Presidents, did not often involve himself in specific trade questions. He recognized the political sensitivity of the oil import program for a Texan, and told Stewart Udall to handle it in Interior. His free-trade views — part of the heritage of moderate Southern politicians, particularly of those who shared the national outlook of Sam Rayburn and Cordell Hull — had seldom been challenged during his years of representing Texas in Congress. Kennedy, representing Massachusetts, had faced delegations of angry men who spoke for textiles, shoes, rubber goods, machine tools, and a score of other industries straining under foreign competition. That was enough to make a realist of any man. It was difficult to keep repeating one's intellectual faith in the ultimate value of foreign trade — if we are going to sell abroad, we must be prepared to buy from abroad — to men thrown out of business, or out of work, by the import of goods whose labor costs permitted them to be sold at a fraction of ours. Kennedy's intellect prevailed when he sent the 1962 trade bill to Congress, though he knew, more poignantly than the economists who advised him, that the same free trade which helped the general economy was hell on some people.

Twice in 1967 Johnson confronted tough problems that required him to decide between free trade and protecting an American industry — in one case, the makers of window glass, in the other, of watches. Valuable senators and congressmen spoke for the domestic manufacturers. They had all the political clout; the President's trade representative, William Roth, had nothing but sweet reason, statistics, and the argument that we should prepare for the Kennedy Round trade negotiations in 1968 by eliminating those politically inspired duties that most annoyed the Europeans.

In both cases Johnson rolled back the tariffs. The *Times*, in what may have been its last favorable editorial about Johnson until he announced that he was quitting, wrote about "Mr. Johnson's Tariff Courage." The *Washington Post* said: "The voice of the White House has often been raised in behalf of free trade, but President Johnson provided the indispensable element, not the profile, not the rhetoric, but a willingness to stand on principle when the political disadvantages hopelessly outweigh any prospects for gain. That is the essence of political courage."

There were few immediate political advantages, to be sure. But the long-term consequences more than justified what Johnson did. We entered the Kennedy Round with clean hands, and partly as a result, achieved a good agreement. The benefits from that would last for years.

All the memoranda I have quoted were biased. All proceeded from the personal convictions of Johnson's advisors, which we believed he shared. Politicians and journalists often complained that Presidential staffs "shielded" their President from information and opinions he should have. The real danger was that we would weigh it wrong. The very process of reducing a dozen position papers and committee meetings to a three-page memorandum for the President required that we exclude some arguments and data, and emphasize others. We tried to give him both sides, but our judgments colored what we wrote. Presidents are not helpless in such matters; any man who attains the office may be presumed to be familiar, through a lifetime in politics, law, business, or the armed services, with the tendency of staff men to shape what they tell him in accordance with their opinions. Presidents also choose staffs on whose values they believe they can rely. But the danger of bias or omission is always there, and it is unavoidable so long as Presidents make twenty decisions a day on the basis of information they can only receive through the filter of other men's convictions.

TAPPING THE BRAINS: HELLO OUT THERE?

Several times in 1967 Califano, Cater, and I boarded a small Air Force jet and flew to a university town. There, after drinks and dinner, we discussed issues with a group of faculty members — sociologists, political scientists, economists, chemists, physicists, and medical men. The ostensible purpose was to gather ideas for the following year's legislative program. I was equally concerned about the erosion of good feelings between the university community and the Administration. I hoped that the visits would prove we were open to academic opinions; I was even willing to say we were dependent on them.

At Harvard, the conversation was good and the comments were knowledgeable and relevant. Most of the men around the table spent almost as much time in Washington, advising departments and Budget Bureau committees, as they did in Cambridge. They knew what was politically feasible and did not waste time proposing utopian measures. They told us about recent research in education, in the nature of effective community action, the delivery of health services, and so on. They put this in context with current programs and recommended improvements.

Visits to Yale and the Bay Area in California, where professors traveled nearly as often to Washington as did the Harvard men, were also productive. Elsewhere the take was disappointing. For many distinguished scholars, the country's chief problems had to do with insufficient federal money for research in their fields, or unnecessary requirements for fellowship grants. The cities were burning down, the poor were still going without money, good schools, and medical care, the air and water stank; but what really concerned them was that HEW contracted for research with individual professors, and not with the department heads, or the other way around. For several other scholars there was only one problem — Vietnam. All else flowed from it or could not be remedied because of it.

In May of that year, Cater and I suggested to the President that he invite some of the intellectuals who held high office in his Administration to have lunch with him. It was an impressive group. John Gardner; Bob Wood of MIT, the Housing undersecretary; Charles Haar of Harvard Law School, an assistant secretary in HUD; Harold Brown, the physicist and Secretary of the

Air Force; Alain Enthoven, McNamara's premier systems analyst; the Council of Economic Advisors (all three university economists); John Roche; and a dozen others. Most of these men maintained contact with the faculties on which they had served, and with colleagues in other universities and foundations. The majority felt that the war had soured the academic world on the Administration. A few spoke of snobbery toward a Texas politician. Zbigniew Brzezinski, a brilliant, outspoken foreign affairs specialist, said he believed the President's style was the main problem. I had the impression that several palms grew moist at that point. But the President listened thoughtfully, and then defended himself. He had guided into law almost every proposal that the intellectuals thought desirable: aid to public schools and higher education, medical care and research, antipoverty programs, conservation, model cities, civil rights, everything about which they had faulted Eisenhower for resisting and Kennedy for failing to produce. What he had done in Vietnam had been started by other Presidents, and had been vigorously recommended by most foreign policy scholars and analysts. As to his style, he could not change that. Some people told him that he should go on television to discuss all the elements that made the war in Vietnam such a protracted misery, all the sorry options he had faced; but he did not believe the people wished to see their President agonize in public. He needed support from the intellectuals; they produced the ideas, they molded opinion. He hoped that those around the table would explain what he was doing to their colleagues in private life. The session ended inconclusively. People argued in little groups, as after a faculty meeting. I was disappointed. Roche, a veteran of many faculty meetings, was not. He had never expected much from it.

On occasion, when the tirades from the campuses became particularly shrill, I wondered whether it was really important to secure the intellectuals' support. The term itself was vague. By custom it included men of every scholarly discipline, as well as creative artists. Whether a microbiologist, or a lyric poet, should be paid serious attention when he spoke about Vietnam was open to dispute. And though the Democratic party had traditionally attracted many intellectuals, its base was among the grade school and high school graduates; the majority of college graduates voted Republican. FDR and Truman had had their problems with liberal intellectuals — many of whom had been America Firsters, Socialists, Communists, and Henry Wallace Progressives — and still they had won elections. So maybe it was not so damaging when the novelist and the pediatrician and the poet linked arms and marched on the Pentagon. Maybe they were just arrogant *clercs*, with a record of poor judgment on most public issues and with no appreciation for the stakes in Asia. They made news because they were celebrities. They made waves in New York, where the media people were inclined to parrot what they heard at parties, and where many people regarded Johnson as a frightening bully or a gauche boob or both. But maybe their ultimate effect on the wards in Philadelphia, Chicago, and Los Angeles was not as great as I feared. Eric Hoffer, whom Johnson came to know well in his last years in office, was certain that most intellectuals were out of touch with what ordinary people wanted and felt. "They don't know anything about us!" he told Johnson, and by "us" he included the President, as well as himself. That was satisfying to hear, and almost persuasive. I would have found it completely so, if I had been sure that I was one of "us," and not a *clerc* myself. The truth was that the opinions of scholars and writers were terribly important to me, and remained so even in the worst days.

Meanwhile a number of intellectuals were administering programs which they had helped to design. At Brookings Institution, Johnson took pride in that:

> There is hardly an aspect of the Great Society program that has not been molded, or remolded, or in some way influenced by the community of scholars and thinkers . . . and a number of those who

helped to create the new programs have followed their children to Washington.

What was needed now was the exercise of another form of intellectual power — the critical faculty — to evaluate what had been done.

[The intellectuals' critical] judgment may be wrong, and they must live with that knowledge — as other men do who have been chosen by their fellow citizens to exercise the powers of government.

Their judgment may be right, and still not be accepted in the political arena or the editorial room. That is a risk they take — along with everyone else.

But they must provide it; it is [their] obligation . . . no less than the obligation to produce fresh ideas or to serve the Nation in its time of need.

No doubt many intellectuals believed they were providing critical judgment when they called the war mad. Just as surely Johnson had something else in mind.

MESSAGES TO THE HILL:
CRISIS AND SALVATION

Ted Sorensen's drafts for Kennedy's legislative messages to Congress had set high literary standards. Bill Moyers and Richard Goodwin equaled them for Johnson. Goodwin's draft of a 1965 message on the cities was especially fine. ("The problem is people and the quality of the lives they lead. We want to build not just housing units, but neighborhoods; not just to construct schools, but to educate children; not just to raise income but to create beauty and end the poisoning of our environment.")

The writing of messages was a political art form, as orthodox as a classical string quartet. First came the passionate description of a problem — sometimes widely recognized, like crime, urban decay, the paucity of medical care for the poor; sometimes esoteric, like the need to reorganize a government agency or provide a four-year term for congressmen. The purpose of this part was to hit the mule across the forehead, to get its attention. The future was bleak — unless the people chose some expensive commitment to change.

If we stand passively by, while the center of each city becomes a hive of deprivation, crime and hopelessness . . . if we become two people, the suburban affluent and the urban poor, each filled with mistrust and fear for the other . . . if this is our desire and policy as a people, then we shall effectively cripple each generation to come. We shall as well condemn our own generation to a bitter paradox: an educated, wealthy, progressive people, who would not give their thoughts, their resources, or their wills to provide their common well-being.

I do not believe such a fate is either necessary or inevitable. But I believe this will come to pass — unless [now the theme changed to one of rugged hope] we commit ourselves now to the planning, the building, the teaching and the caring that alone can forestall it.

That is why [resolution and principal theme] I am recommending today a massive Demonstration Cities Program. I recommend that both the public and private sectors of our economy join to build in our cities and towns an environment for man equal to the dignity of his aspirations.

Thus began the first message on which I worked. What followed were the nuts and bolts: "special grants amounting to 80% of the non-Federal cost of our grant-in-aid programs included in the demonstration," "planning funds for the coordinated treatment of the regional transportation network," and so on. They were the substance of the program. The rhetoric would last only a day or two; whether the cities would be helped depended on how well the "Urban Problems Task Force" had foreseen real-life problems and designed a practical structure to meet them, which the President could persuade Congress to adopt.

Writing the cities draft was part of a rational process. I worked with the task force throughout the fall of 1965, as it debated technical amendments to the housing laws and sweeping changes in policy; used an excellent memorandum, prepared by Wood and staff, as the basis for the President's message; circulated the draft to Budget, the economic advisors, and Califano (though not to the new Housing Department, which was thought to be wedded to past programs and more responsive to congressional than Presidential goals); and then discussed it at length with the President. He made many changes in language, crossing out and writing in the margins, and many more in substance — "I don't want to say that on page 8; I want to tell 'em to give me a supplemental appropriation right now." He had designed the task force, and had given it its charter. He was aware of what it was doing throughout. His staff was deeply involved, as were his counselors on the budget. There were no last-minute surprises. Altogether the process was a model for the writing of Presidential messages. It was also atypical.

Often I came into the picture at the last minute, when subcabinet officers and experts had drafted proposals whose purpose was evident, but whose origins were buried in a file back at the department. Why a particular approach had been chosen, and not another, was not immediately clear. Whether Congress or the public was interested in the program, whether the mechanism existed or could be created to administer it, where it ranked among priorities in the field — all was a mystery. For many cabinet officers, the important question was whether their department would have the principal responsibility for the new program — not the hard choices that lay hidden within it.

Joe Califano's job was to produce agreement on a viable program. Mine was to put it into "Presidential language" and give it an indiscriminate sense of urgency. Since Kennedy had promised to get us moving again, Democratic writers had forced the pace of everything their Presidents said. Nothing was too small to be termed "urgent." The consequences of inaction were never less than drastic; action would always bring redemption, prosperity or civil peace.

Sometimes the problem was described so severely that the program seemed feeble by comparison. Late one night, as I finished a draft on rural poverty, I realized that its concluding words — "I do not believe we should stand idly by and permit our rural citizens to be ground into poverty, exposing them . . . to the neglect of a changing society"—were somehow out of joint with the program we were proposing. Better planning and community development districts were sensible recommendations, but bloodless. We needed to express our concern in immediate action. What could we do that did not cost new billions or require congressional approval? Well, we could appoint a Commission on Rural Poverty, to tell us how to "share America's abundance with her forgotten people." Freeman accepted the idea, and so did the President. I turned promptly to other things. Months went by before we began to assemble names for the commission and found a director. A year later, we were presented with a thoughtful, 160-page report, recommending programs whose cost was estimated by the Budget Bureau at between twenty and forty billions a year. By then the budget squeeze was on. Expenditures of that size were out of the question. The commission's report — appropriately called "The People Left Behind" — was quietly filed away for a more sanguine time. If the rural poor had been politically organized, and if the media had been more than remotely interested in rural conditions, there would have been an outcry about that. As it was, only its authors — a diverse collection of farmers, businessmen, economists, writers, sociologists, and educators, twenty-five liberals and conservatives who had arrived at a common view of what should be done for fourteen million rural poor — only they seemed to mourn its end. As its progenitor, I was sorry that their work would not be fulfilled, at least by us. But there was no arguing with the budget. And I had another message to draft.

I speculated that writers for conservative Presidents did not have such problems. Their guiding principle was good management, where ours was social change. Good management was an end in itself. It satisfied the need for efficiency that was part of the American ethos. Whether it succeeded was not very important, or even discernible. Social change, on the other hand, was a process — involving the recognition of legitimate needs, the arousal of expectations that they should and could be met, the creation of laws and bureaucracies, and a payoff — money, health care, the right to vote and get a job, better schools. The process could fail at any point — most often at the payoff. It could not even be started unless the needs were recognized and the expectations aroused. To do that, a leader had to raise his voice. He could not engage in an academic debate; he could not take a long view of history, in which crowded cities and poverty seemed in retrospect the benevolent engines of progress; he could not say, "Perhaps it would be wise," but "We must."

In pressing hard for change he took great risks, both for himself and for the country. He had to convey, not only a poignant sense of the misery to be relieved, but confidence that money and organization and skill could relieve it. Otherwise men would do nothing.

If he proposed a law prohibiting certain malign practices — such as excluding Negroes from restaurants and voting booths — he was relatively sure that he could effect the change he sought if the law was passed. If his goal was to provide medical care for the aged and needy, or a college education for poor youth, that required considerably more administration — the resolution of disputes with hospitals, universities, and so forth; still, as checks could be delivered, so could doctors and teachers. But if he proposed to "rebuild the core of our cities," "give men new skills, and thus new hope," or "give the poor control over their own lives," that was another matter. A labyrinth of bureaucratic controls, social workers, planners, deputy assistants, consultants, and acronyms came into being; governors and mayors became at once acquisitive and suspicious; groups of militants, each with a voluble spokesman, formed overnight; Congress, which might have been sympathetic enough to pass the enabling bill, became tight-fisted when it was asked to appropriate money for it; war and other demands elbowed for priority attention; and soon the newspapers, which had faulted the President for "insufficient vision" the last time around, began to ask whether he had promised more than he could produce. The beneficiaries of the programs grew restive, and then angry, when the gap between goals and reality remained as wide as ever. In an age that exalted instant gratification, in a country that gloried in its standing as "the richest, the most powerful in the world," there could be no excuse for failure to deliver swift social change, not when the President had called for it and the Congress had apparently agreed to it.

The Administration could have used more restraint. It could have aimed only at those social and economic injustices which would yield to the ready application of public resources. Instead of training, advising, and seeking to engage the poor, it could have written a monthly check and said it's up to them.

But a new philosophy of government had emerged since New Deal days. In essence it held that our problems were more of the spirit than of the flesh. People were suffering from a sense of alienation from one another, of anomie, of powerlessness. This affected the well-to-do as much as it did the poor. Middle-class women, bored and friendless in the suburban afternoons; fathers, working at "meaningless" jobs, or slumped before the television set; sons and daughters desperate for "relevance" — all were in need of community, beauty, and purpose, all were guilty because so many others were deprived while they, rich beyond their ancestors' dreams, were depressed. What would change all this was a creative public effort: for the middle class, new parks, conservation, the removal of billboards and junk, adult education, consumer protection, better television, aid to the arts; for the poor, jobs, training, Head Start, decent housing, medical care, civil rights; for both, and for bridging the gap between them, VISTA, the Teacher Corps, the community action agencies, mass transportation, model cities.

It was a magnificent design. It would make America the Great Society, where, in the President's words, "the meaning of our lives matches the marvelous products of our labor." It would make, of Kafka's despairing "K," Whitman's robust "I." It would satisfy the philosophers and social scientists, the political bosses and the independents, the moderate Republicans and union Democrats, two-thirds of the voters, and nearly all of the papers.

If it could be done. If government programs could overcome their own inertia, and the limitations of those who ran them. If they were clever and massive enough to divert the course of growth that destroyed virgin land, put up billboards, pandered to commercialism, and cheapened the quality of goods. If they could reach into white hearts where the fear and contempt and hatred for blacks lay almost untouched. If people scattered apart by highways could be given a sense of community — and if they, bombarded by events and hunkered in their individual shelters, really wanted it. If moral commitment could last in the face of bitterness and ingratitude. If public policies could relieve the various torments and hungers of two hundred million souls.

At the end of our time in the White House, I winced at the striving rhetoric I had written at the beginning. By then Nixon and Moynihan and others had all decried the dangers of raising more hopes than one could satisfy. Because the Johnson Administration had done so, they said, it had contributed to violence and disrespect for authority. The inference was that it was better to let sleeping dogs lie unless one had something to feed them.

I thought we might have been more cautious in claiming what we did for our programs. But that we should not have tried to awaken the country to its needs and dangers, and to suggest the means of responding to them, seemed a cold judgment. I would have removed many dramatic phrases from those early messages;

I would have warned that whatever we attempted might fail, or take many years to succeed; I would have wished to concentrate on more conventional goals, and to have avoided such concepts as "community" and "meaning." I might have written as urgently of the need to restrain the worst in man, as to help him become "the best that is within him to become." But I would not have traded Johnson's vast hopes and intentions for another man's bookkeeping prudence.

WRITING AND TRAVELING: AND NEVER LEFT HOME

With the possible exception of King Ibn Saud, no national leader traveled abroad with such a retinue as the American President's. Baggage-handlers, communications experts, Secret Service agents, secretaries, reporters, press officers, foreign policy specialists, military aides, a protocol chief, pilots and stewards, valets, advance men, and speech-writers — all crowded into Air Force One or the "back-up" planes and took off for the world, ready for anything.

In the early fall of 1966, Moyers, Roche, Jim Symington — the Chief of Protocol — and I led a party around the rim of the Western Pacific, preparing the way for Johnson. We flew to Samoa, Wellington, Canberra, Manila, Bangkok, Kuala Lumpur, Seoul, and back to Washington in eight days. Moyers arranged facilities for the press at each stop, Symington got the dignitaries straight and found quarters for the President, Roche and I talked politics with local scholars and journalists, and a remarkable man named Marty Underwood made sure there would be enthusiastic crowds along the route. Underwood was a broad-faced, genial politician who remembered everything, and got his way — rather, the President's way—more often by ingenuity than by threat. (Once in Mexico City, desperate to produce a great reception for Johnson on two days' notice, he persuaded an official to snarl the transportation system at the rush hour shortly before Johnson arrived, and so created a massive captive audience in the center of the city.) In much of Asia, his talents were unnecessary to produce a crowd; the Asians saw to that. His job was to get Johnson through the waving multitudes in time to meet a king or a president.

Thirty-six hours after we returned home, we left again with Johnson. From notes along the way:

SAMOA: Hot. Reception line of a hundred local leaders and their wives. Average weight two hundred fifty pounds. Each couple places leis of flowers and shells around the Johnsons' necks, which midway through line begin to sag. Our advance man (whom Moyers's plane had dropped off on previous trip), perspiring happily, says Samoan mothers teach their daughters one hundred positions for making love, called ami-ami. Men do not need to move unless they feel like it.

Johnson makes a speech, written on the plane. Follows classic pattern: You have reduced (measles, illiteracy, dependence on us), you are doubling (GNP, use of fertilizer, dependence on us), you have built (factories, classrooms, new society), you have stood fast against (communism, tides of despair, voices that say). Eyes of the world are upon you. Samoans listen respectfully, thinking about that. Johnsons go off to see educational television experiment. I stay to watch native dances, thinking about ami-ami. Two hours later the Great White Chief gathers up his assistants and boards a plane on whose sides are the words UNITED STATES OF AMERICA. Jim Cross, the pilot, turns on full power and we start to climb out over the blue-green bay, our obese happy wards still waving on the strip below.

WELLINGTON, NEW ZEALAND: We come down over a windy harbor and find Governor General Sir Bernard Fergusson, wearing a monocle, and Prime Minister Keith Holyoake waiting for us. Big bands, a ceremonial guard, thousands of people making thumbs-up signs along fence. Johnson delivers shoulder-to-shoulder speech: we were together in World War I, World War II (recounts own wartime experiences: flew with zero visibility into Auckland Bay, became ill in New Guinea, was cared for by New Zealanders on Fiji). Doesn't mention Vietnam — we have word that several hundred demonstrators are waiting for us downtown. The following day, as he is on his way to Parliament, demonstrators push through great friendly crowd to hold up banners reading STOP THE WAR. They chant — something firm but respectful, none of that Hey Hey LBJ stuff — and while officials make nervous apologetic sounds, Johnson turns around on the steps outside Parliament House and makes a "V" sign. Crowd behind the demonstrators roars. That's the stuff.

Next morning at five, shaving in a bathroom I share with Underwood, I hear a woman's voice in his room. "Oh sir that's really too nice." Underwood: "Well, you've been so good to me, I want you to have it." Woman: "I'll always treasure it sir." Underwood: "Now maybe you'll take care of my friend Mr. McPherson next door." "Oh indeed I will sir." Criminy. Five in the morning, maybe three hours before we get breakfast on the plane, and Underwood's sending . . . There is a knock at the door. I open it and find a big plain girl in a maid's uniform, holding out a silver tray with muffins, jam, and tea upon it. I take it gratefully and notice that her right hand is firmly clasped about an LBJ ballpoint pen.

CANBERRA, AUSTRALIA: Are all planned capitals handsome and dull? I hear Brasília is; Washington was at the beginning and for a long time thereafter. Canberra's streets are wide and empty. Its shrubs are clipped. Its vistas are logical ("You see, the war memorial is the apex of a triangle that begins at Parliament . . .") It is spacious and sane and altogether as exciting as a size twenty flowered print dress. Of which there are many in evidence.

Johnson draws a big crowd in Sydney. A few demonstrators

break through to throw paint on his car. That becomes *the* news of the Australian trip: not the tens of thousands yelling "Good on you, Lyndon!" but the red paint exploding on the car and on millions of television screens and retinas, spreading out until nothing else can register. Good news is no news, Lyndon.

He makes a good many extemporaneous speeches, which become progressively richer with the imagery of World War II. You stood fast! . . . while just across the Owen-Stanley range in New Guinea the enemy waited to give the knock-out blow. (Listening, I remember the face of the Zero pilot in the movies, fiendishly grinning to his wing man and pointing downward to where the big red cross marked the hospital.) The survivors of that thwarted Japanese army are now our best trading partners and the Bulwark of Asian Democracy. Glad we aren't stopping there.

Night at Brisbane airport. Johnson takes a speech I wrote on the plane and mounts a floodlit platform. Our local consul, reading a copy, chokes with horror. Johnson is to say, "I am told that something like a million Americans passed through Brisbane during World War II." That has a special libidinal meaning for Australians. It is certain to provoke knowing laughter among the women and grinding of teeth among the men. I alert Moyers, who runs up to cross out the sentence just in time.

Into town through a hundred thousand cheering people. Good on you, too. Early next morning, a Sunday, we leave the hotel at high speed, bound for the airport. Suddenly the caravan stops. A thousand people are waiting at a suburban crossroads. Johnson can't pass them by, any more than he could a thousand Blanco County farmers. I see him standing high in the bubble-top car, smiling and waving in that curious, straight-fingered way, his hands bobbing like duck bills. Alongside, fathers in pajamas hustle by, carrying small children on their shoulders. Two young priests fly past, alternately hitching up their cassocks and holding down their hats. The morning light is soft, the air is cool, the

Australians are laughing and cheering. One could do worse than end up here.

Midday in Townsville. Johnson was briefly stationed in Townsville, back when the Japs were poised across the Owen-Stanley range. A Western-movie town, dusty and hot. We go to church. One of the prayers is Niebuhr's, reminding us that our lives are dependent on the courage and integrity of others. The familiar hymns, the Church of England prayerbook, these people who look like us and share our language — all this is comforting, and suggests that we have an anchor in the Western Pacific. But for what purpose? The Australians talk about their responsibilities in Asia, but they are importing Eastern Europeans to do their scutwork; they have admitted far fewer Asians than we have. "Together, we . . ." shall what? Fight Asia's wars? Fight her age-old enemies, poverty, disease, etc.? What are white men doing out here on this stalagmite of a continent, praying the ancient English prayers and talking about a war between brown men four thousand miles away? Presumably making sure that North Vietnamese or Chinese troops do not someday camp in the New Guinea mountains across the Coral Sea. At the moment, as we stand on the baked, barren ground at Townsville, that seems farfetched.

MANILA: We are escorted over Manila Bay by a squadron of Philippine Air Force F-4's, flying terrifyingly close to our wingtips. I hope Cross is telling PAF headquarters to get them the hell away. You can see the pilots' faces. I think of all those speeches about how Asians can take responsibility for their own defense, if we only give them the means. Well, there they are, about to knock off one of our wings with the means we gave them. One must have faith. Men of all races can fly F-4's thirty yards from your wing-tips. At last they peel off and we land. Better to talk about Asia's defense on the ground.

The humidity is oppressive. How can anyone work here?

Broad faces, the smell of poverty, stucco peeling from the buildings along the bay. The country is sinking under the weight of graft and official corruption and wet air. The murder rate is so high that customers in the bars are asked to check their guns before entering. In a hotel elevator, I stand next to a wispy man under whose shiny black suit bulges a small automatic. I suppose the Secret Service agents, Clint Hill and Rufus Youngblood, can handle him, or anybody else; but he is part of an atmosphere of simmering violence that makes me nervous and ill-tempered. It affects others in our party. One of them, drunk and enraged by a crowd of leftist students picketing our hotel, drops a water-bomb out the window. Like the offshore cannon-shot into Africa in *Heart of Darkness.* Johnson is sore when he hears about it and has somebody admonish the aide.

At sunset I talk to several Filipino scholars who've been invited to the embassy. One says his people have no identity. The Spanish made them Catholic and antimaterialist and we made them democratic and venal. We should not have left until we showed them how to prosper and run a good government. Another says we should never have come. Better to have left them untouched by Western values, another Sarawak or Borneo. I look out through the grill of a French window onto Manila Bay. Horizon and distance are indistinguishable in the glowing saffron light. I can just make out the silhouette of a freighter, weightlessly at anchor in the bay. A launch moves slowly toward it. Maybe to loot it, with the cooperation of its crew. Hundreds of millions of dollars in goods are expropriated out there each year. An informal aid program, with a highly restricted list of beneficiaries.

There is a party at the Palace one night. Fried plantain, rice, and superb *cabrito.* Philippine beer is delicious. Why is it that poor tropical countries like this one and Panama make better beer than we do? Probably some minor form of poetic justice. The Johnsons come in, riding in a donkey cart and followed by

President Marcos and his glamorous wife. Strings of lights in the trees, a lively orchestra, a great crowd of the swells moving about. All the men, even our agents, wear *barong tagalogs*, the sheer embroidered shirts that mercifully replace tuxedos in the Manila nights. The time could be 1902, with Governor William Howard Taft instead of Johnson up there on the bandstand.

It is different in the tunnels of Corregidor. Bare light bulbs hang in the dank passageways. Over here was the infirmary. Here is where they kept food. Here was Wainwright's command post. Here were the gates that the Japanese shelled day after day. Out there were our cannon and graves.

One million Filipinos died as a result of the war. Manila was devastated. And not for independence; we had already promised that eight years before, to take effect in 1946. The suffering came because we were not prepared to fight the Japanese successfully. If we had not been there at all, if we had not regarded the invasion of the Philippines as a threat to our vital interests in the Pacific, and if (as would have followed from such an American view) the Japanese had not attacked us directly at Pearl Harbor, the conquest of these islands would have been swift and relatively bloodless. But we believed we had much at stake in the Philippine Islands. So we fought doggedly to hold them and violently to regain them. They paid the price of our interest and our lack of preparation to defend it. After which they received their independence on schedule.

When I get back to the hotel Johnson has left on a surprise trip to Vietnam. I thought that was coming later, when we got to Thailand. I wait around. In the evening there is a call from the plane. The President wants me to meet him on his return to Manila. We get into his car. He wonders why I wasn't there earlier, when he needed me. Nobody told me you were going. We argue heatedly through the narrow streets. I wonder why Lyndon Johnson interrupts a time of high adventure, a coup of wartime leadership, to complain about the absence of a speech-writer? It is as if nothing can satisfy him that does not exercise the full range of his emotions — triumph, gratitude, resentment toward those who unjustly fail or refuse him.

BANGKOK: Early one evening, I take a speech to Johnson's quarters in the Palace. He is asleep. I wait in an elegant parlor outside. French provincial furniture beneath a high domed ceiling. Maybe Anna slept here, between classes for the king's children. I'd like to. I am tired and rumpled from a month of travel.

Johnson wakes up and goes in to shave. In the center of the bathroom is a sunken bath, four feet deep and ten feet long. The spigot is a water-buffalo head in silver. I tell him that would go well in Texas. Hmmph, he says. We sit down with the speech. It is Ben Wattenberg's draft for the university next day. Johnson is easy and patient, trying to be interested in one more collection of words to be spoken before another foreign audience. Mrs. Johnson comes in and gently reminds him that the state dinner is at eight, ten minutes from now. He thanks her and returns to the speech. She comes back in ten minutes, growing more concerned. The king and queen will be waiting at the foot of the stairs below. He looks at her for a long time. Then he asks, "What are they going to do?" Good question. At length he stands up and is zipped into his formal clothes by his valet. There's one good reason for being President. I start to leave, but he has more to say about the speech, and the three of us go out toward the stairs. The young king and his pretty wife wait pleasantly below. We start down the steps between rigid guards-at-arms. Halfway down, Johnson turns and hands me the speech. Then king and President meet warmly and walk toward a receiving line. In my wrinkled suit I stand between the drawn swords and marbled eyes of the guards, feeling that I should issue an order.

Stag dinner next night. I sit across from a prince who had parachuted into Thailand with a CIA team during the Japanese occupation. Tough old bird. He thinks Thailand ought to send many more troops to Vietnam. What do the Thai people think about that? He asks me to repeat the question. When I do, he looks at me quizzically, as if the idea had not occurred to him. "The Thais accommodate," says a man in our embassy. "To the French, the British, the Japanese, and if necessary to the North Vietnamese and the Chinese. They don't think the last is necessary now, so long as we are willing to supply arms to them and treat them as protected property under SEATO. They haven't been anybody's colonial possession for a thousand years, but they've accommodated."

So much for history. I have a toast to write. "Tonight we stand as allies in a common cause. At this very moment, Thai forces are assisting the South Vietnamese in their struggle against armed aggression alongside the forces of the United States of America."

Next day we leave Bangkok. The streets are lined with Chinese lingerie shops, Honda agencies, and gigantic movie ads — in one of which a looming black-shirted hero, gun in each hand, looks very much like Marvin Watson. We hustle along the AID-built highway toward the airport, as if trying to make up for all the time we had set aside here for traveling to Vietnam and did not use. Water buffalo — live ones this time — stand knee-deep in the rice paddies. Frail children look up beside them, open-mouthed as ten great limousines rush by at seventy miles an hour. And then go back to switching the buffalo. There is another world out there, beyond the Palace and the imaginary garden of my speeches.

KUALA LUMPUR: International airports are the Esperanto country. They are Nowhere and Everywhere. This one is prettier than most, but it might as well be in Guatemala or Kenya for what it tells you of Malaysia.

Troops in khaki shorts and knee socks, Malaysian ladies with parasols. All proudly British. After the welcoming ceremony we drive through rubber plantations into the capital, under Malay banners stretched over the highway. Clark Clifford gravely translates them into worshipful English.

K.L. is a clean city, prosperous by Asian standards. Tin and rubber did that. And the industrious Chinese. There are three million of them in Malaysia, and they control most of the incountry commerce. Many of the Malays would like to cut them into small pieces. But the Tengku—the Edwardian poker-playing gent who runs the country—keeps his fellow Malays under wraps.

"Amok" is a Malay word.

The President makes a "you have demonstrated" speech. Here it appears they have. With British help the Malayans fought a tough war against Chinese Communist guerrillas, and defeated them; those whom they did not kill or capture they isolated. The government resettled half a million Chinese, to break the threat of further insurgency, and started a number of agricultural communes through which it hopes to make the jungle areas more productive and secure. Sir Robert Thompson, a British expert on the Malayan campaign, believes it has lessons for Vietnam. He stresses the policing aspects of counterinsurgency — gathering intelligence, keeping the guerrillas off balance by surprise raids on their redoubts, establishing the government's presence in all the principal towns. It is an interesting idea, but are the situations analogous? The Malayans had several things going for them which the South Vietnamese do not: racial animosity between Malays and Chinese, which denied the guerrillas a foothold in the Malayan masses; the ability to choke off troops and supplies from without — there was no Communist North Malaya across the border. The lesson of Malaya in the fifties seems to be that sudden small-unit actions in the countryside, together with effective police administration in the towns, can defeat a vastly outnumbered guerrilla force drawn from a minority ethnic group separated from the nearest friendly power by fifteen hundred miles.

I sit in an office, looking out on green hills and the graceful turreted buildings from which British governors and Malay sultans ran the peninsula for centuries. A land development man shows charts, pictures, and maps which demonstrate the government's success in improving rural living conditions. I think about the silver water-buffalo head in the Thai palace, and the real water buffalo along the airport road. What's the relationship between these figures and graphs, and the slow sweating life of a rubber plantation worker? Does the man before me know? Or does he deal in plans and numbers, as I do in words and ideas, hoping they connect with reality? What would he do if someone burst in here to report a full-scale rebellion on the plantations? Probably extend the production line sharply downwards, as I would change Johnson's speech from "You have mastered a mortal challenge" to "You are facing" one.

SEOUL: Looks like they turned out the country. All the way in from the airport the students were two or three deep on both sides, carrying flags of both countries (Underwood?) and friendly signs (HEY THERE TEX JOHNSON, YOU SURE LOOK FINE; HODY COWBOY BIG FRIEND LBJ). Here in the Plaza people are packed like grains of sand. Office workers stand precariously near the roof-edges of their buildings. From bunches of balloons overhead, the largest flags I have ever seen — maybe a hundred feet by seventy-five — are suspended, almost touching the heads of the crowd.

There are issues to be made and avoided, but the speeches on both sides almost write themselves. This, after all, is our baby. We saved it in the fifties, at great cost in American lives. We have kept fifty thousand men and squadrons of fighter aircraft here ever since. The economy is growing, there is no internal subversion, and with our subsidy they have sent two divisions to Vietnam. Where, we hope, the same results will obtain — though we know the war there is even less analogous to Korea's than to Malaysia's. Anyway, South Korea works. In many respects it is a model for the "New Asia" we think we see coming into being. And our relationship to it is what our statesmen would like to have, at least transitionally, with other countries in the region.

The Malaysians appear almost ready to apply for United States citizenship, but surely that is because the British have announced their intention to quit east of Suez. The Australians and New Zealanders, the Filipinos, the Thais, Malaysians and Koreans, the Japanese and Indonesians — all are glad to have a counterweight to China in the region. All say, publicly or privately, that resistance to the Communists in Vietnam is terribly important to them. Then why has none of them, except for the Koreans, sent substantial numbers of troops there? Because we have. If the strongest, richest, etc. country in the world proclaims that stopping North Vietnam is critical to its own security, surely that makes it unnecessary for lesser countries to contribute much to that fight? Prime Minister Holt is a stalwart friend of America's and LBJ's; he thinks it is important to fight in Vietnam, and has said so; but he could not survive the deficits and long casualty lists that would follow a deeper commitment — so long as America is there. Nor could Marcos in the Philippines. Here, President Park is in a stronger position. His country is still on a kind of war footing, against a Communist enemy; and he counts his divisions in Vietnam as insurance that a grateful America will not forget him if another invasion comes. He needs us, and for the time being we need him. Not that our relationship is without friction. He asks for more than we are prepared to give him, and settles for less; he wants to respond to incidents along the 38th parallel with force, and we warn him that we cannot support him in that. But he is tough and confident and reasonable enough, and his people care about their country.

We stay at Walker Hill, overlooking the plain of the Han. The press is there too, and on the last night everybody turns loose for the first time on the trip. Bill Bundy and Rostow and I go out on the town as guests of several Korean cabinet ministers. Through a haze of rich food, incense, and whiskey I see Bundy, a towering splinter of a man, leaping about in a New England waltz step while his tiny partner runs to keep up; Rostow in the lotus position next to me speaks solemnly of takeoffs into the fourth stage of economic growth, and I bang my head on a radiator as I collapse into a beatific state — beyond speeches, ceremonies, reducing or doubling or standing fast. We drive back to Walker Hill through the dark city, barely missing a drunk who is obviously not contributing to the New Asia.

ANCHORAGE, ALASKA: One more river to cross. There are traces of early snow in the forests, the streams are running full and the firs are wet in the bleak twilight. Andrew Wyeth in the Far North. Then the city. Utilitarian on the outskirts, the downtown gaudy with neon bar signs and a bonfire set for Johnson. The chill in the air is the first we have felt since leaving Washington.

The President speaks next day about the Manila Conference. The "partnership" there, among the seven troop-contributing countries, "will endure long after those of us who met there have passed from the scene. It is permanent, because it is built on a foundation of historic necessity." I think of Thieu, Ky, Marcos, Park, and the others at Manila, and of Johnson, an "equal among equals," as he declared himself to be. Like Gulliver, just one of the boys on the beach.

Long bumpy flight home. The turbulence makes Mrs. Johnson uneasy, and an aide puts his arm around her for comfort. That wouldn't be enough for Liz Carpenter, who is panicky about any kind of flying and insists that people perform skits, sing, make speeches, do anything to be distracting. Symington obliges with a musical reprise of the trip. While the wings of Air Force One creak ominously in the storm, he has us in tears of laughter with songs of a mythical fiefdom that could be anyplace from Samoa to Seoul.

We land at Dulles, at night, in the rain. Johnson begins to speak once more, but I see my family, grab up the children, and go home.

Six months later. Punta del Este, Uruguay, in the huge Hall of the Americas, at a "summit" meeting.

"Haiti." A pale French-Negro took the microphone, and for nearly an hour pleaded for understanding of his island's peculiar social and political heritage. Our people are poor, illiterate, and bewitched, he said. Hence a regime such as Duvalier's was necessary. Or at least inevitable.

Throughout the morning at Punta del Este the presidents of Latin America had recounted, with a passion that survived translation, the urgent needs of their peoples. The democrats, chief among them Eduardo Frei of Chile, concentrated on social justice. Generals Stroessner of Paraguay and Onganía of Argentina thought the first requirement was public order. Some of the speakers looked to the United States as the ultimate benefactor, one which could, if it only would, provide sufficient development funds and trading opportunities to save the continent. The Ecuadorian president was particularly sharp in his attacks on United States policy; apparently this had to do with our withholding aid until something was done about the seizure of our tuna fishing boats. Other leaders thought their salvation lay in their own hands.

After the first dozen speeches it became clear that Latin America's problems and attitudes were wildly diverse. The near universality of the Spanish language, and the presence of the English-speaking giant of the North, obscured that for a time. But beyond language and formal religion, the oil-rich Venezuelans and the desperately poor Indians of Bolivia had as little in common with each other as both did with the people of Massachusetts and Idaho. The Germans of Chile, the Italians of Argentina, the descendants of the Mayas in Guatemala, the white rich and brown poor of Peru — might have lived on separate continents, so different were their backgrounds and prospects.

There was some impetus toward creating a common market and ending their long isolation from one another. It was accepted that people should be able to call Buenos Aires from Santiago without going through New York. There ought to be roads and railroads across the continent — so that, for example, components made in Peru could be easily shipped to Brazil for assembly. Tariff and quota walls ought to come down. Procedures for doing business should be simplified. Most of all, chauvinism and mistrust of others should give way, if not to a sense of brotherhood, at least to a desire for practical cooperation. It was not easy for the elected leaders of parliamentary democracies to associate with the self-imposed leaders of military juntas. But if they were to prosper separately as well as jointly, they would have to. Meetings such as this one were useful in taking the edge off that idea.

Speech followed speech. Morning became afternoon, and still the rhetoric flowed on under the blinding lights of television. People fought to stay awake. Several presidents, apparently shielding their eyes from the lights or studying documents on the table, slept soundly.

Johnson spoke last, after the Haitian. As at Manila, it was the only way by which he could avoid the appearance of directing the others through the incomparable weight of American power. He commended the new proposals in trade and communications, speaking of them as if they were settled policies that required only time and will and money to be consummated. In part that was cheerleading encouragement; in part it reflected Walt Rostow's inclination to regard theoretical conclusions as accomplished facts. Rostow had promoted the common market idea, and he could discern selflessness and cooperation between the Latin nations where other observers saw nothing. Thus he sometimes misled as to actual conditions. But enthusiasm such as his for a regional market was essential if it were ever to become a reality. At the end of the eighteenth century it was necessary that some Americans should talk about national unity as a present phenomenon, long before it actually existed — when our states and communities were as remote from one another as La Paz and Recife are today. What they wished to achieve could not otherwise have been done. So it was important, in encouraging what ought to be in Latin America, to emphasize the few instances in which it already was.

And talking first of the Latins' achievements and commitments permitted Johnson to urge them to greater efforts. "Each of us must engage in some introspection and ask ourselves . . . what are we doing to take on the hard problems of tax reform and land reform, to create new jobs and economic opportunities for the people we presume to lead; to clean out the red tape and act with the sense of urgency that our times require; above all, to . . . follow through on the plans we have made?" That was about as far as a United States President could go without giving fruitless offense.

I was prepared to have him blast the dictators, the rich who sent their money to Switzerland, the conservative churchmen who resisted family planning, the legislators who denounced United States investors without attending to the misery in the barrios, the soldiers who insisted on sophisticated weapons when their people needed food and medicine. But to what end? The Alliance for Progress was built on the idea of concurrent economic progress and political reform. Some economic progress had been made, though the rate of population growth threatened to nullify it; there had been little political reform. Colombia and Venezuela and Chile had managed to transfer power by election, but elsewhere more generals were in office than before; and what was to be gained now by attacking them about the table in Punta del Este? Not much, it seemed, except to unite them in resentment: the American President is impolitic and understands nothing of our situation. One had only to imagine the leader of Honduras or Uruguay using such a conference to chastise us for the poverty, discrimination, tax inequities, great hereditary fortunes, and military spending in our own country, to understand their sensitivity to *Yanqui* preachments.

Each afternoon at Johnson's quarters, a succession of Latin delegations got down to more practical business. We need an allocation for our residual oil in the United States market. We need approval for fish flour under the Food and Drug Act. Higher coffee prices. Greater control over some extractive industry without risking a cutoff of aid. A larger sugar quota. An Export-Import loan. Johnson used the time between meetings to be briefed on the facts. He knew this world very well, and he handled himself with confident authority. And then went back to the conference for more rhetoric.

There I heard almost nothing about our intervention in the Dominican Republic. I attributed that to the violent anticommunism of the military presidents, and the equally strong objections to Cuban trouble-making among the democratic leaders of Venezuela and Colombia. Our gunboat diplomacy had few active proponents among the Latin governments; Castro had none.

Under Johnson and Tom Mann, the Assistant Secretary of State for Inter-American Affairs, the American government had moderated the transcendental language of the early sixties, and had settled for realism. We had abandoned the old Wilsonian arguments against recognizing undemocratic regimes, those who seized power through force; after a seemly pause we took the traditional English course and recognized them. We dealt with those in office, and did not, as a matter of expressed policy, cultivate the opposition. We maintained, and indeed increased, the flow of dollars to the south. No wonder the leaders at Punta del Este were reasonably satisfied with our policy.

Yet as we left, I was conscious of disappointment in the big conference hall. Something was missing which could not be supplied by quotas, aid, or higher prices, and which had nothing to do with a common market or improved communications. An excitement, a sense of mission and destiny that united all these Spanish, Portuguese, Indians, Africans, and Italians. Something grave as death and lively as blood. Ideals; nobility; sex. We had adopted more modest and obtainable goals than reforming Latin society, but we had forfeited inspiration along with the challenge.

Coming back, we landed in Surinam to refuel. The equatorial night exploded with sudden rain, but there was a large gathering at the airport — even here, for an hour's stop, there had been an advance man — so there had to be a speech. Johnson spoke briefly about Punta del Este, and complimented his audience for the country's racial harmony. "Remarks at the Airport in Paramaribo, Surinam" is one of 577 items in the 1967 *Public Papers of the President*. It demonstrates as well as any that Presidents are called upon to speak too often, manufacturing words of no lasting significance for gatherings of little consequence to them. There is a Gresham's Law of Presidential Rhetoric, that too much of it spoils the effect of all of it. In defiance of that law, wherever the President moved microphones were set up, crowds invited, the press alerted, and a speech-writer assigned to produce appropriate language. Even if the speech was tolerably good, it was quickly forgotten; the President climbed back into his plane, the press boarded its own, and his words and audience vanished as quickly as the tropical squall at Paramaribo Airport.

I went with Johnson to Bonn, for Adenauer's funeral, and wrote not a word. That was a ceremonial gathering of the Western chiefs, and the somber drama of their rites — the mass in Cologne cathedral; the flotilla of ships, one bearing Adenauer's body, heading south against the Rhine's current, their red, black and yellow streamers clear in the twilight — made Presidential prose inadequate.

Perhaps it always was before a foreign audience, unless one could call on a magic phrase — like Kennedy's "Ich bin ein Berliner" — to convey something deeper than an idea, something that touched the immediate interests and emotions of the crowd. In El Salvador, in 1968, Johnson spoke at a teachers' school out in the country. I had visited the school the day before and talked with several students — none of them older than twenty — who would soon be leaving to teach in the mountain villages. I tried to reflect what I heard from them in the speech. "The starvation of education — with its third-class citizenship for teachers, its narrow circle of students, its dull, mechanical drilling of facts into young minds was never good enough. It is a prescription for disaster today." The new teachers were going to use educational television, and so they would not be cut off from the intellectual resources in the capital and elsewhere in Central America. But the teachers themselves were the indispensable elements, the liberators; as the Salvadoran anthem had it, "In each man there is an immortal hero," and it was their task to release the hero in each village child.

As the speech went on, the students became restive — still polite up front, talkative and boisterous toward the back, Johnson's words and the rapid flat translation falling upon them like annoying motes in the sultry air. I walked out and looked at the black earth and the ring of mountains about us, and wondered what I might have written that would have interested them. That would have bridged the chasm between young Central Americans headed for a life of respectable poverty in the villages, and the American President — whose cars and agents stood waiting to speed him away to Washington.

Maybe words could not do that. John Kennedy might have done it through personality: young, elegant, Catholic, liberal, he was what they dreamed of being. Robert Kennedy, by identifying with those who stood for change in Latin America — the dissident clergy, the intellectuals, the political opposition —

expressed the students' impatience with their society more effectively, and more safely, than they could themselves. But Presidents, unlike senators, could not take up the opposition's cause during official visits abroad — if indeed they wished to. They were stuck with "appropriate" rhetoric, and that, unless it was infused with personal magnetism, did not translate to the foreign heart.

There was a last, mighty trip, a kind of Phineas Fogg adventure that proved little more than the speed of Air Force One.

In December 1967, Prime Minister Harold Holt drowned in Australia. His death was a hard blow for Johnson. Of all the Pacific leaders — except for the South Vietnamese themselves — Holt was the most deeply committed to the war. And he was Johnson's friend. He was unashamed to be allied with one who aroused hot feelings in the Australian left, as in the American. Johnson — harassed by de Gaulle, unsure of Wilson, knowing that the Asians at the Manila Conference were minnows when whales were needed — treasured his relationship with Harold Holt. For an Australian broadcaster he recalled him poignantly:

> I don't think I have ever known a man whom I trusted more, or for whom I had greater affection and respect — [My impression of him] is associated with his country, the impression of candor, frankness, courage, tenacity, doing what is right and staying with you all the way through if you are right and never starting with you if you are wrong.
> . . . It has been one of the saddest things that has happened to us in Washington since we have been here — to have had the message . . .
> . . . Mrs. Johnson will go through with the affairs we had scheduled here during Christmas week, but I just had to go. I will be leaving at 11 o'clock in the morning.

I left with him, along with the usual coterie and Mr. and Mrs. Charles Engelhard — close friends of Holt, and the owners of a great fortune.

The funeral service in Melbourne was standard Anglican, devoid of spectacle until we left the cathedral and the crowds outside began to strain for a look at the leaders who had come all that way for a final tribute to their prime minister. Afterwards there was a stately wake, in which I found myself matching drinks with a lugubrious South Vietnamese.

At this point, the conventional thing to do was to go home. Instead, we went north to Darwin, and thence to an air base in Thailand. There we slept for a few hours until, shortly before dawn, the President addressed a crowd of pilots and crewmen gathered before a hangar. From time to time Thunderbolt jets roared off into the darkness, and Johnson rationalized their mission: "A mere handful of you men are pinning down several hundred thousand North Vietnamese. You are increasing the cost of infiltration. . . . Air power is providing the mobility which meets and matches the stealth of an enemy whose tactics are based on sudden, hit-and-run attacks. . . . Your missions are bringing closer every week the time of peace for which we and all of your fellow countrymen pray each day." A sergeant, hands in pockets, asked for a light, and I told him to wait until the President had finished. I did not want to be distracted; I wanted to see the reaction of these uniformed Americans, eight thousand miles from home, to their commander-in-chief's unapologetic justification of what they were doing. I assumed that here, if anywhere, he could speak decisively, making few bows to the doubters in his audience. He could be the war leader, bringing cheers from his troops. Even the skeptical reporters, sleepily making notes by the light of the hangar, would have to acknowledge that. The *Times* editorial board might complain about his "bellicosity," but most people would approve; they would not expect him to launch a new peace initiative before an audience of their fighting sons.

It did not work out that way. The airmen were courteous, but they gave no sign that they were now ready to clobber the enemy with redoubled force. It was not that kind of war.

The men did their jobs faithfully and well. The fighter-bomber pilots, as professionally able as any who had ever served American arms, took off for their elusive targets hundreds of miles away. Yet words from their President could not inspire them to feel what few other Americans felt by December 1967: that the war in which they were engaged was critical to the safety of their homeland; that unless the trucks and pack-carrying soldiers of North Vietnam could be prevented from entering South Vietnam, America itself would be endangered. I could understand that. I had begun to feel the same way.

But I thought we might get a keener reaction in Cam Ranh Bay, later that morning, and we did. Johnson made a speech, thanking the men for the sacrifices they had made, assuring them that "All the debate that you read about can never obscure the pride [that the people back home feel in you]. The slogans, the placards, and the signs cannot diminish the power of their love." He presented medals to Westmoreland, Bunker, and a number of other officials. Afterwards the soldiers gathered around him reaching for a handshake, laughing and yelling. It was show biz; but he was their President, and he had come a long way to tell them that the risks and discomforts they endured had meaning. When he went back to his plane, Johnson's face was glowing with pride — in himself, and in the men on the field. It occurred to me that this would have been a bad time to discuss a new peace proposal.

Now it really made sense to go home. Instead we headed west, over the Bay of Bengal and India, and landed for fuel in Pakistan. The rumors were true. We were going to see the Pope. On the airstrip at Karachi, Valenti and Hugh Sidey of Time-Life argued about that. Sidey, a sensitive and experienced observer of the Presidency, thought this kind of impulsive diplomacy demeaned the office, diminished the integrity of the trip's original purpose, which was (one could barely remember) to attend Harold Holt's funeral — and all for nothing, except to put Johnson in the Vatican on Christmas Eve. The Pope, the universal desire for peace, Christmas, Catholic votes — it was too much. Valenti replied that Sidey, like many White House correspondents, had once again crossed the line between reporting the President's moves and second-guessing him. Wait and see what happens, he said; don't let your annoyance at being kept away from home at Christmas prejudice you against what may be a useful move. It was a stand-off. Valenti got aboard Air Force One, griping about the presumption of the press; Sidey climbed into the back-up plane, griping about the President's shameless politicking.

Most of us waited at an Italian military base outside Rome while Johnson, Valenti, the American ambassador, and several others packed into a small helicopter for the trip to Vatican City. What happened there was the subject of later dispute, but it seemed that Johnson had explained his requirements for stopping the bombing, and asked the Pope's help in freeing our imprisoned pilots in Hanoi. What Pope Paul replied was not clear; those who had heard the discussion were more inclined to repeat Johnson's words than to recall the Pope's.

Coming home, we landed in the Azores, after midnight. Someone arranged for the small post exchange to be opened, so that the passengers and crew might shop for presents. Johnson remained asleep aboard the plane. There was a spectral scene in the PX: twenty-five tired people, just in from Vietnam and Rome, shuffling about among cut-rate blenders and luggage; Jane Engelhard advising Secret Service agents and baggage-handlers on the merits of various perfumes, writing up sales tickets, making change; a growing crowd outside in the damp balmy air. Suddenly Johnson came in, wearing a turtleneck sweater. He picked up a guitar and began to play it. A few secretaries sang along with him, and the local crowd applauded. We became giddy. I walked out and told someone that I had last been to bed in an air base in Thailand. What effect I expected this disclosure to have, I cannot remember. Next morning in Washington — with my body still somewhere west of Rome — I went down to the White House and wrote a radio address which the President delivered that evening, five days after we had left for Australia. The effect of this address was equally uncertain.

As was that of the trip itself. If it had been extended, as Sidey suspected, in order to shore up the President's political fortunes before the 1968 campaign, it was not a success. The New Hampshire primary, and his announcement that he would not run again, followed within three months.

WRITING FOR HOME: FINDING THE PUNCH LINE

Many people found it disappointing that Presidents employed speech-writers. It disturbed them that they could never be sure whether the man whom the majority had elected, or some faceless assistant known but to God and his associates, had composed a famous Presidential metaphor. But (1) if Presidents wrote the drafts of all that they were required to say, they would have had little time left for the main business of their office, that is, governing; (2) Presidents did not ordinarily speak, or write, Presidentialese — that exalted language in which, custom had it, great public issues should be discussed; (3) speech-writers did not last unless they had a good idea of what their Presidents wished to say; (4) when it counted — when the President was preparing a major address — the final product usually belonged more to him than to his writers.

It was part of the speech-writer's code that he should not assert his authorship of what the President said. A knowing shrug was permissible, but only just. When John Kenneth Galbraith and several other contributors to President Kennedy's speeches began to claim credit for particular lines in them, Art Buchwald wrote an urgent message to the director of the National Parks. Watch out for a tall, thin man with a chisel in his hand, Buchwald warned, especially if he gets near the Kennedy gravesite.

The clear inference was that "Ask not what your country can do for you" might soon be followed by "J. K. Galbraith, 1961."

But it was impossible for some Presidential writers to conceal themselves behind a screen of anonymity. Richard Goodwin, who was probably the best writer to serve a President since Roosevelt's day, did not bother to try. He saw his role as far more than that of a creative amanuensis; he meant to influence the direction of government. His advice to me, before he left the White House, was to wait until the last possible moment before submitting a draft to the President and the bureaucracy. In that way, he said, you can make your ideas almost a *fait accompli;* there will be no time for them to secure an alternative draft, and they must bargain with you to temper what you've written — instead of your arguing at the end for a bold variance from accepted policy. By the time I became the principal speech-writer, there was little range for striking initiatives. My job was to make staying with it in Vietnam, and in the ghettos, sound compelling and necessary.

I drew on many sources for speech drafts, chiefly on material supplied by the departments. There, buried in language that human beings never used except in communicating between large institutions, were the outlines of policy. I tried to turn them into Presidentialese.

That was a strange dialect, meant to fix in the listeners' minds the impression that something profound and memorable had just been said. It made heavy use of alliteration to catch their attention. Two examples, neither of them mine: "[The Dominican people] want, as we do, an end to slaughter in the streets and brutality in the barrios." Second, about the Middle East: "This is a time not for malice, but for magnanimity; not for propaganda, but for patience; not for vituperation, but for vision." I was told that Johnson admired this sort of thing; I thought it put up a wall between him and his audience, and made him — already the artful politician — seem the more contrived.

Roosevelt could explain a complicated question of economics

by telling a simple story. Johnson, trying to simplify, was often painfully artificial: "I have talked to you about a six-point program . . . Food — that is 'F.' Recreation — that is 'R.' Jobs and wages and income — that is 'I.' Education — that is 'E.' Increased social security, Medicare, and nursing homes for older folks — that is 'N.' And a strong nation that will defend us and help us get peace — defense — that is 'D' . . . that spells 'friend.'"

Still, he was often at his best when extemporizing. I thought that nothing Goodwin or I ever wrote for him compared with a talk I had heard Johnson make one morning years before in Abilene, Texas, to a group of REA district managers. While he ate a bowl of oatmeal, they told him about their problems with the banks and the Department of Agriculture. Johnson finished his breakfast, and in a low, compelling voice advised them they should join with the unions, the home builders, and all others who needed low interest rates; separately their power was inadequate, together they would force the government into lowering the rates. The idea of uniting with Walter Reuther and David Dubinsky, as Johnson recommended, must have seemed strange to those West Texas farmer-managers, but they cheered him vigorously.

He was just as good before an audience of Jews in the Catskills, where he dedicated a hospital in the summer of 1966:

The B'nai B'rith wanted to give me an award because they were very pleased at the civil rights program I had enunciated. And so finally, reluctantly, I agreed to go out of the White House to a hotel to receive this award.

And I went out and I made, I thought, the greatest speech of my life. And they stood and applauded me and took my picture and gave me the award. And I came on back home and worked hard the next morning — and picked up the afternoon paper and I saw "B'nai B'rith Denounces Johnson's Education Bill." And I was rather distressed.

And then the next thing I heard, some of the Catholics were upset because they couldn't get the books and because of provisions in the bill that were obnoxious to them. And so we talked to a few Cardinals and we worked very hard on the matter and we worked out an arrangement where everybody could get a peep at the book a little bit and we got them adjusted. And I thought, "Now if this line just holds for a few hours, maybe I can get a roll call."

And lo and behold, a friend of mine down in Texas — a very prominent doctor who is a leader of the Baptist faith — heard about what had happened and they, the Catholics, were going to get to see some of these things. He called up one of my assistants, and said, "What in the world has happened? Has the Pope taken the President over?" My assistant said, "No one has taken him over. The President is out swimming."

"Well," my friend said, "I've got to talk to him on the phone." It was the middle of the day. And my assistant said, "Well, I can go out and interrupt him — he is swimming."

"What's the President doing swimming in the middle of the day, with all the work he's got to do?"

"Well," said my assistant, "he's out there swimming with Dr. Graham."

And he said, "Which?"

My assistant said, "Dr. Graham."

He said, "Is that *our* Billy?"

Well, it was "our Billy," one of the great religious leaders of this country.

So before the sun went down that night we had the Cardinals and we had the Rabbis and we had "our Billy." They were all aboard — and the greatest educational measure ever to be considered by any legislative body became the law of the land.

It was hard to think of a base that did not touch.

Most of what Presidents said passed unremarked into the obscurity of the Archives. Unless the occasion itself was momentous, hardly a paragraph survived a copyeditor's desk. For a speech-writer, the trick was to find an arresting phrase, something that would be "news" in itself, and would not embarrass the President later on. Some writers could do that almost automatically, whatever the subject. I needed to care; autointoxication did not work for me: I had to hate somebody, some idea or condition, and hope that a compelling phrase would suddenly appear on the page without design. Writing about the death of Mrs. Liuzzo at the hands of the Klan, I put down "hooded band of bigots" almost before I knew it, the words squeezing out of rage and contempt; that afternoon they were across every front page. The same emotions produced headlines for an election-eve statement in 1966: "White backlash is dangerous because it threatens to vest power in the hands of second-rate men whose only qualification is their ability to pander to other men's fears." In an AFL-CIO speech in 1967, "wooden soldiers of the status quo," referring to Republicans in Congress, caused a stir. Maybe the lesson was not so much that rhetorical art came from real feelings, as that attacking anyone from a Presidential platform was guaranteed coverage in the press.

Writing a political speech was hard work. Television spots were reducing political issues to subliminal clichés, but there were still fund-raising events where Presidents were expected to ring the familiar changes. The pressure was on the writer — so he thought — to produce classic effects. The models for Democrats were Bryan's "Cross of Gold" speech, Roosevelt's "Happy Warrior," Truman's giving 'em hell.

In fact, speeches before Democratic dinners were often little more than recitations of achievements before a dazed crowd of party-goers. I remembered a dinner in the late fifties, at the Washington Armory, as the nadir of political communication. There was supposed to be one principal speaker. Five other men were to make brief remarks. As it happened there were six speeches, each half an hour long. By midnight, the audience had dwindled to a few hundred. Garbage trucks drove onto the floor at both ends of the cavernous hall, and waiters, many of them staggering from leftover booze, began tossing plates, glasses, and food onto the truck-beds. Majority leader John McCormack chose that moment to survey the Republican legislative record during the Eighty-sixth Congress. "On the farm bill," he said, in his flat Boston voice, "one hundred fifty Republicans voted to recommit, while only thirty-six . . ." From a table of South Carolinians directly in front of McCormack, a tall man in a summer tux swayed to his feet, tucked a bottle under his arm, and shouted, "Jee-sus *Chrahst!*"

Democratic politicians traditionally broke the bonds, struck the shackles, lifted up, gave new hope, made possible. "They" — the Republicans and other skeptics — thought we would fail, fold, give up, but "they" had another think coming. We had not come this far to quit in sight of our goal. Answer the following rhetorical question: Shall we quit trying to feed the poor, train the uneducated, heal the sick, just because it is hard and costly? (One hoped for a chorus of "No's," but usually there was only silence. By 1967, one was satisfied if no one yelled "Yes!") Of course it was hard; but we would win because the people loved us for what we had tried to do. In the great tradition of Franklin D. Roosevelt! Harry S. Truman! And so on.

Johnson stumping was the best of all — when he was good. He made a political speech in Morgantown, West Virginia, shortly before the 1968 election. He had a brief text, but his juices were flowing and the audience was appreciative, so he spoke for more than an hour, flavoring politics with country tales. "We like this democracy so much, this freedom so much, we want everybody to have a little taste of it. It is like the fellow who had a few too many drinks. He came home, and he got to sleep and woke up in the middle of the night. His mouth was burning and he said to his wife, 'Get me some ice water.' And she got the pitcher of ice water and brought it to him and he took a drink. Then he said, 'Honey, this is so good, go wake up the kids and give them some of it.'"

That kind of story might not travel well. Certainly it was not meant for national television. But it had the color and smell of life, in a way that prepared rhetoric did not. It came very close to representing the man himself, and that, after all, was what people wanted to see, whether they supported or hated him. He made a pretty good speech for an ethnic group luncheon in New York — the "All Americans Council of the Democratic National Committee" — comparing Humphrey in 1968 with Truman twenty years before. Breslin wrote that it was probably the best Democratic performance of the campaign, not so much because of the speech, as because of Johnson's personal politicking — carrying his grandson Lyn through the crowd, conveying a sense of the President as a man as well as a politician.

Political speech-writing was never good enough. It never matched what a good politician could do with the right metabolism, the right relationship between himself and an audience. But it was usually necessary — not just to give the politician a frame to build on, but to lay out what he thought or hoped his people believed.

Somewhere in every serious political speech were the markers by which a party defined its course. Their colors ran back to Jefferson and Hamilton, to Rousseau and Hobbes and the old debates over man's capacity for sensible judgment. They were cast in either/or terms: crime resulted either from murderous living conditions, or from the society's unwillingness to impose firm sanctions on antisocial behavior; poverty was either a social crime of the rich, or a psychological failure of the poor; prosperity should trickle down or bubble up.

Inevitably the distinctions that brought the loudest cheers at political dinners seemed the most inadequate and simplistic the next morning. Sober, thinking people did not see the world in either/or terms. Everything was true in life; energetic choices were made in a storm of contradictions. Political words offered a rationale for otherwise chaotic events. They helped to unite people of very different sensibilities behind common policies, and thus they helped government to function. But they rarely gave an accurate reflection of reality. Their writers, joining in (and sometimes leading) the applause that followed their ringing phrases, could easily forget that.

And communicating fairly and precisely was not the only question. Out beyond the convention centers and the Hilton hospitality rooms, beyond the cars pulling up with lobbyists and their clients, were citizens whose problems did not yield to any words at all.

10

Cities Aflame

> I know the Negro race has a long road to go. I believe that the life of the Negro has been a life of tragedy, of injustice, of oppression. The law has made him equal, but man has not. And after all, the last analysis is, what has man done? — And not what has the law done? I know there is a long road ahead of him before he can take the place which I believe he should take. I know that before him is sorrow, tribulation, and death among the blacks, and perhaps the whites. I would do what I can to avert it. I would advise patience; I would advise tolerance; I would advise understanding; I would advise all those things which are necessary for men who live together. — Clarence Darrow, final plea in the *Sweet* case, 1926

April 1965

AT five o'clock the nurse came in, carrying a bland hygienic dinner which she proceeded to place carefully in a patch of afternoon sun. Bored by three days of hospital routine after a minor operation, I promptly went to sleep. At six I woke up to the cheerful face of Pat Moynihan. Under one arm he held a bottle of Scotch, under the other a blackbound pamphlet bearing the title, *The Negro Family: The Case for National Action*. For the next four hours we talked and read and drank.

The Negro Family report had been prepared by Moynihan and his assistants in the Labor Department. The copy he had brought along was one of a hundred, and bore the warning "For Official Use Only." I was accustomed to security classifications on papers at Defense and State; to find one on a sociological treatise from the Labor Department was surprising. Halfway through I saw why. *The Negro Family* was politically charged.

Because it became so famous and occasioned so much controversy, it seems unnecessary to recall now what it said. Yet it is necessary, for the controversy obscured its purpose almost beyond recognition.

In sum, the report described a rapid deterioration in Negro family stability, as measured by the number of working fathers living at home. For many years the number of families receiving help under the Aid for Dependent Children program had tracked with the unemployment rate for Negro men. But two years before the report was written, the Negro male unemployment rate had fallen, while the number of families on AFDC had continued to rise. Most of the increase reflected the absence of fathers from the home. Thus the expectations on which family welfare were based — that higher male employment would reduce the dependence of families upon the state, with assistance needed mainly in periods of recession — were suddenly undermined by a frightening set of statistics.

At the time the report was written in early 1965, more than a quarter of Negro families were headed by women. "The typical AFDC mother in Cook County, Illinois," said a 1960 study, "was married and had children by her husband, who deserted; his whereabouts are unknown, and he does not contribute to the support of his children. She is not free to remarry and has had an illegitimate child since her husband left." Almost 90 percent of Chicago's AFDC families were Negro.

In many Negro families, the father was present and worked, but in a menial job; the mother was the principal money-earner. This operated "to enlarge the mother's role, undercutting the status of the male and making many Negro families essentially matriarchal." Where the parents were together but both were unemployed, a subtle denigration worked against the father.

"Consider the fact that relief investigators or case workers are normally women and deal with the housewife. Already suffering a loss in prestige and authority in the family because of his failure to be the chief breadwinner, the male head of the family feels deeply this obvious transfer of planning for the family's well-being to two women, one of them an outsider. His role is reduced to that of errand boy to and from the relief office." *

Hundreds of thousands of Negro youth grew up with "little knowledge of their fathers, less of their fathers' occupations, still less of family occupational traditions. . . . The white family, despite many variants, remains a powerful agency not only for transmitting property from one generation to the next, but also for transmitting no less valuable contacts with the world of education and work. . . . Children . . . learn patterns of work from their fathers even though they may no longer go into the same jobs. White children without fathers at least perceive all about them the pattern of men working. Negro children without fathers [in areas where male unemployment is catastrophically high] flounder — and fail." The effects were everywhere: poor performance in school and on intelligence tests (surveys had shown that the IQ's of children with fathers in the home were consistently higher than those whose fathers had left); high rates of delinquency and crime; trouble in holding jobs and enduring frustration; failure to pass the Armed Forces Qualification test.

The last deserved elaboration. Many white Americans remembered their military service as a joke or a hazard or both. Many others welcomed it as a time for shifting gears between school and work, an obligation that fortunately delayed their choice of vocation; so it was for me. For Negro Americans, the stakes were higher. Moynihan wrote to me later: "The biggest opportunity to do something about Negro youth has been right under our noses all the time. Above all things, the down-and-out

---

* Edward Wright Bakke, *Citizens Without Work* (New Haven: Yale University Press, 1940), quoted in the Moynihan report.

Negro boy needs to be inducted into the male American society. Nothing can better give him the sense of more inclusive identity that Erik Erikson talks about. Nothing could give him more direct, working skills. . . . The country has caught on to the fact that serving in the Armed Forces is by and large an advantage, and typically, the Negro has been excluded." The Civil Rights Commission had found that "Negro enlisted men enjoy relatively better opportunities in the Armed Forces than in the civilian economy in every clerical, technical, and skilled field for which the data permit comparison." The arguments for bringing more Negroes into the service seemed conclusive.

Yet in 1963, 56 percent of Negro youth failed the mental test for induction. Steve Ailes, the Secretary of the Army, testified that almost 60 percent of the volunteers rejected each year had deficiencies that could be corrected. Moynihan and others proposed that the tests be changed to compensate for the difficulty which Negroes (and Southerners generally) had with them. The idea offended Senator Russell, who worried about lowered standards in the service. Many professional officers feared a tide of unequipped soldiers in a military environment that demanded more and more technical competence. *Sotto voce,* they carried their concerns to the Hill.

Secretary McNamara, with Johnson's blessing, subsequently announced a program for inducting 100,000 men who had narrowly failed the test. But military service was only one answer. The whole thrust of *The Negro Family* was that a massive effort, treating Negro problems as interrelated, was necessary to avert calamity. "Three centuries of injustice have brought about deep-seated structural distortions in the life of the Negro American. At this point, the present tangle of pathology is capable of perpetuating itself without assistance from the white world. The cycle can be broken only if these distortions are set right."

I "knew" much of this, in the sense that I knew there was malnutrition and religious hatred throughout the world. But to see it displayed systematically, as it was in the report, brought it home. One conclusion was obvious. Despite the civil rights acts, the awakening of white conscience to the injustices in Southern Negro life, and the Medicare, education, and antipoverty programs from which Negroes would benefit, living conditions for millions of black Americans were growing steadily worse.

We were in the last of that period in which we thought real progress was made each time a white Southerner stood up to be counted for racial justice. In which men like Bull Connor and Sheriff Jim Clark and George Wallace seemed to be the principal enemies of the Negro race. And from which, we believed, the Negro would emerge, freed of the social and political disabilities of his past, to share in America's promise. But the report said that while positive acts of injustice were the cause of the Negro's peculiar suffering, ending them would not stop that suffering. Legal remedies were not enough; a vigorous economy was not enough. Only new and painful exertions would do. The report did not suggest what would happen if the "tangle of pathology" was not unwound, but two things seemed inevitable: the fiscal cost of welfare would rise dramatically; so would the social cost of delinquency.

How would the public react to the report? Obviously it touched on matters of deep political and private sensitivity: mounting welfare rolls, illegitimacy, "shiftlessness," crime. I was chiefly concerned that conservative politicians and writers would use it to prove the inherent corruption of Negro life. Surely it would provide them with arguments: that after all the furore about civil rights, after "all that these people have had done for them," they were retrogressing to a state of immoral dependency. I could not understand why a hundred copies had been printed. So many guaranteed that some would find their way into unfriendly hands, so few suggested that there was something to hide, which would be hotly pursued by enterprising reporters. What was apparently a compromise intended to get the report into circulation within government, without provoking an uninformed public debate upon it, seemed sure to have the latter effect.

As it happened, the report attracted its sharpest criticism from the left — from a number of Negro spokesmen, and from white activists, principally clergymen, who saw in it a racist attack upon Negro mores and particularly upon female-headed families.

Following the President's historic speech in June at Howard University — built around the report, and drafted by Richard Goodwin after long talks with Moynihan — we began a series of discussions in preparation for a White House conference, which the President had announced in the speech. Social scientists like Erik Erikson, Talcott Parsons, Urie Bronfenbrenner, James Q. Wilson, Tom Pettigrew, and Robert Coles came in for long afternoon talks in the west wing conference room. Bayard Rustin came, too — the most astute Negro leader I had ever met — and it was from him that we heard the first expressions of doubt about centering the conference on *The Negro Family*.

In New York, where Rustin lived, a group of Protestant churchmen had drawn up a manifesto against the report. One of them, a Dr. Payton, had issued a particularly egregious statement accusing Moynihan of avoiding the "real" issues — jobs, housing, the enforcement of civil rights. (In fact the report was a four-alarm call to provide jobs and training so that Negro men might sustain their families.) Floyd McKissick of CORE raised a cultural objection: "My major criticism of the report is that it assumes that middle class American values are the correct ones for everyone in America. Just because Moynihan believes in middle class values doesn't mean that they are good for everyone. . . . Moynihan thinks that everyone should have a family structure like his own. Moynihan emphasizes the negative aspects of the Negroes and then seems to say that it's the individual's fault [?] when it's the damned system that needs changing." * Even Clarence Mitchell, the brilliantly effective lobbyist for the NAACP,

---

* Quoted in Lee Rainwater and William L. Yancey, *The Moynihan Report and the Politics of Controversy* (Cambridge: MIT Press, 1967).

thought Moynihan was implying that "it was necessary for the improvement of the Negro community to come from within." * Marcus Raskin took McKissick's point a step further. In a letter to me, he urged "as a part of the theme of the conference an investigation of which mores and values which dominate the Negro lower class could be adopted or emulated by the rest of the society . . . there is great danger in pressing for a restructuring of the Negro family toward the middle class. The only result of such a thing will be the further enlargement of the cop role for the social worker class. It will appear that its monopoly will be protected by the Federal government to spy, exploit, and interfere." Rustin, true to his labor movement background, said, "We must talk about the poor family, not simply the Negro family." †

Day after day, as we met in the west wing, expressions of dissatisfaction with the report came in. There were rumors that the conference would be picketed or even disrupted, if we based it on *The Negro Family.*

I was reluctant to yield to what I believed to be misconceptions, if not downright distortions of what Moynihan and his staff had written. Looking at the social indices of Negro life, I had been frustrated by their endless interconnections. Bad housing was related to unemployment, which was related to poor education, which was related to the cultural and financial poverty of the home, which derived from unemployment. Ad infinitum. Treating any one of these problems as a *ding an sich* was a prescription for failure.

Where they were all present, they formed a condition in which people simply did not hope. One afternoon, tutoring in a settlement house, I grew impatient with four teen-aged Negro girls who did not know the meaning of "physical," "mental," "social," "significant," "deprived," or "disaster" — all words that theorists and politicians had used in describing lives such as theirs for a generation. I asked them, "How do you ever expect to become a

---
* Rainwater and Yancey, p. 200.   † *Ibid.*

secretary? How do you expect to help your children become businessmen or teachers?" The expression on their faces was incredulous. The idea of becoming productive members of the society, or of seeing their children do so, had never occurred to them. Only one of the four came from a home in which the father was present, and that father was unemployed. Two mothers were domestics, the other two were on relief.

The family was a still point in this turning world. If we set about trying to strengthen it, we would have to do all that the critics of the report believed should have first priority: see that jobs and job training were available, improve the schools, build new housing, insist on fair treatment. We could measure our progress by family cohesion. We would succeed if we stopped the rise in AFDC clients, in separations and abandonments. Stabilizing families should lead to less delinquency — to fewer street crimes, illegitimate births, and less dope addiction. It would give shape to the random days of the ghetto young.

Moynihan believed in the critical importance of a father in the home. So did I. He believed in "middle-class values" — ignoring, for the moment, the connotations of prudishness and self-righteousness that are attached to that term. He thought a society became healthier the more its people were willing to work, bear responsibility, endure petty frustrations, and plan for the future. So did I. No doubt there were beneficent values in Negro lower-class life, as Marc Raskin suggested. But there was also an abundance of crime, brutality, idleness, and poverty, and not much hope of better. The adoption of at least some middle-class values seemed indispensable to changing that. Anyway, it was certain that middle-class taxpayers, black or white, would not wish to pay for the preservation of a "value system" that tolerated illegitimacy and male irresponsibility. We were to see many variations on that truth in the years to come.

During the fall of 1965, a friend grumbled about the government's "god-like" manipulation of Negro family life. His concern was misplaced. Some of us wished to manipulate it, but so many people complained about our intentions that we were compelled to drop the idea. The report's implicit program — that the government's efforts should be devoted to enabling fathers to remain with their families — was abandoned in favor of a more traditional approach to Negro problems. Not, as Rainwater and Yancey believed, because the Vietnam war had devoured the huge resources that encouraging family stability would have required. (The Administration, according to their view, had welcomed the controversy as a cloud behind which to escape its Howard commitment.) As it turned out, the cost of programs recommended by the civil rights conference probably exceeded that of the family allowance program that Moynihan talked about so often. No; we would have pursued the family concept, its ramifications and remedies, if the civil rights groups had supported it. (King and Wilkins were enthusiastic about the Howard speech at the time; but they were in no position to urge consideration of the Moynihan report when the activists in their ranks began to denounce it. Leaders do not divide their own forces unnecessarily.)

Scholars often think of a President as one who can, through the power of his office and personal persuasion, steer the "right" course against the current of public opinion. Sometimes he can, if he is actively supported by key interests. But where the very groups for whom his policy was designed reject it, and where the country is not ready for the expenditures it requires, he is wise to alter his policy toward one of wider acceptance. So it was that we turned to jobs, housing, education — matters about which there was still debate, but which were more familiar, having a constituency that included business executives as well as sociologists.

The war in Vietnam was beginning to put a damper on expenditures for social purposes, but it had not yet limited our aspirations. If the support had been there, we would probably have aspired to a family allowance as well as to plentiful jobs.*

---

* As President Nixon did in 1969.

It was not easy to get public agreement on that much. The "liberal consensus" — in this case, the middle-class sense of fairness — had supported the ending of official discrimination, and of some private (in job placements, hotels, restaurants, and theaters). It was willing to free the Negro from certain obvious and obnoxious restrictions. Once that was done, the American idea was that every man was on his own. No one was supposed to get special treatment. The Irish hadn't: the Italians hadn't; the Jews hadn't. What made the Negro special? It required a generally sympathetic press, a few enlightened (or well-advised) businessmen, activists in the universities, the civil rights organizations, and a President willing to commit himself and his administration to the work, to keep the idea alive — that whites in the Negro's history had made him a special case; that the civil rights acts had not met all his legitimate demands; that the riot in Watts had not discredited the help that had been given, but had only put it in perspective. At the heart of the problem — of building a new consensus for action — was the absence of observable cruelties which could be effectively forbidden by law. When Negroes were forced to ride in the back of buses, refused service in restaurants, or told to come back next month to register, that could be seen or felt by people everywhere, who then cried out for a federal remedy. Such indignities had elements of drama in which there were palpable villains. There were no villains — at least none that strangers could identify — in the broken homes of the Northern cities where men "chose" to be unemployed, women chose welfare, and young people chose heroin. In time, a national commission found the villain, with consequences I will discuss later on.

The riots in Watts and Newark and Detroit, and the movie-gangster rhetoric of Rap Brown and Stokely Carmichael, strained the patience of the "permissive" whites; depressed the responsible blacks; and disorganized the white liberals. A few of the latter excused the riots as inevitable, and even justifiable. Nothing could have been better calculated to undermine the consensus.

Johnson knew better. Speaking to a conference of equal employment workers shortly after Watts, he said:

We shall never achieve a free and prosperous and hopeful society until we have suppressed the fires of hate and turned aside from violence — whether that violence comes from the night riders of the Klan, or the snipers and the looters in the Watts district. Neither old wrongs nor new fears can justify arson and murder. . . . The brave story of the American Negro is related to the struggle of men on every continent for their rights as sons of God. It is a compound of brilliant promise and stunning reverses. Sometimes, as in the past week — as the two are mixed on the same page of our newspapers and television screens [Negroes in the South had just begun registering under the new Voting Rights Act] the result is baffling to all the world. And it is baffling to me, to you, to all of us. . . . Always there is the danger that hours of disorder may erase the accumulated goodwill of many months and years. I warn and plead with all thinking Americans to contemplate this for a due period.

Our instinctive reaction to the Watts riot was to look to the civil rights organizations for mediation and leadership. But neither the NAACP, the Urban League, nor King's Southern Christian Leadership Conference, had much of a base in the Northern and Western ghettos. King's genius, as Charles Silberman wrote to me, lay "not in organization, but in mobilizing white sentiment . . . he, Wilkins, and Farmer could not have afforded to have gone to Los Angeles during the riots; their appearance there would only have dramatized how small a constituency they really have." Moynihan's warning that the "Negro problem" was no longer one of race, but of class — involving the same pathologies which had afflicted "under-classes" in the past — seemed borne out in the photographs of looters in Watts, as in *The Negro Family*'s statistics. Sending Ramsey Clark to Los Angeles, and talking about regenerating the local poverty program would not do much to remedy the problem, or even to make Watts a less desolate community; but there seemed to be no alternative at the time.

Meanwhile, there was a conference to be run. The controversy over *The Negro Family* made it certain that we could not be ready by November 1965 as we had planned, and so we converted the fall meeting into a planning session for several hundred activists. Much of their rhetoric was furious, full of contempt not only for the repressive society outside the Washington Hilton, but for the government's efforts to date. The "family" question was reduced to one seminar among many, and was devoted in good part to a defense, by women civil servants, of the existing social welfare agencies. Elsewhere the planners vied with one another in demanding more and more extreme reparations for the Negro's wrongs.

At Howard, the President had talked about a new stage in the struggle — moving beyond opportunity to achievement, beyond the possibility of equity to equity itself. After the planning session, the danger was that this movement, with all its potential for resentment, would be controlled by a small army of abrasive men whose language alienated the moderate center. To the point men in this army, the moderates were prisoners of the past — prejudiced, complacent, and yet vaguely fearful; they didn't know where it was at, and would have to learn quickly if they were to be spared future riots. That this was a fairly accurate indictment did not diminish its power to annoy and even to repel. And if it repelled the moderates — if they could not see beyond the rhetoric to the broken streets of the ghettos and the threat to themselves and their children — then there would be no help. Not by the violence which some of the activists talked about so casually; that would be met by superior violence. Not by the passage of laws to redistribute wealth and advantage; there would be none. If we were to move on to the next stage, the leadership would have to be returned to the centrists, to the sensitive establishment — to business, labor, Wilkins and Young. The question would have to be changed from "What will you do to expiate your guilt?" to "What can we do to make a tolerable society?"

So we turned to Ben Heineman, the president of the Chicago and North Western Railway, for a new chairman, We got up a council which included the chief executive officers of Lockheed, Cummins Engine, and Textron; George Meany; and the vice president of the steelworkers' union. The businessmen — particularly Heineman — were far out in front of the Congress in their comprehension of urban problems, and their success in making money suggested to the public that they were not revolutionaries or mere theorists. Most of them attended a number of weekend meetings, flying in aboard private jets to talk about people whose children ate the paint off windowsills. There was a certain éclat in demonstrating social consciousness after attending to corporate business; certainly it did not hurt them in their other dealings with a liberal government; but they also cared about social peace in their communities, and in the nation. Heineman announced that the June conference would be concerned with "how to do it. . . . The idea is to enlist segments of society that perhaps have not been motivated or shown the opportunity of making the Negro an equal partner in society." So far as we were concerned, that was the right note.

As the conference neared, dissonant sounds became louder. Jesse Gray, the Harlem rent-strike leader, circulated a statement: "The black ghetto and the black South need no more conferences with the two-faced white power structure to understand its problems. What sense does it make to take our problems to the very people who are responsible for them in the first place? What sense does it make to trust Lyndon Johnson who raises one billion dollars for India in two days while ignoring homeless people from Mississippi camping on his front lawn?" SNCC, it was said, planned a demonstration on the floor during the final dinner. We asked the Washington police for black officers in mufti, but that struck them as inappropriate for a national conference. We asked the FBI for black agents, but most of those were assigned to sensitive jobs around the country. It seemed we might have to do the job ourselves — dubious prospect — until Louis Martin came up with a solution. Martin, a political genius who shared the discontent of his people and yet retained a sense of humor about all mankind, asked Howard University for a number of its most attractive young women in formal gowns, to serve as hostesses. 'That'll make those SNCC boys think twice about raising hell," he said. It did; the dinner was as restrained as a Chamber of Commerce convention.

There were pickets outside the Sheraton Park. So much was going on inside that their protest lacked point. Still, they were the focus of considerable television coverage, as cameras were not permitted in the meeting rooms. Berl Bernhard, the conference director, went out to meet their leader. There were parties going on upstairs, and the pickets wanted an opportunity to share in them. That was arranged, and the small but vocal group disappeared. It was interesting to know that civil rights groups were not entirely programmatic — that like trade association and "40-and-8" conventions, this one was not confined to committee work and formal debates.

Despite Jesse Gray's misgivings, thousands of people attended the conference. The Heineman council's report and recommendations — one hundred pages — were adopted, with many additions. Several impromptu proposals were rejected in committee — for example, to require General Motors to hand over its Chevrolet division to black ownership — but there was a spacious air about the place, reflecting a sympathetic Administration and a general optimism about solving The Problem. It was, indeed, a time of determined hopefulness. The mayor of Baton Rouge had written to the President that he could not attend the conference, but "I have carefully read the Council's Report and Recommendations and highly recommend that every aspect of the report be pursued to realization."

The principal recommendations called for action by the federal government. That was not surprising, since most of the gains of the recent past had resulted from, or in, the enactment of national laws. Afterwards the Chamber of Commerce complained about the emphasis on government, and the slighting of the private sector. The chamber was right about that. But business had not been broadly responsive to the needs of the Negro poor, and it was understandable that a conference such as this would not focus on gifts from a stranger.

On the last day we spent a lot of time debating whether the President should address the closing dinner. A hostile demonstration was still a possibility; though it could only come from a tiny minority, it would, given the laws of reporting, dominate the news — like the red paint thrown on his car in Sydney. The impression would be left that the group for which he had done so much, and promised so much, had repudiated him; and that would hurt the Negro's cause no less than him.

Around six o'clock the chances for peace seemed good, and I shaped up a draft I had prepared a few days before. Johnson's entry into the hall set off a tremendous ovation. Throughout the past week we had been dealing with the sensitivities of famous spokesmen, mediating, placating, and amending our plans; we — or at least I — had scarcely noticed that the majority of the conferees were church people, NAACP, and Urban League members, the moderates of the movement. I should have known that Louis Martin would not leave the selection of delegates to chance. On and on they chanted, "LBJ! LBJ!" and once — following his extemporaneous pledge to "give my days — and such talents as I may have — to the pursuit of justice and opportunity for those so long denied them," they were back on their feet and shouting. The trump card was his introduction of Thurgood Marshall, who told the crowd — his crowd, for whom he was exemplar and father figure: "Thirty years ago when I started in this business, you just didn't hear things like that." When Johnson left, I followed him out to congratulate him. In the light of his car his eyes were large and his face almost incandescent with the pleasure of an unexpected and flawless triumph. It was about the last one he would have.

> *The problem was there for all to see —*
> *The fractured Negro family.*
> *And just the man to coin a plan*
> *Was Daniel Patrick Moynihan.*
> *His data made the pundits swoon.*
>   *(But where are the snows of yesternoon?)*
>
> *To LBJ 'twas clear the polity*
> *Demanded we have real equality.*
> *At Howard he said, "Let us gather*
> *All the experts; let them blather.*
> *Bring on the Irish and the Jews*
> *And all the militants you choose.*
> *Give me your ideas, foreign or native,*
> *Just so they're fresh and innovative."*
> *Everybody said, "How keen!"*
>   *(But where are the snows of yestere'en?)*
>
> *'Tis better, they say, to light a spark*
> *Than sit around and curse the dark.*
> *And so they did in Watts, L.A.,*
> *And lit a fire as bright as day.*
> *(Baby, baby burning bright,*
> *In the ghetto late at night,*
> *Say, what studies, what commissions*
> *Will ever really change conditions?)*
> *Everybody studied Watts*
> *And said, "We'll have to change their lots;*
> *Then they will neither burn nor thieve."*
>   *(But where are the snows of yestereve?)*
>
> *Came November and sweet sessions*
> *Of silent thought and loud professions.*

*Scarcely a man is now alive
Who planned those sessions in sixty-five
For who is loved by LBJ
In December as in May?
Where went our blood, our sweat, our tears?
(Gone, with the snows of yesteryears.)*

*Off with the old, on with the new!
Face the future with derring-do!
Sometimes the dice must come up sevens,
Notwithstanding Novak and Evans.
And for the old snows shed no tear,
For there'll be snow-jobs all next year.**

Clifford Alexander and I were appointed chairmen of an interdepartmental committee, with the goal of implementing as much of the conference's work as seemed appropriate. Its members — John Doar, Roger Wilkins, and LeRoy Collins among them— endorsed most of the recommendations, as might be expected; their departments had prepared many of them, working with outside experts who had often served as consultants to government. Some proposals were sweeping. Most called for relatively minor changes in administration.

After our first few meetings, I began to wonder about the recommendations. If they were so sensible, as both the conference and the committee seemed to think, why hadn't they been adopted before? Because of political objections — in Congress; in the states, through which most federal benefits for the poor were disbursed; in the departments themselves, where secretaries and bureaucrats competed for control over the administration and direction of remedial programs; in the White House, where money was tight and already committed. And as formal comments came in, other realities emerged to challenge the hortatory

---

* From Harold Fleming, "Ode on a Broken Crock, Civil Rights 1965," published by permission of the author.

language of the conference. "Recommendation: The Administration should adopt a firm and vigorous policy to utilize all the programs and resources of the Department of Housing and Urban Development and other agencies to promote and implement equal opportunity and desegregation." Commend from HUD: "This recommendation fails to give consideration to the legislative and administrative structure of those housing programs administered by HUD and other Federal agencies — the almost total control of the initiation and implementation process by non-Federal public bodies and private builders. The corollary of this fact is that the Federal government does not 'utilize programs' but makes its aids available to those local entities concerned with homebuilding and community redevelopment." That seemed to have been dictated through pursed lips, but its point was valid. "Recommendation: The Federal government should assume responsibility for the quality of education in all parts of the United States." How? We had forsworn federal control only a year before, in the aid-to-education bill. Otherwise we could not have passed it. Anyway, a year or two later many of the people who had attended the conference would be calling for community control of the schools.

One of the disabilities of the conference as a producer of useful ideas was that its voice was essentially lyric — a single voice, pursuing its ends without real opposition — and not dramatic. It did not reflect a conflict with competing goals and interests. No one would have dared to suggest, at the conference, that incompatible purposes might be equally legitimate; we had decided what was our most urgent national problem, and we were committed to resolving it. Whatever did not contribute to that end should be changed. It remained for the postconference meetings to deal with obdurate matters. And the farther we got from the conference and its echoes of applause — the more impregnable the budget became to new ventures — the less purposeful our meetings were.

A few of the recommendations found themselves worked into programs. Most did not. We continued to meet sporadically until the end of 1968. I was interested in preparing an executive order requiring federal agencies to locate new buildings in areas of high unemployment, or where they might be conveniently reached by workers and clients from such areas. Johnson was agreeable to the idea at first. But all the various agency objections had not been met by December of that year, and when I discussed it with him again, he said it was too late. He did not want to impose such a requirement on a new Administration, so close to the transition.

Roger Wilkins had written, at the beginning of our meetings:

In earlier decades, the overwhelming majority of Negroes retained a profound faith in America, her institutions, her ideals, and her ability to achieve someday a society reflecting those ideals. The flaws were in the white people — their meanness, their funny stupidity or their inconsistency — but not in the institutions. Now, however, there is a growing and seriously held view among some young militant Negroes that white people have imbedded their own personal flaws so deeply in the institutions that those institutions are beyond redemption. . . .

Apart from the militant minority's rejection of the institutions, there is also, I believe, a subtler, but more general and growing, Negro skepticism about the commitment and sensitivity of even "good" white people. I feel safe in saying, for example, that there is widespread belief among Negroes interested in civil rights that there will be no significant follow-up to or implementation of the recommendations of the Conference by this Administration.

The White House Conference "To Fulfill These Rights" was only one aspect — and for many reasons, one of the least productive aspects — of the Johnson Administration's effort to improve living conditions for Negroes. Simply to list some of the programs — many of whose beneficiaries were black — which it began or augmented, gives an idea of what was attempted. In the Office of Economic Opportunity, Head Start. Community Action. Neighborhood Health Centers. Upward Bound. Legal Services. The Job Corps. The Neighborhood Youth Corps. *VISTA*. In HEW, Title I of the Elementary and Secondary School Act, the basic program of assistance to schools attended by poor children, the Title III, the source of funds for special and experimental programs. Medicare and Medicaid. Scholarships and work-study programs in the colleges. In the Labor Department, the Manpower Development and Training program. In the Justice Department, enforcement of the Civil Rights Act of 1964, the Voting Rights Act of 1965, and the Fair Housing Act of 1968. In HUD, the rent-supplement program. In Defense, Project 100,000, for the near-successful on the induction tests. In Budget and the Council of Economic Advisors, economic programs geared to the constant expansion of job opportunities. Associated with the White House, the private-sector JOBS program.

On occasion I became involved in the administration of some of these programs, when political issues filtered up that threatened trouble between the President and the Negroes. The Child Development Group of Mississippi was one such issue. CDGM combined elements of the Delta Ministry, Mississippi Summer, and black farm women in a Head Start program of considerable quality. It operated in rural areas where the need was desperate. The trouble was, it had failed to account for a large quantity of federal funds; it was riddled with nepotism; some of its employees had used government automobiles to campaign against sitting members of Congress; and its response to criticism from Washington was evasive. Sargent Shriver threatened to cut off the support of the Office of Economic Opportunity. At once the Northern friends of CDGM began to assail him as a craven prisoner of the reactionaries, that is, of Stennis, Eastland, Whitten, and William Colmer, all of whom had power to harass and undercut his agency. Moderate friends in Mississippi warned me that CDGM's political activities would destroy any chance the national Democratic party might have to carry the state in 1968. They were anxious to put together another organization, with more conventional black and white leadership, which could replace CDGM as the local manager of Head Start.

I talked with two leaders of CDGM in the White House, and found them dedicated and sensible people. It was a dilemma. The results of CDGM's work were clearly good; yet the issue had become one of the respectable management of public money. (Most people thought it was outrageous when the managers of programs for the poor were revealed to have diverted them to their own purposes. This was especially true when the managers were themselves poor. I could understand that feeling because I shared it. Intellectually I could agree that the poor, having been denied the gravy so long, should be entitled to spread some of it around in unorthodox ways; viscerally I could not. I had found it more offensive to be presented with a civil rights leader's questionable entertainment and telephone bills, which he had charged to the White House conference, than to pay indirectly for those of a corporate official — which I would do, by making up for his company's deductions with my taxes. It was irrational, bigoted, bourgeois; but it was a fact of political life. When Johnson, at the end of his term, addressed a roomful of Negro appointees and said, "When you look at the long list you will not find one that ever abused the President's confidence or ever betrayed him or ever brought any blush of shame to his cheek," I was shocked, for the moment, at what I took to be patronizing; but he was right to have been concerned that scandal among black officeholders would have undermined programs for the black poor.)

Friends of CDGM argued that organizing their clients against incumbent officeholders was the most useful service anybody could perform for them; that only coherent political action would force the government to treat black people decently. Stennis and the others replied that federal appropriations ought not to be used to arrange the defeat of those who voted them. For Shriver, the question came down to whether CDGM was so effective that, as a matter of principle, it should be supported despite its peccadilloes of management, and the damage its opponents in Congress might do to the entire antipoverty program. His answer was no. I agreed. Later he effected a compromise in which both CDGM and the "moderate" group undertook responsibilities for Head Start in Mississippi, but not before he and the White House — because of my role in supporting him — were roundly denounced in the liberal weeklies.

7 p.m., Monday
September 12, 1966

FOR THE PRESIDENT

The civil rights movement is obviously in a mess. Partly as a result of that, this year's bill is lost. White resentment is great and still growing; the Negro community is fragmented.

. . . You are the principal civil rights leader in the country — in a time of turmoil, as in a time of unity and progress. This was of powerful assistance to you in 1964. You cannot shake it off. The very fact that you have led the way toward first-class citizenship for the Negro, that you are identified with his cause, means that to some extent your stock rises and falls with the movement's.

If you do nothing to exercise your leadership, you will be damned by the Negroes, who will turn increasingly toward extremist leaders, and by the whites, who will still identify you as the Negroes' protector. The pressure will grow for you to silence the protests, to take vigorous action to "bring the Negroes into line." At an earlier stage in history this might have worked. But the Negro is not about to return to subservience now. He has won new rights; white people are having to pay attention to him; he is being urged to seek a better job, to participate in the society as a full member, to take part in the general scramble for consumer goods. He will not listen to — and will bitterly resent — those who tell him to stop where he is now and consolidate his gains.

Part of the problem is that the civil rights acts, while profoundly meaningful to the Southern Negro and symbolically meaningful to the Northern Negro, did little to bring about progress in education, housing, and employment. Expectations were aroused by breakthroughs in political rights. Economic rights are much harder to achieve; but that fact does not placate people who are anxious for a share in the bounty.

Another part of the problem is the increasing age of the responsible Negro leaders. Mr. Randolph is in his seventies, Roy Wilkins in his sixties. Even Whitney Young and Martin Luther King have been around so long that they seem old school to the young militants. When you look at where the greatest unrest is, among the teenagers and people in their twenties where unemployment is disastrously high, you know that the young on the streets will not always respond to advice from middle-aged and elderly men. Our lines of communication run generally (and from the White House, only) to the older establishment. We have very few contacts with younger Negro leaders. We *must* develop those contacts.

I believe you should seek the best advice you can get on where the movement should go now. I think you should call in a dozen people who can offer good advice, and let them speak their minds. Nobody can pretend to much wisdom about the matter; but a few things are sure:

1) the way to a decent life for Negroes lies through peaceful change;

2) the Negro is threatened by riots — immediately, because they usually take place in his neighborhoods, and long-term, because the white community turns against him and will not support peaceful change;

3) the task of Negro leadership is to make these points clear to their people;

4) *young* leaders must also be brought along; that is the task of the established leaders . . .

. . . Louis Martin, Cliff Alexander and I agree that there is a need for this meeting. I have not spoken to Nick Katzenbach. [President's note: do so at once.]

We recommend the following people:

Randolph, King, Wilkins, Young, Leon Sullivan of Philadelphia, State Senator Barbara Jordon of Texas, Father Baroni (a liberal priest in Washington), Bill Miller of Textron, Juanita Stout (Judge of the Court of Common Pleas, Philadelphia), Jesse Hill of the At-

lanta Life Insurance Company, Dorothy Height of the Negro Women, Federal Judge Leon Higginbotham.
There is no longer any need to have SNCC and CORE represented.

Nick Katzenbach replied:

While I agree with much of what you say, I don't agree with your recommendation as to a meeting with the President at this time. . . . The President does not strengthen the leadership of Roy Wilkins or Martin Luther King when they are made to appear his lieutenants or apologists. Indeed, whatever appeal the extreme groups have is based upon arguments that the older leaders are the pacific captives of the administration-establishment and are thus not sufficiently militant.

All the responsible leaders understand and have publicly stated the first points you make and have argued vigorously against violence and for peaceful change within the system. Their success in making these points clear is not going to be enhanced either by our agreement with them or by a meeting devoted to that subject. In fact, I think it would be weakened. . . . I believe that if a meeting were to be held at this time on these subjects, even the most conservative civil rights leaders would find it politically necessary to take issue publicly with the President on our failure to deliver sufficient results in any of the areas in which the problems are obvious.

I have the most difficulty with your point that we should establish contact with young leaders. The fact is that the younger leaders who now exist are precisely those whom you say should not be included and who have consistently chosen an "outside course"; that is, Stokely Carmichael, et al. We are not going to reach these people except through results. And the extent that we do reach them in the meantime is close to the same extent to which we corrupt them as leaders.

"I do think, however, that there is a problem here for the civil rights groups themselves. I can see considerable merit in the Big Three establishing a militant but peaceful organization of young people who could successfully compete with SNCC . . . but to launch it at the White House would be to kill it before it was born.

And I answered:

You say, "The fact is that the younger leaders who now exist are precisely those whom you say should not be included and who have consistently chosen an 'outside course'; that is, Stokely Carmichael, et al." Surely the next generation of Negro leadership does not have to be dominated by Carmichael. In my opinion no amount of results is going to "reach" Carmichael; not rebuilding the slums overnight or employing every Negro male in America. Carmichael right now doesn't care a damn about being "reached."

The question always comes back to who is a leader. Carmichael can lead a riot or a march but he is not, for that, a leader whose constituency is broadly based.

. . . Why not establish some kind of communication with people who might emerge as responsible leaders? Is Presidential interest the kiss of death for them? I grant that it may be, in the eyes of those who are stirred by Carmichael and to most extremists. I don't think it is to the majority of Negroes. The President has a high rating among Negro people generally, and I believe he stands to enhance, rather than to risk it, by a meeting. . . .

. . . I expect some complaints about delivering sufficient results in employment, education, etc. I would not expect the President to get off unscathed. But the fact is it would have been hard to pass the Emancipation Proclamation in the atmosphere prevailing now. White people are scared and sore and the consensus is running out — has run out. *That,* not the question of why the President won't do this or that to change Negro life, is the principal dilemma for President and Negro leaders alike.

There was no meeting. The President agreed with Katzenbach that the established Negro leaders had to keep some distance between themselves and him, if they were to retain credibility. As a politician he was sensitive to that. Once, following an amicable private discussion with one leader, he had asked him what he intended to say to the press on leaving the White House. "Just that we talked over some problems of mutual concern," was the answer. "You can't do that," said the President. "You've got to have demanded action on something. What about Annapolis?" "Annapolis?" "Yes. The Naval Academy's only got a handful of Negro midshipmen. You brought that to my attention, and I said I would see to it that the Navy changed and got some more black faces in the officer corps. I'll do it right now." Johnson called the Pentagon, and told a startled Navy Secretary that he wanted immediate action on a problem which a fellow who was sitting in his office right now had brought to his attention. The Negro leader went out to meet the press, and described the situation at Annapolis by reading from a list of figures Johnson had just handed to him.

Game-playing was all right in the days when we all knew what was needed and believed we were going to get it.

Rioting began in earnest in 1967. Califano and I found ourselves in familiar roles — working with Cy Vance on a chronology of violence. Vance had been sent to Detroit as the President's observer shortly after the rioting began there in July. Governor Romney and Mayor Cavanagh asked for federal troops, and they were dispatched to a nearby air base; but during the evening of the second day the local leaders became divided over whether troops were needed, or would only make a tense situation worse. Then it became worse by its own momentum, and soldiers were committed.

I went off upstairs to write a Presidential statement for television, announcing that the army was moving in. When I returned to the Oval Office the President was reading over a statement he had already written with the help of a Washington lawyer. It was tough. It contained no reference to the desperate conditions from which the riot had burst. I was asked for my judgment of it. The hour was late, around ten o'clock. J. Edgar Hoover stood beside the President, silent and dour. McNamara was hunched over the news ticker. Johnson and the lawyer waited for my reaction. I was troubled by something in the statement, but I thought it was the absence of compassion for the Negroes of Detroit, and I was reluctant to start an argument about that when the cameras were waiting and the men around me wanted a decisive call for order. Anyway, this wasn't a fight between George Wallace's Alabama cops and civil rights workers. This was an attack such as no society could tolerate. There would be time to ask why it happened after it was stopped. I said O.K. The lawyer said, "Really?" Yes, O.K.

We went into the television studio, and shortly before midnight the President made the statement. Suddenly I heard what was wrong. "I am sure the American people will realize that I take this action with the greatest regret, and *only because of the clear, unmistakable and undisputed evidence that Governor Romney of Michigan and the local officials in Detroit have been unable to bring the situation under control*. . . . The Federal government in the circumstances here presented had no alternative but to respond, since it was called upon by the Governor of the State *and since it was presented with proof of his inability to restore order in Michigan.*" * In days to come we would all contend with the press that the emphasis on Romney's inability to quell the riot was meant to lay a legal foundation for the President's action in committing troops. After all, in our constitutional system local authority had the responsibility of dealing with local disorders; it was extraordinary that national authority should supplant it. Perhaps that — and not Romney's candidacy for President — explained the statement. But my doubts were as deep as those of the reporters I tried to persuade.

Aug. 1, 1967

For George Christian

. . . I've been wondering what we can do to repair our position. I'm afraid we look awfully programmatic and legalistic.

We talk about the multitude of good programs going into the cities, and yet there are riots, which suggests that the programs are no good, or the Negroes past saving.

We talk too much about the necessity for this or that step by the governor or the mayor, and for confirmation by our representative on the scene, before our troops can be sent in. . . .

---

* Italics added.

We keep pounding the Congress on the rat bill [a rat control program which Congress had hooted down] but I think that will sooner or later lose its electrical charge and just leave Congress sore. I think we ought to quit beating up on Congress unless and until we are willing to go before them in joint session and state the case for America's cities. . . . If we want to make programs for the cities the major issue now, let's go up and tell Congress so face-to-face, instead of kicking it in the shins via third-party conversations — speeches and statements of one kind or another.

As for "rewarding" the rioters, that is a hollow issue if ever there was one. In the first place, we will help to feed, heal and house everyone who needs it, regardless of his moral position during the riots; in the second place, we don't have enough money to "reward" anybody, if "reward" means the massive rebuilding of slum areas. We didn't have it before the riots and we don't now.

What to do? The only thing that occurs to me now is to go into the Newark area with Governor Hughes [a Democrat and a friend of the President]; look at the destruction; talk to some Negroes and white store owners, hold an off-the-record session with poverty workers, etc.

There is, of course, the security problem. If the place is swarming with cops and troops, it would be worse than not going (to visit one of his cities in broad daylight, the President needs a bloody army.) But with some skill it ought to be manageable.

Christian showed this memo to the President. What his reaction was I never heard. Probably that since there was little he could do, there was no point in entering the ruins while they — and the feelings of the people who lived there — were still smoldering.

What to do? A scholarly friend of John Roche's wrote to him:

First of all, we must make rioting more expensive for the rioters. We've *got* to do this, because if today's white political authorities do not, a massive white backlash will put in new authorities who will, in the savagery of their repression, brutalize the entire nation.

Actually, shooting rioters is probably of little avail. When a riot is on, people are a little crazy, and shooting will as easily inflame as intimidate them. And if, after the riot, they're dead — well, their relatives are bitter, and the message certainly is lost on *them*. I think it's better to use as little force as possible — but to follow a riot with *stiff jail sentences.* (A year? Two years?) Sure, some of our liberal friends will say that if you jail a kid for rioting, you only turn him into a hardened criminal. But I know of no sociological evidence to this effect. I should think he's more likely to become a criminal if, after looting stores and shooting at cops, he gets away scot-free.

Above all, I'd jail the extremist leaders who incite the riots. At the moment we put them on television during prime time. This does not strike me as such a good idea as jailing them.

Of course, our same liberal friends, after every riot, are quick to assert that it is clear the "moderate" Negro leadership has lost touch with the masses, that it is the militant Mau-Maus who now speak for the "grass roots" (!), etc., etc. *But it is in the nature of a riot to dispossess responsible leadership.* Does anyone believe that, if vengeful whites in Detroit took to the streets with shotguns, they'd look to Walter Reuther and Mayor Cavanagh for leadership? We cannot stop this kind of political dispossession *during* a riot; but we can prevent the extremist leaders from consolidating the blessings that a riot bestows upon them. And we must do this; otherwise, it is *we* who will be destroying all possibility of moderate Negro leadership in the country. We have already gone a considerable way toward this goal by funding extremist groups with anti-poverty (and especially Community Action) programs.

Obviously the moderate Negro leaders would denounce such jail sentences on their extremist competitors — who are, after all, fellow Negroes. That's all right with me. I can't think of a nicer subject I'd care to disagree with them about.

But more has to be done, too. I do think it can be said against the present Administration that it has unwittingly teased and taunted Negro aspirations. It has talked grandly about abolishing poverty and transforming slum education — and has instituted a congeries of programs that are complicated, marginal, sometimes invisible in their consequences. We've got to deliver something big, substantial, tangible — not another acronym! We've got to come up with a program that may not promise much, but which delivers *all* of it, right now, in a hurry. . . . Simplicity is of the essence; because only simplicity can evoke credibility.

I was ready to join him in throwing the book at the extremists — particularly Carmichael. Ramsey Clark said that he had put lawyers in every division of the Justice Department to work on the evidence against him, but that they had come up empty-handed. Given the public's animosity against Carmichael, an indictment for inciting to riot seemed assured. But the evidence for conviction was not there, and acquittal, Clark believed, would exalt Carmichael as nothing else. I thought that Clark — whom I admired greatly, and who never dropped the libertarian torch — was responding more like a Supreme Court justice than like a political officer of the government whose responsibilities included those of a prosecutor as well as a judge. I would have liked to see him publicly angry and determined to put incendiaries like Carmichael behind bars. Not because Carmichael was a clear and present danger, though he shouted to crowds in the restless slums, "Black power cannot mean the power of the ballot box, because the vote has never been and never will be beneficial to the survival of black men in this country. . . . Mao Tse-tung said, and I agree, that political power goes out of the mouth of a gun. The vote means nothing unless you've got the gun behind it." Not because of his rhodomontade, but because he was helping to destroy the consensus on which progress depended. If we were to preserve it, we would have to be seen to set our face against the advocates of violence. Clark had too much integrity to strike an empty pose, and as he said, acquittal, or even special attention from government, would make Carmichael a hero. I was worried that unless Carmichael were prosecuted the government, with its commitment to peaceful change, would be made a goat. I believe Johnson had the same concern, but he abided Clark's judgment.

What to do — if you were a black civil rights leader, faced with riots among black people and backlash among the whites? If you had succeed in impressing Congress with the need for civil rights laws, and were now confronted with black people looting appliance stores? If you had depended on middle-class whites for support, and now found them shocked and silent?

If you were Martin Luther King, your advisors urged massive

civil disobedience, aimed at forcing the government to produce what it had long promised. But a black friend argued with him: "Given the mood in Congress, given the increasing backlash across the nation, given the fact that this is an election year, and given the high visibility of the protest movement in the nation's capital, I feel that any effort to disrupt transportation, government buildings, etc., can only lead, in this atmosphere, to further backlash and repression." The situation had been different in 1963, during the march on Washington. Then the movement's objectives were clear and widely accepted. They were not clear now; there was neither a critical bill, nor a dependable constituency on whom the effort could be pressed.

King went to Memphis in support of a garbagemen's strike. Coming home late one evening, I took a call from Ramsey Clark. King had been shot. Nobody knew how seriously. On the way back to the White House I heard that he was dead.

We sat in Califano's office, trying to decide on a plan of action. Johnson was hesitant. He knew how serious a loss this was, not only to Negroes, but to several million whites. Yet King had recently attacked the Vietnam war with moral fervor — partly, we thought, because enthusiasm for the Negro cause had declined, and the liberals who had supported him were obsessed with the war. The assassination had come less than a week after Johnson's announcement that he would not seek reelection, and in so short a time it was hard for him — deeply committed to the justice of the war — to untangle his feelings of resentment and dismay. Then the weight of it hit.

We called the other Negro leaders. There would be a meeting at ten in the morning, and a memorial service in National Cathedral. We found Rustin between planes at Dulles Airport, and just before dawn we spoke to King's bedridden father. "The President is very sorry. He prays for you and your son's family." The answer came back out of an old reserve of suffering and endurance: "You tell the President I am praying for him."

At ten we met in the cabinet room, and after an hour — of which I remember nothing, except the drained faces of Randolph and Rustin — we left in a procession of cars for the cathedral. On the way out I talked on the radio-telephone with Louis Martin, who had remained behind to deal with Floyd McKissick. Stokely Carmichael had not been invited to the meeting, and McKissick was protesting that. There was no end to politics, not even at a wake. I thought of Ed O'Connor's Mayor Skeffington in Boston, and of his retainers making points over the faithful departed. Vanity, intrigue, the thrust for recognition and place — life triumphant over death.

We returned to the Oval Office and discussed programs, each leader stressing those about which he cared most: Young, jobs; Wilkins, civil rights; Judge Higginbotham, the courts. I found it hard to concentrate. I thought of King and his warm handshake, his kindness and openness when one day in an airport years ago I had introduced myself and told him that I was a Southerner and supported what he was doing. He was preachery in formal gatherings; many sophisticated Negroes called him "The Lawd," mocking a style they had left behind a generation before. He was in many respects a man like any other. But what bravery! He sensed the dangers and pitfalls about him, feared them, and yet endured them. And he spoke to the hearts of more Americans than anyone, white or black, left behind in that room.

Walter Washington — the new mayor of Washington — went out periodically to take urgent telephone calls. There had been trouble in the city the night before, a few fires, some vandalism. When he returned from one call he asked to see the President privately. Califano and I joined them. The situation had grown rapidly worse. Gangs were breaking windows along Pennsylvania Avenue. In several black commercial areas, where whites owned the stores, there was widespread burning and looting. The police were already overtaxed. Very likely we would need troops. The President called the Army Chief of Staff and told him to station forces in readiness across the river. I suggested the Park Police, under the jurisdiction of the Interior Department, as an interim reinforcement. Stewart Udall was out of town, and the undersecretary was new. Johnson told him to look into the matter and report back at once. The new man caught his breath and said he would. Welcome to Washington. In office for a few weeks, learning all about Indians and irrigation, and now charged with helping to contain a city riot.

Throughout the afternoon we sought agreement on committing the army. Ramsey Clark's views on that were well known. He thought it heightened tensions. Warren Christopher, the deputy Attorney General, was traveling in one riot area; the director of public safety, Patrick Murphy, was in another. The mayor was at City Hall. Communicating between them was frustrating. One said troops were needed — then no, the situation had changed, the police seemed to be in control; another said no, then yes. At last we had agreement and the troops moved across the river, under Johnson's admonition not to shoot except in extreme situations. As at Detroit, the soldiers' performance was disciplined and effective.

Six months before, I had told the President about a conversation with three young Negroes, all from welfare families, whom I had known for many years. I had asked them about the possibility of a major riot in Washington. They thought there was almost no chance of that. "There'll be a lot of little riots, but nothing like Newark or Detroit." Why? "It's the capital. They won't let it happen here." Now it was happening. A brown cloud rose beside the Capitol building as Johnson took a call from Mayor Daley, who asked for troops in Chicago. In the evening, as he talked to other mayors and governors, the sky outside his window was red with the fires of Washington.

That day — Friday, April 5, 1968 — arrangements were made for the President to address the Congress and to present "suggestions for action — constructive action rather than destructive action — in this hour of national need." At the time there was no accord among his advisors on what those suggestions should be.

Charles Murphy, a wise Carolinian and a veteran of the Truman Administration whom Johnson had brought back to the White House, thought we should ease restraints on spending. That would mean a higher rate of inflation, but it was more important to fund our social programs and improve conditions in the cities. Joe Fowler, the Secretary of the Treasury, disagreed. Inflation was hardest on the poor, he said. To aggravate it would hurt them more than social spending would help. Besides, Wilbur Mills was demanding a cutback in spending as the price for a surtax, which was necessary to make up part of the war-caused deficit. Gardner Ackley, chairman of the Council of Economic Advisors, called for a Bill of Economic Rights, a reordering of priorities "toward the critical problems of the poor, at the expense of programs which can wait, such as the SST, space exploration, and public works." The case for that rested "on both justice and self-interest. Even people who can't be appealed to on the basis of conscience ought to recognize that the choice is between assuaging the thirsts of the poor or repressing their violent protests at incalculable cost." Joe Califano wrote the President: "As of last evening, there has been violence in the Negro areas of over 50 American cities since the assassination of Dr. King. Something is clearly wrong in this country and I believe the people (as well as the Congress) are looking for a lead as to what to do about it." He recommended the same kind of total reassessment of our policies toward spending cuts, the balance of payments, and budget priorities that had preceded the President's changed position on Vietnam. His assistants, Larry Levinson and Jim Gaither, produced a $5 billion list of new social expenditures which the President might announce to Congress. It would require new taxes, which in the common emergency people should be prepared to pay. Charles Zwick, the new budget director, suggested instead that there be no budget cuts in programs for the cities; that $2 billion be reprogrammed from other purposes to provide new jobs. That way no new taxes would be required, "and the Polish factory worker won't have to pay for the riots."

Meetings continued throughout the weekend. Gaither: new programs won't stop riots now. The question is whether we can buy some peace for the next generation. Cater: the question is whether the cities will survive. If they don't, neither will civilization. Berl Bernhard: we must ask people to compare the cost of our social programs with the cost of riots. Walt Rostow: people in the riot areas must be given the means of doing for themselves. Congress must act to provide those means. Citizens who can must pay for them. Cliff Alexander: our programs aren't doing much for the rioters themselves. We help their neighbors, but not the people with the guns and firebombs. Gaither: but why have law and order broken down now, when we've begun to move? McPherson: because we've begun to move. It's always been this way. Louis Martin: because of human misery. It's still there and it has hardly been touched. Murphy: the President should come forward with major expenditures, not to reward the rioters or even to stop the riots, but because it is right.

Alexander: the President should go to Congress and ask the members to stay in session until his program is enacted or defeated. Bernhard: he should speak to the nation, and not only about the pending program. John Roche: the objective is national reconciliation. Maybe he should speak at the Lincoln Memorial. Arthur Okun: no — he should go to Congress. There should be no more rhetoric. He should call for programs and money now. Matt Nimetz, an aide to Califano: he must speak to the nation. That's where the problem is, in the people.

Elsewhere the President was hearing from Congress. It was willing to pass a fair-housing bill in the aftermath of King's death. But with the budget running a heavy deficit, with angry constituents demanding that the government restore law and order before paying out more tax dollars for programs whose effect appeared to have been minimal or even conducive to riot, Congress would not commit new funds. Not if new taxes were needed to provide them. Not in the wake of a request by Johnson, only the week before, for a surtax to check inflation. Not for a lame-duck President.

Extraordinary that there should have been such a vast difference between the conversations in the White House and attitudes on the Hill. The country both institutions served was threatened by the riots, and by a consequent increase in race hatreds that would make it politically more difficult to repair the slums and thus to avoid future trouble. The right response to this threat, the President's staff believed, was the appropriation of new billions by Congress. What was wrong with the old programs was that they were starved for money. That must be remedied. Men, especially young men, must be given hope of decent jobs and adequate incomes, else they would strike out again and again. On the Hill, and probably for a majority in this country, this seemed dangerously like a protection racket. And while most congressmen and senators understood that conditions in the inner cities were so poor as to encourage violence, they were not convinced that public funds and programs would be more successful in changing them in the future than in the past. Taxpayers — their voters — were already burdened enough, without supporting new bureaucracies. The members were angry and frightened by the fires that came so near their doors, but most of them were not "racists"; the passage of the fair-housing bill testified to that. They simply saw no relationship between the issues of racial justice with which they had wrestled for a decade, and people stealing television sets from gutted stores. They would have presented a cold audience for a departing President who sought fresh funds from an overdrawn account.

So the speech was canceled.

Martin Luther King's death provided the final impetus for one

370 A POLITICAL EDUCATION

more civil rights law, just as the abuse he bore during his life had helped to persuade the nation, and then the Congress, that the earlier laws should be passed. After his jailing in Birmingham, when dogs and hoses were turned on his followers, the Civil Rights Act of 1964 was adopted; after Selma and his march to Montgomery came the Voting Rights Act of 1965. His suffering was an agency through which white America began to change its behavior toward black citizens, began purging the wrongs of two centuries that still soured the air in 1968. But we could not change enough — not yet. The laws were on the books, but the blacks were still in the slums. And as Clarence Darrow said, "The last analysis is: what has man done? — and not what has the law done?"

Riot Lessons
May 1, 1968

1) Adequate numbers of security forces (not less than 10,000)
2) Minimum force necessary (arrest, not shooting)
3) Army's training has paid off in discipline and ability to move quickly
4) Early use of tear gas useful
5) Early curfew useful
6) Pre-planning for integration of Federal, state, and local efforts
7) Adequate communication between all units
8) Early access to data for decision-making (developed by local police)
9) Mobilizing local businesses to meet emergency needs and provide services
10) Pre-planning for arrests (getting papers with arrestees, preparing courts to handle large numbers)
11) Providing information to people, squelching rumors

FOR THE PRESIDENT

Louis, Cliff and I spent the weekend in Harlem and Bedford-Stuyvesant.

The people we talked to in Harlem felt there would be no major riot there this summer. Several reasons were advanced:

— Federal, state and local money has been coming into Harlem in substantial amounts.
— HARYOU, and a number of neighborhood groups, are making gains with a great many people. Two men said: "When the baby's got his mouth on the nipple he can't holler."
— good police work, at least in the 28th precinct that covers central Harlem.
— the sophistication of the business community. Negroes are coming to own a good deal of it, and some white businessmen — notably Jack Blumstein, the owner of a department store on 125th — have been leaders in the inter-racial field for years. These people want quiet.
— the inter-relationship between organized crime and civil order. The numbers and vice people want it to stay cool. Their business suffers when a lot of cops and Guardsmen are on the street-corners. We heard of a conversation between Rap Brown and a Negro rackets boss. Brown had made a strong speech, and when he came by Frank's Chop House later the boss told him: "I agree with a lot of what you said. Except I don't want any riots. I've got to raise $60,000 to buy off some people downtown on a narcotics rap. I can't do that if there's a riot. You start a riot and I'll kill you." Brown is said to have left town the next day. The story may be apocryphal but it is widely believed.

Factors working for a riot are:

— the difficulty of reaching enough young people. The unemployment rate for Negroes in the 17-21 bracket is very high — one in three or four.
— agitators like the Rev. Kendall Smith and Charles Kenyatta of the Mau-Maus. They have a hard time raising a crowd most days, but they are looking for opportunities to make trouble.
— housing. It is awful in most of Harlem. Empty lots piled high with rubbish, breeding rats by the thousands; filthy streets, broken doorways (affording no security), trash in the halls, condemned buildings where junkies sleep overnight and sometimes start fires that threaten the whole neighborhood. Even in the much-acclaimed 114th Street area, where rehabilitation has been

going on under an experimental program for the past two years, the air shafts are piled high with sickening trash.

— not enough Negroes on the police force. Precinct 28 is authorized 330 men and has 270 on duty, of whom only 40 are Negro. The cops live in the Bronx, Queens, and Jamaica. They are "outside authority" and resented. However good New York cops are — and compared to police in other cities, they are pretty good — they don't relate to Harlem Negroes. For many years Harlem was a desirable beat for them. The graft was so great that each block had its own price. Harlem people still regard the police as outsiders with night sticks, probably on the take.

We talked with Inspector Arthur Hill, the Negro chief of the 28th Precinct, between 2 and 3 Sunday morning. "I talk to everybody," he said. "I move around among the leaders. If trouble starts, I get there in a hurry. By the time I arrive 30 white officers may be trying to control a situation involving two or three hundred Negroes. I get the officers out of there fast. If somebody drops a bottle on them from the roof-top, they'll start swinging, and things will get out of hand in a hurry."

We asked him about the principal trouble-makers. "Last year it was the '5 percenters' — a wild bunch of kids. Their leaders sat here for an hour. It was fantastic — they had been sent from Allah for revenge, and all that. I didn't think anybody could reach them, but during the winter a man in Lindsay's office did. They're working with some city program this summer, and they tell me they don't want any trouble." (Lindsay is highly regarded in Harlem. He has been booed and heckled sometimes, but he keeps coming back. He or his representatives are in the area several times a week.)

Hill thinks police standards should be changed — "not lowered, but changed" — to permit more Negroes to qualify. There is a natural reluctance to do this within the police hierarchy. But he feels that educators and behavioral scientists, working with police authorities, could come up with tests that capable Negroes could pass, and that would still exclude incompetents and undesirables.

I have never met a more impressive police officer.

. . . Harlem is the capital for Negro Americans. Depressing as it is, it is also alive, tumultuous and racy. It has an exciting gaminess that communicates even to a visiting WASP. Whites are afraid of it, and I saw only two others all weekend, if you don't count cops; but I felt no hostility toward me — maybe because I was with Cliff and Louis. Harlem is permissive. And there are a great many attractive Negro people there.

Bedford-Stuyvesant is another matter. Low buildings stretching for miles. Bars, liquor stores, store-front churches, rubbish, hair-straightener parlors, a poverty-war office here and there. Every tenth car — as in Harlem — is a Cadillac Eldorado or Buick Riviera, double-parked before a busted decaying house. "You can't get one honestly," Louis said. "It's got to be numbers or something like that."

At Fulton and Stuyvesant, there was a meeting in a small park. Two hundred people were standing in a light drizzle, listening as a heavy Negro woman harangued them about the persecution of the RAM leaders — the people who are thought to have plotted against Roy Wilkins' life. She was terrific. When she spoke of the need for black violence to meet white violence, the crowd applauded vigorously. Then she asked for contributions toward the leaders' defense. A number of people, maybe 50, left. She lit into those who remained. She pointed out one heavy-set man smoking a cigar—called him by name, and said, "Everybody knows how you got that war-on-poverty job. They're paying you $11,200 a year over the table and God knows how much underneath. You ought to give some of that to your brothers." Applause and laughter. She said, "You union members — make them give some of your dues money to your own people. Let's hear it from No. 1184 — 303 — 6 — and 3, and the laundry workers and the restaurant workers. Let's hear it from the Negro Shriners — they owe us something after they picked a white girl for their queen out of 38 beautiful sisters." I would bet she knows her neighborhood better than any organization politician in it. The crowd was attentive, relaxed and easy, cat-calling as she fingered people. There were a dozen young people in dashikis collecting money, a number of Negro cops on the edge of the crowd, and a car full of white detectives on a corner nearby.

Up and down the streets, drunks, derelicts, kids at loose ends. But also many church people — the voters, Louis calls them. Hundreds of them in starched shirts and dresses were heading for buses to take them out of the Bedford-Stuyvesant hellhole for a Sunday outing or an organized trip to Washington.

—Suggestions:

1) HARYOU, the anti-poverty office, is closed on weekends. It ought to be open. Many people can come there at no other time.

2) The Federal presence ought to be emphasized. People have only a vague idea that Federal money is behind this or that project. The most obvious way to dramatize it would be by putting up a great Federal office building in Harlem.

3) More Administration officials should go up there, and have lunch or dinner with Harlem leaders. Several people said that you could pay an unannounced visit without danger. One man said, "The President's number one up here. Everybody knows what he's done."

4) The only answer to the housing problem I can imagine is massive public housing and massive tax incentives to encourage private building. . . .

5) Ways must be found to clean the streets and vacant lots. It breaks the spirit, this ugliness of waste everywhere. There are a few "Clean-Up Committees" around, but from the looks of things they aren't doing much. Public programs that hired local people to clean up would make a tremendous difference in the way people live.

Recollections:

—in the second floor of a YMCA, a terrific din of sound. A band of six, mixed Negro and Puerto Rican, is blaring out something that sounds like Latin rock-and-roll. They are greasy-haired poor city kids, duded up, absolutely and seriously preoccupied with making a pounding roar of electronic sound. In front of them, a Puerto Rican is teaching two good-looking girls an intricate dance. Apparently they're getting ready for a show. The room is sweaty and alive with New Yorkers putting on a performance and working hard to make it good. In the window, a sign says this is a HARYOU deal.

—standing in the doorway of Precinct 28, a huge Negro cop is getting some air. He is of West Indian extraction. (Do all Negro leaders derive from the West Indies? Inspector Hill does; so do Louis, Cliff, Ray Jones, Adam Powell, and Stokely Carmichael. The sociologists say this has to do with the fact that West Indian families were not broken up under the islands' system of slavery; the fathers were around to help raise the children.) Anyway, at 11 p.m. there are three girls, about 10 or 12 years old, hanging around the big cop. "Why you come around here?" he asks them. "To see you is why," one of them said.

A number of us went out from the White House in 1967 and 1968 to spend a few days in the Negro neighborhoods of New York, Chicago, Cleveland, Baltimore, and other Northern cities. We knew we could not learn much about them in the course of a long weekend. What we hoped to gain was a sense of how the people who lived there felt about their future: specifically, whether they thought conditions might be improved through peaceful processes, or only through violence; or that nothing would help.

It was a desultory way of getting information about the black poor to the President. He might have been better served if he had maintained a political apparatus in each city, through which intelligence flowed continuously to his office. But few Presidents had created such an apparatus anywhere, and most of those were limited to the regions from which they came. Some of the prevailing city machines were useful. FDR had his Boss Flynn; Mayor Lawrence of Pittsburgh and Mayor Daley of Chicago were good sources of information for Kennedy and Johnson. Such men were rare. And even they were not comprehensive. The President heard more about conditions in most cities from the federal bureaucracy than from the mayors who led them or the congressmen who represented them. It was sobering. If you considered that the majority of civil servants were white, middle-class, and defensive about the work of their agencies; that the President, like all his predecessors in the twentieth century, had no roots in the contemporary life of a great city; that the cities were changing rapidly, their political systems weakening as their traditional populations fled to the suburbs; that visitors to the White House were likely to tell the President good news about his programs, or to describe conditions in terms of unrelieved gloom, in the hope that he would respond with massive action — you wondered how he could understand what was going on in the urban areas to which most of his efforts were addressed.

I believe he was aware of the intelligence problem, and as a practical man did not let it worry him overmuch. I know that he thought years would pass before the black poor took a full part in the prosperous society. Until they did, there would be violence and suffering, as there had been for the Irish and the Jews. In the meantime, if men of good will kept their eyes on the main thing, he would pass the laws that would speed the process. As he had said in the Catskills, "If this line just holds for a few hours, maybe I can get a roll call."

The report of the Kerner Commission on civil disorders threatened the line in two ways. First, it called for expenditures that Johnson believed he could not make, given the pressures on the budget. Thus it intensified arguments about the war, raised impossible demands, and implicitly diminished the significance of what was already being done. Second, it found, in white racism, the proximate cause of the riots. Thus it provoked the deepest resentment among white workers whose unions had helped to pass the laws of the Great Society. The charge against white racism was true — but so was the bitterness of white families, who lived and worked among blacks, when they were told that they were responsible for the sacking of the cities. An officer of the American Jewish Committee made this point in the *New York Times*, and suggested that the commission had weakened the liberal bloc by charging part of it with crimes against the other. "That's what I've been trying to tell you," Johnson said. "There aren't that many of us that we can afford to set some of us against the rest of us. That kind of talk [placing the principal blame on white racism] only hurts us when we try to pass laws for the Negro." Bayard Rustin, putting it just as simply, told an interviewer that he would rather have a job program for blacks than a psychoanalysis of whites.

By turning "law and order" into "code words for racism," the liberal leadership further deepened the split between itself and the voting public.

I was one of the last staff members to respond to the growing alarm about street crime. I *felt* the threat of crime, and in 1966 moved my family out of the Capitol Hill area to a safer community in Maryland. But I thought about the policing of criminals almost entirely in terms of civil rights. I could write, in the draft of a "Message on Crime in America," that "public order is the first business of government." But I believed more strongly in the words of a contemporaneous "Message on Equal Justice": "We want public order in America, and we shall have it. But a decent public order cannot be achieved solely at the end of a stick, nor by confining one race to self-perpetuating poverty."

I was concerned that Johnson, having earned recognition as the country's preeminent civil libertarian, might be forced to become its chief of police. I told Richard Scammon one day in 1967 that I wanted to write a speech decrying police brutality. Nothing, I believed, was more dangerous to civil peace; nothing so alienated young Negroes from the society. It made a mockery of our protestations of concern for their well-being. "They take you and rap you with their knuckles," a young Negro friend had told me. "They bounce you off the walls so you won't show any marks on you. Then if you complain about that in court, they lie about it. They just take the stand and lie." The Kerner Commission, the Eisenhower Commission, the Civil Rights Commision, all documented the effect of police brutality on the consensual arrangements between citizens and their government.

"Do you really want to help the President?" Scammon asked. Of course, "Then get him photographed with a man in blue." I laughed. But Scammon was serious. He talked about a "social issue," which he believed might dominate the 1968 elections. The voters were becoming quietly enraged by crime and disorder, and by what they regarded as permissiveness on the part of institutional authority. Politicians who wanted to escape that rage should identify themselves with the forces of law and order. It was not necessary that they countenance ruthless acts of suppression, or even that they defend the police against the charges that had been made against them. Just that they show whose side they were on: the mugger, the looter, the sniper, the violent protester, or the law enforcer. If there was any doubt in the voters' minds about that, all the magnanimity and progressivism in the world would not suffice to save the candidate. If the doubt was removed, the candidate was free to promote whatever liberal schemes he wished. The analogy with the "Communists in government" issue in the late 1940's was obvious.

It scarcely needs saying that Johnson understood this without my telling him. He was a political animal, not an ideologue. He had never been infatuated with the police, and regarded many of them as thick-headed bumblers. But he could feel the political earth quiver with impatience about crime and riots; so he got himself photographed with a man in blue. With a whole convention of them, at Kansas City, in the fall of 1967.

I wrote the draft of his speech, and got a measure of satisfaction out of hearing him say, to the International Association of Chiefs of Police, "Self-righteous indignation [about crime] is not a policy. It is a substitute for a policy. What America needs is not more hand-wringing about crime in the streets. America needs a policy for action against crime in the streets. Let us repair as many shattered lives as we can. Let us do it within the American system of due process and in keeping with our tenacious regard for the blessings of individual freedom."

The chiefs were pretty quiet up to that point. But then:

> This summer, some of you experienced a new kind of disorder in your cities. You faced, not individual acts of violence or thievery, but massive crimes against people and property. Much can explain — but nothing can justify — the riots of 1967. [Applause. Cheers. Headlines.]

". . . The violence of this summer raised up a new and serious threat to local law enforcement. It spawned a group of men whose interest lay in provoking others to destruction, while they fled its consequences.

These wretched, vulgar men, these poisonous propagandists, posed as spokesmen for the underprivileged and capitalized on the real grievances of a suffering people. [Applause. News stories. Editorials.]

And the vast majority of those people believe that obedience to the law, in Abraham Lincoln's phrase, must be our religion here in America. . . . They have seen the law change. They have seen it become more just, their rights more established. They know that the law in a democratic society is their refuge.

We must redeem their faith in the law. We must make certain that law enforcement is fair and effective — that protection is afforded every family, no matter where they live — that justice is swift and justice is blind to religion, color, status, and favoritism. [Silence.]

[Sudden extemporaneous thought.] We cannot tolerate behavior that destroys what generations of men and women have built here in America — no matter what stimulates that behavior, no matter what is offered to try to justify it. [Ovation. Long hoarse cheers. Whistles.]

[Back to the text.] Neither can we abide a double standard of justice, based on the color of a man's skin or the accent of a man's speech." [Silence.]

It was a special audience, but all of us knew, by then, that there was nothing special about its reaction. Scammon was right. The extemporaneous sentence — about behavior that destroys what generations have built — was a perfect expression of the "social issue." The lusty response to it, and the silence that followed the President's call for fairness to all races, remained with me for months to come.

Americans were upset about disorder. But what about violence? The Saturday Night Specials in Houston and Hough; the private armories in Westchester County and southern California; the mass killers; the killers of blacks in the South; the wife, neighbor, and storekeeper killers; the drunks on the road at ninety miles an hour; the rioters and violent demonstrators, and the violent cops and guardsmen who responded to them; the hired guns of the movie Westerns, scowling that this town, this life, is too small for you and me, let's settle it once and for all. There was so much casual killing all about us, so much romanticizing of extreme behavior, that it almost seemed we were in love with violence.

For a few days after Robert Kennedy was assassinated, people talked about violence in America. As President, Johnson needed to reflect the national self-analysis, without indicting the entire country for Sirhan's act.

Tonight this nation faces once again the consequences of lawlessness, hatred, and unreason in its midst. It would be wrong, it would be self-deceptive, to ignore the connection between that lawlessness and hatred and this act of violence. It would be just as wrong, and just as self-deceptive, to conclude from this act that our country itself is sick, that it has lost its balance, its sense of direction, even its common decency. Two hundred million Americans did not strike down Robert Kennedy last night any more than they struck down President John Kennedy in 1963 or Dr. Martin Luther King in April of this year.

But those awful events give us ample warning that in a climate of extremism, of disrespect for law, of contempt for the rights of others, violence may bring down the very best among us. A nation that tolerates violence in any form cannot expect to be able to confine it to just minor outbursts.

My fellow citizens, we cannot, we just must not, tolerate the sway of violent men among us. . . . There is never any justification for the violence that tears at the fabric of our national life; that inspires such fear in peaceful citizens that they arm themselves with deadly weapons; that sets citizen against citizen or group against group.

A great nation can guarantee freedom for its people and the hope of progressive change only under the rule of law. So let us resolve to live under the law. Let us put an end to violence and the preaching of violence.

Let the Congress pass laws to bring the insane traffic in guns to a halt, as I have appealed to them to do. That will not, in itself, end the violence, but reason and experience tell us that it will slow it down; that it will spare many innocent lives.

Let us purge the hostility from our hearts and let us practice moderation with our tongues. . . .

Working with Johnson and Justice Fortas on that address was an excruciating experience. I knew Robert Kennedy and liked him. He was a driving, and yet self-amused politician; confident in a way that seems reserved for the very rich or the extremely gifted; impatient with both smug conservatives and mawkish liberals. I thought he was intelligent and concerned enough, though there was a dark absolutist streak in him that I found disturbing. I opposed him politically. I knew something about the searing animosity and mutual suspicion between him and President Johnson. I suspected that for Johnson, Robert Kennedy's murder stirred such a hurricane of emotions that it was difficult for him to speak about it. Yet he had to speak, and in a way that acknowledged, but did not succumb to, the numbed horror that struck millions of Americans — supporters and opponents of Robert Kennedy — after his savage death.

Johnson was determined to do something more, and in the (by now) traditional way, he established a commission. This one, to be chaired by Milton Eisenhower, was to examine the causes of violence in America. "What in the nature of our people and the environment of our society makes possible such murder and such violence?" It was a staggering question. There were no multiple-choice answers to it, nor any answer at all that might prevent another Sirhan from firing at another Bob Kennedy, or a Jones from shooting a Smith. Except by depriving them of guns.

Standing beside Johnson on the evening before Kennedy's death, I saw part of the research data for the Eisenhower Commission. The three television sets in the Oval Office were tuned to the major networks. On the middle set Frank Mankiewicz, Kennedy's press secretary, was reading the latest medical bulletin on the senator's condition. On the left set, a cowboy threw away a cigarette, hitched up his belt, and walked out to a gunfight. On the right, a friendly agent — presumably CIA — waited behind a door to cosh an enemy. Mankiewicz read on, trying to keep his voice steady, while to the left of him puffs of smoke rose in the western street and bodies crumpled; on the right, the friendly agent had been decisively coshed himself, and in the commercial break a pickup was showing real speed over a plowed field.

All this was politically irrelevant. The networks could prove that their "adventure" shows had no more effect on the level of American violence than did Laurel and Hardy. It was just entertainment. And we viewers — we entertainees — we knew what was causing crime and disorder in this country.

The President's speeches and messages became increasingly absorbed with the "social issue." I was determined that so far as I had anything to do with them, they would not neglect the wretchedness from which most violent crime emerged. A columnist friend complained about that. Just make it clear that you're against crime and disorder, he said. Forget the sociology. People want the government to make the streets safe, stop the arsonists, lock up the muggers. Afterwards they'll listen to the explanations and the programs.

He was right. Johnson might have said Stop! No more! and then stopped himself, before calling on the country to repair the human damage in the slums. If, like Canute, he could not have reversed the tide of lawlessness, he might have improved his own political standing and more effectively argued the case for social reform.

But he was a liberal, and he found it distasteful to join the loud chorus that called for "law and order." And — I see now — there was another pressure upon him, to which he and his speech-writers accommodated. The war in Vietnam threatened to estrange the Democratic party from the President. If he was to retain the support of the national Democrats — by and large a liberal army — he would have to remain a liberal at home, talking less of stopping crime than of its causes.

What irony: that because of the war, he should have to forgo political advantage on the social issue, or lose any hope of retaining the support of his party's loyalists. For it was (in part) because he was a liberal himself, and the leader of a liberal party, that he had entered the war in the first place.

11

Democracy Fights a Limited War

The war on the Chinese frontier might have been won if the French of 1947 had imitated their forefathers of the days of the colonial conquest and had plunged into the jungle to fight the enemy hand to hand. But they clung to the roads; they were the prisoners of their own cars and trucks; and they therefore condemned themselves to failure. . . .

. . . in 1948 the French brought up [pacification], because they were unable to bring the Vietminh to a pitched battle and destroy them. Henceforward the great idea was to leave Ho Chi Minh in his patch of jungle and to win all the rest away from him. When the Vietminh no longer had the fertile areas and the close-packed mass of the people on their side they would be more entirely crushed than by any military defeat. They could no longer continue to subsist, and Ho Chi Minh's regulars would then perish, starved and cut off. . . .

. . . The two juxtaposed, intertwined civilizations were at grips with one another in total warfare. At their disposal the French had everything that showed on the surface, the whole of the established society founded upon law. The Vietminh, on the other hand, were just underneath everywhere, present in everything that was hidden. Two sides appealed to two opposing instincts in mankind, the French holding out a normal life, with prosperity and the benefits of the West, and the Vietminh offering pride and revolt. . . . In their bid for twenty million *nha-ques* both the one and the other made use of terrorism. Between the two huge machines the private individual was crushed.

— Lucien Bodard, *The Quicksand War*

I CANNOT remember when I first heard about the fighting in Indochina. In 1952, as an Air Force intelligence officer, I briefed the Tactical Air Command headquarters on the

French–Viet Minh war, in which American pilots were already flying combat support missions. One of the men in the room had just returned from a tour there, and told us that he was often fired upon by farmers around the Saigon airport as he taxied his B-26 down the strip. As I remember, this did not strike us as unusual. We regarded it as typical of the way Communists fought: sneakily. Our response was not to discuss the reasons why farmers should shoot at free-world airplanes; nor to wonder whether bombs would put a stop to it; but to agree that B-26 gunners should be alert at all times.

Dienbienphu was a shock. The Communists were obviously more formidable than most Americans had supposed. Their massed artillery around the French camp was a far cry from the isolated rifle fire of disaffected farmers.

A shock, but not a disaster. It was the French, after all, who had lost it, as they had lost most of their other battles in the twentieth century. Their defeat in Indochina was — or seemed, after the fact — inevitable, even appropriate. The age of European colonialism was over. Whoever resisted that fact risked having it driven home to him on the battlefield.

One felt sure that the American army would not have been routed at Dienbienphu. Of course it would never have been there in the first place. We were not a colonial power. Aiding the French in Indochina was an anomaly, justified by our partnership in Europe and our determination to prevent the spread of communism, under whatever flag, anywhere on earth. Our proper role was in helping weaker states maintain their independence.

Supporting the Diem regime was more in keeping with that role. Pictures of Diem — "the doughty Catholic leader" — talking with white-suited American officials in Saigon, turned up from time to time in the papers, and were vaguely satisfying. Under him, South Vietnam won a secure place on the middle pages of the leading dailies. *Diem Proposes Land Reform Program. South*

Viets Build Strategic Hamlets. U.S. Advisors Teach Anti-Red Tactics. Tide Turning in V'Nam Countryside.

Our commitment to an independent South Vietnam was an expensive one, in dollar terms. Progress there was difficult and slow. But it was still a surrogate war, fought by others for purposes that were important to us. And there was no question about who would win it — particularly after the Kennedy Administration took office. For it was precisely this kind of contest which (the Democratic theorists believed), though immune to Dulles's "massive retaliation" policies, was susceptible to the right techniques of counterinsurgency. With American advisors — trained in jungle fighting, communications, languages, medicine, and psychological warfare, backed by an efficient system of supply, but capable of living off the land for weeks on end — the South Vietnamese army would become more than equal to any guerrilla force.

Robert Kennedy, in Saigon in 1961, said "We're going to win"; Johnson, traveling as Vice President, compared Diem to Churchill. Even when the regime grew dictatorial and oppressive, when several engagements went badly and the first signs of incredulity and pessimism appeared in the American press, the confidence level in Washington remained outwardly high.

Because the war had to be won, and what Americans had to do, they did. President Kennedy was a disabused student of history, sensitive to the limitations of power, and the ironies of fate; but I believe he was as sure of America's ability to impress its will on struggles such as the one in Vietnam as any wahoo congressman. If we had to win, or else face a Communist hegemony in Asia, we would. If we had to get rid of Diem because he was dividing the South Vietnamese and so impairing the war effort, we would see to that by encouraging a coup.

Why did we have to win? A clear expression of the stakes for the United States in Asia appeared in the Sunday, November 3, 1963, *New York Times* "News of the Week in Review." That was two days after Diem was overthrown and murdered.

... The American stake in South Vietnam is large. The country is vital to the whole Western defense position in Southeast Asia.

It is geography that gives South Vietnam its crucial importance in international affairs and explains the great stakes for the U.S. in the country's future. South Vietnam holds the key to the Indo-Chinese peninsula and thus to the whole of Southeast Asia.

Communist control of South Vietnam would almost surely mean the collapse of the shaky coalition regime in Laos; it would put enormous pressure on pro-Western Thailand and on the neutralist regimes in Cambodia and Burma. The lands to the south — Malaya and Indonesia — and the entire Allied position in the Western Pacific would be in severe jeopardy. India, already under pressure along its borders with Communist China, would be out-flanked. Communist China's drive for hegemony in Asia would be enormously enhanced.

... [The wider repercussions]: the loss of South Vietnam to the Communists would raise doubts around the globe about the value of U.S. commitments to defend nations against Communist pressure. It would throw into question the ability of the U.S. to check the kind of campaign at which the Communists are adept — infiltration, subversion, guerrilla tactics and political appeals to impoverished masses.

The impact on revolutionary movements throughout the world would be profound. At best, neutralism in the East-West struggle might spread. [Shades of J. F. Dulles!] In much of Asia there might be a feeling that the Communists — under the leadership and inspiration of Peking — represented the "wave of the future."

Max Frankel — in my judgment, the wisest journalist in Washington — wrote in the same edition that what was really at stake was the ability of the West, and particularly of the United States, to withstand the third major form of aggression attempted by Communist nations since World War II (the first being the threat to Europe from Soviet land armies and the French and Italian Communist parties, the second the invasion of Korea). A large map of Asia, crosshatched to show the extent of the Communist danger, bore markers over Manila (SEATO ALLIANCE WOULD BE THREATENED) and Peking (CHINA'S PRESTIGE WOULD BE ENHANCED).

As for the recent coup in Saigon, the *Times* editorialized: "Fortunately, the new Vietnamese rulers are dedicated anti-Communists who reject any idea of neutralism and pledge to stand with the free world. It is significant that one of their charges against Mr. Nhu [Diem's brother, killed beside him in the coup] is that he tried to make a deal with Communist North Vietnam along the lines hinted at by President de Gaulle. . . ."

To recapitulate, the United States had to prevent the Communists from controlling South Vietnam because (1) all of Asia, from Laos to Indonesia to India, would otherwise be threatened (this was known as the "domino" theory); (2) losing to the new mode of aggression, or failing to resist it, would raise doubts in the minds of others with whom we were allied; (3) our defeat would give the Communists, and particularly the Chinese, a worldwide political advantage. Though it was unfortunate that President Diem had been murdered in the coup, his successors appeared to be staunchly pro-Western, determined to resist a sellout to the Communists.

There was nothing very remarkable about this analysis. It was shared by President Kennedy and most of his advisors. It was accepted by his successor, who took office within three weeks of the *Times* account.

Logically, it followed from this view that the stakes in Vietnam were so great as to warrant almost any American effort to secure them. Complicity in the overthrow of Diem was a minor price to pay if it would forward that effort. Indeed, if this view were correct, the introduction of half a million, or even a million American troops was fully justified. Magnifying the importance of a minor naval incident, in order to arouse public and congressional sympathy for an enlarged American effort, was legitimate; if South Vietnam fell to the Communists, "the entire Allied position in the Western Pacific would be in severe jeopardy"—surely a more disturbing event than the manufacture of a mini–Pearl Harbor.

Years later, many people who shared this view when it was expressed in the *Times* found a hidden proviso in their earlier opinion. They had not really intended that we should endure such tremendous losses of men and resources in order to protect our stakes in Vietnam. Perhaps they truly believed that a struggle of such terrible importance to us, and by inference to the Communists, could be conducted with small loss of life. If so they were unrealistic — as were many of their leaders, who believed that America's might, once introduced on the ground in South Vietnam and into the skies of the North, would bring an early end to the war.

Soon after I joined the White House staff in March 1965, I had dinner on Capitol Hill with the "Szilard group" — members of Congress, staff, journalists, and foreign policy buffs whom the scientist Leo Szilard had brought together years before to talk about ways of ameliorating international conflicts. I was a regular member, and I believe this was the first session devoted entirely to Vietnam.

Hans Morgenthau was the principal speaker. He elaborated what became a familiar dissent to the prevailing view. Our mistake had been to treat the situation in Vietnam in European terms, that is, we had tried to contain China as we had contained Russia. It was not possible to do this in Asia. There were no anchors for containment there, no powerful industrialized states such as there were in Europe.

We had, he said, no vital stakes in Asia. That did not mean we could evacuate Vietnam the next day; no great power could do that. We had to get out through negotiations, with some face saved. If the bombing program was intended to produce such negotiations, it was justified.

We had to face the fact that China was and would be supreme in Asia — not through invasion, but through influence, as were we in Latin America. A realistic statesman would act in the light of that fact. Realism was an advantage in the long run. The British and French were more highly regarded now than when they were clinging to their colonies.

Chalmers Roberts of the *Washington Post* answered that containment should work in Asia; in any event, we would have to draw the line against China somewhere in the region, and Vietnam seemed as good a place as any. Edward P. Morgan agreed, and thought our failure to stand in Asia would have the gravest consequences for our position elsewhere in the world. Donald Zagoria, a political scientist, said there were indications that containment, if it worked, would result in the de-Stalinization of China. Frank Church supported Morgenthau's view that there was nothing on which to anchor a line of containment in Asia; thus he thought we should negotiate a withdrawal as soon as possible. Senator Bob Bartlett supported Church.

I wrote a memorandum about the meeting for the President, but got no response. By then he was engaged, not in philosophic discussions about China's sway over Asia, but in deciding the number of troops to be sent to Vietnam. Questions about the importance of stopping the Communists — the North Vietnamese Communists, supported by China and Russia, the active virus of a disease that might break out anywhere unless contained — had been answered years before by his predecessors Eisenhower and Kennedy, and by himself.

The memorandum must have arrived on his desk about the time Sheriff Clark turned his men loose on King and his marchers at Selma, and a week before Johnson would say, to a joint session of Congress, "We shall overcome." The juxtaposition had meaning for me. I remembered Johnson's reaction years before to the Kennedy bill that would have repealed the loyalty oath requirement to the National Defense Education Act. Liberal Democrats were suspect on the Communist issue. If they wished to pass progressive laws, they had to show that they were firmly committed against the ultimate "progressives" — the Communists. If they were "soft" on Communists, at home or abroad, they would find their legislative programs stopped cold by charges of complicity. If Johnson were to end poverty, abolish racial discrimination, improve education, provide better health care, clean up the highways, put a college degree within the reach of everyone — all of which he proposed to do — he would have to fight Communist armies wherever they stepped beyond their borders. He would not, and need not, invite a war with the great Communist powers — Americans wanted peace before anything else. But he would have to take on the (as we regarded them) third-rate Communist regimes, when they attacked their neighbors — especially neighbors to whom the United States had given its pledge. (Whether we had given our pledge to South Vietnam in the SEATO treaty was the subject of a continuing, and useless, debate — the public believed we had, and successive American governments behaved as if we had.)

Holding such views, succeeding a President who believed in the domino theory ("I believe it. I think that the struggle is close enough. China is large enough, looms so high just beyond the frontiers, that if South Vietnam went, it would not only give them an important geographic position for a guerrilla assault on Malaya but would also give the impression that the wave of the future in Southeast Asia was China and the Communists"), and remembering the years before World War II when, as a young congressman, he had helped Sam Rayburn round up the votes to extend the draft — small wonder that Lyndon Johnson did not wish to argue Hans Morgenthau's views about accepting Chinese supremacy in Asia.

In 1965, others in the White House wrote speeches about Vietnam; I only kibitzed. Goodwin was the author of the President's celebrated speech at Johns Hopkins, in Baltimore, which offered massive assistance to all the countries of Indochina — including North Vietnam — after the war. It also included a systematic defense of our role there, the first that any President had attempted:

We are there because we have a promise to keep. . . . To dishonor that pledge, to abandon this small and brave nation to its enemies, and to the terror that must follow, would be an unforgivable wrong. *We are also there to strengthen world order.* Around the globe, from Berlin to Thailand, are people whose well-being rests, in part, on the belief that they can count on us if they are attacked. To leave Vietnam to its fate would shake the confidence of all these people . . . in the value of America's word. The result would be increased unrest and instability, and even wider war. *We are also there because there are great stakes in the balance.* Let no one think for a moment that retreat from Vietnam would bring an end to conflict. . . . The central lesson of our time is that the appetite of aggression is never satisfied. . . . There are those who say [*vide* Morgenthau] that all our effort there will be futile — that China's power is such that it is bound to dominate all Southeast Asia. But there is no end to that argument until all the nations of Asia are swallowed up.

Our objective is the independence of South Vietnam, and its freedom from attack. . . . In recent months attacks on South Vietnam were stepped up. Thus, it became necessary for us to increase our response and to make attacks by air. This is not a change of purpose. It is change in what we believe that purpose requires.

If the stakes were as great as Johnson and his advisors [and in November 1963, the *Times*] believed, air attacks were not only justified; they were mandatory.

I fully shared their assessment. But I thought much was lacking in the Administration's presentation of its case, and in its ability to understand the public's growing concern about the war. I squirmed when Johnson, at a 1966 Democratic dinner in the Armory, looked down at Fulbright and said, "I am delighted to be here tonight with so many of my very old friends as well as some members of the Foreign Relations Committee"; and then "our people have learned that aggression, in any part of the world, carries the seeds of destruction to America's freedom." The implicit scorn for Fulbright — who had supported Johnson for President in 1960 — seemed unduly harsh, especially before an audience of Democrats. The claim that aggression anywhere posed a mortal danger to America was indiscriminate. I expressed my discomfort in a memorandum that ended:

... I am one who believes we are right to stand in Vietnam. ... But there are questions about Vietnam, and about our appropriate role in the world, that are extremely difficult for me to resolve — difficult for anyone, I think, who gives them close attention. They cannot be shouted out of existence.

Churchill rallying Britain in 1940 is not the only posture a wise and strong leader can assume today, especially an American leader with half the world's power at his disposal. The speeches you make, even on the stump, ought to pay some attention to the complexity and diversity of the questions America faces. To stand or not to stand is simple. After that nothing is. I hope what you say, and indeed, how you say it, will reflect that; for you set the tone for all who follow your banner.

Four days later I had an answer, of sorts. "All I can say to you," the President told a Democratic dinner at Chicago, "is that the road ahead is going to be difficult. There will be some 'Nervous Nellies' and some who will become frustrated and bothered and break ranks under the strain, and some who will turn on their leaders, and on their country, and on our own fighting men. ... But I have not the slightest doubt that the courage and dedication and the good sense of the wise American people will ultimately prevail."

Johnson's rhetorical style, in the Chicago speech and in others he would make over the years, was appropriate to a leader in time of war. If anything, it was mild. In 1943, FDR spoke of bombing the Japanese in terms very similar to those which brought such vigorous condemnation on the head of General Curtis LeMay in the mid-1960's. Churchill's determination to crush the "Nah-zees" was unqualified.

But Johnson's strategy goals were very different. He never asserted a goal of unconditional surrender; he did not even propose to change the form of government in North Vietnam; all he wished to do, as he said, was to force the North Vietnamese to relinquish their aggression against the South, or to render it unsuccessful. American military operations, with the exception of the air attacks on facilities in the North, were strategically defensive. Johnson did not plan to invade North Vietnam or Cambodia in order to cut off the enemy's reinforcements. He rejected population bombing as a means of forcing the pace. As the years passed, he talked more and more of seeking negotiations, and less of fighting aggression.

He was determined, as Kennedy had been, to resist Communist control of Southeast Asia. Yet he spent sleepless nights worrying that American bombs would strike a Russian ship in Haiphong, and he watched nervously for any signs that the Chinese were preparing to send troops into the war.

In short, he sent out confusing signals to the public. We must win; but "victory" was not our goal. The men of Hanoi were the enemies of freedom and democracy, and so serious a threat to America and the free world that we were sending half a million men to resist them in the jungles of Southeast Asia; but our ultimate purpose was to make peace with them, and afterwards to include them as beneficiaries in our program to develop the Mekong Valley.

He was trying to summon up just enough martial spirit and determination in the people to sustain a limited war, but not so much as to unleash the hounds of passion that would force him to widen it. He was trying to thwart China's purposes, by thwarting its deputy, and to get away with that without taking on China directly. He was negotiating with the Russians over a nuclear nonproliferation treaty, and hoped to conclude an arms limitation agreement with them; this while Soviet munitions poured down the Ho Chi Minh trail, aimed at America's sons.

No wonder some people were becoming "frustrated and bothered and [breaking] ranks under the strain." Many of them complained that they were not being told why we were in Vietnam. But since Johnson repeated the themes of the Johns Hopkins speech again and again, it seemed that his listeners were either deaf or willfully ignoring him. Perhaps they simply could not believe that we would have picked that God-forsaken place, with which we had no ties of blood or history, to make our stand — unless there were some hidden motive. The President's reputation as a master manipulator, who often kept his cards face down until the last moment, may have contributed to that. But "not being told why" was, I believe, essentially a euphemism for something else: a sense of confusion growing out of the disparity between America's expressed war aims, and the means we were employing to achieve them.

My own misgivings were of another kind, and in time I came to regard them as impractical and even foolish. I wanted Johnson to reflect those "questions about Vietnam, and about our appropriate role in the world, that [were] extremely difficult for me to resolve" — as I knew they were for many others. I wanted more than restraint in his speeches; I wanted analysis. South Vietnam's corruption and inanition were almost as large an obstacle to the achievement of our goals as North Vietnam's tenacity. I hoped Johnson would say that. We could not help others maintain their independence unless they were able to win and hold the loyalty of their own people. He should say that, too, and for good measure recite the reasons why perhaps the United States ought not to have committed itself to Vietnam at all — to show that he understood the doubts in many citizens' minds. He should deal thoughtfully and respectfully with the criticisms of Walter Lippmann and Senator Fulbright, and ignore the extremist demonstrators, except to say that he could appreciate their concern.

What I overlooked was that we were in a war. Ordinary citizens would have found it strange to hear their President, having just sent several hundred thousand Americans to Vietnam, wondering aloud whether Lippmann was right and the whole affair a tragic mistake. As allies, the South Vietnamese left much to be desired; Saigon in the mid-sixties was not London in the early forties. But one did not publicly chastise one's own side in a war.

Intellectually, the issue was far from clear. Lippmann was a formidable critic, but in half a century his limpid prose had borne many foolish as well as wise judgments. Senator Fulbright objected that the Administration had left Congress in the dark about the war, though in 1961 he had written:

. . . It is my contention that for the existing requirements of American foreign policy we have hobbled the President by too niggardly a grant of power. . . . The overriding problem of inadequate Presidential authority in foreign affairs . . . derives not from the internal relationships with the executive branch, but from the "checks and balances" of Congressional authority in foreign relations.

. . . The Secretary of State and other high officials are obliged to spend prodigious amounts of time and energy in shepherding their programs through the glacial legislative process. . . . The question I put, without presuming to offer solutions, is whether in the face of the harsh necessities of the 1960's we can afford the luxury of 18th century procedures of measured deliberations. It is highly unlikely that we can successfully execute a long-range program for the taming, or containing, of today's aggressive and revolutionary forces by continuing to leave vast and vital decision-making powers in the hands of a decentralized, independent-minded, and largely parochial-minded body of legislators. The Congress, as Woodrow Wilson put it, is a "disintegrated ministry," a jealous center of power with a built-in antagonism for the Executive.*

The *Economist* thought the American commitment was unavoidable:

The Americans . . . have virtually no choice but to resist what China is trying to do. No one else can. It will take the other Asians at least a decade to summon up the strength to look after China themselves. . . . China has nominated Vietnam as a test case for what it claims to be a new kind of war. . . . Those who believe that this technique of "people's war" should be opposed, because its aim is to set up an unacceptable form of society, have little choice but to fight it on their own terms: that is, by a land war. . . . It is not the sort of war that the Americans will be able to bring themselves to fight time

---

* *Cornell Law Quarterly*, 47 (1961).

and time again in other parts of the world. But if it comes out right in Vietnam, it will with luck not have to be fought all over again else where.°

Peregrine Worsthorne, a British journalist who followed Johnson's trip through Asia in 1966, wrote:

Just as President Truman's determination to risk breaking the Berlin blockade strengthened non-Communist Europe's will to unite against Russia, so President Johnson's willingness to risk committing a great army in South Vietnam has ignited a new spirit of Asian resistance to what only a few years ago was regarded as the inevitability of Chinese domination.†

Russell Wiggins, the editor of the *Washington Post*, saw the war in relation to other crises in which America had refused, to its later cost, to join in stopping aggression.

The notion that our armed forces should be used to protect a small country against the aggression of a larger neighbor is greeted as though it were an impulsive invention of President Lyndon Johnson. The theory that we should exert ourselves in a far place, solely for reasons of international morality, and because aggression, however distant, is a threat to our own security, is greeted with derision again in many quarters. . . .

. . . today, 25 years after Pearl Harbor, we have chosen a course that to most Americans is "a great evil," the use of force in a far country where we have no direct or immediate interest — no more interest than we had in Manchuria in 1931. We have chosen it because we prefer it to the greater evil of allowing aggression to go unchecked. . . . Because we were unwilling to risk a little war in 1931 we found ourselves in a great war in 1941; and we are fighting a little war in 1966 because we are unwilling to risk a great war in 1976.‡

These editorial comments — which now seem so ancient that one almost expects to find them illuminated — showed that a number of responsible observers of international affairs believed,

---
° *Economist*, editorial, August 20, 1966.
† *Sunday Telegraph*, November 6, 1966.
‡ *Washington Post*, December 7, 1966.

in 1966, that our engagement in Vietnam was critically important to world peace, then and later. For us, they were friendly beacons in a dark sea, telling us we were on course.

Logically we should not have needed them if we had been certain of our bearings. Every generation has its great scientists and artists who forge ahead with their work, almost oblivious to public acceptance or rejection. But political leadership, while having something in common with both science and art, is precisely neither. To function well, a political leader must be supported by a significant number of those he leads, and by a reasonable share of its active elite — those who think about questions of public policy, and have the means to make their views known or felt. Johnson and his staff heard often enough — and ultimately, almost to the exclusion of all else — that the war was immoral or stupid; that a victory by North Vietnam would not threaten Asia with Chinese domination; and that even if it would, it was none of our affair; that the South Vietnamese, being ineptly and corruptly led and as a consequence disaffected, were not worth one American life, much less many thousands. In the face of such opinions — and having irrevocably committed our troops — it was encouraging to read that some thoughtful persons (outside the bureaucracy) thought the decision was wise. Encouraging? It was much more than that. It was sanity-preserving.

But it was one thing to be justified, and quite another to succeed. We had prevented a North Vietnamese victory early in 1965, and in the next two years we inflicted heavy losses on both the indigenous Viet Cong and the invaders. Still the enemy persisted.

We were deep in a "land war in Asia," the classic quagmire of the strategic thinkers. And it was not, as Korea was, a war of battle lines, in which our colossal firepower might be put to use simply by shooting north. Everyone understood that, but how to deal with it was the subject of a continuing dispute.

Sir Robert Thompson, an expert witness of the Malayan insurgency and a four-year veteran of Vietnam, wrote that

winning . . . demands that the Vietnamese government must steadily regain the countryside, area by area, through a pacification programme, and that it must then restore a functioning civil administrative machine to hold it. Progress in these two fields (as yet almost non-existent), combined with military success, will provide a triangular base on which confidence in the future and a stable government can be built. [As for the effectiveness of bombing]: the automatic progression which is naturally inherent in all bombing offensives has in turn (as it did in the Second World War) "escalated" the objectives. These are now "to deter aggression" and "to bring Hanoi to the conference table" [where at first bombing was justified politically as retaliation to North Vietnamese infiltration, and militarily as a means of slowing down infiltration]. This [escalation of objectives] is the miscalculation which is distracting attention and diverting resources from the development of a winning strategy in the South.*

One evening I spoke to the President about the problems of the pacification campaign, and about the difficulty of rallying the Vietnamese people to the side of a Saigon government they scarcely knew except as a bribe-taking and irresponsible stranger. He turned the conversation to the bombing campaign in the North. "We'll put more and more pressure on them," he said, "until they're ready to talk." Perhaps he thought reform in the South was impossible. More likely, that there was not enough time on the American clock to wait for it. Thompson believed that "only a co-ordinated [land campaign] will reduce and finally deter aggression. Equally, it is only the prospect of defeat within South Vietnam which will bring Hanoi to the conference table. . . ." We were, in fact, vigorously pursuing a big-unit war in the South; but our real hopes seemed to rest with the fighter-bombers in the North.

John Roche saw that, and objected. He wrote to the President in 1967:

---
* "America Fights the Wrong War," *The Spectator*, August 12, 1966.

What has distressed me is the notion that air power would provide a strategic route to victory, and the parallel assumption that by bombing the North we could get a cut-rate solution in the South and escape from the problems of building a South Vietnamese army. . . . The simple military answer to the war is "destroy the enemy," and the military professionals could do a good job of it if you turned them loose, doubled or tripled our commitment, authorized nuclear weapons, etc., etc. In essence, they are like doctors who have a cure for pneumonia but not for the common cold — they therefore have a vested interest in the patient *getting* pneumonia. . . . At the risk of sounding banal, the war in the South can be won in either of two ways: by one to two million United States troops, or by 500–750,000 United States troops *and a well-trained ARVN* [South Vietnamese army]. . . . We have still not done the job [with ARVN] that we did in Korea. Or even started to do it. . . . Assuming as I do that nothing in the limited war range will force Hanoi to negotiate (and that total war is out of the question), we have a force in Vietnam that can buy time and hopefully do something with it; namely, make ARVN into an army.

I knew very little about military strategy. But in late 1966, as I began the first of many speeches I would write about Vietnam, I saw — along with millions of others — America's noble commitment reduced to an outrageous moment on the evening news. Marines were using Zippos to set fire to a village. It was true, but irrelevant, that all wars were brutal. What mattered was that in this one the brutality — of our troops only, since the enemy was not before the cameras — was inescapably laid before every family. One did not have to know much about strategy to understand that repeated doses of that would make Americans wonder whether the national commitment was worth the national guilt.

The razing of villages, and the bombing campaign around Hanoi, epitomized for me all that was fruitless and self-defeating about the war. In March 1967, I wrote the President:

I believe in the policy of bombing the North. But I cannot see where the continued and increasing bombing of areas around Hanoi and Haiphong will get us. If I were on Ho's staff, I would expect it and recommend preparing against it. I would fear being killed myself, but I would try to steel myself against that. I would advise Ho to do just what he is doing: stimulate an outcry around the world, whip up my people for a prolonged resistance, dig shelters throughout the populated areas, and turn down offers to talk made under the threat of intensified bombing of the capital area.

I believe in a policy of punishing armed aggression. I would saturate the area north of the 17th parallel, in North Vietnam and Laos. I would warn the North that I intended to do this: bomb a thirty to fifty mile band north of the parallel. Anything that moved in that area would be hit. My purpose would be to halt the aggression, and still not raise memories of World War II population bombing. My understanding of the post-World War II bombing studies is that sporadic bombing of military targets, such as we are conducting in the North today, was not very effective. Saturation alone succeeded.

After adopting this policy, I would renew the effort to talk, making it clear that as the infiltration diminished, so would the bombing.

It may be that lifting the bombing of the Hanoi-Haiphong area will take some of the heat off Ho Chi Minh and make it easier for him to talk. Continuing the bombing of the North, but limiting it to the border area, would give you military results and would not require you to back away from the requirement for reciprocity.

A year later, something like this was announced. It was not a unique suggestion at the time; McNamara had put men to work on the same idea. It was not adopted then, I believe, because the bombing was regarded as a "bargaining chip." Moderating or ending it would come only after the North had agreed to talk, or to reduce its own efforts in the South.

Its impact on political opinion in America outweighed its apparent military effects on North Vietnam. Rowland Evans told me that there was a feeling, among people he knew, that "the President is bound and determined to bring Ho to his knees by force, that he will escalate to population bombing, and that he is driving us to a LeMay-type resolution in which mighty America bombs little North Vietnam into oblivion. The President's 'six-shooter' image has a lot to do with that." I interjected that the bombing had been, on the President's instructions, incredibly sparing of life. Evans agreed, but he said people still had the sense that the President preferred a solution by hardware to one by negotiations. I thought he simply wanted a solution that satisfied America's war aims — that preserved our stakes in Vietnam. How it came about was of secondary importance.

Rallying public opinion behind the war was an almost neglected task. The U.S. Information Agency and its Voice of America did a competent job overseas; the military lectured its recruits on the dangers of a Communist Asia; but nobody in government, except the President and several members of his cabinet, spoke up for the Vietnam commitment to the two hundred million people whose support or opposition would determine how vigorously we pursued it. Congress had always opposed the creation of a domestic propaganda agency — assuming, I supposed, that in wartime the media and the politicians would be out in front, stirring the necessary emotions. I did not believe that there should be a government news agency or an official channel on television. That was inappropriate in a democracy. But I thought it would strike historians as strange that this nation, having invested so much blood and treasure in a foreign war, heard so few of its leaders speak in favor of that investment, and the majority of those defensively.

John Gardner brought a California businessman to the White House with an interesting proposal. We should draft a brief form telegram, he said — something like "We pledge our support to our brave men in Vietnam" — and create a committee, chaired by Eisenhower and Truman, which would urge people to send it to an office in the Pentagon. With energetic promotion, the number of signatories might exceed the number of marchers in the April 1967 antiwar demonstration. There would be no overt White House involvement. I thought it was worth pursuing. Others thought it would appear contrived, and that the government's hand would show.

A 130-man "Citizens Committee for Peace with Freedom in Vietnam" was organized to support the war effort, and "the policy of non-compromising, although limited, resistance to aggression." Roche helped a number of private citizens put it together, but again in constant apprehension that the government would be seen to encourage the "spontaneous" expression of public confidence. It was an impressive group. Chaired by Paul Douglas, its members included Presidents Truman and Eisenhower, and veterans of the national security establishment like Dean Acheson, Lucius Clay, Omar Bradley, Douglas Dillon, Thomas Gates, and Edmund Gullion; the labor leaders George Meany, Joe Beirne, and Louis Stulberg; academics and writers like James McGregor Burns, Ralph Ellison, James T. Farrell, Oscar Handlin, Eric Hoffer, Ralph Lapp, Allan Nevins, Ralph McGill, Robert Scalapino, Paul Seabury, Ithiel de Sola Pool, and Harold Urey. Its announcement made news, but events overtook it. "A great test is taking place in Vietnam," the announcement read,

. . . that test is whether or not the rulers of one territory can cheaply and safely impose a government and a political system upon their neighbors by internal subversion, insurrection, infiltration and invasion. These are the tactics of the communist "wars of liberation" which depend for success upon achieving their goals at an endurable price and a bearable risk. Our objective in Vietnam is to make the price too high and the risk too great for the aggressor. . . . Our objective as a committee is not to suppress the voice of opposition — [but] to make sure that the majority voice of America is heard — loud and clear — so that Peking and Hanoi will not mistake the strident voices of some dissenters for American discouragement and a weakening of will.

Already, as the committee spoke, the test was changing. It was becoming one of national will — whether, in the face of mounting draft calls and casualty lists, the censure of many nations, and the lack of identifiable progress, the "majority voice of America" would continue to be raised on behalf of perseverance. Millions of citizens — including many of the ablest young — were beginning to ask Ward Just's question, "To what end?" For them, the time was passing when they would listen to, and follow, the traditional advice of older leaders.

In the spring of 1967 I asked the President if I might spend two weeks in Vietnam. If I was going to write speeches about it during the next year — as seemed certain — I wanted to see it first-hand. He agreed, and in mid-May I left for Saigon.

Within a few days I understood that the big issue on the campuses, *whether* we should be in Vietnam or not, was almost beside the point. We *were* there in such enormous force, in such totality, that the fact of our presence was where all discussions began.

At fifteen hundred feet in a Huey on any given afternoon, you could see three Eagle flights of choppers going in to chase VC's; an air strike in progress; artillery "prepping" another area; a division camp here, a battalion forward area there; trucks moving on a dozen roads. Flying north along the road to Danang, you could understand why the highway was secure. Great areas had been scraped off the hilltops every five miles or so and covered with tanks and tents. We had pacified the area by paving it.

I traveled north to the Marines' I Corps, through to the Montagnard country near the Cambodian border, and around the lush river delta in the South. I saw our limitless array of armaments in every region: thousands of choppers, tanks, APC's, jets, and the navy's "riverine" assault boats, looking like relics of the Civil War. If anything had gone awry, it was not the American logistics system.

The announced purpose of my visit was to observe the pacification program — the slow, frustrating work of establishing security in an area, setting up an administrative apparatus, and giving the villagers some reason to identify with the Saigon government. That was ARVN's job, primarily. The Americans made the big sweeps; the South Vietnamese protected the villages from guerrilla attack and won their allegiance.

"They'll never win the people's allegiance," an American civilian said. "For a lot of reasons. Corruption is one. It's everywhere, from the police checkpoint to the license office, from the district chief to the corps commander and the ministries in Saigon." I asked Marshal Ky about that one evening at dinner, shortly after I arrived. "Most of the generals are corrupt," he said. "Most of the senior officials in the provinces are corrupt. That's bad. But getting at corruption takes time. You must remember that corruption exists everywhere, and people can live with some of it. You live with it in Chicago and New York." I accepted his answer at the time, but two weeks later, having seen more of his country, I said, "I don't think you have all that time. And I don't think you can stand even as much corruption as we have in the States. We have a government that people have given their loyalty to, and we can absorb some corruption without shaking their loyalty. The problem here is that people have not committed themselves to the national government, and I don't think they will so long as officials of the government leech on them day and night." Ky agreed at once, which disconcerted me — it was too much like the old Asian game of saying "yes" to whatever the colonial Westerner wanted. I said I thought a Vietnamese leader could create a powerful constituency if he convinced the people that between them — between the leader at the top and the people at the bottom — they would crush the sons-of-bitches in between who were sapping the country's strength. Ky's eyes lit up for a moment, and he said "Yes, yes" — but then he must have thought of the trouble that would entail, because he reminded me "It takes time to get them out. You must be patient."

It was not an academic question. One day in Gia Dinh province, I walked around a hamlet in which a "revolutionary Development" pacification team lived, its bamboo hootch dripping with grenades like walnuts. Frank Scotton — a legendary young civilian, who had spent a lifetime in Vietnam before he was thirty — told me why an RD team had recently moved in here. "A few months ago, the VC came in one night and routed everybody out of bed. They asked these people to identify the police among them — the off-duty police from that checkpoint you saw down the road. For years the police there had stopped the farmers from this region on their way to Saigon, and wouldn't let them pass until they paid a kind of private toll in rice. So when the VC said 'Identify the police,' the people did, and the VC shot them one by one."

Our hopes for ending that kind of small-time debilitating graft in the villages rested in large part with the RD program. One cool morning in Saigon I talked with its administrator, General Thang. He was ordinarily robust and cheerful, in the Fort Leavenworth manner (indeed, in the manner cultivated throughout the foreign military training system).* But on that morning, he was quite unhappy and wanted to quit. I asked him if he was getting enough support from Ky and Thieu. "The problem is not what they say," he answered, "but what they do." Ambassador Bunker had used precisely the same words at lunch the day before, when I had praised the candor of Marshal Ky.

At Vung Tau, on the southern coast, the Revolutionary Development center trained thousands of paramilitary cadres. Their mission was to fight off small-unit VC attacks until reinforcements arrived; to organize a medical service or a market; to get supplies from the provincial capital, and if necessary to teach a school; most important to live in the hamlets as an outward and visible sign of the government's concern. The director of the center, Mayor Nguyen Be, was a charismatic figure, so full of his

---

* Between 1950 and 1968, the United States trained 107,044 East Asian military personnel. Korea, Taiwan, and Japan led the list of trainee nations; South Vietnam was fourth with 14,000 men.

mission that his words jammed up between the blackboard and me. He saw RD as truly revolutionary. It could create the basis for a popular democracy. It could unify the people — unless the politicians in Saigon destroyed it "when they learn what it is that we are trying to do — give the people power." (I had some sign of this from President Thieu, who told me, "Better educated and more patriotic people — army people — ought to be put in charge of every RD team.")

Vung Tau had graduated over fifty-five thousand cadres by May of 1967. They were supposed to move into the hamlets in 59-man teams, each member having a precise responsibility — so precise that it could only have been defined at CIA headquarters in Langley, Virginia, where there was time and money for such enterprises. The average size of the teams in place was thirty. The others had simply left. Hamlet life was boring; the pay was poor—3,500 piastres a month ($35)—and the teams often ran afoul of the district government's corruption and lack of interest. Traveling around Vietnam, I saw teams that had made some progress, at least according to their charts, and others where progress existed solely in the words of the team leader. Scotton said, "Nothing can really work until there is *political* change. Revolutionary Development has been tried before, under Diem. Almost everything has been tried. But until there is a government in Saigon that can gain the people's trust and make its will felt in the provinces, all of these schemes will break apart on the same old rocks — suspicion of the government, corrupt officials, lack of response by those in a position to help."

Fred Weyand, a fine, laconic general whom I had known in the Pentagon, turned a drink in his hand. "Before I came out here a year ago, I thought we were at zero. I was wrong; we were at minus fifty. *Now* we are at zero. We've created a vacuum. We've pushed the VC out of a great many places they used to control. Now the question is, who's going to fill the vacuum?"

It could be us, he thought, with another 200,000 troops. But the more we took responsibility, the more remote the day would become when the ARVN was ready to take our place. I had already sat through a briefing at an ARVN division headquarters where the American advisors did all the talking, and the Vietnamese commanders sat glumly at the rear of the room. I was told that they were shy because their English was poor. Then get somebody to translate for them, I said. "Like to say anything, gentlemen? Mr. McPherson would like your comments." They shook their heads politely, as if reluctant to interfere in someone else's war.

As for the people, no one was quite sure what they thought. A young political scientist, married to a Vietnamese and living quietly in My Tho, in the Mekong Delta, said, "I would guess that not more than 10 to 20 percent of the people around here would voluntarily cast their lot with the VC. Another 20 percent would go with the government. That leaves 60 percent undecided. If there were an honest election in this province, with one VC candidate, one government candidate, and one man who said to hell with both of them, that man would win."

Fear, or its absence, determined politics in most places. The VC often staged reprisals against villages where the chiefs were friendly with the government. On the plains south of Danang, I came upon the wreck of a tiny bus, destroyed by a mine. Several women and children had been killed in it. The blast was a reminder that Saigon could not protect its citizens, even in "pacified" areas. I thought the villagers might have been enraged by that, and determined to find and destroy the VC. "No, they're just afraid," an American officer said. "They know the government can't stop this kind of thing, and they don't want to make it worse."

We were creating fear as well — by bombing, by search-and-destroy operations, by a thousand daily interdictions of Vietnamese life. One afternoon on the Mekong, the lookout on a patrol boat spotted a small sampan moving along the shore. A marksman fired three rounds in front of it, the bullets skipping off the water into the tall grass. The sampan turned toward us. The sound of its tiny outboard was inaudible against the deep roar of the navy craft. Fifty-caliber machine guns were trained on the boatman and his wife as they pulled alongside. On demand he produced their identification papers. These were checked against a list of "known VC" and handed back. A sailor told him to open up the hatch at his wife's feet. He did so, exposing three small fish. "Could have been gelignite or mortar rounds," the sailor told me. He gave the boatman a bar of candy, a few cigarettes, and waved him off. Good God, I thought. This war could go on forever.

In some places people found security against terror for the first time in a generation. It was usually provided by an American unit. In a village in I Corps, a strapping Marine sergeant and his squad had extended their tour for another six months. When they first came to the village, the people were apprehensive, afraid of VC retaliation if they cooperated. But one night four months later, the prearranged warning signal was given — a rattling of cans that told them the VC were in the neighborhood. Thereafter the Marines had trained a Popular Force unit. Its members had shown their mettle by running down a moonlit road during another attack to take up positions with the Marines. "They're good," the sergeant said. "They'd better be. Because what's going to happen when we leave?" What, indeed.

Elsewhere we had created instant security for thousands of people, by moving them out of lands they had farmed for generations into tin-roofed encampments. This was done in order to establish "free-fire zones," where we could make unimpeded use of artillery and air strikes against the Viet Cong. Before I left Washington, Senator Russell had told me, "Look into that free-fire zone business. I don't like the sound of it. The Vietnamese people are animists. They feel very deeply about the land where their ancestors are buried. I suspect we're alienating them by moving them away from their homes, even if it's for their own safety. I know how Georgia people feel about that. When a big dam is dedicated down there, and a lot of farmers have been moved out to make way for the reservoir, I don't go to the dedication. I don't want them to see me up there on a platform built over their land." I asked our commander in Pleiku, in the central highlands, whether he was concerned about that. "Not at all," he said. "These people [the Montagnards] lived in filthy huts. Now they're in sanitary houses. And they're safe from the VC." But near the coast, the Air Cavalry Division commander thought otherwise. "It's the hardest problem we have, knowing whether to move them. I've stopped it, for the time being, even though that limits our effectiveness. I'm afraid we've made a great many enemies in those camps."

The same tough political-military question was raised each time a VC squad entered a hamlet. Should we bring in air and artillery at once? ARVN commanders, I was told, usually said yes; our own officers claimed, "We don't make a move until we have the approval of the district chief." But the district chief was usually an ARVN major with no roots in the area, a military man who wanted to see a high body count as much as MACV [*] did. I spoke to a couple of company-grade officers, thoughtful men who had faced the dilemma of whether to shoot up a village and assure the safety of their men, or practice restraint and risk casualties. They had found no satisfactory answer to it. It was like the war itself, an endlessly compounding riddle. All that was certain — to use Bodard's words about the French and Vietminh — was that "between the two huge machines the private individual was crushed."

A few days before I left, I had a last talk with Ky, and then with Thieu, in the Presidential Palace. I suggested to Ky —

[*] The American military headquarters in Saigon.

whose apparent candor disarmed me, as I was told it did Ambassador Lodge — that the American people would more willingly support the war if the Vietnamese were led by someone with a program for change, rather than by the survivor of a struggle for power. "We'll all have a program for change," Ky said. "We'll all sound like Roosevelts. The question is, who can carry it out? The civilian candidates are too old, and I don't know what Thieu wants to do." It was clear to whom we should have to turn. Ky's problem, he confided, was in keeping his vote from becoming too high. Apparently he meant that the enthusiasm of his friend Nguyen Ngoc Loan, the National Police chief, might produce a 90 percent mandate. Remembering Loan's eyes at dinner one evening, that seemed a real possibility.

Still I thought it might be time for South Vietnam to have a civilian leader. Ky disagreed. "A civilian might try to negotiate with the North, or form a coalition with the VC. That would bring on a coup." When I asked Thieu about that, he assured me that he would never support a coup against an elected civilian. "Mr. Huong" (a civilian, and briefly prime minister during the musical chairs game several years before) "would make an excellent President. I would be glad to serve him as Chief of Staff or Defense Minister." It struck me that he had made a deal with Huong. Divided, Ky could beat them; together, with Huong as President, they would rule. Political officers in the embassy thought this was worth cabling immediately to Washington. I thought I had been permitted a glance into the murky pool of Vietnamese politics. Like many Americans before me, I was mistaken.

Coming back to Saigon one afternoon, we were followed by a rescue helicopter. Corpsmen lifted out a young soldier, about twenty-three, and with an almost womanly gentleness carried him toward a waiting ambulance. He had been hit in the stomach. Two big packs, soaked red, lay on his belly. He was pale, his eyes were open wide, he was scared but holding on. The corpsman yelled in an anguished voice over the whap of the chopper, "He was down for an hour and a half before we could get to him." The soldier's boots and britches were wet from the paddy where he had lain until they reached him.

Driving to my quarters, a wave of grief came over me. What if all we had tried to do was wrong. What if the stakes were not worth this suffering and waste, this effort to build a line of defense in a bog. God Almighty. I did not want to think about that.

"I came back neither optimistic nor pessimistic," I wrote the President, "neither more 'hawk' nor more 'dove.' We are simply there, and we should be."

I laughed each time I thought of Senator Fulbright's phrase "the arrogance of power." I'm sure it applied, and may still apply, to some Americans in Vietnam, who thought we could bring this conflict to an end by the sheer force of military power and the sheer weight of our assistance programs. But when I think of the American major sitting in his fly-specked office in Binh Chanh province, wondering how to get his Vietnamese advisee to do something intelligent for a change, "arrogance of power" makes me laugh. Most of our people in Vietnam know what the limitations of power are.

. . . If our effort is only military, we will lose the big prize. We can have, and indeed have now, a kind of enclave-plus-strike force capability. We can line the roads between the enclaves with soldiers, and in that way "secure" them.

But security in Vietnam, freedom from that feeling that you are in somebody's sights, will ultimately have to be won by something more than military means alone. Leadership, and the political and economic stimulation of the masses of the poor in the rural areas, are just as important to security as live ammunition. That is a platitude back here in Washington. It is as much a reality in Vietnam as the beauty of the women.

One thing you must always insist on is honest reporting by your own people. You must put a premium on candor, and a pox on what is only meant to make you, and other leaders at home, feel confident. . . . There is a natural tendency in the military to feel that things are going pretty well, and will go much better if we only have more bodies and bombs. I am not competent to pass on the more-troops question, but I think everyone who is should be wary of the hungry optimism that is part of the military personality.

Several months later, I heard a mocking echo of that admonition. Tom Buckley, in the *New York Times Magazine*,* wrote about a futile infantry operation near Rachkien, twenty miles south of Saigon. Thousands of rounds of ammunition, small arms, and artillery had been fired — without hitting a single VC, so far as anyone knew. The article concluded:

> It happened that the commander of the third brigade, Col. Charles P. Murray, was also in Rachkien that day. A V.I.P. visitor, a member of the White House staff, was scheduled to fly down from Saigon for a briefing on progress in the delta.
> "We're going slow, but we're getting there," said Murray. "Just think, if each company in each battalion in the brigade could kill one VC a day, why, in a year, they'd equal the strength of the brigade in dead VC."

I remembered Colonel Murray's briefing. It was quite encouraging.

I had planned to return to Washington by way of Israel. After Mike Feldman left the White House, I inherited his role as the resident specialist on Jewish affairs. It was a deeply satisfying assignment, especially as I came to know the Israeli minister, Ephraim Evron, and to treasure his friendship. I looked forward to seeing his country.

But while I was in Saigon the Egyptians closed the Straits of Tiran; the American response was uncertain, and from press accounts it appeared that the U.S.–Israel relationship had become strained. I cabled the President that I would still like to go, and suggested that I might express his personal concern to Prime Minister Levi Eshkol. He agreed.

---

* "The Men of Third Squad, Second Platoon, C Company, Third Battalion," November 5, 1967.

My Air France plane landed at Tel Aviv at three o'clock on the morning of June 6, 1967. The airport was deserted. An embassy officer met me, and drove us north of the silent city to Ambassador Barbour's residence. Just before five I walked out and looked at the Mediterranean, calm under a rose-green sky. The soft air was restorative, but I was aching with fatigue. I went inside and quickly fell asleep.

Three hours later the phone rang. It was Wally Barbour. "You'd better come down to breakfast," he said. "We're in a war." "I've just been in a war," I answered. I thought this was a poor joke, or a bad dream. Then I heard the sirens.

We had breakfast and drove into town. Barbour — a generous, decent man who looked like Sidney Greenstreet in his yellowing Palm Beach suit and brown-and-white shoes — got off a cable to Washington, telling State what we knew about the fighting: nothing. There was another alert, and we hurried down to the underground garage, first making an appointment at the foreign ministry for eleven-thirty.

Shopkeepers were taping windows as we drove through Tel Aviv, but there was no sense of panic among people in the streets. We entered a small nondescript building, and talked briefly with Abba Eban before sitting down with the chief of military intelligence. It was a warm, sunny day. Through the window of the sparsely furnished room, I saw a garden path leading to an underground bunker. No doubt we would go there if there was another alert.

The Israeli general began by describing the terrific buildup of Egyptian tanks and artillery in the Sinai. They had threatened the Negev and Tel Aviv itself. Did the Egyptians attack, we asked? He answered with an order of battle: so many Soviet-built tanks facing so few Centurions, a constant stream of reinforcements crossing the canal, bound for the Israeli border. Did they attack? It was important that President Johnson should know before issuing any statement about the fighting. Yes, he could understand that. Well, there had indeed been reports of Egyptian shelling of the Negev. And the movement of armor was frightening. The sirens wailed again. The general kept talking. Barbour suggested that we might continue the discussion in the underground bunker. The general studied his watch. "No, that won't be necessary. We can stay here." Barbour and I looked at each other. If it wasn't necessary, the Egyptian air force had been destroyed. That could only have happened so quickly if it had been surprised on the ground. We did not need to ask for confirmation, but left at once to cable the news to Washington.

That evening, in a blackout, Barbour and I met with an Israeli official in a downtown hotel. We complained about the absence of information before and since the attack. He expressed his regrets, but suggested that Israel had spared the United States considerable embarrassment by taking matters into its own hands. There was truth in that.

We walked out to the car. As we opened the door the interior light went on, and before we could shut it off an Israeli put his head through the window and rasped, "Never trust the Americans." "Drive on," Barbour said.

Next day the atmosphere had changed. The first reports of victory were confirmed. Egypt's aircraft had been destroyed on their fields, and Israeli armored columns were sweeping the Sinai. There was fighting on other borders, but the Israelis were almost contemptuous of the Syrians and Jordanians. As we drove to the embassy, an old Packard roared by, smeared with mud for camouflage and crowded with soldiers. At a streetlight the soldiers grinned when they saw the small American flags mounted on our fenders. They made thumbs-up signs, and their driver shouted, "Shalom!" before speeding off. "Shalom!" we shouted back.

I went down to Gaza with an Israeli officer. At the border, trucks were parked among the scrub trees, their drivers sleeping or chatting in the shade. "They've a right to rest," the officer said. "They've been working since the night of the fifth." Above the trees, in the direction of the town of Gaza, a black column of smoke rose in the white sky. We were asked to turn back. This was no place for a visiting American bureaucrat.

Near Ben Gurion's kibbutz at Sde Baker, a big jeep passed us, headed toward Egypt. In front sat two husky soldiers, and on benches in the rear, bouncing over the desert road, were two beautiful women. Both of them wore fatigues, but one had on a purple bathing cap, its spangles glinting in the sun, and the other an orange turban. Extraordinary people.

North of Beersheba we stopped beside a police car. Apparently two *fedayeen* had been sighted in the fields nearby. The officer and driver debated whether to get out and help search for them. The driver, a sergeant, spoke excitedly in Hebrew. "He's telling me that you have to get back to Tel Aviv and that I don't know what I'm doing," the officer said. The argument went on for several minutes, until the officer stopped it with what was unmistakably a command. "I think we'd better help find these fellows, if you don't mind. You stay here. We'll be right back." They picked up their compact, Israeli-made automatic weapons, and with the police in tow started up a dusty road. I stood there, watching them go out of sight, and suddenly realized that I would have been wiser to have stayed with them. What if the buggers jump out of those bushes? There were no weapons left in the car, and the keys were gone. I wondered what in the hell I was doing on a deserted road in Israel, in the middle of somebody else's war. If this were Vietnam, the officer might have called in artillery and air strikes on the heads of a "suspected VC concentration." Well, the Israelis seemed to be doing all right without that. I might as well trust in them, and in the ancient God whose territory this was once believed to be. I was glad to see the sergeant trotting back down the road. "Too bad. We saw no sign of them," the officer said. Neither did I, thank God.

At the Weizmann Institute, in Rehovot, there was a faculty party to celebrate the capture of the Wailing Wall in Jerusalem. A physicist offered a toast, and a biologist shouted a response. Meyer Weisgal, the president of the institute and one of the great fund-raisers of the world, raised his glass. "To the Jews in Jerusalem!" he said. "Of course, you'll have to give it back if you want peace," I replied. "Never!" said the physicist. "Jerusalem is sacred to the Jewish people." I could not understand. "Why should you care about seizing these places? You're a rational man, a scientist. You should be more concerned with making peace than with holding on to religious shrines." There was silence for a moment. Then everyone began speaking at once. These "religious shrines" were the symbols of all that had sustained the Jewish people through centuries of persecution, and that had drawn them back to the land of their fathers. They were the mortar in the house of Israel. It would be a sacrilege to give them up, when at last they were back in Jewish hands; it would be political suicide for any Israeli government to try. I staggered to bed after three, unconvinced of the merit of their position, but sure that it was a reality with which statesmen would have to cope.

Two wars, two days apart for me. And as different as if they had occurred in separate centuries. In the one, an exhausted passivity; in the other, a sinewy confidence. In the one, desertions in the army and corruption in the government; in the other, dedication and sacrifice. In Vietnam, ethnic and religious divisions that sapped the national effort; in Israel, a common religion which, under the common danger, bound different nationalities in a unity of purpose.

South Vietnam would never become an Israel, even if it were "unified" under the totalitarian rule of Hanoi. If it was to survive as an independent country, it would have to summon up the will of its people, as it had not succeeded in doing before. That required giving them confidence that the enemy could be beaten, or at least prevented from striking at will. We could help in that. But it also required evidence of integrity in the government, from Saigon to the provincial capitals, and that we could not provide.

12

Dénouement

in the fourth book of the Peloponnesian War
Thucydides tells among other things
the story of his unsuccessful expedition

among long speeches of chiefs
battles sieges plague
dense net of intrigues of diplomatic endeavours
the episode is like a pin
in a forest

the Greek colony Amphipolis
fell into the hands of Brasidos
because Thucydides was late with relief

for this he paid his native city
with lifelong exile

exiles of all times
know what price that is

2

generals of the most recent wars
if a similar affair happens to them
whine on their knees before posterity
praise their heroism and innocence

they accuse their subordinates
envious colleagues
unfavorable winds

> *Thucydides says only
> that he had seven ships
> it was winter
> and he sailed quickly*
>
> —Zbigniew Herbert, "Why the Classics"

VIETNAM became a second consciousness, coexisting with that which was concerned with "normal" things. One thought of friends, and Vietnam; raising a family, and Vietnam; investing in the market, writing a letter, visiting a university, watching television, and Vietnam.

Like an acid, it was eating into everything. It threatened to wipe out public awareness of Johnson's great achievements; it had already corroded his relationships with members of Congress.

Joe Tydings asked me to come up and talk about it. In the Senate, he had been a pretty firm supporter of the war. But it had become such a political albatross in Maryland that "any reasonably good Republican could clobber me if the election were held today." He did not hold the President personally responsible for his troubles; but "every political advisor I have says I can save myself only by attacking him. I won't do that, but I'm going to have to speak out against the war. It's dragging the country down, and Democrats along with it." He said that other senators friendly to the Administration — Bayh, Harris, Muskie, and Hart — had reported the same bitterness in their states. Senator Russell said, "For the first time in my life, I don't have any idea what to recommend."

Senator Stennis did: taking the wraps off the Air Force. That made sense to many people. We were losing hundreds of American lives every week. Their sacrifice would have meaning only if we threw every resource against the enemy and concluded the war successfully. That Russian ships steamed into Haiphong harbor, carrying supplies that enabled the North to kill our men in the South, and that we gave them sanctuary and risked our pilots' lives on inconsequential targets, was madness.

Others recommended an invasion of Laos, to interdict the enemy's supply lines, or an Inchon-type landing north of the demilitarized zone. It was ridiculous to fight the war only in South Vietnam; the invader should be pursued into his homeland. We had not fought the Second War to a conclusion only in France and Poland. We had pursued the enemy to Berlin.

But the President knew that to bomb the Russian ships, or mine the harbor, risked a retaliation elsewhere. Moscow could not passively assent to our cutting off its assistance to North Vietnam. An invasion that threatened the government in Hanoi might well bring Chinese volunteers into the war, as they had gone into Korea. Besides, as Roche suggested, the analogue for an amphibious landing was more likely to be Anzio than Inchon. We could easily bog down a million men in an effort to "take the war to the enemy."

There was an obvious kinship between those who urged greater military pressure, and those who called for longer bombing pauses and the more energetic pursuit of a peaceful settlement. Both rejected the prevailing policy. Both disbelieved Westmoreland and Bunker when they professed to see light at the end of the tunnel. Both thought that the enemy might agree to negotiate — by pressure, or by persuasion.

I knew very little about the many abortive efforts to begin talks with North Vietnam. It was part of the credo, of those who thought them attainable, that Johnson had rejected every overture from the Communist side. Perhaps he was too peremptory on some occasions. But I believed that the Communists did not wish to settle on any terms that we could legitimately accept. The Russians were said to be anxious for an end to the war because it disturbed their bilateral relations with the United States and served the interests of their rival China. But if I had been a Russian leader, and had seen how America's absorption in Vietnam had weakened it elsewhere, brought down upon it the condemnation of Europe, and ripped its own society apart in fratricidal hostility, I would have found the war more amenable than dangerous to my purposes. The Chinese, even in the chaos of their Cultural Revolution, had a great stake in the success of this paradigm war of liberation. And the North Vietnamese — incredibly brave, and fixed in their determination to rid Vietnam of the new colonials — believed they would win.

So the question became, for me, whether we would change our strategy in Vietnam to one of protecting pacified areas, improving the government's effectiveness as an administrator, and avoiding heavy casualties; and in Washington, to removing some of the most vexing elements of national policy. I did not believe we could persuade or force North Vietnam to talk, or that we could win the war. I wanted to cut our losses, get the demonstrators off the streets, and reelect Lyndon Johnson.

Restricting the bombing of the North seemed the most urgent step. In a memorandum to the President I reflected what I was hearing about that around Washington. The bombing of Hanoi had galvanized world opinion against us. We appeared purely vindictive: America and its President were angry at a small adversary that would not come to terms, and though it was apparent that bombing would not produce talks, we were determined to pour it on and punish the North Vietnamese for the frustration they were causing us. It was ineffective in stopping infiltration; studies had shown that North Vietnam was able to meet its logistical needs in the South despite the campaign of interdiction on the trails. If we destroyed 20 percent of their southbound supplies, they increased the flow to 120 percent of their requirements. It was an inadequate sop to the true hawks; even if we destroyed every military and industrial target in Vietnam, these could be rebuilt, and the cry would go up that they should be destroyed again.

If we intended to continue the bombing program, we ought to tell the public why and what we hoped to gain from it. And we should give new consideration to bombing only the area north of the DMZ, and postponing further attacks on Hanoi. I sat back and waited for an answer. Next day Walt Rostow called. The President wanted the two of us to work up a speech justifying the bombing. Neither of us, I believe, had much appetite for that — Rostow because he had other fish to fry, I because I was hoping to write about its termination. We postponed it until it was forgotten.

That was late October 1967. Three months later came the Tet offensive. The question thereafter was not what to do about the bombing, but what to do about the war.

The events of February and March 1968 have been so widely discussed that another narrative seems superfluous. Besides, I was not privy to the crucial discussions about troop levels. What follow are fragmentary impressions of a time that began in confusion and dismay, and ended in hope and renunciation.

• The President had excised a long section of his 1968 State of the Union address which dealt with Vietnam. He preferred to reserve the subject for a later occasion, and instructed me to prepare a draft. After Tet, the need seemed greater than ever. But so was the confusion about what to do. There was a baffling disparity between reports from MACV and the stories that dominated the papers and the evening television screens. On several mornings I arrived at the White House filled with shock and foreboding over what I had seen the night before, and went to Rostow's office to read the cables from Saigon. They were invariably optimistic, full of stratospheric enemy body counts, inspiring stories of South Vietnamese resistance, and so forth. Rostow elaborated on them. The enemy had called out his hidden agents and sympathizers, and they had been decimated. There had been no "popular uprising" in the cities. In the anachronistic language of pre-1940 Oxford, the South Vietnamese were suddenly pulling up their socks, bowing their necks, putting their shoulders to the wheel.

As it happened, there was truth in the assessment that the enemy had not achieved his aims in South Vietnam. But he had convinced the American public that after all the bombing, after all our expenditure of lives and resources, he was still vitally alive, resourceful, and determined.

The horrific pictures of death and destruction kept coming on the tube, making a travesty of phrases like "body counts" and "surfaced enemy assets." As Don Oberdorfer has written in his excellent account of the Tet offensive,*

The cables from Saigon presented a reassuring and bloodless picture snapped from the lofty perspective of high headquarters. They emphasized Communist shortcomings and losses rather than Communist achievements and said little or nothing of the "negative" aspects. Washington did not seek the darker side. It wanted desperately to hear that all was well.

The cables were thus doubly welcome. The leaders in Washington took heart and believed the country would take heart as well. The leaders were mistaken. While they were receiving, reading, and disseminating after-the-fact official summaries of what had happened, the public was *experiencing* the worst of the bloodshed through the new technology of television. The summaries were not believed. The projected experience was.

Oberdorfer suggests that the central event of the period, measured by its influence on public opinion, was the shooting of a bound VC suspect in a Saigon street by the chief of the National Police, General Nguyen Ngoc Loan. Photographs and films of the incident were universally reproduced. In them, Americans saw not only the inhumanity of an ally, but confirmation of an impression that had been building for years: we were sunk in a war between alien peoples with whom we shared few human values.

---
* *TET!* (New York: Doubleday, 1971), p. 159.

I remembered Loan as he sat next to Ky one evening in Saigon, nursing a beer, taking Bob Komer's sharp gibes about his ruthlessness and the graft of his subordinates. Loan the tough cop, Loan the rascal. Now it was Loan the killer, raising his revolver on every channel, turning public doubt into heartsick rage. And carrying us along with him.

I thought of a poem which someone had inserted in the President's toast "to the free peoples of Vietnam and the United States," at a Guam conference the year before. It was written in 1873, by the Vietnamese scholar Bui Vien, and addressed to an American friend in Japan. It read:

> *We pour out wine into glasses at Yokohama in*
> *the ninth month — in autumn.*
> *Turning my head toward the clouds of Vietnam,*
> *I am anxious about my country.*
> *Sea and land — memory and emotion — remind me*
> *of my former journey.*
> *Enjoying myself with you, I regret all the more that*
> *we must part.*
> *Spiritual companion, in what year will we be together*
> *in the same sampan?*

"In 1968," a friend said when I showed him the toast, "and we seem to be sinking."

• On a cold, bright Saturday in February, we left the White House to say goodbye to the 92d Airborne at Fort Bragg, and to a Marine unit in California. Both were being rushed to Vietnam as a precaution against further enemy attacks. Both included veterans of at least one tour in Vietnam. The President was distressed to send them back. But our reserves were stretched thin, and there was little alternative.

That night we landed by helicopter on the deck of the carrier *Constellation*, anchored off San Diego. It had returned only recently from Yankee Station, in the gulf near Haiphong. Horace Busby and I asked to speak with some of the pilots who had flown missions over North Vietnam. Twenty or thirty men filed into the wardroom and sat about a conference table. The President remained in an adjoining stateroom, but I believe he heard at least part of the conversation.

It began conventionally, with senior officers describing the excellent performance of pilots, deck crews, and aircraft, the good recovery rate on crewmen downed at sea, and so on. There was a pause. A young lieutenant with an Irish name broke it. "Permission to speak, sir." "Granted," said a commander. There followed a furious assault on the bombing program. Men were being asked to fly through the heaviest antiaircraft defenses ever seen, in order to bomb meaningless targets. "I've hit the same wooden bridge three times. I'm a damned good pilot. I know I've knocked it out every time. Big deal. It takes them two or three days to put it back. And for that I've flown through SAMs, flak, and automatic weapons fire. I've seen the god-damned Russian freighters sitting there, and the supplies stacked along the wharves. I can't hit them. It might start a wider war. Well, the war is too wide for me right now. And it's stupid." When he was through, other young pilots took up his cause. I replied as best I could, that what they had done had helped to put pressure on the enemy; that hitting the freighters might indeed trigger a third world war. They listened in silence. After they left, I shrugged toward Busby and went off to polish the President's remarks for the following day.

Next morning, before he spoke, Johnson watched films of air attacks on bridges and roads around Hanoi. The briefing officer, an admiral, was especially proud of the "Wall-eye" missile, which carried an image of its target, made by photo-reconnaissance planes, and homed in on whatever matched the image. There was a picture of one wobbling through the sky, and finally zooming down on the pier of a bridge. "Pretty accurate?" the President asked. "Yessir, pretty accurate." "Does it miss sometimes?" "Occasionally it does, sir. It picks up a similar image away from its target, and homes in on that." "So I might be trying to hit a barracks, and hit Ho Chi Minh's house?" "Well, Mr. President, the accuracy rate is high . . ." "I'm trying to find out whether if I tell that thing to hit a Viet Cong, it might hit Lady Bird." "Oh, I'm sure it wouldn't do that, Mr. President." "Uh-huh, O.K., thank you."

• Gene McCarthy lost the New Hampshire primary, but came so close that his campaign against Johnson was given a tremendous thrust forward. Many people whom I knew and admired were enthusiastic about him. I thought I might have been, too — or at least, might have better understood his appeal — if I had not been committed to the man he was attacking, and if I had not retained an impression of his nonchalance from my days on the Hill. I had no doubt about McCarthy's brains and courage, but I had not believed him to be a serious figure. That may have been because I was absorbed in programs, and McCarthy was not. Obviously this was no hindrance to him in his campaign. People were tired of programs, and particularly tired of hearing Johnson recount them. The war, the credibility gap, the alienation of the young, all were meat for McCarthy's cool wit and understanding. He and Johnson had once been friendly, and even after New Hampshire it seemed certain that Johnson preferred to see McCarthy, rather than Robert Kennedy, leading the Democrats of the left.

One day in mid-March, Califano and I had lunch with Johnson on the edge of the Rose Garden. He said he had been giving thought to not running for reelection. We did not respond at once; I thought he was only exhaling his frustration. But he returned to it and pressed us for a response. "Of course you must run," I said. "Why? Give me three good reasons why." We walked back into his office. "Well, if *I* were you, I wouldn't run.

It's a murderous job, and I see no way to change the things that make it so bad, at least not soon. But I'm not you. You have to run." He shook his head. "That's a conclusion, not a reason. What would be so bad about my not running? What would happen?" I answered, "For one thing, nobody else could get a program through the Congress. Nobody else knows how." He shook his head. "Wrong. Any one of 'em — Nixon, McCarthy, Kennedy — could get a program through next year better than I could. They'd be new, and Congress always gives a new man a little cooperation, a little breathing room. I'd be the same old Johnson coming back to the well again, beggin' and pushin' 'em to give me a better bill than last year. No. Congress and I are like an old man and woman who've lived together for a hundred years. We know each other's faults and what little good there is in us. We're tired of each other. Give me another reason." I looked to Califano for help. At that moment Marvin Watson appeared to announce the next appointment. Relieved, we walked back to Califano's office and debated whether Johnson was really serious.

A few days later, I wrote a long memorandum about the political situation, on the assumption that the President would stand for reelection. Its theme was that he was *ex officio* the defender of the status quo, and that was bad. Telling the public to persevere in current policies was like telling a man already deeply in debt to go deeper. People wanted to know how to get out of debt. They wanted change.

George Wallace offered a radical change, and 12 to 15 percent of the people would probably go for it. Nixon would be "just as tough as Wallace on crime, but more 'progressive' on urban problems."

I think he will end up more flexible on Vietnam than we expect him to be today — not more hawkish. And he will blame Vietnam for everything — budget troubles, gold, "a sense of unhappiness." . . . I think Rockefeller will go dove on Vietnam — call for a political settlement, de-escalation, etc. [Wrong.] Kennedy offers a change to a dove policy, together with the reputation of a tough guy who could somehow prevent us from being hurt by following a softer line. . . . He will try to occupy the same relation to you that his brother Jack occupied to the Eisenhower-Nixon Administration: imagination and vitality vs. staleness and weariness, movement vs. entrenchment, hope of change vs. more of the status quo. We will be defending our programs; he will be attacking the tired bureaucrats who run them. We will point to the good we've done; he will point to the people who've been left out — the Mississippi and Harlem Negroes, the Indians, the Appalachian farmers. He will speak before college groups whom no member of the Administration could address without embarrassment. Many young liberals are bitter about his opportunistic entry into the race after McCarthy's strong showing, but Kennedy is cynical enough to believe that they will forget, given time, razz-ma-tazz, and the development of momentum behind his candidacy. He is right about that.

"If you present a stationary target, standing so firmly by the status quo that you seem to eliminate the possibility of change, you will be in grave trouble both at the Convention and in November." I thought he should de-escalate in Vietnam, and undertake to carry out many of the Kerner Commission's recommendations — especially to explore its indictment of white racism. (A foolish suggestion. I feared that Johnson would be accused of avoiding the issue, and that Kennedy would "take it over." I had no sense, then, of its true political abrasiveness, especially among the union rank and file. Kennedy handled it beautifully, managing to make his own convictions clear without dressing his audience in sackcloth.)

I hoped Johnson would travel more often, chiefly to show that he could, also to reduce the contrast between himself and the other candidates. Medium-sized cities offered good opportunities: New Orleans, Kansas City, Cincinnati, Rochester, Salt Lake City, Louisville, Denver. I thought he should concentrate on groups with whom he had been popular in the past — traditional Catholics, women, Jews, organized labor, moderate Southerners, Western farmers.

He had great advantages: political intelligence, experience, achievement, and the office of the Presidency. He could waste them by holding fixedly to his present course. "Maybe people have never had it so good, but neither have they been so uneasy, at least in my lifetime."

Christian called to say that the President agreed with much of the memorandum. He did not say what he had disputed; with my mind set on the campaign ahead, I did not guess that it was its fundamental assumption.

• Phil Carter of *Newsweek* called to talk about Arkansas and the war. "In Durmont, they've attracted a new industry that will use a lot of water. They need money for new wells, pumps, pipes, and storage tanks. They passed a bond issue to provide part of it, and they looked to the Economic Development Administration for the rest. But they've been told that 'because of the war,' EDA money is tight.

"They want an addition to their county hospital. They've been told that Hill-Burton funds may not be available, 'because of the war.' They need a new kind of defoliant, a weed-killer for their cotton crop. But it's in short supply. It's being used in Vietnam.

"Casualties hit these small towns especially hard. Everybody is likely to know the boy who was killed. In Mount Tree, it was the co-captain of the 1965 high school football team. The bank president, the football coach, and one of his teachers all said they had real doubts about the war. The only person I talked to who defended it was that boy's mother, and I think she had to for her own sake.

"A lot of combat soldiers come from the Mount Tree's."

• Lunch at the State Department, a few days before Robert McNamara left office. Rostow, Califano, and I were there from the White House; Rusk, Katzenbach, Bill Bundy, and the newly appointed Defense Secretary, Clark Clifford.

McNamara, obviously on edge, condemned the bombing — North and South. He recited the comparative figures; so many tons dropped on Germany and Japan and North Korea, so many more on Vietnam. "It's not just that it isn't preventing the supplies from getting down the trail. It's destroying the countryside in the South. It's making lasting enemies. And still the damned Air Force wants more." Rusk stared at his drink; Clifford looked searchingly at McNamara, but said nothing.

In mid-March — six weeks after I had begun the first draft of a Vietnam speech, I circulated the fourth draft to the men in that luncheon group. Clifford called to ask what I really thought about the war. I told him. "Old boy," he said, in his measured way — Clifford always began as if he were delivering an opinion from the Supreme Court bench, and then often broke the spell with a salty phrase from Missouri — "Old boy, we have a lot of work to do together. And I think we're going to pre-vail. Let me tell you what I've been doing." He described the cross-examinations he had been conducting in the Pentagon, going to the first principles on which the war was being waged. His conclusion was that it could not be won by the present level of effort, but only prolonged; and as escalation was inconceivable, we should have to "wind it down," beginning with an announcement that we would not commit substantial new forces. "Now you must tell me what you hear over there, and I will keep you advised of my activities. We must be watchful for any sign that the war is to be wound up again, and not down. That would be tragic — for the country, and for the man himself. Keep in constant touch."

I felt like Chill Wills, seeing the United States cavalry on the horizon as it galloped straight for the encircled wagon train.

- Friday, March 22. An extended lunch in the Mansion. Rusk, Clifford, Wheeler, Bill Bundy, Joe Fowler, Richard Helms, Christian, Rostow, me, I think General Taylor. The question was whether to include, in the speech, a cutback in the bombing to the 20th parallel. I do not remember individual contributions, but at the end, Rusk said: "Mr. President, I believe it is the consensus of your advisors that a partial reduction of the bombing would be insufficient to produce talks. The North Vietnamese have always insisted that the bombing be stopped completely, and without conditions, before talking. On the other hand, we cannot stop the bombing altogether, without risking the security of our troops. The North Vietnamese have given no sign that they would not use a total cessation to attack our bases and the cities. Unfortunately, that is the situation." The President shrugged and said, "O. K."

In the living room, Joe Fowler argued for stronger language in behalf of the surtax. At one point during the past month, the need to persuade Congress that it should raise new revenues threatened to increase the troop figure as well; that is, it seemed possible that only national mobilization, with the calling up of reserves, would strike Congress forcefully enough to provoke action on the tax bill — which, in turn, was needed to reduce the deficit created by past expenditures. Now that grim prospect was past. There would be no major troop reinforcement, no mobilization, no significant reserve call-up.

At noon the next day, I sent in a short memorandum recommending a sequence of negotiating steps. We would announce that we had stopped the bombing north of the 20th parallel, and that we had sent representatives to Geneva and Rangoon to await the North Vietnamese. They would say that wasn't enough; we'd have to stop it altogether. We would say that we could not do that so long as men and supplies were pouring down the trail. But we'd say, we will stop it altogether, if you will not mount attacks on the cities in I Corps, or upon Saigon; and if you will stop the shelling of South Vietnam from the DMZ. They'd say there could be no conditions; we must stop all the bombing. We'd express our regret that they had responded in the same intransigent way.

I did not expect it to produce negotiations, but I thought it would show the American people, and people in other nations, that we were truly seeking them. Later that afternoon the President sent for additional copies. That was encouraging.

- At Secretary Acheson's for dinner, on Tuesday, March 26. He had just met with the President, along with the other "Wise Old Men" — George Ball, General Bradley, Mac Bundy, Arthur Dean, Douglas Dillon, Abe Fortas, Robert Murphy, General Ridgway, and Cy Vance. The majority's advice had been to deescalate the war. After dinner the Secretary handed me a long editorial from the *Winston-Salem Sunday Journal and Sentinel* written by its editor and publisher, Wallace Carroll. Its thrust was summed up in this paragraph:

> The war has made us — all of us — lose sight of our national purposes. We need to stand back and get our priorities right. Enemy No. 1 is Russia. Enemy No. 2 is China. The vital strategic areas, in their proper order, are Western Europe (particularly Germany), Japan, the Middle East, Latin America — and only then Southeast Asia. The most crucial priority of all, of course, is the home front.

The newspaper had supported the war in the past. So had Secretary Acheson. Now he said, "This represents my views precisely. I could have written it myself." Next day I sent it to the President.

- On Thursday, five of us met in Rusk's office to talk about the latest draft of the speech — the eighth, I believe. We were Rusk, Clifford, Rostow, Bill Bundy, and McPherson.

Clifford had read the draft, and thought it was totally inconsistent with the reality of opinion in the country. "Now, I make it a practice to keep in touch with friends in business and the law across the land. I ask them their views about various matters. Until a few months ago, they were generally supportive of the war. They were a little disturbed about the overheating of the economy and the flight of gold, but they assumed that these things would be brought under control; and in any event, they thought it was important to stop the Communists in Vietnam.

"Now all that has changed. There has been a tre-mendous e-rosion of support for the war among these men. I do not know exactly what has caused it. Maybe some of them have sons or grandsons who have gone to Vietnam. Maybe they feel that we are unable to do what we must do at home, so long as the war continues to put such great demands on our resources. Maybe it is their reaction to Tet. Whatever the specific reason, these men now feel that we are in a hopeless bog. The idea of going deeper into the bog strikes them as mad. They want to see us get out of it.

"These are leaders of opinion in their communities. What they believe is sooner or later believed by many other people. It would be very difficult — I believe it would be impossible — for the President to maintain public support for the war without the support of these men.

"So I believe that we must change this speech. We must make it point toward peace, and not toward more of the same. We must take the first step toward winding down the war and reducing the level of violence. Then, if Hanoi will just take a step of its own, we will take another. And so on. Maybe they won't do it, although I believe there is an even chance that they will. In any event, we will have put ourselves in a better posture here at home. We will have moved to get out of the bog.

"I believe the first step should be an announcement that we have unilaterally restricted our bombing of the North to the area north of the DMZ. Not that we have paused, but that we have stopped it north of the 20th parallel. Then if there is a favorable response from the other side, we would be prepared to take other steps."

Secretary Rusk asked Bill Bundy what the reaction to such an announcement would be in the allied countries — particularly in

Seoul. Bundy, whose knowledge of the personalities and policies of Asian leaders was encyclopedic, said he thought President Park would not be unduly alarmed, if Ambassador Win Brown had time to inform him before the event. The real problem of course, was Saigon.

I brought up the memorandum I had written the Saturday before, proposing a negotiating strategy. The President had apparently been interested in it. "Yes, we sent that idea out to Saigon," Rusk said. "Bunker thinks the South Vietnamese can live with it." I thought he was referring to my memorandum; a year later I heard that Rusk, on the President's instructions, had sent a bombing-restriction proposal to Bunker earlier in the month, together with Arthur Goldberg's recommendation that the bombing be completely stopped. It was assumed that Thieu, confronted with a choice between two evils, would choose the lesser.

Amazingly, the conversation thereafter was concerned with the mechanics of informing our commanders and allies, and with redrafting the speech — not with whether the country should instead be rallied to sustain the effort. No one argued for a continuation of the bombing around Hanoi, or for committing large numbers of fresh troops. Here were five men, all associated with the war; all of whom had either urged its prosecution, helped to form its strategies, argued its rationale, or written its leader's speeches; and not one of whom spoke out against "winding it down" — which would mean, inevitably, accepting a result that was less than satisfactory by the standards they had set for it.

Why should that have been? Clark Clifford was one of the most persuasive men in Washington; his contacts with the major figures in American society were unequaled by the others in that room. But something more than Clifford's style and contacts must have caused men like Dean Rusk and Walt Rostow — staunch believers in the justice and necessity of the war — to acquiesce. Something like conversations with President Johnson, who had, in turn, been talking with Congress.

The President had long been aware of the disaffection in the country. He knew that the "credibility gap" had become an abyss, when the sanguine assessments of his Administration, rendered in the fall of 1967, were mocked on the television screen during Tet. But he believed we could not quit the field until the purpose for which we had entered it had been served: to assure the independence of South Vietnam under Communist attack. The majority of the members of Congress thought so as well, until they began to feel that the achievement of that purpose was not in sight, and that their people would not indefinitely abide the effort to reach it. They did not want us to "withdraw precipitously," as the expression went; our pride and stature as a nation, and the deaths of our men, would not allow that; but they were totally unwilling to vote for a greater commitment. The chairman and most of the members of the Senate Foreign Relations Committee were opposed to the war. The Senate majority leader was opposed to the war. The chairman of the House Ways and Means Committee would not impose new taxes to reduce the war-inflated deficit, unless steep cuts were made in federal spending — including spending for the social programs which the Congress had enacted under Johnson's leadership.

If the street demonstrations could not convince the President to alter his course, word that the Congress no longer supported it could. Along that armature between the Capitol and the White House, the current flowed — not, this time, from President to Congress to country, but in reverse.

This I believe he must have communicated to his most trusted advisors, Rusk and Rostow. And this, more than Clifford's logic and the impressive sources of his information, must have caused them to talk of "how," instead of "whether," after he spoke.

Whatever the reason, it was decided that I should write a different speech. I would send it to the President, along with the current draft, as an alternative. There was not much time. It was Thursday, March 28. A television slot had been reserved for Sunday, March 31.

I left the State Department wanting to holler. Whom could I talk to? Celebrate with? No one. That would have to come later. I wrote into the night, and marked the alternative draft "1A." Next morning the President called. "Now, I don't want to say that on page 3 . . . ," he began. I looked quickly through both drafts. He was talking about the alternative. We were on our way.

• Saturday, March 30. All day, and into the evening, we worked on the draft in the Cabinet Room. The President sat, coatless, tie pulled down, painstakingly going over each word. Katzenbach was there for Rusk, who was on his way across the Pacific; the others included Clifford, Wheeler, Bill Bundy, Rostow, and Christian. There were long discussions about replacement troops — 13,500 were to be sent — and about the language describing the geographical limitation on the bombing. I had made it the 20th parallel. Katzenbach argued for describing it in functional terms:

Tonight, I have ordered our aircraft to make no attacks on North Vietnam, except in the area north of the demilitarized zone where the continuing enemy buildup directly threatens allied forward positions and where the movements of their troops and supplies are clearly related to this threat.

That would better explain it to the American people, and perhaps make it easier for the North Vietnamese to accept it as an adequate basis for talks. The change was made.

We finished around nine. The President asked, "Where's the peroration?" That morning, Clifford had called and said, "Old boy, you've been sticking that same old peroration on these latest drafts, and it's out of line with what now goes before. Why don't you do another one?" There wasn't time before the meeting, so I had simply removed it. "I didn't like it, Mr. President. I'm going upstairs now to write another. I'll make it short. The speech is already pretty long." He smiled. "That's O.K. Make it as long as you want. I may even add one of my own."

When he left, I turned to Clifford, who was gathering up his papers. "Jesus, is he going to say sayonara?"

"What?"

"Is he going to say goodbye tomorrow night?"

Clifford looked at me with pity, as if I were too tired to be rational.

• The new peroration was cast, not in terms of steadfast commitment as the old one had been, but of retrospective satisfaction. "I believe that a peaceful Asia is far nearer to reality tonight because of what America has done." That was the justification for the war, if there was one. What had seemed inevitable four or five years ago — the rising of the Red Star over Asia — was no longer so. Indonesia, South Vietnam, Thailand, Malaysia, the Philippines — had at least been given time to strengthen themselves; whether they had made sufficient use of it only the future would tell.

• Sunday in the White House. The President was in the mansion, working with Horace Busby on an additional peroration. I felt sure I knew what it would say.

Looking over the speech, I became troubled about the bombing language. We had removed any reference to the 20th parallel, and the limitation now read as if we intended to bomb only in the immediate vicinity of the DMZ. What if we bombed near the 20th, up around Vinh? Wouldn't the critics say that we had deceived the North Vietnamese? I thought we ought to restrict the raids, at least during the next few days, to the DMZ and its environs. I called Clifford. He did not think the North Vietnamese would quibble about that; we were, after all, ending the bombing in areas where 90 percent of their people lived. Besides, the mission orders had probably already gone out, from CINCPAC in Honolulu, and would be difficult to retrieve. This struck me as peculiar, but I accepted it.

Around five, Johnson called and asked if I thought the speech was any good. I thought it was. Would it produce negotiations? Maybe; even if it didn't we would look much better. He had his own ending to the speech. So I had heard. Did I know what he was going to say? I thought so. What did I think about that? "I'm very sorry, Mr. President."

"Well, I think it's best. So long, podner."

I went to the home of a friend, a robust, irreverent man named Owen Smith, and began to drink. Charles Maguire called, breathless with astonishment, to say he had just read the last paragraphs on the Teleprompter. Did I know what they said? Yes. After a while they came on, the words I knew as well as my own name, and then the unfamiliar ones: "Finally, my fellow Americans, let me say this . . ."

Around ten Doug Cater called. The President was going to Chicago next day, to speak to the National Association of Broadcasters. Cater had drafted a speech. The President wanted me to come down and work on it. I started to laugh. There was no end to it. I had a last drink with Smith, and called the White House garage for a car.

• Inevitably, our planes bombed near the 20th parallel the next day. Senator Fulbright blasted the Administration. How could the North Vietnamese accept the offer to talk under such circumstances? It was hard to know where to direct one's ire: toward the military for clumsily jeopardizing the peace initiative, or toward Fulbright for giving North Vietnam a respectable excuse for declining. When the response from Hanoi was favorable, Fulbright confessed that his wife had scolded him for "talking too much." On this occasion, that seemed indisputable. The experience taught us several lessons, one of the more important being that we could expect continuous domestic criticism of our negotiating position, sincerity, and good sense, until an agreement was reached or the war otherwise ended.

- Disagreement over a site for the negotiations continued for weeks. We proposed Geneva, Vientiane, Rangoon, Djakarta, and New Delhi; the North Vietnamese, Pnom Penh and Warsaw. The President was damned if he was going to send his negotiating team into a capital where communications were difficult or the environment was hostile; that would guarantee that most of what leaked to the press from the conference room — the "atmospherics," the hints, the rumors of dissension within the delegations — would favor the other side.

I sat with him by the pool of the Kaiser estate in Honolulu, which had been lent to us for a meeting with President Park of Korea. We tried to think of other acceptable sites for the talks, in countries not too firmly associated with our side: Colombo, Kabul, Katmandu, Vienna, Helsinki, and so on. By God, nobody could say we weren't trying to get them started. "How many are there now?" "Fifteen."

In time, Paris became the leading contender. But apparently because of de Gaulle's opposition to United States involvement — and copious intelligence that Frenchmen had long played a dog-in-the-manger role in their lost colony — Johnson was reluctant to agree.

Clifford took me aside at a party. "Old boy, we've got more work to do. We must keep up the momentum. We must convince our friend that he should end this argument over a site. People are hungry for peace. They want us to get on with the talks." I agreed, and phoned my secretary to dictate a memorandum to the President.

Next morning at 8:30 the President called. He was hopping mad. Who had put me up to that memorandum? He was trying to keep from turning over the keys to the house and if his aides and advisors would just give him a little room, he might succeed. I was furious. Nobody had put me up to it! I shouted. I did not want to see him charged with blocking the initiative he had begun. Nobody would understand why he had rejected Paris! He began again, much quieter, patiently explaining why he had to move cautiously.

When he hung up, I called Clifford to warn him that "our friend" was in a high dudgeon.

"Uh . . . when would you estimate that he called you?"

"Exactly at 8:30."

"My notes show that the President and I finished a telephone conversation this morning at 8:29."

Throughout the summer and early fall, a struggle went on over stopping the bombing completely. The North Vietnamese delegation in Paris insisted that it must be stopped before substantive talks could begin. Our ambassadors — two tireless public servants, Averell Harriman and Cy Vance — pressed Washington to agree. Clifford argued increasingly for further de-escalation, and for thrusting more responsibility for the fighting onto the South Vietnamese. His comments became known as "Cliffordisms" by those on the other side of the debate — those who asserted, with Rusk, Rostow, and Bunker, that the enemy's acquiescence in the talks signified his exhaustion; that continuing the military pressure would produce an increasingly compliant response; or (contra) that our intelligence had warned of an imminent new attack, making a total cessation of the bombing very dangerous. They taught it round or flat.

The story is told, correctly so far as I know, in *The Roots of Involvement*, by Elie Abel and Marvin Kalb.* For me, it was a painful period — one of the few times in my association with Johnson in which I was almost totally unsympathetic with his position.

He had his reasons for delay. He thought that he was entitled to something more than a North Vietnamese agreement to talk. He had said, at San Antonio in 1967, "we assume that while discussions proceed, North Vietnam would not take advantage of

---
* Chapter 9, "Winching Down the War," pp. 257–271.

our cessation . . ."; and on March 31, "Even this very limited bombing of the North could come to an early end — if our restraint is matched by restraint in Hanoi." He wanted their commitment that they would not attack the cities or shell from the DMZ. In the end — on October 31 — he settled for their understanding, communicated through the Soviets, that this was what we expected. Before he accepted that, many of us, especially Hubert Humphrey, grew gray hairs.

Johnson was also concerned that a cessation during the campaign would be regarded as a cheap political maneuver — making him look narrowly partisan and exposing the Democrats to charges that their President played with soldiers' lives for votes. Harriman was a devoted party man; it seemed clear that some of his enthusiasm for an early cessation was related to Humphrey's fortunes. Certainly mine was. I wanted to see Humphrey win, and I wanted Johnson to go out in the favor of his party. I thought that Democrats would have found it hard to forgive one of their own who failed to act on reasonable odds.

The South Vietnamese were balky to the last. Bunker, in his seventies, spent almost three days and sleepless nights seeking to win their approval. There was evidence that overzealous Republicans had urged the South Vietnamese embassy in Washington to delay agreement, in order to deny Humphrey a last-minute advantage. But President Thieu probably needed little encouragement in dragging his feet. From New Hampshire through Chicago and into the campaign, it was obvious that millions of Democrats were prepared to jettison the war — and South Vietnam — as soon as possible.

How strange it seems now, that we should have been so concerned with South Vietnam's approval of an American bombing halt. But shortly before the election, a cry of protest from Saigon would have given credence to a Republican charge that we had acted politically, without regard to our troops or allies.

So we sat around, waiting for word from Bunker. It seemed

wise to me to move swiftly with our election only a few days away; if Thieu was going to protest our intentions, as had been reported, better to get the benefit of the act first, and take the condemnation later. At last we did.

Then there was a controversy over the seating arrangements in Paris, which ended only four days before the new President's inauguration. Then the "substantive" talks began. Then . . .

Was the war a kind of mirror, in which the strengths and weaknesses in our own society were revealed? We seemed to have acted out before it our mastery, and our dependency; our ability to "face the facts," and our absorption in rhetoric; our power, and its inefficacy.

Thomas Jefferson warned that public men "should from all student disputants keep aloof, as you would from the infected subjects of yellow fever or pestilence. Consider yourself, when with them, as among the patients of Bedlam, needing medical more than moral counsel. Be a listener only, keep within yourself the habit of silence, especially on politics. In the fevered state of our country, no good can ever come from any attempt to set one of these fiery zealots to rights, either in fact or in principle. They are determined as to the facts they will believe, and the opinions on which they will act. Get by them therefore, as you would by an angry bull; it is not for the man of sense to dispute the road with such an animal." *

One would have liked to get by them, but by 1968 they had left the road for the fields, and there was no avoiding them. For a long time I thought it was strange that liberal students were so violently opposed to Johnson. Student activism in the sixties began in the South, with sit-ins, Freedom Rides, and voter registration drives; Johnson had negotiated the passage of laws guaranteeing the rights for which the students worked and demonstrated. The students were angry about the prevalence of poverty

---

* Letter to Thomas Jefferson Randolph, 1808.

and the lack of services for the poor; Johnson had persuaded Congress to pour billions of dollars into remedial programs. The students assumed there was corruption in the upper reaches of government and industry; the Johnson Administration was remarkably free from scandal. Many students needed financial assistance to complete their college training; the Johnson Administration produced an array of scholarship, loan, and work-study programs. I even hoped, in the mid-sixties, that the students, despising totalitarianism, would support the war in Vietnam.

From the perspective of 1968, these expectations seemed quite naïve. There was, between Johnson and the students, an unbridgeable generation gap.

Marty Lipset of Harvard described the generation gap in the terms of Max Weber. Young people identified with an "ethic of absolute ends," older people with an "ethic of responsibility." The young judged the society in the light of its professed ideals, or of their own, and invariably found it wanting. Older people thought it was usually necessary to compromise in order to make any progress at all.

If ever a man believed in the "ethic of responsibility" and the necessity to compromise, it was Lyndon Johnson. As a congressman and senator, he had made deals with left and right, accepted crumbs when half a loaf was unattainable, remained silent about his own views until those of others were known and therefore manipulable. As President, he committed himself to a program of social action; but inevitably his judgment of its results was biased by his authorship of it, and by the need to sustain confidence in our ability to solve our problems by parliamentary and institutional means. The poverty and social injustice that persisted, despite efforts to end them, were a challenge to do more — not an indictment of the entire system.

Like most politicians — better say, like most men — he dissembled, and never doubted his own good intentions, while admitting errors of fact or inadequate information. The students put great store in candor, even to the point of self-effacement. To them, it was the quality most likely to be missing in professional politicians.

He was a poor performer on television, and for a generation raised on it, that was inexcusable. He had no apparent interests outside government and politics — not the theater, nor books, music, sports, automobiles, handicrafts, stamp collecting, the study of history, anything that would connect with the curiosities and pastimes of private citizens. Breeding cattle did interest him, but that was arcanum to most people. (This was not so much a generational problem for Johnson as a political one.) He was a manipulator of men, when the young were calling for everyone to do his own thing; a believer in institutions such as government, universities, business, and trade unions, when these were under constant attack on the campuses; a paternalist, in a time of widespread submission to youthful values and desires.

Most important, he had come to political maturity in the late thirties, when Fascist power threatened the world; the threat of Russian power followed; there had never been a time, from his election to the House to his accession to the Presidency, when the democracies were not threatened by somebody. He had no doubt about the human evil of communism, nor about Soviet and Chinese aggressiveness.

To the young, the experience of the thirties and forties might as well have occurred during the Renaissance. Even the Hungarian Revolution was a historical abstraction. When Moscow and Peking began to claw at one another, it seemed obvious to them that there was no one left to fear. Yet here was the United States, fighting "communism" in Southeast Asia — sending American youth, who had no quarrel with the peasant guerrillas of Vietnam, to kill them and to die at their hands because its leaders were locked in the past and terrified of change. Paradoxically, those who took part in violent campus demonstrations against the war were least likely to be required to fight it; there would be few names on the memorial plaques of college chapels after this war. But the sense of outraged impotence before a government that steadily escalated a bad commitment was genuine enough. So was the sense of being deceived. For though the Establishment had put the stakes high from the beginning, it had given the impression that they could be preserved by a relatively small number of professional soldiers. And now there was the draft.

So convinced were the students that United States power was the principal evil in the world that they could not assimilate the events in Prague in 1968. Senator McCarthy understood that, and his cool response reflected the students' own. Only when the Soviet presence in Czechoslovakia was related to ours in Vietnam did it find its way into speeches at Berkeley and Cambridge and Grant Park.

There were millions of young people to whom these comments do not apply. Richard Scammon and Ben Wattenberg have pointed out that for every student "leftist" there was a young Wallace supporter. There were the 4-H Club members, the manual workers, the squares in the small colleges (I had been one), and the blacks. Johnson invited many representatives of these groups to White House ceremonies, hoping to dispel the impression that he had no contact with young America. Each time he did, I felt the gap all the more; I thought the really important young were those who marched outside the White House gates.

Like the "legitimist reformers" of whom Brzezinski wrote — "In a revolutionary situation, they are particularly concerned with not being stamped as counterrevolutionary conservatives" * — I spent many hours with student government officers, editors, members of political science seminars, and so on, trying to convince them that we understood their concerns and were moving to assuage them. In the environment of the White House, the students were restrained. And they seemed much better in-

---

* "Revolution and Counterrevolution," *New Republic*, June 1, 1968.

formed than my contemporaries and I twenty years before. They were intensely ideological, but they appreciated candor; when I said we could not take a particular step because it would be politically costly, they seemed to welcome the admission — though whether that was because I had been honest with them, or had only confirmed their suspicions, was hard to say.

I agreed with much that I heard from them. They were no more free of cant than we were, and they were rather less tolerant. But they were unafraid to remind us that the Administration was not meeting the standards it had set for itself, and that, for bureaucrats whose visitors were usually too deferential to be pointed, was useful.

The student activists were helping to form a new politics in America — a more divisive and impatient politics, "radicalizing" opinions on both sides. Many liberal people who should have known better adopted the most extreme views of the student left. Many moderate people, shocked by the violence, destruction of property, and anti-intellectualism of the left, looked to the conservatives for answers. They could not quite believe, with Tom Wicker at Chicago, that it was "our children" out there, yelling "Off the Pigs!" If it was, they thought they should be punished, not emulated. Johnson, speaking in Texas in May, said "Those who glorify violence as a form of political action are the best friends the status quo ever had. They provoke a powerful conservative reaction among millions of people. They inspire, among many people, a blind allegiance to things as they are — even when those things ought to be changed."

Humphrey paid the price for that. He was the main target of the leftist militants; carrying the can for Johnson and the war, he was heckled unmercifully — and still was not able to convert the incivility he endured into a groundswell of voter sympathy. There was bitter irony in that. He had as much appetite for controversy, and as much genuine interest in reform, as any man in public life. And there he was, being shouted down by a petulant mob, while the voters went off to find someone less "sympathetic" to the troublemakers.

Only Edmund Muskie seemed to be able to convert a confrontation into votes. Self-confident and steady, he dominated his hecklers with a mixture of tolerance and firmness. He required his audience to be silent while a representative of the militants stated their position, after which he gave his own. Thus he turned an emotional climate into a rational one. It was a fatherly performance, winning him the admiration of millions for whom the central question of 1968 was how to deal with unruly and even unlawful behavior.

Richard Nixon was virtually ignored by the militants, perhaps because he had no identification with the war, or because they expected little from him. He was not "their" candidate; he did not pretend to be troubled by what troubled them; he was invulnerable to their complaints. He would never have said, as Humphrey once did, that he could understand why people whose children were constantly attacked by rats might riot, he might do it himself in the same situation. He did not need to establish his sympathy for the concerns of the antiwar demonstrators, while abhorring their excesses. He needed only to wait patiently for that "powerful conservative reaction" to elect him President.

Two years before, answering a press conference question about the 1966 elections, Johnson said, "Although my delightful friend, Senator Dirksen, optimistic as he is, feels that there may be a [Republican House] gain of 75, I notice the chronic campaigners, like Vice President Nixon, have begun to hedge and pull in their horns." That afternoon I congratulated him for the phrase. Democrats needed a little partisan slugging from time to time, to keep their spirits up. "No, it was a stupid mistake," he said. "I probably nominated him" — meaning that he had singled Nixon out of the other Republican contenders, Romney, Rockefeller, Reagan, et al., for special attention.

Once he announced his retirement, Johnson did very little in public for Humphrey until the last few days of the campaign, when he made several speeches and television tapes. What he did privately I do not know, though I believe he helped raise some funds for the campaign. His feelings appeared to be mixed. On the one hand, an old and deep affection for Humphrey; his own lifelong fidelity to the Democratic party; and surely a desire that the Administration's record be vindicated by the election of its Vice President. On the other, apprehension that Humphrey was preparing to repudiate the war policies for which he had once been such a zealous advocate; the desire to remain "above politics" in the search for peace; and, surely, resentment that another man now carried the banner that was his by right of achievement?

Moving away from Johnson and the war, as many of Humphrey's advisors told him he must do, was sure to provoke the kind of angry reaction in Johnson and his supporters which Stevenson had aroused in Truman in 1952. Furthermore, Johnson had given Humphrey the nomination, in the sense that delegates friendly to Johnson were the core of Humphrey's strength in the convention. So there was a moral obligation, as well as a personal one, not to renounce the President.

But the extensive help which the Administration might have given Humphrey during the campaign was missing. The machinery of government was not transformed, during the 1968 campaign, from neutral-bureaucratic to partisan-political. And the President would not bend, would not take the crucial step of ending the bombing until moments before the election; the entreaties of Humphrey's friends seemed only to make him more unyielding — as if he thought the final discrediting of the war (and of himself) would come if he seemed to be managing it for political purposes. For Humphrey, and for many of us in the White House who were close to him, it was a bitter time.

The last few months of 1968 saw a steady diminution of Presidential power. There was no point in preparing a massive legislative program for the next year, since the new President would urge his own. So the lines of demand and response between the White House and the departments grew slack. There was no sense of anticipation, nor fear of sanctions.

"I do understand power," Johnson said, "whatever else may be said about me. I know where to look for it and how to use it." Now, for the second time in a decade, he was suffering its loss.

He asked members of the cabinet to come in for long individual sessions, in which they discussed the work of their departments during the past five years. Records of these meetings were to become part of the Johnson Library collections, in Austin. Califano and I attended many of them. Inured though I was to talk about federal programs and achievements, I was astonished by the range and depth of what had been done or at least assayed. Few human problems had escaped attention by an Administration whose leader had truly meant to improve the way people lived.

The data on conditions among Negroes were startling. In 1965, 19 percent had incomes equal to the national median; in 1966, 23 percent; in 1967, 27 percent; and outside the South, 37 percent. The Negro median level in education had been 10.8 years in 1960, one and half years less than that for whites; now it was 12.2 years, about a half year behind. Seventy-seven percent of urban Negro families had lived in the "poverty areas" of large cities in 1960; 56 percent lived there in 1968. For many Negroes, life was worse than before. But for millions of others, the sixties had been years of new hope and unaccustomed well-being.

Once the cabinet members had recited the achievements of the Great Society, they retired to farewell parties, to arrange the transition of authority to their successors, and in a few cases, to make administrative decisions which the President had either specifically or inferentially asked them not to make. Ramsey Clark, Stewart Udall, and Bill Wirtz all took actions that as a matter of policy, or of comity toward his successor, the President was dead set against. Great antitrust suits were filed, vast lands were absorbed into the federal system, the manpower program was more nearly federalized. It was a carnival of last-minute activity, a release of wills reminiscent of the first days after Johnson left the Senate majority leadership.

The President delivered a last State of the Union message, its proposals falling as flat on congressional ears as if they had been parts of a doctoral thesis. But there was a deep welling of sentiment in the Hall when he said,

Most all of my life as a public official has been spent here in this building. For thirty-eight years — since I worked on that gallery as a doorkeeper in the House of Representatives — I have known these halls, and I have known most of the men pretty well who walked them.

I know the questions that you face. I know the conflicts that you endure. I know the ideals that you seek to serve.

I left here first to become Vice President, and then to become, in a moment of tragedy, the President of the United States.

My term of office has been marked by a series of challenges both at home and throughout the world. In meeting some of these challenges, the Nation has found a new confidence. In meeting others, it knew turbulence and doubt, and fear and hate.

. . . I believe deeply in the ultimate purposes of the Nation — described by the Constitution, tempered by history, embodied in progressive laws, given life by men and women who have been elected to serve their fellow citizens.

He thanked the men with whom he had worked — Humphrey, and McCormack, and Carl Albert; Mansfield, Russell, Dirksen, and Gerry Ford. There were rounds of applause for each, perhaps for the years they had spent listening to Johnson, being swayed to do his bidding or resisting, making the arrangements with him through which countless bills had been passed or defeated, governing with him.

That was about it. There was a party in the Mansion on the last night. It was a little subdued; we were giving up our lease.

I thought back to that first meeting on the Senate floor — almost thirteen years ago — and of how in those years Johnson had become like one of my family, not to be judged by me as others judged him, in the aesthetic terms of like and dislike, but more deeply, in love, rage, and grief; knowing what he wished to do, proud of what he did, dismayed by his tragic failures.

Next day we saw him off at an air base. I was officially powerless, and glad it was over.

Epilogue

THE lessons of my political education are in this book. My point of observation during these years was unusual; my conclusions about the politics of government and its practitioners are by comparison pedestrian.

I saw America chiefly through the abstractions of policy. My world was contained in a quadrilateral, running from the Capitol, to the Pentagon, to the Department of State, to the White House, and back to the Capitol. Within those few square miles I saw much that gave promise that the country would become what its founders believed it already to be, the best hope of mankind; and much that portended discord and failure. Apparently it had always been this way. Henry Adams, writing of the America of 1800, said,[*]

The city of Washington, rising in solitude on the banks of the Potomac, was a symbol of American nationality in the Southern States. The contrast between the immensity of the task and the paucity of means seemed to challenge suspicion that the nation itself was a magnificent scheme like the federal city, which could show only a few log-cabins and negro quarters where the plan provided for the traffic of London and the elegance of Versailles.

Washington had become grand and powerful in the intervening century and a half. There was no longer any "paucity of

---

[*] *History of the United States of America During the Administrations of Jefferson and Madison* (New York: Boni, 1930), p. 30.

means," but there were serious questions about their use. And the task, while no greater than that faced by Jefferson and his contemporaries, was more complex.

Perhaps the most serious question of all was whether we could learn from our experience and shorten the lag between events and our response to them. Nearly twenty years passed from the time black Americans began leaving the South, until the national government began to respond to their unique problems in the Northern and Western cities. Our apprehension of the danger to us in the unification of Vietnam under Hanoi's rule was the same in 1963 as it had been in 1954. Our political leaders, like the rest of us, dealt with new phenomena on the basis of prevailing assumptions. Usually the assumptions were changed only by bitter experience, not by analysis and foresight. The public's reluctance to think new thoughts had much to do with that; so did their faith, which their leaders shared, that as a nation we were immune to history. We believed we could afford the lag, with our cushion of power, wealth, and resourcefulness. Detroit and Tet told us otherwise.

It was Lyndon Johnson's fate to be President at a time when the cost of the lag came home. On the whole, he paid it bravely, without "whining on his knees before posterity," or accusing his "subordinates, envious colleagues, unfavorable winds . . . ." He finished the old agenda, and by painful example taught us something about the new.

Other men will deal with that — men just as ambitious, faulted, and responsible as he was. There will always be a species of the human animal that can find satisfaction only in the heat and glare of elective office. And there will always be young men who want to witness what they do, and to do good themselves, to cast a shadow in Washington — men like Moyers, Califano, Cater, and McPherson.

John Adams wrote to his friend Dr. Warren in 1774, "Politics are an ordeal path among red-hot ploughshares. Who, then, would be a politician for the pleasure of running about barefoot among them? Yet somebody must."

Doubtless that was an honest view in the years before we were a nation; doubtless there are still distinguished men who regard political office as a burdensome responsibility which they must bear as gifted citizens. But most of the men I knew in Washington hungered for it, and would not have been happy without it.

By the end of 1968 I was (like most of the country, I think) tired of political issues. I was tired of seeing every dispute turned into an apocalyptic struggle between good and evil, tired of looking at life through a political lens. I needed a respite from my political education — a sabbatical, not a retirement. As Democrats out of office have done for the past generation, I settled back into the private life of Washington — dismayed to observe, over morning coffee, what the wretched Republicans were doing to the country we had left them.

Postscript, 1988

A GENERAL rule: you are what you were, if you were once a senior aide to the President. Former Johnson aide says, joins, succeeds, goes to jail, retires. It fixes one vividly in the social universe, as "a lawyer" or "from Washington" cannot.

Whether that is a help depends, to a considerable degree, on the President's reputation in subsequent times, and among various groups. Franklin Roosevelt is almost universally admired, and so my friend Jim Rowe, one of his first White House assistants and thereafter a fixture in the Democratic Party and the life of Washington, benefited from being "former FDR aide" to the end of his days. The public's fondness for John Kennedy, surviving a series of tabloid disclosures that would have spoiled the memory of a less favored politician, cast a warm glow about his former staff as well. Even the dour among them were presumed to share some measure of his charm.

For the Johnson crowd, it was different. Among blacks and those whites for whom civil rights was still the paramount issue in America, Johnson's standing was high, all the more so as Nixon and Reagan seemed to ignore the ghettos; and that fondness for "a President who cared" extended to those who had helped him shape and articulate his programs for the black poor. Many Texans, too, and thousands of his fellow Washington provincials — people who had observed him at close range throughout his career — remembered him fondly, and there were journalists who, while deploring his flaws, missed his extravagant self.

But in the South, a lot of whites who had voted for Johnson in 1964 (helping to make him the only Democratic nominee in the ten Presidential elections since the death of Roosevelt to win as much as 50 percent of the nation's white vote) regarded him as a renegade. In their minds, whether he truly believed in the civil rights cause or only espoused it for reasons of politics made no difference. When he cried "We shall overcome" in 1965, he allied himself with a "we" that challenged, and embittered, much of the white South.

In the mid-seventies, when Sam Ervin announced his retirement from the Senate, I urged Congressman Richardson Preyer, a gentle, decent moderate, to run for the seat. I said I would go to North Carolina and write speeches for him, ring doorbells, raise money, whatever. He seemed warmly appreciative, but said he thought he would remain where he was. A few weeks later I heard that he had told a kinswoman, "I was touched by Harry's offer. I'm sure he doesn't understand that if anyone in Carolina heard that he was working for me, it would defeat me." In later years, the black vote was openly courted in Southern Congressional elections; but the sense of Johnson's betrayal lingered in many Southern hearts.

As among other Americans there developed the conviction of his prodigality — his tendency to "throw money" at intractable social problems, as carelessly as he had thrown empty beer cans from his speeding Lincoln. The Great Society became identified with impracticality and waste, with catering to, and thereby spoiling, the improvident poor. With respect to a few of the programs launched by the Johnson Administration, including some that I had a part in, the indictment was probably justified. It was often enough stated.

But it was hardly a fair summing-up. For millions of Americans

— the infirm old and those who cared about them, young people enabled to attend college, children given a modest chance to overcome the conditions they were born to, blacks required to be treated fairly — the Great Society had brought tangible benefits that could not be discounted, at least in their eyes, by the editorials of the *Wall Street Journal*.

Whether they identified Johnson with the provision of these gains is hard to say. After my White House days I seldom heard from the beneficiaries of his programs. As a Washington lawyer I lived among businessmen and professionals who, though they rather admired Johnson's forceful personality, disparaged his agenda, and, like millions of other people throughout the country, identified him with the tragedy of Vietnam.

It was "Vietnam" that I thought I saw in the eyes of strangers when I was introduced as former counsel to Johnson. Even with groups inclined to be friendly because they shared the liberal faith, I learned to expect, after a ritual acknowledgment of the good he had done, a kind of pained probing of the reasons why this President, otherwise so shrewd and crafty, could have thought the war worth fighting, worth sacrificing so much for. Surely there was some compelling circumstance, unknown to the public, that caused him to risk so many lives, America's standing in the world, and history's verdict on his Administration. Otherwise, how obvious to all was the futility of that tortured effort!

The war had become identified with Johnson, and he with it. Often I protested that he had not originated the American commitment to protect South Vietnam. That he had not introduced the first ten thousand soldier-advisors into the country. That when he became President, the prevailing view in Congress, in the Administration, and in the media was that a North Vietnamese–Chinese victory in South Vietnam would jeopardize all of Southeast Asia, and must somehow be prevented. Johnson's role was to give substance to that view. His fate was to advance a tragic process toward its end.

If this was so, if he had entered upon the stage *in media res* — the result foreordained by a generation of war and the political imperative to resist Communist expansion anywhere — then the harshest judgment of his countrymen should fall on history itself, not on Johnson. His choices should be measured not retrospectively, after the last American was lifted off the roof in Saigon, but in the light of what was known in 1965; what he and his predecessor, their cabinet, Congress, and the public believed to be the stakes in Southeast Asia in the early 1960s; and what was then thought to be the danger of inaction, and of still more decisive action . . .

No doubt this sounded to many people like a jury speech: the crime wasn't the defendant's fault, and if it was, there were plenty of reasons why he had been compelled to commit it. And America, having lost almost sixty thousand of its sons in a miserable war, needed to pin the responsibility on someone.

So it was "Johnson's war." I thought that was like renaming the Pleistocene epoch for one of the great mammoths that roamed the icebound earth. It centered on one head accountability for the acts of many others as well as his own.

But it is the burden of national leaders to see their names attached to disasters, just as it is often their luck to be identified with successes of which the causes are numerous. Many of the triumphs of the Great Society had their beginnings in the Fair Deal of Truman and the New Frontier of Kennedy, in the big unions, in environmental groups and educational organizations; most people associate them now with Johnson, who pressed them through to enactment. "All those great things he did," goes the common refrain. "What a shame he led us into that war."

I've learned to hear this without launching into my jury speech. I accept it as essentially well-intentioned. What riles me, and always will, is the "Johnson and Nixon" pairing — by which is intended Johnson's war, Nixon's Watergate. Two dark Presidencies, two precipitous fallings-off from the halcyon days of Kennedy, even of Eisenhower. To match one caught in the toils of a calamity, who earnestly if vainly sought the best course out of it, with Nixon, whose White House was debased by a corruption of his own making, is more than unjust; it is intellectually lazy. Both Presidencies ended prematurely (though Johnson says, in his memoir *The Vantage Point*, that he had not intended to serve more than one term). Both men won landslide elections and enjoyed a period of exhilarating public approval before seeing it vanish. But the story of one has elements of tragedy, the other of bitter farce.

I asked Johnson, after the 1968 election, what he thought of Nixon. He said, "He's dumb." I didn't ask him to elaborate, and wish I had. Others have told me the opposite — that Johnson respected Nixon's intelligence. I'm sure he admired his stamina, but my guess is that he detected in Nixon the kind of imprudence that would cause him to engage in the Watergate business, and to try to conceal it while preserving the tapes that would confirm it.*

What Johnson and the other Senate "whales" of whom I wrote in this book would have thought of the principal Democratic politicians of the 1970s and 1980s seems clearer, even without an exchange such as the one about Nixon. George McGovern was a back-bencher — a reliable vote when a Democratic majority was needed, otherwise a farm-state radical about whom there clung the peculiar righteousness of the breed: sometimes right on target, sometimes priggish, always unwilling to be seen taking a cheerful part in political horse trading.

---

* Three former Nixon aides are striking exceptions to the "you are what you were" rule: my friend Moynihan, who sought to make of Nixon a conservative social reformer, in the mold of Disraeli, and later championed reform *pro se*, in the Senate; Henry Kissinger; and Leonard Garment, Nixon's counsel and friend, afterward the expert defender of a series of beleaguered Reagan Administration appointees.

Within the Senate, McGovern's influence was modest. Humphrey had been the liberals' leader, their negotiator with entrenched power. Muskie was one of the most esteemed members, the parent and protector of the nation's environmental laws. Even Kennedy, McGovern's equal as a campaigner in the primaries and caucuses, had been a more significant gear in the Senate's machine.

But McGovern was an early and outspoken critic of the Vietnam war. Humphrey — despite his sunny disposition and early sponsorship of the Peace Corps — was tarred by his association with "Johnson's war," for which he had, in fact, been a vigorous apologist before he put distance between himself and it, during the 1968 campaign. Muskie spoke of Vietnam in the language of what was feasible, while McGovern caught the spirit of the activists: cosmically condemning. Muskie's was the ethic of responsibility, in Max Weber's terms;* McGovern's, that of absolute ends. The one was suited for legislative and executive leadership, the other, as it turned out, for winning the nomination. It was not the first time such skills were separated, and it would not be the last. Indeed, the new party rules governing the nominating process almost required the distinction.

My law partner, Berl Bernhard, chaired the Muskie campaign in 1972, and I saw its frustrations through his eyes. After the Iowa caucuses, I gravely suggested that less attention should be paid to winning endorsements from the mighty, and more to building grassroots support. "What do you suppose we've been trying to do?" he asked. "It just isn't there." The emotionally energized were for McGovern; the rank and file — the union members, the civil rights groups, the party regulars — were split between Muskie and Humphrey, for whom old loyalties remained strong.

That fall I was introduced to Gary Hart, McGovern's campaign

---

* See p. 444.

manager, and liked him. Over drinks in a club we argued about what it would take to beat Nixon. He thought McGovern had the potential to do it. I did not. Two weeks before the election he asked me to stop by his office, and suggested that I manage the transition.

"From what to what?" I asked. Hart described the keys to victory, chief among them the commitment of McGovern's workers. They would get voters to the polls in numbers the Nixon campaign could not match. I looked closely at Hart and grinned. He sat back, boots on his desk, and returned the grin, with a difference: O.K., maybe this is bull, it said, but wouldn't it be fine if it weren't? And why accept the conventional wisdom, if all it gets you is another term of Nixon? (How often Gary Hart must have sent that kind of signal as he recruited his campaign team against Mondale, and then against Dukakis in the wake of his self-crippling.)

With two weeks to go in 1972, I said I would play the game. We agreed that I should recruit a committee for the purpose, one that provided the appropriate race and gender mix, and we settled on a half-dozen names. I bought as many black notebooks, in which the résumés of prospective McGovern administration officials would be filed, but I bought no paper. That would have treated the game too seriously.

Conventional wisdom won, and there was no transition. But for the politically curious, there was always something to do. I was invited over to the Democratic National Committee, where Bob Strauss, rolling strips of the *Times* into balls and energetically chewing them, told me that he was creating a policymaking council of elected officials. He had won a tough battle for the chairmanship of the committee, and he was looking for interesting things to do.

It was a familiar notion, a cousin of the Senate Democratic Policy Committee in which I had begun my life in Washington. Parties ought to take positions on the issues so that voters might choose rationally between them, and hold them accountable thereafter. Debate about ideas was also consistent with the post-1968 Democratic Party. Bosses and money, the determinants of politics past, were discredited. The future belonged to ideas and bold programs. Besides, the list of desiderata begun by Truman, amplified by Kennedy, and accomplished by Johnson — at least in the form of signed legislation — needed replenishing.

What about the danger, foreseen by Johnson and Rayburn in the 1950s, that a policywriting group of Democrats, keen on winning the White House but insensitive to the special politics of Capitol Hill, would drive conservative Democrats out of the party?* Strauss's solution was to compose the council of members of Congress, mayors, governors, and other elected officials whose survival instincts were strong. He asked me to chair a "domestic task force" to advise the council. Averell Harriman, a political addict undaunted by a generation of losses and slights suffered at the hands of lesser men, chaired a foreign affairs task force. We met on weekends, examining long papers in search of ideas that might interest — whom? Others like ourselves. The elected officials — our advisees, as it were — normally approved what we proposed, if they could be found. After a time the spuriousness of this exercise became apparent, and I complained to Strauss. The party wasn't really trying to generate new ideas, I said. The politicians didn't take the council seriously, and neither did the press. It was a waste of everybody's time. "Damn!" said Strauss. "I thought you, of all people, would understand what I'm trying to do. I'm trying to throw some meat to these silly people" — the McGovernites and other enthusiasts of the new politics, whose interest in the National Committee he had formally welcomed — "so they'll go after it and leave me alone to get something done for this party." His eyes widened in mocking entreaty. "You and Harriman please try to help me, and quit worrying about whether anybody takes you se-

---

* See p. 160.

riously. *I* take you seriously," he promised, and chewed on a fresh strip of the *Times*.

One morning in January 1976, George Stevens, Jr., the filmmaker, called to say that he had given dinner the night before to "the next president of the United States": Jimmy Carter. Several Kennedy supporters had wanted to test him out, and George provided the location. Carter had come through brilliantly. I laughed. Carter's standing in the polls was still in the low single digits.

A year later I understood what George Stevens had seen that evening. A hand-held camera recorded the New Hampshire primary, and in the resulting film were several Washington friends of mine on the primary trail: Mo Udall, Fred Harris, Birch Bayh, Scoop Jackson. And then there was Jimmy Carter. His persona, as it was filmed in a series of encounters with New Hampshire voters, was quite different from the others'. He seemed to connect with every person he met in a relaxed but interested way, as if he had the time and inclination to hear each distinctive story. The members of Congress seemed stagy by comparison, amiable enough, but out of sync. They were accustomed to receiving citizens in their Capitol offices, where their help, or at least their understanding, was implored. The Hill was their ground, and they moved on it with assurance. On the chill, wet sidewalks of Manchester, it was different.

Carter had been out of office for a while, living among the folks in Iowa and New Hampshire, hearing and using their speech patterns. Meantime the members had been speaking Congressese — transforming simple ideas into rhetorical abstractions, assuming that every difficulty was, or was thought to be, the potential subject of legislation. This did not translate as well in New England as the Georgian's faded drawl, which despite its incongruity expressed the realities he found about him. Small wonder, I thought, that he had won.

And he was quick-minded. When, as President, he announced

his famous "moral equivalent of war" energy program, designed to make the United States less subject to the pressures of OPEC, he mastered every feature of it — geology, taxes, price controls, international politics — before sending it forward to Congress. One morning I visited Representative Barber Conable, a thoughtful New York Republican, just after he heard Carter, at the White House, brief Congressional leaders on the program. Carter had needed little help from his cabinet officers. Conable was impressed. "He's really very bright," Conable said. "Will he get it through Congress?" I asked. "I don't know," he replied. "He's got no agents up here." Agents — friends among the members — put your bills through even when your standing in the polls was at rock-bottom. Johnson still had them in 1968, and could count on much of his legislative program being reported by committee members who responded to the simple statement, "Lyndon wants this."

Carter neither had them, nor appeared to want them very much. He gave an impression of distaste when speaking of Washington, whereupon many politically interested people in Washington more or less went on strike.

For a time this was amusing, as court politics can be. After a while its serious consequences became apparent. If Carter could not make government work effectively — because he lacked, or was unwilling to use, political manners within its institutions (in contrast to his performance on the streets of New Hampshire) — then the voters would very likely turn him out, and perhaps many valuable senators and congressmen with him. The Washington regulars might smirk, but opportunities for public good, as Democrats perceived them, would be lost.

Strauss had joined the government as Special Trade Representative, and soon became an informal political counselor to the President. Surprisingly (for few men were less alike), he became fond of Jimmy Carter. He thought to shield him from the consequences of his success as a primary campaigner — from the impression he gave of a Christian engineer: moral and precise, the opposite of the Washington of Watergate, and unfortunately of other Washingtons as well.

A symptom of this problem was Carter's insularity, and that of the group of Georgians around him. Strauss sought to persuade the President, through his long-time advisor Charles Kirbo, that he should reach out to the very crowd he had scorned in his campaign and ignored at the outset of his Administration.

On a gray afternoon in late 1977, five of us arrived at Strauss's office to render counsel to Charles Kirbo. We were four Washington lawyers, Jim Rowe, Lloyd Cutler, Clark Clifford, and I, and an excellent trade association officer, Lloyd Hackler. Strauss asked only that we be candid.

Rowe thought Carter should abandon his cardigan sweater routine and seem more Presidential, as people preferred in their chief executives. Cutler and Hackler spoke encouragingly, and rather mildly, about the President's political difficulties. I thought we were letting a splendid opportunity pass us by, and so when my turn came I criticized what I described as the moralizing tone, and the concurrent lack of resourcefulness and energy, of the Administration's first year.

Kirbo frowned at the floor and said not a word. I compared Carter's techniques unfavorably to Johnson's, and it struck me that Kirbo might well be reflecting that we hadn't finished up strong enough in 1968 to have earned the right to censure his man. Fair enough; but at some point he would have to address my criticism on the merits.

Clifford cleared his throat, and as was his custom when speaking *ex cathedra*, brought his fingertips together. "Mr. Kirbo," he said, his voice like a woodwind, "the people of the United States have been weighing the question of whether one with no experience of

Washington, or of the Federal government, who shows little interest in working with the Congress, or the bureaucracy, and who is surrounded by men who also have little or no experience with this city, can be expected to succeed as he attempts to carry out the awesome responsibilities of President of the United States." Then a brief pause, in which I waited with delight and admiration. "The answer they give, as of this moment, is a resounding *No.*" Kirbo frowned harder but remained silent. Clifford, and then the rest of us, made a few suggestions, and after a while we stood to leave.

At last Kirbo spoke. "I'll just say this. Many people have written off Jimmy Carter at different times in his career. He's been down before. But he always comes back. He always overcomes his adversaries." (It seemed pretty certain that some of us had made that team, in Kirbo's eyes.) "And he will again. I have no doubt of that." End of comment. We shook hands cursorily and left.

Outside we compared notes. It was not unusual that a political leader should have, among his close advisors, an old shoe with whom he felt comfortable, though others might shake their heads in wonder. It was more than a little disturbing that a President so isolated by inexperience and choice should have retained, as his close counselor, such an impenetrable provincial as Kirbo.

That meeting, and others Strauss conducted during this period, had at least one consequence for me. A political realist, Anne Wexler, was installed in the White House to communicate with the Washington regulars and with business groups around the country. She invited a number of us to meet with her once a week, to take the Administration's political blood pressure. We were the Wednesday group, and we came to the Roosevelt Room either early over coffee, or at midday, with limp sandwiches supplied by the White House mess.

What good we did the President through these staff discussions is unclear. They were a tonic for me, however, providing, for an hour or so every week, an occasion for the evacuation of my political glands at a time when other lifelong Democrats were simply dismayed by the Carter Administration's performance, and could find no satisfactory way to express themselves. That was about the extent of it. I genuinely wished to be helpful, but despite our weekly proximity to the Oval Office, I felt remote from its tenant and from most of the crises that absorbed him and his staff. It is usually so, with advisors brought late to court.

I had only a few encounters with President Carter himself. One balmy afternoon in the Rose Garden, he told me that he had read this book, and introduced me to his wife as its author. That was pleasing, and for a moment I thought we might speak as Southerners who liked to read and relish the comedy that is political life. But he said nothing in judgment of the times or the persons I wrote about, and it crossed my mind that he may have been a little embarrassed by Johnson, may have felt that he had to live down the Southern rogue who had occupied these quarters a decade before. "I'll never lie to you" had become the most significant thing this President could say to the people. Not "I'll get you an education bill, and a civil rights bill, and a bill to care for you when you're old." Purging adultery from the heart was more important than cutting a deal.

Carter appointed me to his commission to investigate the nuclear accident at Three Mile Island. I rather expected to hear his views of nuclear power during the course of our investigation. As a protégé of Admiral Rickover, he surely had such views, but he never shared them with me or, as far as I know, with others on the commission. When at the last we reported to him, it was to describe a culture of carelessness in the nuclear industry, and inattention in the agency assigned to regulate it. He received us with equanimity, and if what we said perturbed him, he gave no sign of it. I waited for some expression of impatience, outrage, or transparently phony interest masking one or the other; or of warm gratification for a job pretty well done that cast no blame upon his Administration; or of barely contained energy, ready to be spent on reorganizing the agency, lobbying a massive reform bill through Congress, winning promises of better performance from industry executives, and of cooperation from labor; and then it occurred to me that this was Carter, not Johnson. In the photographs of this occasion, I appear bemused. I was, by the passage of time and the mortality of leaders.

On a bright day in 1979, I was asked to join the President and a few of his aides in the Lincoln bedroom of the White House. The subject was Teddy Kennedy's challenge to Carter for the Democratic nomination. While we waited for the President, I walked about the room, remembering that twilight, years before, when a rumor flew about the pressroom that Johnson had suffered a heart attack. To prove it false, Johnson invited several reporters to join him as he toured the White House with a group of Hispanic-American politicians. One of the reporters, the veteran Merriman Smith, had rushed to the White House from a party, and he was wobbly, apologetic, but nevertheless determined to examine Johnson closely for signs of bad health. As Johnson stood by the Lincoln bed, gesturing about the room, the diminutive Smith stood behind him, eyes fixed on Johnson's lower back. Suddenly the President turned around, and Smith, forced backward, fell onto Lincoln's bed. Johnson stared down speechlessly upon the dean of the White House press corps, the trusted hand at the wire service ticker; Smith, equally uncertain what to make of the moment, rested. The politicians stirred uneasily. A curious scene in the room of the exalted Lincoln.

As was this one: a new President and his assistants — pollsters, image refiners, men with skills that neither Lincoln nor Johnson had brought into the White House — sitting about a nineteenth-century table, talking about primaries, caucuses, polling techniques, momentum from one state to the next. I was out of place in such a discussion. Carter was not. He was articulate and confident. He had no doubt whatever that he would defeat Kennedy's challenge. The contrast between an uncertain President, fumbling his way through a period of almost Weimar-like inflation, crippling interest rates, Iranian captivity, and this firmly commanding politician who knew exactly how to cope with an attack on his left flank, was both striking and instructive.

Most of the best political leaders I have known would have been no match for Jimmy Carter and his team in the winter wars of Iowa and New Hampshire. A number of them were better than he at the arts of government. Though he succeeded in putting a Canal treaty through Congress — over the violent objections of the Zonians whose affairs I had overseen years before* — and helped Israel and Egypt come to terms, he left few accomplishments at home, and conveyed a fatal sense of uncertainty in dealing with the Russians. The Cabinet he chose on entering office was experienced, capable, and public-spirited; yet he treated with them as if they were remote nobility — or worse, as if they were "Washington." He had, in Stuart Eizenstat, a broad-gauged chief of domestic policy, and in Zbig Brzezinski, an aggressive player of the foreign policy Go game. Neither man was lost in the capital.

And yet Carter was. Quite smart enough not to be, very likely the only Democrat among the candidates in 1976 who could have won the race against Gerald Ford (so out of touch with the necessary South and Southwest had the Democrats become), and favored with a Democratic Congress, he was lost — purposeless, it seemed, filling out multiple-choice questions because it was his turn to do so. He could not lead, perhaps because he wasn't led himself, by any mastering theme. Events smashed down upon him, and all he had for a shield was the fixed smile that had served him so well in seeking the job, and now mocked his efforts to fill it.

I left the President and his aides that day in 1979 and walked across Lafayette Square, headed for my law office. I had now been

---

* See pp. 207–210.

out of government for almost a dozen years. At four-year intervals I had offered counsel to an old friend who either lost the nomination or declined to pursue it. In 1972 the friend had been Ed Muskie, who became almost encyclopaedic in his grasp of domestic and national security issues, and never found the tonic chord that might have converted many well-struck notes into music.

In 1976 it was Hubert Humphrey. I joined him in his office on the day before the filing deadline for the New Jersey primary at a time when, despite widespread doubts and several primary defeats, Carter had almost sewed up the nomination. Max Kampelman and Bob Short were there, close friends of Humphrey's for many years; Fritz Mondale and the equable Dick Moe, both raised in Humphrey's political house, the Minnesota DFL; two or three others. The issue was whether Humphrey should enter this last primary and show, with a victory, that the party wasn't really behind Carter and wanted an open convention. Then labor, the teachers, and civil rights groups, all those with whom Humphrey had marched in the cause of social justice, would rally behind him and help him seize the prize once more.

Humphrey was unusually reticent as the afternoon waned. He had entered the race late in 1972, and fragmented Muskie's vulnerable support in the party's middle. As a result some Democrats thought him a spoiler. He didn't wish to confirm that opinion, he said. We all nodded in agreement and resumed the debate — which inevitably concerned how to spoil Carter's long and careful pursuit of the nomination. There were bulls who thought it was do-able. There had always been bulls around Humphrey, animated by his good cheer and eloquence. There were bears, like Dick Moe, who thought it too late, too divisive, too costly. I watched the subject of this argument pensively, with affection, as always. He was not long past a bout with cancer. Three times before he had sought the nomination. Now he was a respected senator again. Why not be content to have that place, to be venerated by his colleagues and the nation for the qualities of mind and spirit, voice and imagination, that he had exhibited for three decades? Why not, if the cancer should return, savor the last years in relative peace?

Surely he felt all this. But not to run meant acknowledging the end of the lifelong quest — not just for office, but for the highest rostrum from which to be heard, the best command post from which to promote humane laws for the nation.

I thought his nomination was unlikely, and said so. It was much likelier that he would divide the party and elect Gerald Ford.

And I knew that there were reasons to worry about a Humphrey Presidency: his difficulty in saying no, the uneven quality of his friends, the unsettled question of whether his inspirational gifts would translate into executive competence. Yet for every concern, there was an offsetting ground for admiration, a memory that offered hope. Years before, when I worked for him and Mike Mansfield in the Senate, I heard him describe his first days as mayor of Minneapolis, in the late 1940s. He had been toughest, he said, in dealing with his own people. They had been out of office for a long time, and many of them hungered for the gravy of power: appointments, contracts, contributions. Mayor Humphrey called his boys together and declared this rule: no one was to put his hand in the cash register until he knew that the mayor had been there first and had gotten his. If someone was so greedy as to go before him, he said, he would slam! the drawer on the guy's hand and break it. Humphrey never took that first step, and Minneapolis had clean government. He was like a merry *capo* as he told the tale. I liked to think it was essentially true, and at least suggestive of his performance in the White House.

Sometime around eight in the evening it was agreed that I would prepare an announcement statement, for use the following morning. I went home and did the job — not a bad one, considering my doubts. Humphrey went home, talked to Muriel, and made the right decision: not to run. Eighteen months later he was dead with cancer.

Fritz Mondale inherited a double helix — the generous Minnesota liberalism of Humphrey, and four sobering years of living with America's limitations, under Carter. One coil told him that no challenge was too daunting; the other, that neither our economy nor our personnel abroad could be made altogether secure from greed and anti-American malevolence. Though they carried opposing messages, they might have produced, as audacity and caution often do, a successful leader. But Mondale ran against a popular figure in a time of prosperity, at the head of a party whose program no longer contained many elements of magnetic appeal. What had driven the Democratic Party from the mid-thirties into the late sixties — an urgent sense of public needs to be met and justice to be done — had been diminished: partly by accomplishment; partly by misgivings about government's ability to remedy many social ills; partly, I believe, by the continuing destructive power of racial antagonism in American life.

Democrats had been, at least since the days of Al Smith, the including party. Moderate Republican leaders were forever counseling their party to reach out beyond the white male constituency that was its base. For many years this was difficult to do, not only because Democrats already occupied much of the wider territory, but because that Republican base was where power had resided throughout most of American history, and there was little incentive to risk it by courting others.

Not that the base felt secure. White men had run America since colonial days, and they were still the most active and influential part of the electorate. But they had seen their power slowly attenuated by the extension of suffrage first to women, then to blacks. Democratic administrations had done the extending, in 1920, with the adoption of the Nineteenth Amendment, and then, in 1965, with the Voting Rights Act. In a sense, they had watered the white male stock, thereby empowering others, who responded by supporting them and — such is my conjecture — progressively alienating the white male stockholders.

After Mondale's defeat in 1984, the scholar Samuel Popkin pointed out that the Democratic nominee had now lost the majority of white votes in every election since the death of Roosevelt, save for Johnson's victory in 1964; and after Johnson, only Carter among Democrats had won as much as 40 percent of that vote. So it had required two Southerners to attract large numbers of white voters, and neither, in all likelihood, could have done it a second time (as Carter showed). Many of those who rejoiced in the punch that Southern blacks carried in local and congressional elections missed the significance of this trend. They kept the faith that liberal coalitions — blacks, activist women, Hispanic Americans, the white working class — could overcome. But in 1984, the number of white males who voted for Reagan equaled Mondale's entire vote, and Reagan carried a majority of white women as well. The liberal coalitions were indeed successful in the off years. In the race for the White House, their nominee had been rejected in four of the five contests since 1968.

No doubt part of this rejection, at least in recent years, stemmed from the Democrats' perceived weakness in matters of national security. White men cared about such things, and Democrats often seemed either to consider the willingness to negotiate to be a sufficient mode of defense, or to be incompetent in the use of force, as in the aborted rescue mission to Tehran. Virtually every Democratic candidate for the presidential nomination made it his business to understand the three-level chess game that is arms control negotiations. Routinely the voters preferred a Republican who made simple bellicose pronouncements about the Soviets and other adversaries, so long as he seemed rational enough not to provoke a war.

A deeper reason, I believe, lay in the white man's view that Democrats had cast their lot with black Americans, to the ultimate disadvantage of whites. Thoroughgoing racism, commonplace in America before the 1960s, was much less prevalent in the 1980s. But the multiplying calamity of black children born out of wedlock, fated, more often than not, for lives of illiteracy, dependency, involvement with drugs, and unwed parenthood — if not imprisonment — produced white reactions quite unlike the ones of earlier years, which acknowledged and sought to atone for the role of white racism in black suffering. This time the suffering seemed self-induced, though the costs were society's — and not just to the Treasury, but to the morale of whole cities. No one knew what to do about it. The situation was clearly beyond "private initiative," as the Reagan years proved; but the party of government, which had helped free black Americans from institutionalized bigotry, was just as confounded for answers. When Pat Moynihan carried his report into my hospital room in 1965,* something like a quarter of black families were headed by women. Poverty followed them like a pack of hounds. By the late 1980s, the percentage had doubled. And no one knew what to do.

Yet political language dies slowly. In addressing urban poverty — which to most Americans connoted black life in the central cities — Democratic speakers normally used terms of exhortation ("We must") and chastisement ("We cannot continue"), excoriating greed and indifference and praising commitment. Harking back to the language of Presidential commissions in the explosive sixties, they warned of two societies — which, to millions of Americans, was exactly what was wanted, and in most places already existed. What was not wanted, by those of both races who had moved out of the central cities, was responsibility for the mess left behind — often now presided over by black mayors and their friends, who in most cases had no more precise standards of rectitude than their white predecessors.

---

*See p. 344 and following pages.

So despite the general lack of agreement about what might usefully be done; the prevailing skepticism, amounting to mistrust, about the value of large social expenditures in the hands of big bureaucracies; and the reluctance of "conventional" families to come to the rescue of people whose misfortunes were at least partly of their own making — despite these sobering political realities, Democratic primaries and conventions often rocked with the language of rebuke. Very like, it has occurred to me, the language many wives use in speaking to their husbands, particularly toward the end of marriages. You never think of the children, or of my mother, or of me; only of yourself. Substitute the ignored disadvantaged, the homeless, people trapped downtown. The reaction among husbands, for whom read "white male voters," is what is normally provoked by attempts to burden people with a sense of guilt. In an era in which divorce is common, many men can be expected to have heard such charges, and to be alert to politicians who touch the same nerve. Some of the more intense women who have been active in Democratic politics in recent years may have found the precise point at which the pressure of asserted guilt, both sexual and societal, is most exquisitely objectionable to white males, and therefore most likely to drive them to the more comfortable GOP.

Candidate Reagan made full use of the opportunity. His attacks on the welfare queen in her Cadillac resounded in millions of breasts. Democrats might scoff about the insignificance of welfare costs, compared to the sums that Washington paid out to agribusiness each year. They were right, and irrelevant. Politically, there was no comparison. Everyone had a welfare-abuse story, observed or passed on; few people knew much about farm subsidies beyond an occasional stunning report in the papers, which read like an account of Iran–Iraq casualties: awful, remote, soon forgotten.

Reagan seemed truly to believe that undeserved benefits to big-city malingerers had very nearly bankrupted the government. Many Americans were apparently willing to accept the notion, not being pressed to consider alternatives. They did not have to ask — Reagan did not have to say — which party had passed the laws, provided the funds, and still argued the case on behalf of welfare recipients. The President's views about impoverished masses of people were vaguely censorious; his sensitivity to individual cases of need was real; in both respects, as in his tremendous credulity about the lives of unwitnessed others, he was at one with those who elected him.

A dilemma indeed. The including party, having extended the suffrage to women and blacks, has lost the original voters, the white males, and with them the potent leverage of the Presidency — by which it might, in time, help to lift the weight of poverty off the newly included.

The dilemma won't be solved by regression. The party can hardly repudiate the people or the causes for which it has worked, and who now regard it as theirs, quite as Southern judges and Chicago politicians once did. It would be suicidal to try, since minorities and women make up much of the voting power that perpetuates Democratic control of Congress. Above all it would be vain, since no one of any political persuasion would believe it.

Once I put some equally perplexing quandary to Johnson. If he took one course, he faced certain trouble. A second, grief. In between lay a third that combined the worst of the others. I sat back, sadly sympathetic, but pleased that I had described these miserable options well — much as a professor might feel satisfied after giving an eloquent lecture on the Black Death. Johnson waited for me to continue, and when I didn't, asked, "Therefore?" It wasn't enough to describe a dilemma. One should offer answers, even if they were only relatively good, only better than nothing.

Hence these thoughts. Race — in the narrow political sense,

meaning attitudes toward the participation of blacks in American society — has always been a highly charged issue, whether or not explicitly raised in the course of a campaign.*

Throughout most of American history, the participation question asked whether blacks were granted the same political and legal rights enjoyed by other Americans. Beginning in the mid-forties and continuing through the late sixties, a powerful combination of forces secured virtually every legal right for blacks that black leadership had fought for and that reasonable whites were willing to endorse or abide. A Southern President, part of that combination of forces, recognized that these legal rights were necessary, but by no means sufficient, for the enormous task of insuring full participation by blacks in the country's economic life. He believed that the lingering effects of slavery and oppression made this task particularly difficult, and achievable only through the expenditure of great sums directed specifically, though not exclusively, toward the black poor. White guilt was the motive force; black inclusion was the stated goal; the liberal agenda of the Democratic Party, embracing reforms and entitlements in many fields, was the means.

From the beginning there were skeptics. Many millions outside the South were themselves the children of immigrants, for whom slavery and its residual guilt were like planets light-years away. It was all right with them if blacks participated fully in the economy, so long as they earned their way. The reforms and entitlements were all right, too, so long as their benefits were shared by all who needed them and "deserved" them by virtue of their efforts, however failing, to be self-supporting. Participation and benefits were not, in their minds, to be given out as compensation for the sufferings and injustices of past generations or as rewards for antisocial conduct. The all-explaining theme of guilt was in a key they could

---

* My encounters with the political issue of race are described in Chapter 10, pp. 334–383.

not hear, and the more it was invoked to justify unearned demands and excuse bad behavior, the more irritated they became.

Affirmative action programs came to symbolize the injustice of the guilt indictment. For the most part the programs simply called for special efforts to recruit and train minorities and women. But every white male had heard, or thought he had heard, of a case in which an unqualified, newly hired black or woman had been promoted over a competent veteran white male, all to make up for slavery and discrimination. And in his mind, that case became a metaphor for "civil rights" each time the issue was raised in a political campaign.

If, as the election data tell us, the social-justice coalition is weak — and if white males have abandoned it more or less for the reasons I've suggested — it will do little good to continue trying to instill a sense of guilt, and a corresponding obligation, among people who don't feel it. To the contrary. The coalition will grow still weaker, and the condition of the underclass will grow still more desperate — grotesquely relieved, here and there, by the counterfeit affluence of drug dealing.

If guilt is no longer effective as the engine of change, perhaps a sense of civic pride and responsibility might serve? A sense that the heart of great cities should not be left to spoil? Throughout the country, developers are reclaiming neighborhoods of decayed buildings, to the great satisfaction of city governments. Office towers are soaring out of the rubble. Every block, it seems, has an ethnic restaurant and a photocopying store. Money is being made, taxes are being paid.

All to the good. But a few blocks away the ghettos remain; the number of people without legitimate competence grows; crime proliferates, together with welfare, prisons, the lot. The economy has rudimentary needs for service workers, and has trouble meeting them. It has more complex and ultimately much more serious needs for skilled workers, who can handle the materials and processes with which America competes in an aggressive world. If we cannot educate and train great numbers of currently uneducated and untrained people to do these jobs, the economy will decline. So will living standards for the rest of us.

In recent months, Democratic senators have pushed through a welfare reform bill. It imposes new work and child-support requirements, and ultimately it should help both welfare families and the larger society. What struck me about the debate, as conducted by Senators Moynihan and Bentsen, was the general absence of preaching, of guilt dispensing. Their message was practical: a system that moves people off welfare dependency and into self-support is to be preferred not only for the moral health of the recipients, but for the sake of the American economy, which needs them. Further efforts to make ours a more wholesome society should be based on the same functional grounds.

The consequences of slavery endure. Racism is still the most debilitating virus in the American system. It should be addressed directly and indirectly, in schools, on the job, in every form of social intercourse where generosity of spirit is exemplary. But massive public attacks on its consequences will require political consensus, or at least majorities; and those will not be obtained from defensive people who resent being addressed as racists. Cool heads, and restrained language, will be needed in composing the next liberal agenda.

As I write this — at the summer equinox, 1988 — Dukakis has a narrow lead over Bush in the early polls, and Democrats are beginning to consider that they might elect a President this year. Few of them are willing to be exhilarated about it yet — partly, I suspect, because Dukakis and exhilaration are not paired concepts in anyone's mind; partly because the pessimistic instinct is strong, for the reasons I've suggested, or for other reasons Democrats use when they rationalize how the party of the people is so often rejected in its bid for the Presidency. The actor fooled us. Money. McGovern and the flower children. Poor Jimmy Carter. Johnson's war. The perceived dominance of interest groups whose demands were not negotiated in the interest of winning wider acceptance, but were simply accepted by the Democratic candidate.

No doubt all of these have contributed to Democratic losses since 1968. Their legacy, and the concomitant steady loss of white votes, makes any Democratic nominee an underdog in the structural sense (as unemployment is described as either "structural" or "cyclical"). With the nation at peace and jobs plentiful, Republicans should have the cyclical edge as well.

It is possible that Bush cannot exploit these advantages. And if that should be so, what kind of environment will Dukakis enter in January of 1989?

He will find, unhappily, very little money for dealing with the sorts of problems that Democrats are drawn to contend with. His reputation is for competent management. It is much needed, and obviously missing from the White House in recent years (unless, as Stockman suggests, we were managed into a black hole of debt in order that Democratic big-government spenders could not practice their passion for decades to come). But good management practices are chiefly admired by accountants, not by masses of people needing affordable housing, job training, anti-drug-abuse programs, better education for their children, and the like. If he means to launch costly efforts in these fields, he will need first to establish his fiscal prudence, bordering on parsimony. I've thought about what Johnson would do if he were to follow a Republican who left him a two-trillion-dollar debt. I believe he would begin as he did in 1963, turning off White House lights, risking jeers for the sake of making a point: I am not about to waste the people's money; I will spend it only to meet the people's needs.

Dukakis could capitalize on the public's skepticism about Pentagon spending, making cuts in redundant weapons, in the fleet, and maybe in a few officers' amenities; but he would need to demonstrate his support for the military in apposite ways (such as backing a new and useful weapons system that had been ignored by the Reagan Administration, if one is conceivable) before pruning it. When he has shown his care for the taxpayers' dollars, then he can do what he must, what Reagan has been so frivolous not to do, and ask Congress to raise taxes in order to reduce the deficit.

He will find Congress a very different place from the one I worked in many years ago. The staffs are vastly larger, and raising political money is much more preoccupying. As I look back over these pages, I am struck by their almost total silence about money. It was partly my innocence about it that made them so. I had overheard Bobby Baker talking about the availability of oil and gas contributions with an excited New England liberal; and I remembered Senator Francis Case's outburst about a gas lobbyist's gift to his campaign just prior to the 1956 deregulation vote.* I had few other encounters with moneyraising in those days. Most congressional staffs were divided between people who worked on bills and issues, as I did, and those who raised money in election years and tended to its contributors at other times.

But the book is also silent about money because raising campaign funds in the fifties and sixties was not the absorbing matter that it has become in the eighties. At least it was not so publicly absorbing. The advent of political action committees, of "disclosure," of spectacularly expensive campaigns, has done much to eliminate the reticence that used to surround the subject — much as the advent of the movie rating system has made explicit sex viewable in mixed company. So much money is raised now, from such heterogeneous sources, and incumbents have so many technological and staffing advantages, that members of Congress are pretty much free to be independent. Many choose not to be, and

---

* See pp. 92–94.

as a result the system, being pushed to and fro by vectors of interest, often becomes jammed.

I began this book by describing my arrival in Washington more than thirty years ago — excited by the monumental scene spread before me on a cold January night, and by the prospect of working, for a few years, in the office of Senator Lyndon Johnson. I concluded it as Johnson left Washington aboard *Air Force One*, headed for the ranch at Stonewall, Texas, after a Presidency in which tremendous achievements were mixed with baffling failure.

That was the beginning of a parenthesis, of which the last of the Reagan years would appear to be the end. All within has been a commentary, to one degree or another, on the Great Society and what it represented: the belief that an activist, spending government is necessary to the well-being of the many. Nixon and Reagan, though they could not (and perhaps would not) undo much that was begun in the Johnson years, found it difficult to express themselves politically without that pro-government belief to assail. Even Carter needed it, as exemplifying the compassion of the tradition he had inherited and the excesses he meant to avoid.

Johnson knew Reagan well — at least generically. He had trounced his less glamorous forerunner, Goldwater, and for three decades he fought, mocked, and sometimes placated the well-to-do Texans whose philosophy found its fulfillment in Reagan. The two were in many respects mirror opposites: Johnson the spectacularly successful persuader in private sessions, drawing on an inexhaustible supply of argument; Reagan the three-by-five-card reader, the joke teller. Johnson the stiff, almost sanctimonious (and hence hard to believe) speaker before the barren eye of television; Reagan the warm, avuncular performer from Hollywood's family entertainment era, reassuringly uninterested in the details. Johnson the relentless tinkerer with the engine of government; Reagan the rested, knowing that popular presidents do not spend much time below decks. Johnson the often mistrustful manipulator, the bearer of grudges, striking fear into the hearts of those in his Administration who might, by some misdemeanor or stupidity, visit grief upon him; Reagan the benign, the unflappable, apparently unperturbed by either bad judgment or cupidity around him. Johnson would have been astonished by Reagan's lack of absorption in legislation. Reagan would have known better than to contest with Johnson within the halls of Congress. He would have relied on the camera and opinion polls as his tools of persuasion.

Both men drew politically energetic people into government to work for them and their causes. Though Reagan began his first term by declaring that government was not the solution but the problem, very likely that depressed the spirits only of lifetime bureaucrats — most of them Democrats anyway. It did not discourage vigorous ideologues from seeking government employment, as eager to accomplish conservative ends as liberals had been to achieve theirs, during much of the preceding half century.

Indeed, one of them will no doubt shortly begin a memoir of his political education. I hope he will have found that the rough edges of his opinions have been a little, but not altogether, filed down by events, and that he has rather enjoyed the humbling experience. So it was with me, and so I think it will always be.

Index

Abel, Elie, 441
Acheson, Dean G., 257, 403, 433
Ackley, Gardner, 269, 367
Adair, E. Ross, 282
Adams, Henry, 152; quoted, 453
Adams, John, quoted, 454-455
Adams, Sherman, 14
Adenauer, Konrad, 320
Aiken, George D., 79, 92; descriptive note, 69
Ailes, Stephen, 210, 217, 218, 219, 337
Albert, Carl, 283, 451
Alexander, Clifford L., Jr., 350, 356, 368, 370, 373, 374
Anderson, Clinton P., 35, 49, 50, 158; descriptive note, 27-28

Bagehot, Walter, quoted, 62-63
Bailey, Joseph W., 121
Baker, Robert G. ("Bobby"), 31, 43, 146, 160, 175, 183, 192, 199; position, 24-25; legal trouble, 200, 201
Bakke, Edward Wright, quoted, 336
Ball, George W., 230, 433
Barbour, Walworth, 414-415
Barkley, Alben W., 34, 66, 75, 175; descriptive note, 28
Baroni, Father Geno, 356
Bartlett, E. L. ("Bob"), 136, 390
Battle, Lucius D., 226, 232, 233, 234, 236
Baxter, William M., 163, 164, 165, 214
Bayh, Birch, 420
Beirne, Joseph A., 403
Bennett, Wallace F., 133, 134
Benson, Ezra Taft, 27, 37, 79, 130
Benton, William, 7
Bernhard, Berl, 368
Bible, Alan, 28
Bilbo, Theodore G., 31
Black, Charles L., Jr., 151
Black, Hugo L., 90
Blumstein, Jack, 371

Bodard, Lucien, quoted, 384, 410
Borah, William E., 48, 161
Bradley, Omar N., 403, 433
Brammer, William, 24, 121
Breslin, Jimmy, 271, 332
Bricker, John W., 117; descriptive note, 69
Bridges, Styles, 37, 110, 127; descriptive note, 69-70; and natural gas bill, 91-92, 94
Bronfenbrenner, Urie, 339
Brown, H. Rap, 343, 371
Brown, Harold, 293
Brown, Winthrop G., 435
Bryan, William Jennings, 330
Brzezinski, Zbigniew, 294; quoted, 446
Buchwald, Art, 326
Buckley, Tom, quoted, 413
Bui Vien, quoted, 425
Bundy, McGeorge, 216, 230, 256, 433; as special assistant, 257; and Vietnam, 258-259
Bundy, William P., 314, 315, 430, 431; and Vietnam speech, 433-437 passim
Bunker, Ellsworth, 324, 406, 421, 435, 441, 442
Burns, James McGregor, 403
Busby, Horace, 426, 438
Bush, Prescott S., 70
Butler, John Marshall, 132; descriptive note, 78
Butler, Paul M., 159-160
Byrd, Harry F., 15, 21, 27, 30, 43, 49, 51, 54, 116, 117, 236; descriptive note, 28-29
Byrd, Robert C., 174

Califano, Joseph A., Jr., 219, 221, 223, 226, 292, 427, 428, 430, 450, 454; position, 252, 254-256, 298; and civil rights violence, 359, 364, 365, 367
Cannon, Clarence, 33

Capehart, Homer E., 42; descriptive note, 70-71
Caraway, Paul W., 211-212, 214
Carmichael, Stokely, 343, 365, 374; "outside course," 357, 358, 362-363
Carpenter, Elizabeth S., 315
Carroll, John A., 134
Carroll, Wallace, quoted, 433
Carter, Philip, quoted, 430
Case, Clifford, 78
Case, Francis, 80; descriptive note, 71; and natural gas bill, 92-93, 94, 99
Castro, Fidel, 319
Cater, Douglass, 292, 293, 439, 454; position, 269-270; on riots, 368
Cavanagh, Jerome P., 359, 362
Chavez, Dennis, 43; descriptive note, 29
Christian, George E., 430, 431, 437; position, 265, 270; memo to, on riots, 360-361
Christopher, Warren M., 366
Church, Frank, 25, 117, 145, 162-163, 390
Churchill, Winston S., 53, 386, 393
Clark, James Gardner, Jr., 338, 390
Clark, Joseph S., 20, 32, 44, 69, 80, 116, 117, 119, 188; on Calendar Committee, 17; descriptive note, 29; on missile gap, 118; and Johnson, 169, 190
Clark, Ramsey, 344, 364, 366, 450; and Carmichael, 362-363
Clay, Lucius D., 403
Clements, Earle C., 13, 183; descriptive note, 30
Clifford, Clark M., 273, 312, 430; on Vietnam, 431, 441; and Vietnam speech, 433-438 passim; and peace-talk site, 440-441
Cohen, Morris R., quoted by Fulbright, 149-150
Coles, Robert M., 339
Collins, LeRoy, 350
Colmer, William M., 353
Connally, John B., Jr., 253
Connor, Eugene T. (Bull), 338
Cook, Donald C., 13, 287
Coombs, Philip H., 234
Corcoran, Thomas G., 171
Cramer, William C., 284
Cross, James U., 304, 307
Curtis, Carl T., 106, 117

Daley, Richard J., 366, 375
Daniel, Price, 30
Dardis, Thomas, 11
Darrow, Clarence S., quoted, 334, 370
Dean, Arthur H., 433
de Gaulle, Charles, 322, 440
Delaney, James J., 196
Diem. See Ngo Dinh Diem
Dillon, C. Douglas, 157, 403, 433
Dingell, John D., Jr., 283
Dirksen, Everett M., 20, 60, 69, 130, 135, 182, 448, 451; on James Murray, 47; local base, 66; descriptive note, 72-73; political problems, 106
Doar, John, 350
Dodd, Thomas J., 228
Dompierre, Oliver J., 20
Douglas, Paul H., 15, 29, 69, 103, 116; assistants, 20; descriptive note, 30-31; character, 32, 35, 39, 44, 59; local support, 64; liberal support, 88; natural gas bill, 91, 93; defense appropriation bill, 117; pork-barrel bills, 125; civil rights bill, 145, 148, 154; Citizens Committee for Peace with Freedom in Vietnam, 403
Douglas, William O., 90, 177
Dubinsky, David, 328
Dugger, Ronnie, 30
Dulles, John Foster, 101, 105, 116, 120, 122, 387; "massive retaliation," 104, 386
Dungan, Ralph A., 201, 219, 220
Duvalier, François, 316

Eastland, James O., 69, 116, 117, 146, 182, 194, 353; subcommittee, 21; descriptive note, 31-32; power, 49, 51
Eban, Abba, 414
Edmondson, Ed, 283
Eisenhower, Dwight D., 35, 37, 51, 70, 72, 78, 79, 105, 120, 131, 158, 160, 182, 183, 193, 245, 294; position, 4-5; support for, 7, 110-111; and Knowland, 74; vetoes, 99, 126, 130, 168, 170, 189, 279; meetings with congressional leaders, 112-113; civil rights bill, 142-143, 147; controversial positions, 196; as chief of state, 263; and Vietnam, 390; citizens' committees for Vietnam war, 403
Eisenhower, Milton S., 381

INDEX 489

Eleta, A. Fernando, 223
Ellender, Allen J., 49, 116, 117, 130, 135, 182; descriptive note, 33-34
Ellison, Ralph, 139, 403
Engelhard, Charles W., 322
Engelhard, Jane (Mrs. Charles W.), 322, 325
Enthoven, Alain C., 294
Erikson, Erik H., 337, 339
Ervin, Sam J., 185; descriptive note, 34; civil rights bill, 145, 146, 148, 154
Eshkol, Levi, 413
Evans, Rowland, Jr., 144n; quoted, 158-159, 401-402
Evron, Ephraim, 413

Farmer, James, 344
Farrell, James T., 403
Feldman, Michael, 20, 235, 255, 273, 413
Fergusson, Sir Bernard E., 304
Finney, Thomas, 20, 197
Fleming, Harold, quoted, 349-350
Fleming, Robert J., Jr., 207, 217
Flood, Daniel J., 208
Flynn, Edward J., 375
Fogarty, John E., 284
Ford, Gerald R., 451
Forrestal, James V., 59
Fortas, Abe, 381, 433
Fowler, Henry H. ("Joe"), 367, 431, 432
Frankel, Charles, 232
Frankel, Max, 387
Frear, J. Allen, Jr., 134, 135; descriptive note, 34
Freeman, Orville L., 255, 299
Frei Montalva, Eduardo, 316
Frost, Robert, 182
Fulbright, J. William, 7, 45, 103, 117, 135, 136, 156, 172, 203; descriptive note, 34-35; local support, 64; natural gas bill, 89, 91, 93; brief amicus curiae in *Aaron* v. *Cooper*, quoted, 149-150, 151; Bureau of Educational and Cultural Affairs, 228, 232, 233; and Vietnam, 392, 395, 412, 439; quoted on foreign policy, 396

Gaither, James, 367, 368
Galbraith, John Kenneth, 326, 327
Gandhi, Indira, 260
Gardner, John W., 293, 402

Garner, John Nance, 179
Gates, Thomas S., Jr., 403
George, Walter F., 36, 94; descriptive note, 35
Goldberg, Arthur J., 435
Goldman, Eric, 270
Goldwater, Barry M., 80, 117, 158, 247, 264; descriptive note, 73-74
Goodwin, Richard N., 296, 327, 328, 391
Gore, Albert A., 17, 103, 116, 136
Graham, Rev. Billy F., 329
Gray, Kenneth J., 284
Gray, Jesse, 346, 347
Green, Theodore Francis, 36, 53; descriptive note, 35
Gruenther, Alfred M., 282
Gullion, Edmund A., 403

Haar, Charles M., 293
Halleck, Charles A., 216
Hand, Learned, 186
Handlin, Oscar, 403
Hannum, Calvin S., 227
Harriman, W. Averell, 441, 442
Harris, Fred R., 23, 420
Hart, Philip A., 117, 162, 420
Hartke, Vance, 162
Hayden, Carl T., 54, 80, 94, 103, 171; descriptive note, 36; power, 49, 50, 65; land claims bill, 280-281
Height, Dorothy, 357
Heineman, Ben W., 346, 347
Heller, Walter W., 269
Helms, Richard, 256, 431
Hennings, Thomas C., Jr., 133; descriptive note, 36
Herbert, Zbigniew, quoted, 245, 419-420
Hickenlooper, Bourke B., 106, 182
Hickey, Edward J., 19, 57
Higginbotham, A. Leon, Jr., 357, 365
Hill, Arthur, 372, 374
Hill, Clint, 308
Hill, Jesse, 356
Hill, Lister, 40, 56, 64, 132, 135, 172; descriptive note, 36-37; health research bill, 186
Hiss, Alger, 109
Ho Chi Minh, 384, 401
Hodges, Luther H., 198
Hoffer, Eric, 295, 403
Holland, Spessard L., 69, 136; descriptive note, 37

Holmes, Norman, 122
Holt, Harold E., 314, 322, 324
Holyoake, Keith J., 304
Hoover, J. Edgar, 359
Horn, Stephen, 20
Horwitz, Solis, 157, 263
Howe, Mark de Wolfe, 108
Howland, Harold E., 231
Hughes, Philip S. (Sam), 283
Hughes, Richard J., 361
Hull, Cordell, 291
Hummel, Arthur W., Jr., 231, 236
Humphrey, George M., 5
Humphrey, Hubert H., 15, 29, 69, 79, 199, 203, 448; descriptive note, 37-39; and Johnson, 38-39, 451; candidacy for 1960 Presidential nomination, 52, 169, 170, 173-174, 175, 176; natural gas bill debate, 90, 93; on military aid, 105; possible disarmament agreement, 119; farm issues, 130, 172; and H. R., 3, 133-134; and civil rights bill, 148; foreign policy programs, 198; Vice Presidential nominee, 1964, 228; Presidential candidate, 1968, 332, 442, 447-448, 449
Huong, Tran Van, 411

Ickes, Harold L., 177
Irving, Frederick, 231

Jackson, Henry M. ("Scoop"), 118; descriptive note, 39-40
Jacobsen, Jake, 253
Javits, Jacob, 69, 79, 185
Jefferson, Thomas, 332, 454; quoted, 443
Jenkins, Walter, 23, 176
Jenner, William E., 110, 116; descriptive note, 78; and H. R. 3, 132, 133
Johnson, Gerald, 78
Johnson, Lady Bird (Mrs. Lyndon B.), 178, 214, 304, 310, 315, 322
Johnson, Lyndon B.: staff, Senate, 5-6, 13, 23-25, 68, 121-123; images of, 6-7; leadership of Senate, 7, 50-51, 52, 109, 157, 162, 187, 203-204; and Eisenhower, 7, 110, 112; and Democratic senators, 1956, 28, 29, 30-31, 34, 35, 36, 43, 44, 48, 54, 58, 59; and Humphrey, 38-39, 228; and J. F. Kennedy, 41-42; on Kennedy-Johnson legislative program, 48; candidacy for 1960 nomination, 51, 52, 142, 170-178; relation to Texas, 64-65, 121, 123-124, 134; Vice Presidential nomination, 75, 178-181; and Republican senators, 1956, 76, 80-81; natural gas bill, 89, 90, 94, 99-100; political philosophy, 97-98, 444-445; military aid, 103, 105; foreign aid, 106; and communism, 106-110, 390-391, 445; defense preparedness, 118, 119; pork-barrel bills, 126; Senate building bill, 127; party unity, 130, 135; farm issues, 130; civil liberties, 132-134; "Johnson Procedure," 158-160; Senate problems, 168-170; and Mansfield, 183; as Vice President, 184-185, 190-192, 200; aid to education bill, 196; and Baker, 200; advice on Pentagon position, 201; accession to Presidency, 213-216, 247-248, 262-264; Canal Zone disturbance, 219; press and public relations, 248-250, 259-267; speech style, 249-250, 327-329, 331-333; and Bill Moyers, 252-253, 265; office staff, 251-258, 265; legislative staff, 267-268; specialists, 268-273; Special Counsels, 273, 282-285, 292; legislation, 274-281; and veterans' hospitals, 281-282; Presidential power, 285-288; labor problems, 288-290; trade problems, 290-292; and intellectuals, 293-296; legislative messages, 296, 298, 299; foreign travels, 303-326; decision not to run again, 326, 427-428, 439; and R. Kennedy's assassination, 380-383; and Israel, 413, 414; and 1968 campaign, 427, 428-430, 448-449; credibility gap, 427, 436; student opposition, 443-447; on Nixon, 448; loss of power, 449-450; last State of Union message, 451; summary, 454; mentioned, 16, 32, 45, 72, 88, 116, 167, 230, 235, 337, 346

CIVIL RIGHTS AND RACIAL PROBLEMS: position on, in Senate, 136-142, 152-155; civil rights bill, 142-149; equal accommodation bill, 194-195; and Army test, 337; Howard University speech, 339, 342, 345; "To Fulfill These Rights" conference, 348-349;

new programs, 352-353; memos to, on, 355-357, 370-375; proposed meeting, 356, 358; riots, 359-360, 361, 363, 376-379; reaction to King's death, 364-369; information on black poor, 375-376
  VIETNAM: policy, 386, 388, 390-392, 399; goals, 393-395; criticism, 395, 398, 420-421; and bombing of North Vietnam, 422-423, 439, 441-443; conversation with veterans, 426-427; speech on bombing and farewell, 431, 433, 435-439; peace talk site, 440-441, 443
Johnson, W. Thomas, 265
Johnston, Felton McLellan ("Skeeter"), 33, 36, 132
Johnston, Olin D., 25, 38, 59, 64, 130; descriptive note, 40-41; on Hawaiian statehood, 136-137
Jones, Peter, 197, 198, 199, 200
Jones, J. Raymond, 374
Jordan, B. Everett, 198
Jordon, Barbara, 356
Just, Ward S., 404

Kalb, Marvin L., 441
Katzenbach, Nicholas deB., 193, 430, 437; and planned civil rights meeting, 356, 357, 358
Keating, Kenneth B., 69
Kefauver, Estes, 14, 52, 116, 136; subcommittee, 21; descriptive note, 41
Kennedy, John F., 20, 27, 57, 59, 72, 156, 162, 294, 298, 321, 375, 429; descriptive note, 41-42; and Johnson, 41-42, 178-179; legislative program, 48, 188, 189-190, 191, 192, 196, 197, 198, 200; basis of election, 51-52; candidacy for 1960 Presidential nomination, 52, 169, 170, 172-173, 174, 175, 176, 178, 179; political positions, 103, 105, 116, 117, 118, 119, 148; loyalty oath repeal bill, 108-109, 390; pork-barrel bills, 125; local interest, 126; Johnson compared with, 177, 248; inauguration, 182-183; and Negroes, 193; staff, 200, 252, 253, 257, 271, 272, 273, 296; Canal Zone flag policy, 210, 217, 222; and Vietnam, 213, 386, 388, 390, 394; assassination, 213-214, 262, 380; impact of, 216, 245-247; press relations, 261, 264; as chief of state, 263; trade problems, 291; speeches, 326
Kennedy, Joseph P., 178
Kennedy, Robert F., 178, 191, 194, 248, 253; and Latin America, 321-322; assassination, 380-382; on Vietnam, 386; 1968 candidacy, 427, 428-429
Kenyatta, Charles, 371
Kerr, Robert S., 20, 28, 29, 34, 35, 44, 132, 134, 182, 200; descriptive note, 42-43; power, 49, 50; attention to legislation, 51; pork-barrel bills, 126; expertise, 172; and trade bill, 197
Khrushchev, Nikita S., 85, 110
King, Martin Luther, Jr., 142, 154, 193, 342, 356, 357, 390; Silberman on, 344; assassination and aftermath, 363-364, 365, 367, 369-370, 380
King, Martin Luther, Sr., 364
Kirwan, Michael J., 284
Knowland, William F., 5, 20, 69, 72, 80, 88, 94, 132; descriptive note, 74-75
Komer, Robert W., 425
Kuchel, Thomas H., 20, 79, 80; descriptive note, 75
Kurzman, Dan, 220-221
Ky, Nguyen Cao, 315, 406, 425; quoted, 405, 410-411

LaFollette, Robert M., 161
Langer, William, 76
Lapp, Ralph E., 403
Larsen, Roy E., 233
Lausche, Frank J., 117, 134, 204
Lawrence, David L., 375
Lehman, Herbert H., 19, 29, 103; descriptive note, 43
LeMay, Curtis E., 393
Levinson, Lawrence E., 367
Lewis, Anthony, 134
Lewis, John L., 287
Lichtenstein, Gene, 199
Lincoln, Abraham, 152, 251
Lindsay, John V., 372
Lippmann, Walter, 395, 396
Lipset, Seymour M., 444
Liuzzo, Mrs. Viola Gregg, 330
Lodge, Henry Cabot, Jr., 411
Lodge, Henry Cabot, Sr., 111
Loeb, William, 70

Long, Huey P., 33, 43
Long, Russell B., 46, 49, 135, 282; descriptive note, 43-44
Lucas, Scott W., 14-15, 24
Luce, Henry R., 266-267

MacArthur, Douglas, 50
McBride, Donald O., 20
McCarthy, Eugene J., 117, 446; Senate power, 198-199; 1968 campaign, 427, 428, 429
McCarthy, Joseph R., 80, 81, 85, 88, 110; censure, 7, 58, 131, 178; descriptive note, 76-78
McClellan, John L., 131, 132, 133; descriptive note, 45-46
McCone, John A., 256
McCormack, John W., 330-331, 451
McCulloch, Frank W., 20
McCune, Shannon, 212
McFarland, Ernest W., 15, 47
McGee, Gale, 162
McGill, Ralph, 403
McKay, Douglas, 5
McKissick, Floyd B., 365; quoted on *Negro Family*, 339, 340
McMahon, Brien, 118
McNamara, Patrick V., 190; descriptive note, 46
McNamara, Robert S., 206, 223, 226, 230, 254, 256, 273, 284, 294, 359, 430; and Army test failures, 337; on Vietnam, 401, 431
Magnuson, Warren G., 17, 39, 132; descriptive note, 44; power, 49, 50
Maguire, Charles, 439
Malone, George W. ("Molly"), 134, 196; descriptive note, 76
Manatos, Mike, 267
Mankiewicz, Frank F., 381-382
Mann, Thomas C., 219, 319
Manning, Robert J., 219, 221
Mansfield, Mike, 69, 182, 192, 197, 200, 204, 281, 451; descriptive note, 44-45; as majority leader, 45, 183-184, 190, 194, 201, 202; and Vietnam, 74-75; political positions, 103, 116, 117; speech on cloture, 186-187
Mao Tse-tung, 363
Marcos, Ferdinand E., 309, 314, 315
Marshall, Burke, 193
Marshall, Thurgood, 348

Martin, Edward, 219
Martin, Edwin McC., 78, 80
Martin, Louis, 347, 348, 356, 365, 370, 373, 374
Maybank, Burnet R., 25
Meany, George, 288, 346, 403
Mennin, Peter, 233
Meyer, Karl E., 161
Miller, Clement W., 203
Miller, Francis Pickens, 236
Miller, G. W. (Bill), 356
Mills, Wilbur D., 283, 367
Minton, Sherman, 90
Mitchell, Clarence M., Jr., quoted, 339-340
Monroney, A. S. ("Mike"), 20, 197; descriptive note, 46-47; natural gas bill, 90, 91, 92, 93, 100
Mooney, Booth, 24
Moore, Pauline R., 24, 183
Morgan, Edward P., 390
Morgenthau, Hans J., 389, 390, 391, 392
Morse, Wayne L., 17, 28, 44, 48, 69, 126, 169, 188, 198, 200; descriptive note, 47; political positions, 90, 103, 116, 117; aid to education bill, 195
Moss, Frank E. (Ted), 162
Moyers, Bill D., 200, 270, 296, 303, 306, 454; and author, 235-236; and Johnson, 252-253, 265
Moynihan, Daniel Patrick, 286, 302; on racial problem, 153; *The Negro Family*, 334, 340, 341, 342, 344; quoted, 336-337
Mundt, Karl E., 108, 109
Murphy, Charles S., 273, 367, 368
Murphy, Patrick, 366
Murphy, Robert D., 433
Murray, Charles P., 413
Murray, James E., 47
Muskie, Edmund S., 117, 420; Senate power, 198-199; 1968 campaign, 448

Neely, Matthew M., 48
Nelson, Steve, case of, 131, 132
Neuberger, Richard L., 103; descriptive note, 48
Neustadt, Richard E., 285
Nevins, Allan, 402
Ngo Dinh Diem, 385, 386, 388, 407
Ngo Dinh Nhu, 388
Nguyen Be, 406-407

Nguyen Cao Ky. *See* Ky
Nguyen Duc Thang, 406
Nguyen Ngoc Loan, 411, 424-425
Nguyen Van Thieu. *See* Thieu, Nguyen Van
Nimetz, Matthew, 368
Nixon, Richard M., 185, 302; in 1960 campaign, 170, 178, 181, 182, 193; in 1968 campaign, 428, 448
Norris, George W., 48, 161
Novak, Robert D., 144n; quoted, 158-159
Nugent, Patrick Lyndon, 332

Oberdorfer, Don, quoted, 424
O'Brien, Lawrence F., 190, 192, 193, 267
O'Connor, Edwin, 365
O'Daniel, W. Lee ("Pappy"), 6
O'Donnell, Kenneth P., 252
Okun, Arthur M., 269, 368
O'Mahoney, Joseph C., 103, 145; descriptive note, 48
O'Meara, Andrew P., 218, 219, 220
Onassis, Jacqueline Kennedy, 44
Onganía, Juan Carlos, 316

Park, Chung Hee, 314, 315, 435, 440
Parker, David S., 217-218, 219
Parsons, Talcott, 339
Pastore, John O., 27, 42; descriptive note, 53; local base, 66; positions on legislation, 91, 103, 126
Paul VI, Pope, 324-325
Payne, A. C., quoted, 208
Pell, Claiborne, 53
Pepper, Claude D., 57
Perry, Arthur C., 24, 124
Pettigrew, Thomas F., 339
Pool, Ithiel de Sola, 403
Powell, Adam Clayton, 143, 374
Prettyman, E. Barrett, 282
Proxmire, William, 32, 64, 130, 188; pork-barrel bills, 125, 126; and Johnson, 169, 190; filibuster, 203-204

Raborn, William F., Jr., 256
Rainwater, Lee, 339n, 340n, 342
Randolph, A. Philip, 356, 365
Rashish, Myer (Mike), 197
Raskin, Marcus, 340, 341
Rauh, Joseph L., Jr., 148, 188, 216

Rayburn, Sam, 112, 160, 161, 171, 179, 190, 291, 391; on Johnson's relations to staff, 122-123
Read, Benjamin H., 20, 226
Reagan, Ronald, 448
Redmon, Hayes, 254-255
Reedy, George E., Jr., 23-24, 146, 157, 159
Reis, Harold F., 193
Reischauer, Edwin O., 213
Reston, James, 247; quoted, 246
Reuther, Walter P., 328, 362
Ridgway, Matthew B., 433
Rivers, L. Mendel, 276, 284, 290
Roach, Josephine, 286-287
Roberts, Chalmers McG., 389-390
Robertson, A. Willis, 116, 117; descriptive note, 53-54
Roche, John P., 64, 294, 303, 361, 368; position, 270-272; on Vietnam, 272-273, 399-400, 421; citizens' committee, 403
Rockefeller, Nelson A., 428, 448
Romney, George W., 448; and Detroit riots, 359, 360
Rooney, John J., 232-235, 236
Roosevelt, Eleanor (Mrs. Franklin D.), 160
Roosevelt, Franklin D., 24, 31-32, 35, 41, 75, 88, 142, 160, 176, 247, 287, 375; and Johnson, 6, 7; racial issue, 135; aides, 251; veto, 279; and intellectuals, 295; speech style, 327, 330; on bombing Japan, 393
Roosevelt, Theodore, quoted, 261
Rostow, Walt W., 256, 314, 368, 423, 430, 431, 433, 436, 437; position, 258; on Vietnam, 258-259, 435, 441; on Latin American common market, 317
Roth, William, 291
Rowe, James H., Jr., 216
Rusk, Dean, 228, 256, 430, 431, 437; State Dept. staff meetings, 230; budget requests, 235; on North Vietnam bombing, 432, 441; and Johnson's Vietnam speech, 433, 434, 435, 436
Russell, Richard B., 15, 19, 34, 36, 38, 58, 69, 111, 118, 130, 132, 136, 167, 182, 261, 290, 337, 451; committee staff, 21; power, 49, 50, 65; attention to legislation, 51; descriptive note,

Russell, Richard B. (*continued*)
54-56; position on legislation, 116, 130; defense appropriation bill, 117; and H. R. 3, 133; civil rights bill, 145; expertise, 172; cloture debate, 187, 188; on Vietnam, 409-410, 420

Salinger, Pierre, 261
Saltonstall, Leverett, 78; descriptive note, 79
Scalapino, Robert A., 403
Scammon, Richard M., 377, 379, 446
Schlesinger, Arthur, Jr., 271; quoted, 200
Scott, Hugh, 179-180
Scott, W. Kerr, 56
Scotton, Frank, 406, 407
Seabury, Paul, 403
Semer, Milton P., 283
Sheffey, John P., 227
Shriver, R. Sargent, 353, 354-355
Shuman, Howard, 20
Sidey, Hugh, 324, 325, 326
Siegel, Gerald W., 13, 89, 134, 146, 157
Silberman, Charles E., 344
Sirhan, Sirhan B., 380
Sitterson, John, 213, 214
Smathers, George A., 27, 117, 134, 135, 136, 200; descriptive note, 57
Smith, Howard W., 14, 131, 133, 196
Smith, Kendall, 371
Smith, Magnus, 227
Smith, Margaret Chase, 145, 158
Smith, Owen, 221, 439
Sobeloff, Simon E., 136
Sorensen, Theodore C., 20, 252, 273, 296
Sparkman, John J., 38, 40, 64, 103, 135; descriptive note, 56
Spellman, Francis, Cardinal, 196
Stennis, John C., 49, 117, 118, 127, 182, 225, 353, 354; descriptive note, 57-58; on Vietnam, 420
Stevenson, Adlai E., 135, 148, 160, 449; 1960-candidacy for nomination, 175-176
Stimson, Henry L., 257
Stout, Juanita K., 356
Strauss, Lewis L., 158
Stroessner, Alfredo, 316
Stulberg, Louis, 403
Sullivan, Leon, 356

Sweeney, John L., 286-287
Symington, James W., 59, 303, 315
Symington, Stuart, 20, 116, 119; candidacy for 1960 nomination, 52, 170, 175, 176; descriptive note, 59; on military aid, 105; defense appropriation bill, 117
Szilard, Leo, 389

Taft, Robert A., 50, 88
Taft, William Howard, 309
Talmadge, Herman E., 17, 35
Taylor, Maxwell, 431
Teague, Olin E. ("Tiger"), 282
Teller, Edward, 118
Thieu, Nguyen Van, 315, 406, 410, 435, 442; quoted, 407, 411
Thomas, Albert, 33
Thompson, Sir Robert, 312; quoted, 399
Thurmond, J. Strom, 40, 116, 117, 145, 195; descriptive note, 59-60; and Hawaiian statehood, 136-137
Thye, Edward J., 78, 94; descriptive note, 79-80
Tillich, Paul J., 214
Tito, Josip Broz, 106
Tocqueville, Alexis de, 100
Trujillo, Rafael (Ramfis), 105
Truman, Harry S., 14, 59, 78, 88, 160, 173, 330, 332, 397, 449; internal Communist problem, 107, 109; racial issue, 135; and intellectuals, 295; citizens' committee, 403
Tully, Grace G., 24
Tydings, Joseph D., 420

Udall, Stewart L., 281, 290, 366, 450
Underwood, Marty, 303, 305
Urey, Harold C., 403

Valenti, Jack J., 270, 324, 325
Valenti, Mary Margaret (Mrs. Jack J.), 214
Valeo, Francis R., 44
Vance, Cyrus R., 201, 210, 433, 441; and Canal Zone disturbance, 217, 218, 219; and civil rights violence, 359
Vance, Zebulon Baird, 34
Vaughn, Jack H., 223
Vinson, Carl, 118

INDEX 495

Wainwright, Jonathan M., 309
Wallace, George C., 56, 338, 359, 428, 446
Warren, Earl, 75, 215
Washington, Walter E., 365
Watkins, Charles, 19-20, 188
Watson, W. Marvin, 251-252, 253, 428
Wattenberg, Ben, 310, 446
Weisgal, Meyer W., 417
Weisl, Edwin L., Sr., 201
Welker, Herman, 78
Westmoreland, William C., 324, 421
Weyand, Frederick C., 407
Wheeler, Burton K., 48, 161
Wheeler, Earle G., 431, 437
White, Harry Dexter, 109
White, Lee C., 235, 273, 274
White, Theodore H., quoted, 176-177
Whitten, Jamie L., 255, 353
Wicker, Tom, 189, 447
Wiggins, J. Russell, quoted, 397
Wiley, Alexander, 80
Wilkins, Roger, 350; quoted, 352
Wilkins, Roy, 138, 154, 342, 344, 345, 356, 357, 365, 373

Williams, Harrison A., Jr. ("Pete"), 162
Williams, John J., 216; descriptive note, 80-81
Wilson, Charles E., 5, 117, 120
Wilson, Harold, 260, 322
Wilson, Henry H., 267
Wilson, James Q., 339
Wilson, James W., 127, 157, 158
Wilson, Woodrow, 251
Wirtz, W. Willard, 450
Wofford, Harris L., Jr., 193
Wood, Robert C., 293, 298
Worsthorne, Peregrine, quoted, 397

Yancey, William L., 339n, 340n, 342
Yarborough, Ralph, 64
Yarmolinsky, Adam, 223
Young, Stephen M., 66, 117
Young, Whitney M., Jr., 345, 356, 365
Youngblood, Rufus, 308

Zagoria, Donald, 390
Zentay, John, 20
Zwick, Charles J., 367